Migraine in Women

Elizabeth Loder, MD, FACP

Assistant Professor
Department of Medicine
Harvard Medical School
Boston, Massachusetts

Dawn A. Marcus, MD

Associate Professor
Department of Anesthesiology
University of Pittsburgh Medical Center
Pittsburgh, Pennsylvania

2004
BC Decker Inc
Hamilton · London

BC Decker Inc
P.O. Box 620, LCD 1
Hamilton, Ontario L8N 3K7
Tel: 905-522-7017; 800-568-7281
Fax: 905-522-7839; 888-311-4987
E-mail: info@bcdecker.com
www.bcdecker.com

Sales and Distribution

United States
BC Decker Inc
P.O. Box 785
Lewiston, NY 14092-0785
Tel: 905-522-7017; 800-568-7281
Fax: 905-522-7839; 888-311-4987
E-mail: info@bcdecker.com
www.bcdecker.com

Canada
BC Decker Inc
20 Hughson Street South
P.O. Box 620, LCD 1
Hamilton, Ontario L8N 3K7
Tel: 905-522-7017; 800-568-7281
Fax: 905-522-7839; 888-311-4987
E-mail: info@bcdecker.com
www.bcdecker.com

Foreign Rights
John Scott & Company
International Publishers' Agency
P.O. Box 878
Kimberton, PA 19442
Tel: 610-827-1640
Fax: 610-827-1671
E-mail: jsco@voicenet.com

Japan
Igaku-Shoin Ltd.
Foreign Publications Department
3-24-17 Hongo
Bunkyo-ku, Tokyo, Japan 113-8719
Tel: 3 3817 5680
Fax: 3 3815 6776
E-mail: fd@igaku-shoin.co.jp

UK, Europe, Scandinavia, Middle East
Elsevier Science
Customer Service Department
Foots Cray High Street
Sidcup, Kent
DA14 5HP, UK
Tel: 44 (0) 208 308 5760
Fax: 44 (0) 181 308 5702
E-mail: cservice@harcourt.com

Singapore, Malaysia, Thailand, Philippines, Indonesia, Vietnam, Pacific Rim, Korea
Elsevier Science Asia
583 Orchard Road
#09/01, Forum
Singapore 238884
Tel: 65-737-3593
Fax: 65-753-2145

Australia, New Zealand
Elsevier Science Australia
Customer Service Department
STM Division
Locked Bag 16
St. Peters, New South Wales, 2044
Australia
Tel: 61 02 9517-8999
Fax: 61 02 9517-2249
E-mail: stmp@harcourt.com.au
www.harcourt.com.au

Mexico and Central America
ETM SA de CV
Calle de Tula 59
Colonia Condesa
06140 Mexico DF, Mexico
Tel: 52-5-5553-6657
Fax: 52-5-5211-8468
E-mail: editoresdetextosmex@prodigy.net.mx

Brazil
Tecmedd
Av. Maurílio Biagi, 2850
City Ribeirão Preto – SP – CEP: 14021-000
Tel: 0800 992236
Fax: (16) 3993-9000
E-mail: tecmedd@tecmedd.com.br

India, Bangladesh, Pakistan, Sri Lanka
Elsevier Health Sciences Division
Customer Service Department
17A/1, Main Ring Road
Lajpat Nagar IV
New Delhi – 110024, India
Tel: 91 11 2644 7160-64
Fax: 91 11 2644 7156
E-mail: esindia@vsnl.net

Dedication

For my father, Thomas Wentz, and in memory of my mother,
Janet Wentz (1937–2003), a beloved wife, mother and grandmother,
politician, speaker of the North Dakota House of Representatives,
and devoted and lifelong advocate of opportunities for women.

EL

Contents

Preface

———

The benign headache disorders, especially migraine, are widely and correctly recognized as problems that disproportionately affect women in comparison with men. Media stories about chronic headache almost invariably feature women.[1,2] Women comprise the majority of patients seeking medical evaluation of headache,[3] are more likely to use prescription medications for headache,[3] are the majority of subjects in clinical research trials of headache treatments, and are more likely than men to be severely disabled by headache.[4] Although social and cultural roles undoubtedly influence care-seeking behavior, with women more likely to report and seek evaluation of both acute and chronic pain, recent work has highlighted the disproportionate burden of primary headache on women.[5] Despite this, there has been no single, authoritative medical textbook devoted to the many special topics important in the care of women with headache.

Headache in Women emphasizes recognition and management of migraine, the most frequent primary headache disorder for which women seek medical care. Tension-type headache and cluster headache, although less likely to prompt medical visits among women, are also discussed. Secondary causes of headache that are unique to, or more common in, women are thoroughly reviewed, including the headaches of preeclampsia, cerebral venous thrombosis, and benign intracranial hypertension. Subjects of special importance in treating women with migraine receive detailed examination. Among others, these include the use of oral contraceptives and estrogen replacement therapy in the female migraineur, avoidance of treatment-induced weight gain, and the management of migraine during pregnancy, infertility treatment, and lactation.

This book is aimed at headache specialists and primary care providers, including nurse practitioners, obstetrician-gynecologists, and others who are looking for an in-depth, single-volume resource on headache in women. Standard textbooks on migraine consider diagnosis, treatment, and complications of the disorder from a gender-neutral view. Important information relevant to the care of women with migraine is generally compressed into a single chapter, making it difficult to provide sufficiently detailed diagnostic and treatment recommendations. With *Headache in Women*, we provide a comprehensive, thorough source of detailed and practical information about all aspects of migraine in women. The approach is evidence-based but, where gaps in research exist, our world-renowned authorities provide advice based on expert consensus and clinical experience.

Our sincere expectation is that you will find this book useful and relevant in your everyday clinical practice. Beyond that, we hope it stimulates your interest in headache, and in helping those women and men who suffer from it.

Elizabeth Loder
Dawn Marcus
December 2003

REFERENCES

1. Adler J, Roger A. The war against migraine [cover]. Newsweek January 11, 1999:46–52.

2. Gorman C, Park A. The new science of headaches [cover]. Time October 7, 2002:76–82.

3. Lipton RB, Stewart WF. Migraine in the United States: a review of the epidemiology and health care use. Neurology 1993;Suppl 30:S6–10.

4. Stewart WF, Lipton RB, Simon D. Work-related disability: results from the American Migraine Study. Cephalalgia 1996;16:231–8.

5. Verbrugge LM. Gender and health: an update on hypotheses and evidence. J Health Soc Behav 1985;26:156–82.

Contributors

Sheena K. Aurora, MD
Co-Director
Swedish Headache Center
Swedish Neuroscience Institute
Seattle, Washington

Jan Lewis Brandes, MD
Clinical Instructor
Department of Neurology
Vanderbilt University School of Medicine
Nashville, Tennessee

Robin L. Brey, MD
Professor
Department of Medicine
University of Texas
San Antonio, Texas

Roger Cady, MD
Director
Headache Care Center
Springfield, Missouri

Merle L. Diamond, MD, FACEP
Clinical Assistant Professor
Department of Medicine
Finch University Health Sciences/Chicago
    Medical School
Chicago, Illinois

Kathleen B. Digre, MD
Professor
Department of Neurology and
    Ophthalmology
University of Utah
Salt Lake City, Utah

Kathleen Farmer, PsyD
Adjunct Faculty
Department of Health Psychology and Pain
    Management
Forest Institute of Professional Psychology
Springfield, Missouri

Lynne O. Geweke, MD
Clinical Assistant Professor
Department of Neurology
University of Iowa
Iowa City, Iowa

Joanna Kempner, MA
Doctoral Candidate
Department of Sociology
University of Pennsylvania
Philadelphia, Pennsylvania

Gay L. Lipchik, PhD
Director
St. Vincent Health Psychology Services
Erie, Pennsylvania

Elizabeth Loder, MD, FACP
Assistant Professor
Department of Medicine
Harvard Medical School
Boston, Massachusetts

Sylvia Lucas, MD, PhD
Clinical Assistant Professor
Department of Neurology
University of Washington
Seattle, Washington

E. Anne MacGregor, MBBS, MFFP, DIPM
Director of Clinical Research
The City of London Migraine Clinic
London, United Kingdom

Lisa K. Mannix, MD
Headache Associates
Cincinnati, Ohio

Dawn A. Marcus, MD
Associate Professor
Department of Anesthesiology
University of Pittsburgh Medical Center
Pittsburgh, Pennsylvania

Loretta Mueller, DO, FACOFP
Associate Professor
Department of Family Medicine
University of Medicine and Dentistry of
    New Jersey/School of Osteopathic Medicine
Moorestown, New Jersey

Beau K. Nakamoto, MD
Chief Resident
Department of Neurology
University of Utah
Salt Lake City, Utah

Jeanetta C. Rains, PhD
Adjunct Assistant Professor
Department of Psychiatry
Dartmouth Medical School
Lebanon, New Hampshire

Stephen D. Silberstein, MD, FACP
Professor of Neurology
Department of Neurology
Thomas Jefferson University/Jefferson Medical
    College
Philadelphia, Pennsylvania

Gretchen E. Tietjen, MD
Professor and Chair
Department of Neurology
Medical College of Ohio
Toledo, Ohio

Richard G. Wenzel, PharmD
Clinical Assistant Professor
Department of Pharmacy Practice
University of Illinois/College of Pharmacy
Chicago, Illinois

CHAPTER 1

Highlights

Elizabeth Loder, MD, FACP, and Dawn A. Marcus, MD

This chapter provides an overview of information presented in each of the chapters of this book. Additional details about treatment can be found in the respective chapters, along with references.

MENSTRUAL HEADACHE

What is menstrual migraine?

- Migraine occurring within 2 days before to 3 days after the onset of menstrual bleeding.
- Women should record diaries for 2 to 3 months to ensure headaches are exclusively/primarily linked to menses, rather than coincidental.

How should menstrual migraine be treated?

- Most women respond well to acute care therapy (eg, triptans or nonsteroidal anti-inflammatory medications) taken with headache symptoms.
- Short-term scheduled prophylaxis may be used in women with regular menstrual periods and inadequate response to acute care therapy.
- Short-term prophylaxis begins 1 to 2 days before anticipated headache and continues for a total of 5 to 7 days.
  - Naproxen sodium 250 mg to 500 mg twice daily
  - Magnesium 360 mg daily
  - Estradiol patch 100 μg
  - Sumatriptan 25 mg every 8 hours
  - Naratriptan 1 mg twice daily
  - Frovatriptan 2.5 mg twice daily
- Continuous oral contraceptives, with placebo only every 3 months

ORAL CONTRACEPTIVES (OCs)

Are OCs contraindicated in migraineurs?

- Headaches may be initiated or worsened by OC use in some women.
  - Headaches related to OCs typically occur during the placebo week.
  - Migraine with aura is more likely to worsen than migraine without aura.

- OCs increase risk of stroke (both thrombotic and hemorrhagic). Migraine is an additional independent risk factor for stroke, with the greatest risk in those with migraine with aura.
  - OCs should be used cautiously in women with migraine with aura.
  - OCs should be discontinued in women who develop a migraine aura after using OCs.
  - Migraineurs using OCs should reduce other cardiovascular risk factors: obesity, high cholesterol, nicotine use, and hypertension.
  - Consider discontinuing OCs in migraineurs after age 40 years, when stroke risk increases.

PREGNANCY AND HEADACHES

Should headaches go away during pregnancy?

- Headache improves for about one-half of pregnant women.
  - If headaches will improve during pregnancy, improvement should be expected during the first trimester.
- Hormonal changes may trigger headaches for some women.

When should an imaging study of the head be ordered for the pregnant patient with headache?

- In general, magnetic resonance imaging is believed to be relatively safe during pregnancy.
- Additional testing (eg, blood tests and radiographic studies) should be considered for women with atypical headache patterns, headaches failing to respond to therapy, or abnormal physical examinations.

What treatments are safe to use during pregnancy?

- Safe acute care treatments:
  - As for nonpregnant women, acute care medications need to be limited to a maximum of 3 days per week to avoid the development of analgesic overuse headache.

- Acetaminophen
- Antiemetics
- Intermittent, short-acting opioids (eg, hydrocodone)
- Safe preventive treatments:
  - Relaxation, biofeedback, stress management
  - Beta-blockers
  - Selective serotonin reuptake inhibitors
  - Gabapentin, in early pregnancy
    - Discontinue in later pregnancy because of influence on bone development
- Dietary restrictions (eg, tyramine-free diet) are not recommended during pregnancy because the majority of women will not experience headache improvement and these diets can restrict calcium and other nutrients needed during pregnancy.

What treatments are safe to use when breastfeeding?

- Those medications used during pregnancy can usually be continued during breastfeeding.
- Injectable sumatriptan can be used during lactation if the mother expresses and discards milk produced during the 4 hours following a sumatriptan injection and supplements her baby with stored milk or formula.

MENOPAUSE AND HEADACHES

Should headaches go away when women reach menopause?

- Chronic headaches are experienced by 14% of postmenopausal women.
- Headaches often worsen during the perimenopausal period, when women experience other somatic symptoms, such as hot flashes.
- Migraine improves for 67% of women after spontaneous menopause.
- Migraine worsens for 67% of women after surgical menopause.

Should migraineurs receive estrogen replacement therapy?

- Migraine is not a contraindication to hormone replacement therapy (HRT: estrogen plus progestin replacement).
  - Three percent of women experience new or worsening of chronic headache after starting estrogen replacement therapy (ERT).
- HRT results in improvement of headache in some women and worsening of headache in others.
  - If headache worsens after taking HRT, decrease dose or change formulation of estrogen component.
  - Cutaneous estradiol patches are least likely to aggravate chronic headache.

- Benefits and risks from hormonal replacement help determine when they are prescribed for individual patients.
  - ERT
    - Increases thromboembolic risk
    - Unclear cognitive benefits
  - HRT
    - Increases risk of ovarian and breast cancer
    - No clear reduction in cardiovascular risk
    - Reduces risk for vertebral and nonvertebral fractures by 25%

NONPHARMACOLOGIC THERAPY

Are psychological symptoms important in chronic headache sufferers?

- Depression occurs in over 30% and panic disorder in 11% of migraineurs.
- Patients with chronic headache and comorbid psychological symptoms have a poorer prognosis for headache improvement and require more aggressive therapy.
  - Severe psychological symptoms will need specific targeted therapy.
- Simple and quick paper or online screening tools are available for clinical use to identify comorbid psychological symptoms.

Do psychological treatments only help people who have serious psychiatric problems?

- Typical nonpharmacologic treatment, such as relaxation, biofeedback, stress management, and cognitive restructuring, is as effective as standard migraine-preventive medication therapies.
- Nonpharmacologic therapies are equally effective for hormonally-related or nonhormonal headaches.

Which non-medication treatments really work?

- Thermal biofeedback is effective and can be learned with minimal therapist contact.
- Coping skills, cognitive restructuring, and stress-management are each effective when administered by trained personnel.
- Diet/substance use:
  - Avoid nicotine.
  - Limit caffeine to two 6- to 8-ounce servings daily.
  - Limit alcohol to two drinks daily.
  - About 30% of patients notice headache reduction when avoiding tyramine-rich foods.
- Herbals and vitamins:
  - Riboflavin 400 mg daily
  - Magnesium 500 mg to 750 mg daily
  - Feverfew one capsule 3 to 4 times daily
- The combination of medication plus non-medication therapies maximizes overall treatment efficacy.

CHAPTER 2

The Epidemiology of Primary Headache in Women

Sylvia Lucas, MD, PhD

CASE

ML is a 53-year-old woman who began to experience migraine attacks at age 13 years, coincident with menarche. She recalls frequent motion sickness as a child, and both her mother and maternal grandmother had regular "sick" headaches. A younger brother had similar but less intense headaches. Her 24-year-old daughter is also a headache sufferer. ML had significant improvement in headaches during pregnancy, but the headaches returned soon after her daughter was born. In fact, for a period of 19 years following her daughter's birth, ML had some degree of headache almost daily, with superimposed episodes of severe headache associated with nausea and vomiting. ML works as an architect; when she was in her thirties and forties, she missed work due to headaches one day a month, on average, and functioned at less than full capacity at work and home much of the rest of the time. Four years ago, ML underwent spontaneous menopause, and her headaches returned to an episodic pattern; severity has also decreased.

This case illustrates some common epidemiologic features of migraine, the headache disorder for which women are most likely to seek medical treatment. ML comes from a "headache-prone" family, developed the common migraine precursor of motion sickness in childhood, and had changes in the pattern of her headache coincident with the hormonal milestones of menarche, pregnancy, and menopause. For a large portion of her otherwise productive adult years, ML has experienced significant social and occupational disability as a result of migraine.

All of the primary headache disorders, with the exception of cluster headache, are more common in women than in men. Migraine, in particular, is a prevalent and disabling disease that most severely affects otherwise healthy women during the middle years of life. This chapter reviews the epidemiology of the primary headache disorders with special attention to the disproportionate burden they impose on women.

KEY CHAPTER POINTS

- Migraine is the primary headache disorder for which women are most likely to seek medical treatment; the personal and public health burden it imposes on otherwise healthy women during the middle years of life is substantial. Hormonal influences may explain why it is more common and disabling in women than in men.
- Tension-type headache is the most common form of primary headache, but it does not often prompt medical consultation. It is more common in women than in men, but the gender discrepancy is less pronounced than for migraine.
- Cluster headache is rare in both sexes but more common in men than in women; recognition of the disorder in women may be increasing.

THE INCIDENCE AND PREVALENCE OF MIGRAINE

Incidence

Incidence of migraine is a rate determined by the number of new cases of migraine that develop in a population over a defined period of time. Most incidence studies examine large cohorts of individuals and estimate the incidence from cross-sectional or prevalence data; however, several problems are associated with this approach. First, most such studies do not include children, despite the fact that migraine can begin at a very young age. Second, even if young children are included in epidemiologic surveys, migraine may be underrecognized in them. This is largely attributable to the difficulty of obtaining the historical information necessary to make a migraine diagnosis but may also be due to differences in migraine presentation in children and adolescents as compared with adults. Children may be more likely to have abdominal variants of migraine, such as cyclic vomiting, and seem to have markedly shorter headache episodes as well. In fact, the revised 2003 International Headache Society (IHS) criteria have reduced headache duration requirements and allow inference of photo- and phonophobia.

Two retrospective studies have assessed the incidence of migraine based on reported age of migraine onset. The largest involved telephone interviews of 10,169 residents of Washington County, Maryland.[1] Migraine was identified in 392 males and 1,018 females. Onset in both peaked in adolescence, then declined over time. Of note, migraine incidence peaked earlier in boys than in girls, and the peak incidence of migraine with aura in both genders occurred earlier than migraine without aura. In boys, peak incidence of migraine with aura was 5 years of age, whereas in girls it was 12 to 13 years of age. For migraine without aura, peak incidence in boys was between ages 10 and 11 years, and in girls it was between 14 to 17 years of age.[1]

Another study examined a random sample of 1,000 men and women aged 25 to 64 years drawn from the National Central Person Registry in Copenhagen.[2] Using IHS criteria to define migraine, an age-adjusted annual incidence was estimated as 5.8 new cases per 1,000 person years in women and 1.6 new cases per 1,000 person years in men. However, this study did not look at age-specific incidence and had an older age distribution.

One prospective study on migraine incidence has been reported.[3] One thousand seven members of a health maintenance organization between ages 21 and 30 years were interviewed, 98% of whom completed a 3.5 and 5.5 year follow-up study. The estimated 5.5 year cumulative incidence was 2.4 new cases per 1,000 person years in women and 0.6 new cases per 1,000 person years in men.

Prevalence

Migraine prevalence is easier to determine than incidence, and many studies exist.[4–14] A few methodologic problems should be noted. First, study size may influence results. In general, larger studies more accurately reflect the prevalence of migraine in the general population but are costlier than smaller trials and may

involve application of study criteria through questionnaires or standardized interviews conducted by workers with no special expertise in headache. Smaller trials, in contrast, are more prone to bias related to non-representative study samples, but often involve more thorough, individualized, and expert diagnostic evaluation of subjects.

The period of time covered by the study is also of importance. Surveys, questionnaires, and interviews all generally ask respondents to recall headache events over a lifetime or for a certain time period prior to the study. For example, the lifetime prevalence of migraine refers to the proportion of individuals in a population who have ever had migraine at any time during their lives. One-year prevalence refers to the proportion of individuals in a population who have had migraine at some time during the year prior to the survey. Because of the episodic nature of migraine and the difficulty many people experience in remembering remote pain problems or characteristics, memory for events occurring closest to the time of evaluation may be more accurate. In addition, the age of the population evaluated affects the results; prevalence estimates will be lower in younger populations because migraine has not yet become manifest in all who will ultimately develop the disorder.

Prevalence estimates generated from epidemiologic studies of migraine have converged more closely since the IHS criteria have become more widely used. These independently obtained, similar results increase our confidence in the validity of estimates despite the methodologic problems outlined above. A meta-analysis of 24 epidemiologic studies published before 1994 concluded that most of the variance in prevalence rates among the different studies could be explained by the different definitions of migraine in the different studies.[15] Only five studies used IHS criteria. A later meta-analysis examined 18 population-based studies that all used IHS criteria to define migraine and showed increased agreement among results obtained from these studies.[16] In these studies, as before, migraine was shown to be more prevalent in women than in men, with peak prevalence occurring in women between ages 35 and 45 years.

Table 2-1 shows the prevalence estimates for migraine obtained from methodologically rigorous studies of migraine conducted using IHS criteria. There are five such studies from North America,[6,8,9,11,12] one from Japan,[14] and five from Western Europe.[4,5,7,10,12] The mean lifetime prevalence of migraine in these studies[5,6,9–12,14] is 22.6% for women (range 13–32%) and 10.5% for men (range 6.6–22%). The one-year prevalence of migraine in women is 17.4% (range 15–19%) and in men is 7.0% (range 5.7–9%).[4,5,7,8,13] One-year prevalence estimates show less variability than do lifetime prevalence estimates.

Table 2-1 Epidemiologic Studies of Headache Prevalence

Study	Sample	Methodology	Size (n)	Age (years)	Time Period	Women (%)	Men (%)
Breslau et al, 1991[6]	HMO USA	Interview	1,007	21–30	Lifetime	16.3	7
D'Allessandro et al, 1988[4]	Gen pop Italy	Interview	1,144	> 7	1 year	18	9
Edmeads et al, 1993[9]	Gen pop Canada	Interview	2,737	> 15	Lifetime	23	9
Gobel et al, 1994[10]	Gen pop Germany	Questionnaire	4,061	> 18	Lifetime	32	22
Henry et al, 1992[7]	Gen pop France	Interview	4,204	> 15	Several years	17.6	6.1
O'Brien et al, 1994[11]	Gen pop Canada	Interview	2,922	≥ 18	Lifetime	25	8
Rasmussen et al, 1991[5]	Gen pop Denmark	Interview, exam	740	25–64	Lifetime / 1 year	25 / 15	9 / 6
Russell et al, 1995[12]	Gen pop Denmark	Interview, exam	3,471	40	Lifetime	24	12
Sakai and Igarashi, 1997[14]	Gen pop Japan	Interview, questionnaire	4,029	> 15	Lifetime	13	6.6
Stewart et al, 1992[17]	Gen pop USA	Questionnaire	20,468	12–80	1 year	17.6	5.7
Stewart et al, 1996[13]	Gen pop USA	Interview	12,328	18–65	1 year	19	8

exam = examination; gen pop = general population; HMO = health maintenance organization.

The calculated female to male *lifetime prevalence ratio* for migraine generated from those studies obtaining such data is 2.46:1 ($n = 11$). The calculated female to male *one-year prevalence ratio* calculated from the same sources is 2.58:1 ($n = 5$). These statistics are the origin of the frequently heard statement that "women are roughly three times as likely as men to have migraine."

HORMONAL INFLUENCES ON MIGRAINE

There is an intriguing relationship between migraine incidence, prevalence, age, and gender. Migraine incidence is higher in prepubertal boys than girls,[1,2] so prevalence prior to the onset of puberty is highest in boys. Prevalence rises more rapidly in girls during adolescence, presumably because the onset of menarche drives the incidence peak seen in girls of this age. Most experts believe that the association between peak migraine incidence and menarche is a causal one, but the exact mechanisms through which menarche triggers the onset of migraine are unknown. Speculation centers largely on the belief that cyclical hormonal changes, especially fluctuating levels of estrogen, have important pro-migraine effects on the central nervous system. That these effects may be permanent is supported by the fact that at all ages after puberty, even late in life when hormonal cycling has ceased, migraine prevalence remains higher in females than in males. The female to male ratio for migraine prevalence increases from menarche until approximately age 42,

where it peaks at 3.3:1; thereafter, it decreases,[8,9] perhaps owing to the gradual onset of ovarian failure and the declining provocative influence of hormonal cycling,[18] but also due to the nonspecific beneficial effects of aging on migraine.

The distribution of migraine attacks throughout the menstrual cycle is not random. A study of 52 women that obtained data on 512 migraine attacks[19] showed that the peak occurrence of individual attacks was 2 days before the onset of menstrual flow. Another study[20] of 55 women who charted migraine attacks occurring over a period of three menstrual cycles found the highest frequency of attacks occurring during a window of time from 2 days before to 2 days after the onset of menstrual flow. Falling estrogen levels during the luteal phase of the menstrual cycle have been implicated in this menstrual spike of migraine attacks (see Chapter 10, "Menstrual Migraine").

Despite the decline in migraine prevalence that occurs over time, headache, especially migraine, remains a common, often troublesome, symptom of perimenopausal and menopausal women. Natural menopause is a process that occurs gradually over several years, not an abrupt event. Possibly because of less regular hormonal fluctuations, the period of time surrounding cessation of menstruation (perimenopause) may be particularly problematic for women with migraine. One study[21] noted a high prevalence of migraine in a specialty menopause clinic, with migraine affecting 29% of patients in the preceding

3 months and fully 57% of women reporting any form of headache during that time. Other situations in which hormonal changes occur are also associated with changes in migraine frequency or intensity, although the effects vary from improvement to worsening and have not been systematically or rigorously studied.[22] In particular, the use of exogenous hormones in the form of hormone replacement therapy (HRT) or oral contraceptives (OCs) has been associated with improvement, worsening, or no change in migraine, depending on the regimens and doses employed. Pregnancy often, though not invariably, improves migraine, perhaps through the beneficial effect of non-cycling levels of estrogen.

SOCIODEMOGRAPHIC FACTORS AND MIGRAINE

In addition to gender and age, sociodemographic factors affect migraine prevalence. A large population-based study in the United States[13] found migraine prevalence lowest in Asian-Americans (9.2% in women, 4.8% in men), intermediate in African-Americans (16.2% in women, 7.2% in men) and highest in Caucasians (20.4% in women, 8.6% in men). Differences in genetic susceptibility to migraine presumably account at least to some extent for these results, although other factors such as response to stress, cultural attitudes toward pain, or differing diet and alcohol consumption might play a role.

Migraine prevalence may be related to socioeconomic status. In the United States, migraine prevalence has been shown to increase as income or highest level of education decrease.[8,23] In other studies, however, a positive relationship between migraine prevalence and income was found.[10,11] Rasmussen found no relationship between primary headaches and employment status, category of industry, education, or marital status between those living in an urban or a rural environment.[24]

PERSONAL AND PUBLIC IMPACT OF MIGRAINE

The personal and socioeconomic burdens of headache disorders are underappreciated. At least some of this may be due to the fact that those most frequently affected by headache are women, who until recently were not especially visible in settings outside the home. Certainly the impact of headache is well understood by those who have personal or family experience with the disorders. They realize that all phases of an individual headache attack are disabling. For migraine, these include commonly experienced prodromal symptoms of irritability or decreased concentration; the disabling pain, nausea, vomiting, and sensory sensitivity of the fully established attack; and the unpleasant postdromal "headache hangover" symptoms of lethargy and lingering head pain. Even between attacks, the fear or anticipation of dysfunction and suffering and uncertainty about when the next attack will occur contribute to depression, missed social and occupational opportunities, and misuse of medication. The impact of these lost opportunities may seem insignificant for an individual attack, but result in substantial and cumulative negative effects over a lifetime of attacks.

The American Migraine Study attempted to quantify the individual impact of migraine through a telephone-based interview of 1,748 migraineurs.[25] Eighty percent reported that their attacks usually involved severe or very severe pain. More men reported severe pain (46%) than women (38.9%), but more women reported very severe pain (43.3%) than men (31.8%). Men and women reported similar occurrences of photophobia (76.5% in men and 83.5% in women) as well as phonophobia (72.9% and 79.3%, respectively), but 62.1% of women complained of nausea compared with 47.3% of men. Though the median number of attacks was the same for both sexes, at one to two per month, attacks were of longer duration in women (71% reported migraines usually lasting over 24 hours, compared with only 48% of men).

The economic and healthcare impact of migraine is also substantial. Economic costs are generally divided into indirect costs, which arise from lost productivity, and direct costs, attributable to healthcare expenses related to headache diagnosis and treatment. Many of the indirect costs of migraine are difficult or impossible to quantify; for example, the indirect cost of a migraine attack due to decreased productivity of the migraineur's co-workers is hard to estimate.

Patients with migraine make more physician visits for all reasons, not just headache, than patients without migraine,[26] although emergency department visits are not common. Population-based one-year estimates of emergency department visits in the United States owing to migraine are 5% in male migraineurs and 3% in female migraineurs[27]; not unexpectedly, emergency department visits are more common in those patients who use prescription medications.[28] Hospitalization rates specifically for treatment of refractory headache are low,[29] but migraineurs are more than twice as likely as members of the general population to be hospitalized for any reason.[26] Finally, direct costs of care of migraineurs, as expected, are proportional to the severity of the headache.[30]

For migraine, direct costs pale in comparison to indirect costs. Although it is difficult for studies to capture all costs over a lifetime of headache, work loss is a major source of indirect cost and can be fairly well estimated. A simple measure of actual work loss days (absenteeism) tends to underestimate work-related disability because many patients with migraine often stay at work through the headache, whether treated or not, but perform less effectively (a phenomenon termed "presenteeism").

A study of actual lost work days and an estimate of decreased productivity was reported in 1996 using data from a self-administered Headache Disability and Health Care Questionnaire.[25] This study attempted not only to identify lost work days from absenteeism but to add an estimate of decreased productivity that, if multiplied by the number of days of severe headache, is a "lost work day equivalent." The sum of these two numbers is the lost work day equivalents (LWDE) and was evaluated in 1,663 migraineurs 18 years of age or older with severe headache. Results showed that actual lost work days from absenteeism and decreased effectiveness at work contributed equally to total LWDE. In this sample of migraineurs, 74% of women and 56% of men had at least one LWDE per year because of migraine. However, 90% of the total LWDE could be accounted for by a subgroup of 51.1% of the women and 38.1% of the men migraineurs who had 6 or more LWDE per year. The authors drew special attention to this "compression of disability" and suggested that this highly disabled subgroup of migraineurs might be an important target for treatment aimed at decreasing migraine-attributable costs. Even a slight improvement in their situation would presumably yield significant and exponential cost savings.

Interestingly, the average number of missed workdays per year in these migraineurs was 3.8 in men and 8.3 in women, despite no reported difference in severity or frequency of the headache. In women, headache duration was the strongest predictor of LWDE, while in men the pain level was most closely associated with LWDE.[25] Women were less likely to miss work if they had a higher level of education or higher income. One might speculate that this is due to a higher level of responsibility at work or higher levels of job satisfaction and thus a lower tendency to avoid work for any reason. In a self-reported study of the impact of migraine on work, 14% of migraineurs felt that their headaches placed an extra work burden on co-workers, 7% reported their belief that headaches were responsible for lower work salary or missing raises, and 16% felt that headaches resulted in lower performance evaluations at work.[31] Twenty-eight percent of these migraine sufferers reported working fewer hours because of headache, 24% chose less demanding work because of their headaches, and 8% actually changed their employment because of their headaches. The final conclusion of this study was that migraine costs US employers approximately 13 billion dollars per year owing to absenteeism and decreased work productivity.

The concept of "quality of life" (QOL) refers to the personal perception of general health and well-being. It is a subjective measurement that is influenced by cultural, social, economic, and spiritual factors. There are many general health-related QOL questionnaires, including a few that are headache- or migraine-specific.

Migraine-specific QOL questionnaires have been used to measure the personal impact of this condition on sufferers, during a single attack or over variable periods of time. Health-related QOL questionnaires are now standard in clinical trials of new medications for migraine. As such, most health-related QOL studies are clinic based, and probably measure the QOL of patients with more severe headache who are more likely to participate in clinical trials.[32] Not unexpectedly, these studies have lower QOL results than population-based studies.[33,34]

In population-based studies, migraineurs report lower QOL scores than non-migraineurs in areas of physical, social, and mental functioning.[35] Lower QOL scores are seen as migraine frequency and disability increase.[35,36] Approximately one-third of migraineurs must cancel social or family activities, and over one-half say their headaches affect their relationships with family members.[37]

The majority of subjects identified in one large study as having migraine reported that they had never been diagnosed by a physician as having the disorder. Women were more likely than men to have received a formal diagnosis (41% vs 29%, respectively), as were subjects who reported aura, vomiting, or disability. However, many of the undiagnosed patients reported significant levels of headache-related disability, suggesting that efforts to improve recognition and treatment of migraine are needed.[38] Recognition of migraine in primary care settings is especially important; data suggest that when primary care clinicians make a diagnosis of migraine, they are nearly always correct (98% of migraine diagnoses were confirmed on expert review), but that many patients diagnosed with non-migraine headache in fact have migraine that has been missed (79% of non-migraine diagnoses were migraine on expert review). Almost 90% of patients in primary care settings who present with a chief complaint of headache are diagnosed on careful examination to have migraine; the likelihood of migraine is probably not sufficiently clear to many practitioners, who understandably worry about secondary causes of headache such as brain tumor or meningitis. In fact, secondary causes of headache are rare in this setting.[39]

COMORBIDITY AND MIGRAINE

Comorbidity refers to the existence of two conditions in an individual with a frequency greater than would be expected on the basis of chance.[40] Comorbid relationships between migraine and a variety of somatic and psychiatric or behavioral conditions have been reported. The implications of comorbidity are substantial, both for our understanding of the disease process and because it may have an important effect on treatment choices. Efforts to study migraine comorbidity face many of the same challenges involved in other epidemiologic studies of headache, particularly the difficulty of arriving at precise definitions for all of the disorders involved. Because some of the conditions of interest are less common than migraine, study populations must be large enough to have the statistical power needed to detect an association; this means that smaller clinical or case studies are particularly at risk of showing no association because of low sample sizes and insufficient statistical power. In addition, people who have more than one condition may be more prone to seek medical care or less prone to participate in epidemiologic studies, resulting in over- or underdetection of any association between two disorders.

Despite these difficulties, a number of studies have been conducted that suggest migraine is comorbid with a number of disorders including depression, anxiety, panic, stroke, and epilepsy. As with migraine, affective and psychiatric disorders are clinical diagnoses, generally made using criteria outlined in the *Diagnostic and Statistical Manual of Mental Disorders (DSM)*,[41] which, like the IHS[42] criteria for headache disorders, require the fulfillment of a certain number of conditions before a diagnosis can be made. The most convincing comorbid associations for migraine are with affective disorders in general, especially depression and anxiety. A large community study of 591 patients in Zurich, Switzerland,[43] found that depression and anxiety were more common in migraineurs than in non-migraineurs, with an odds ratio of 2.2 for depression and 2.7 for anxiety. A community-based study of over 1,000 young adults in a Michigan health maintenance organization had similar results, with an odds ratio of 3.6 for depression and 1.9 for anxiety in migraineurs versus non-migraineurs.[6] A subsequent prospective study of this community[44] calculated a relative risk of 4.1 for subsequent onset of major depression in patients who had migraine at baseline. If a patient had a history of major depression at baseline, the relative risk for subsequent onset of migraine was 3.3 compared with a cohort of non-depressed subjects. This "bidirectional association" was interpreted by the study authors as evidence that migraine is not a cause of depression or depression a cause of migraine—instead, underlying factors in the central nervous system seem to predispose affected subjects to the development of both disorders. Interestingly, this relationship between headache and affective disorders did not emerge for other types of primary headache disorders and thus appears to be specific to migraine.[45] Other studies have reported similar odds ratios for depression and anxiety.[46–48]

The Zurich study also examined the order of onset of depression, anxiety, and migraine. Rather than occurring in random order, they observed that onset of anxiety disorder generally preceded the development of migraine (in approximately 80% of cases comorbid with migraine) with onset of migraine preceding that of depression (in 75% of comorbid patients).[43]

The occurrence of comorbid conditions may make it more likely that a patient would see a healthcare professional. In a large population-based telephone survey of over 10,000 patients between the ages of 12 and 29 years in Washington County, Maryland, 14.2% of females and 5.8% of males who had a headache in the prior year consulted a physician for their headaches. Of this patient subset, 15% of females and 12.8% of males had a history of panic disorder. Not surprisingly, women with panic disorder who did see a physician were likely to have the most frequent, severe, longer, and more disabling headaches.[49]

Several epidemiologic studies have demonstrated that migraineurs have an increased risk of stroke compared with people without migraine.[50,51] Numerous explanations for this increased risk have been suggested but not proved, including platelet abnormalities[52] and mitral valve prolapse.[53] A recent Finnish cohort study of patients with chronic unspecified headache showed that the risk of stroke in this group was significantly elevated and persisted up to 25 years.[54] The risk appeared to be twice as high for men as for women, and, in fact, in women the higher stroke rate was not statistically significant.[54] Unfortunately, the study did not obtain information about the type of headaches the patients had, making it difficult to know if the increased risk of stroke was in patients with migraine or not.

TENSION-TYPE HEADACHE

Tension-type headache is the most prevalent of the primary headache disorders. Both the chronic and episodic forms of the disorder are more common in women than in men, but the gender discrepancy is less marked than for migraine. Prevalence estimates of tension-type headache have varied widely, even among studies that used IHS criteria for diagnosis, because most of these studies were small. A large telephone interview survey comprising over 13,000 interviews, however, has recently yielded data that seem highly reliable.[55] This study shows that, as with migraine, the prevalence of episodic tension-type headache (ETTH) peaks during middle age (30–39 years) for both men and women, and the disorder is more common in Caucasians than in African-Americans. The overall female to male prevalence ratio for ETTH is 1.16:1, a less pronounced gender ratio than seen in migraine. Almost three-quarters of patients experience 30 or fewer headaches per year, or once or twice a month, on average. Pain severity is generally rated as mild or moderate, with a mean intensity of 4.98 on a 10-point scale described by subjects in that study. The authors noted other differences between the epidemiology of migraine and tension-type headache, among them the fact that tension-type headache is less strongly related to age than is migraine, as well as a positive correlation of ETTH with educational level, rather than the inverse correlation seen for migraine and socioeconomic status.

Chronic tension-type headache (CTTH) is much less common than ETTH, with an overall prevalence of 2.8% in women and 1.4% in men. Mean pain intensity for patients with CTTH was 5.55 on a 10-point scale. The disability attributable to CTTH was much greater on an individual level than that for ETTH, but because ETTH is so common, it contributes more to the overall societal burden of headache than does CTTH. In women, the age distribution of CTTH was shifted toward older groups (over age 50 years).

CLUSTER HEADACHE

Clinically, cluster headache (CH) is the most distinct and easily recognizable of the primary headache disorders. It is more common in men than in women, but recent reports suggest that the gender ratio is changing, with more women than ever being diagnosed with the disorder. Whether this is attributable to improved recognition of CH in women or to environmental factors that have increased the likelihood that women will develop CH is not clear; both factors may be operating. There is controversy over whether CH is familial; its rarity makes twin studies and other genetic investigation difficult. Epidemiologic studies also face the challenge of studying a rare disorder because very large populations must be studied in order to identify enough cases to permit a reliable estimate of prevalence. However, the diagnostic difficulties faced in epidemiologic investigations of other primary headache disorders are less of a problem with CH research because it is such an easily recognized diagnosis.

Of the handful of large studies of CH epidemiology that exist, prevalence estimates vary from 0.03% (30 per 100,000) in an Ethiopian community study, to 0.092% (92 per 100,000) in a sample of 18-year-old Swedish military recruits.[56] A study of the entire male population of the republic of San Marino yielded a prevalence of 0.056% (56 per 100,000) and an incidence of 2.4 per 100,000 each year.[57] A study in Minnesota suggested an age-adjusted incidence of 15.6 per 100,000 per year for men and 4 per 100,000 per year for women. Peak incidence in men was between 40 and 49 years, although almost one-half of the patients were in their twenties and thirties at onset.[58] Only five women were included in that study, so reliable incidence data cannot be generated; of those five women, three developed CH after age 50 years.

Explanations for the male predominance seen in CH have centered on hormonal factors, but associations with low testosterone levels in men and menstruation, pregnancy, hormonal manipulations, or menopause in women have not been convincingly established.[59] Researchers in Italy have commented on a progressive decline in the male to female prevalence ratio for CH, although considerable controversy exists as to the accuracy of these observations.[60] These researchers suggested that changes in environmental exposures among women might account for an increase in CH. This disorder is associated (causality has not been demonstrated) with smoking and alcohol exposure[61]; social forces mean that those behaviors are now more common among women. Skeptics, however, suggest other explanations for this changing gender ratio, the most plausible of which is that chronic migraine with prominent autonomic features (more common in women) may be increasingly recognized and confused with chronic CH.[62]

REFERENCES

1. Stewart WF, Linet M, Celentano D, et al. Age- and sex-specific incidence rates of migraine with and without visual aura. Am J Epidemiol 1991;134:1111–20.

2. Rasmussen BK. Epidemiology of headache. Cephalalgia 1995;15:45–68.

3. Breslau N, Chilcoat H, Andreski P. Further evidence on the link between migraine and neuroticism. Neurology 1996;47:663–7.

4. D'Alessandro R, Benassi G, Lenzi PL, et al. Epidemiology of headache in the Republic of San Marino. J Neurol Neurosurg Psychiatry 1988;51:21–7.

5. Rasmussen BK, Jensen R, Schroll M, Olesen J. Epidemiology of headache in a general population—a prevalence study. J Clin Epidemiol 1991;44:1147–57.

6. Breslau N, Davis GC, Andreski P. Migraine, psychiatric disorders, and suicide attempts: an epidemiologic study of young adults. Psychiatry Res 1991;37:11–23.

7. Henry P, Michel P, Brochet B, et al. A nationwide survey of migraine in France: prevalence and clinical features in adults. Cephalalgia 1992;12:229–37.

8. Lipton RB, Stewart WF, Diamond S, et al. Prevalence and burden of migraine in the United States: data from the American Migraine Study II. Headache 2001;41:646–57.

9. Edmeads J, Findlay H, Tugwell P, et al. Impact of migraine and tension-type headache on life-style, consulting behavior, and medication use: a Canadian population survey. Can J Neurol Sci 1993;20:131–7.

10. Gobel H, Petersen-Braun M, Soyka D. The epidemiology of headache in Germany: a nationwide survey of a representative sample on the basis of headache classification of the International Headache Society. Cephalalgia 1994;14:97–106.

11. O'Brien B, Goeree R, Streiner D. Prevalence of migraine headache in Canada: a population-based survey. Int J Epidemiol 1994;23:1020–6.

12. Russell MB, Rasmussen BK, Thorvaldsen P, Olesen J. Prevalence and sex-ratio of the subtypes of migraine. Int J Epidemiol 1995;24:612–8.

13. Stewart WF, Lipton RB, Liberman J. Variation in migraine prevalence by race. Neurology 1996;47:52–9.

14. Sakai F, Igarashi H. Epidemiology of migraine in Japan: a nationwide survey. Cephalalgia 1997;17:15–22.

15. Stewart WF, Simon D, Schechter A, et al. Population variation in migraine prevalence: a meta-analysis. J Clin Epidemiol 1995;48:269–80.

16. Scher A, Stewart W, Lipton R. Epidemiology of migraine: a meta-analytical approach. [Submitted]

17. Stewart WF, Lipton RD, Celentano DD, Reed ML. Prevalence of migraine headache in the United States. JAMA 1992;267:64–9.

18. Silberstein SD, Merriam GR. Sex hormones and headache. In: Goadsby P, Silberstein SD, editors. Blue books of practical neurology: headache. Boston: Butterworth Heinemann; 1997. p. 143–76.

19. Dalton K. Progesterone suppositories and pessaries in the treatment of menstrual migraine. Headache 1973;13:151–9.

20. MacGregor EA, Chia H, Vohrah RC, Wilkinson M. Migraine and menstruation: a pilot study. Cephalalgia 1990;110:305–10.

21. MacGregor EA, Barnes D. Migraine in a specialist menopause clinic. Climacteric 1999;2:218–23.

22. MacGregor EA. "Menstrual" migraine: towards a definition. Cephalalgia 1996;16:11–21.

23. Lipton RB, Stewart WF. Migraine in the United States: a review of the epidemiology and health care use. Neurology 1993;43(6 Suppl 3):S6–10.

24. Rasmussen BK. Migraine and tension-type headache in a general population: psychosocial factors. Int J Epidemiol 1992;21:1138–43.

25. Stewart WF, Lipton RB, Simon D. Work-related disability: results from the American Migraine Study. Cephalalgia 1996;16:231–8.

26. Clouse J, Osterhaus J. Healthcare resource use and costs associated with migraine in a managed healthcare setting. Ann Pharmacother 1994;28:659–64.

27. Linet MS, Stewart WF, Celentano DD, et al. An epidemiologic study of headache among adolescents and young adults. JAMA 1989;261:2211–6.

28. Celentano D, Stewart W, Lipton R, et al. Medication use and disability among migraineurs: a national probability sample survey. Headache 1992;32:223–8.

29. Stang P, Osterhaus J. Impact of migraine in the United States: data from The National Health Interview Study. Headache 1993;33:29–35.

30. Lipton RB, Stewart WF, Von Korff M. Burden of migraine: societal costs and therapeutic opportunities. Neurology 1997;48 Suppl 3:S4–9.

31. Hu X, Markson L, Lipton RB, et al. Disability and economic costs of migraine in the United States: a population-based approach. Arch Intern Med 1999;159:813–8.

32. Lipton R, Stewart W, Simon D. Medical consultation for migraine: results of the American Migraine Study. Headache 1998;38:87–90.

33. Solomon G, Skobieranda F, Gragg F. Quality of life and well-being of headache patients: measurement by the medical outcomes study instrument. Headache 1993;33:31–58.

34. Osterhaus J, Townsend R, Gandek B, et al. Measuring functional status and well-being of patients with migraine headache. Headache 1994;34:337–43.

35. Terwindt G, Launer L, Ferrari M. The impact of migraine on quality of life in the general population: the GEM study. Headache 2000;55:624–9.

36. Lipton RB, Hamelsky S, Kolodner KB, et al. Migraine, quality of life and depression: a population-based case-control study. Neurology 2000;55:629–35.

37. Pryse-Phillips W, Findlay H, Tugwell P, et al. A Canadian population survey on the clinical, epidemiologic and societal impact of migraine and tension-type headache. Can J Neurol Sci 1992;19:333–9.

38. Lipton RB, Stewart WF, Celentano DD, Reed ML. Undiagnosed migraine headaches: a comparison of symptom-based and reported physician diagnosis. Arch Intern Med 1992;152:1273–8.

39. Tepper SJ, Newman L, Dahlof C. The landmark study. Cephalalgia 2002;22:590–1.

40. Feinstein AR. The pre-therapeutic classification of co-morbidity in chronic disease. J Chronic Dis 1970;23:455–68.

41. Diagnostic and statistical manual of mental disorders: DSM IV-TR. 4th ed. Washington: American Psychiatric Publishing Inc.; 2000.

42. Headache classification committee of the international headache society (1988). Classification and diagnostic criteria for headache disorders, cranial neuralgia, and facial pain. Cephalalgia 8:1–96.

43. Merikangas KR, Angst J, Isler H. Migraine and psychopathology: results of the Zurich cohort study of young adults. Arch Gen Psychiatry 1990;47:849–53.

44. Breslau N, Davis GC. Migraine, physical health and psychiatric disorder: a prospective epidemiologic study in young adults. J Psychiatr Res 1993;27:211–21.

45. Breslau N, Schultz LR, Steart WF, et al. Headache types and panic disorder: directionality and specificity. Neurology 2001;56:350–4.

46. Merikangas KR, Risch NJ, Merikangas JR, et al. Migraine and depression: association and familial transmission. J Psychiatr Res 1988;22:119–29.

47. Merikangas KR. Sources of genetic complexity of migraine. In: Sandler M, Ferrari M, Harnett S, editors. Migraine pharmacology and genetics. London: Altman; 1996. p. 254–81.

48. Moldin, SO, Scheftner WA, Rice JP, et al. Association between major depressive disorder and physical illness. Psychol Med 1993;23:755–61.

49. Stewart WF, Shechter A, Liberman J. Physician consultation for headache pain and history of panic: results from a population-based study. Am J Med 1992;92 Suppl 1A: S35–40.

50. Merikangas KR, Fenton BT, Chengh SH, et al. Association between migraine and stroke in a large-scale epidemiological study of the United States. Arch Neurol 1997;54:362–8.

51. Carolei A, Marini C, DeMattaeis G. History of migraine and risk of cerebral ischemia in young adults. Lancet 1996;347:1503–6.

52. Kalendovsky Z, Austin JH. Complicated migraine: its association with increased platelet aggregability and abnormal coagulation factors. Headache 1975;15:18–35.

53. Petty GW, Orencia AJ, Khandheria BK, Whisnant JP. A population-based study of stroke in the setting of mitral valve prolapse: risk factors and infarct subtype classification. Mayo Clin Proc 1994;69:632–4.

54. Jousilahti P, Tuomilehto J, Rastenyte D, Vartiainen E. Headache and the risk of stroke: a prospective observational cohort study among 35056 Finnish men and women. Arch Intern Med 2003;163:1058–62.

55. Schwartz BS, Stewart WF, Simon D, Lipton RB. Epidemiology of tension-type headache. JAMA 1998;279:381–3.

56. Ekbom K, Ahlborg B, Schele R. Prevalence of migraine and cluster headache in Swedish men of 18. Headache 1978;18:9–12.

57. Tonon C, Guttmann S, Volpini M, et al. Prevalence and incidence of cluster headache in the Republic of San Marino. Neurology 2002;58:1407–9.

58. Swanson J, Yanagihara T, Stang P, et al. Incidence of cluster headache: a population-based study of Olmsted County, Minnesota. Neurology 1994;44:433–7.

59. Finkel AG. Epidemiology of cluster headache. Curr Pain Headache Rep 2003;7:144–9.

60. Manzoni G. Male preponderance of cluster headache is progressively decreasing over the years. Headache 1997;37:588–9.

61. Levi R, Edman G, Ekbom K, Waldenlind E. Episodic cluster headache II: high tobacco and alcohol consumption in males. Headache 1992;32:184–7.

62. Rozen T, Niknam RM, Schecter AL, et al. Cluster headache in women: clinical characteristics and comparison with cluster headache in men. J Neurol Neurosurg Psychiatry 2001;70:613–7.

CHAPTER 3

Pathogenesis of Migraine

Sheena K. Aurora, MD

—•••—

CASE

DM is a 28-year-old woman with a 12-year history of intermittent, severe headaches that are generally throbbing, located over her right temple, and associated with vomiting as well as extreme sensitivity to light and sound. DM has been diagnosed with migraine, but she is reluctant to accept that diagnosis. She believes that a dangerous medical cause of headache has been overlooked because "there just has to be something seriously wrong for my head to hurt this much."

DM is not alone in her belief that the severe pain of migraine cannot be benign but instead means that something—either in the brain or in the blood vessels

surrounding it—is seriously wrong. What is the cause of recurrent episodes of severe pain and other symptoms that characterize migraine, and how is it that a "benign" process can be so painful?

Much progress has been made in understanding the mechanisms in the brain and surrounding structures that generate the recurrent episodes of severe pain and other symptoms that we recognize as migraine. The current view is that abnormalities in central pain control systems, genetically controlled, but strongly influenced by environmental factors, determine susceptibility to migraine.

KEY CHAPTER POINTS

- **Migraine is an inherited, functional disorder of the brain and not a vascular problem. Migraine is the result of an imbalance in activity in brainstem areas that control pain transmission and regulate blood flow in the brain.**
- **The hyperexcitable occipital cortex of the migraineur can be activated by a variety of environmental and endogenous events to cause a depolarizing neuroelectric and metabolic brain event known as "spreading cortical depression" (SCD) that produces aura in some patients and sets in motion the events that lead to headache.**
- **SCD triggers the release of neurotransmitters that activate peripheral trigeminovascular and brainstem pathways and cause blood vessel dilatation, inflammation, and further nerve activation.**
- **Steroid hormones influence brain structure, development, and function, and may explain why migraine is more prevalent and more severe in women than in men.**

BRAINSTEM ACTIVITY IN MIGRAINE

Genetic factors have an important influence on susceptibility to migraine. Concordance for migraine in monozygotic twins, for example, is greater than that in dizygotic twins.[1] Studies of families with a rare autosomal dominant form of migraine with aura, known as familial hemiplegic migraine, have identified an amino acid substitution in genes that affect the pore-forming and voltage sensor regions of neuronal calcium channels. Other mutations have also been identified, some affecting other ion channel or neuronal control systems.[2] What these mutations appear to have in common is an effect on excitability of aminergic centers in the brainstem that control sensory input and exert a neural influence on cranial vessels.

The now-supplanted "vascular theory" of migraine suggested that vasoconstriction and brain ischemia were responsible for symptoms of the migraine aura (in the 15% of migraineurs who consistently experience it), and that rebound vasodilation of blood vessels in the meninges activated perivascular sensory nerves to produce the pain of headache.[3] It is easy to understand how the vascular theory of migraine arose out of clinical observations of the migraine attack. The vasoconstriction and reactive vasodilation described by vascular theory, for example, appear to explain the pulsing or throbbing pain of severe migraine attacks. Stimulation of intracranial blood vessels in awake patients is known to cause an ipsilateral headache, further suggesting that blood vessels are involved in similar spontaneous headache attacks. Finally, treatment—particularly with drugs such as ergots, known to be powerful vasoconstrictors—was felt to provide strong clinical evidence for vascular mechanisms as the primary cause of migraine.

Although a vascular explanation for migraine seems to make clinical sense and even explains some migraine characteristics, it does not explain all features of the migraine attack and is not supported by results of newer and more sophisticated methods of measuring brain blood flow and function. The vascular theory does not adequately explain the prodromal features and associated neurologic findings seen in many attacks of migraine, for example. In addition, aura occurs in only 15% of patients; even in those patients, it is present with some attacks and not in others, undermining the credibility of vasoconstriction as an important or necessary feature of migraine. Finally, new medications exist that are effective in treating migraine through mechanisms that have no effect on blood vessels. Although reduced cerebral blood flow can be demonstrated during aura, it persists well into the headache phase of migraine.[4] Clearly, then, blood flow changes alone are not sufficient, or even necessary, to explain what occurs in migraine.

In contrast to vascular mechanisms, brainstem involvement in migraine is well established. Positron emission tomography (PET) scans during migraine show increased blood flow in the cerebral hemispheres in cingulate, auditory, and visual association cortices, as well as in the brainstem (periaqueductal gray, locus coeruleus, and dorsal raphe nucleus). The only site with persistent activation, after complete relief of headache symptoms was attained with an injection of sumatriptan, was the brainstem. These findings suggest that pathogenesis of migraine is a result of an imbalance in activity of brainstem nuclei regulating pain relief and vascular control. Further support for brainstem involvement comes from a migraineur, in whom brain oxygenation was measured during visual aura using T2-weighted magnetic resonance imaging (MRI). The subject's typical aura (a left homonomous quadrantanopia) was accompanied by activity in bilateral regions of the occipital cortex and brainstem areas, including the red nucleus and the substantia nigra bilaterally.[5] Activation of these brainstem areas seems to be unique to migraine because head pain induced with injections of capsaicin does not produce such changes.[6]

Neurons in many areas of the brain and brainstem seem to be hyperexcitable in migraineurs, making it easily possible for a variety of environmental and endogenous triggering events to activate them. Transmagnetic stimulation shows differences between the occipital cortex excitation threshold of migraineurs and normal controls. The proportion of migraineurs who developed visual abnormalities known as "phosphenes" was significantly greater than normal controls, with the mean threshold level of stimulation required to cause these phosphenes being significantly lower in the migraine group. These results provide strong evidence that neuronal hyperexcitability predisposes individuals to migraine.[7]

Many factors, alone or in combination, may result in increased neuronal hyperexcitability. The amino acid glutamate has been speculated to promote hyperexcitability, particularly in the occipital cortex. Abnormal glutamate metabolism in the form of decreased glutamate turnover, increased release, poor reuptake, or incomplete enzymatic inactivation could play a role. Glutamate-induced spreading depression can be inhibited by magnesium, providing an explanation for the observed beneficial effect of magnesium treatment in some forms of migraine, particularly menstrually-associated attacks. In addition, intracellular magnesium levels are decreased in the brain of migraine patients during an attack.[8]

Hyperexcitability may also be caused by the release of neurotransmitters as a result of opening of voltage-dependent calcium channels, with subsequent calcium ion accumulation in the cell.[8] Notably, if neuronal hyperexcitability is an important mechanism in migraine, treatments that act to reduce it should be helpful. This could be accomplished either by inhibition of excitatory neurotransmission or by enhancement of inhibitory neurotransmitters that suppress abnormal cortical activity.[9]

SPREADING CORTICAL DEPRESSION

Most clinicians now agree that the aura associated with migraine is a result of neuronal dysfunction. Lashley's experience of his own visual aura led him to suggest that the rate of progression of the cortical phenomenon producing it was around 3 mm per minute.[10] The correlation between this calculated rate and that demonstrated for a phenomenon known as SCD, a wave of cortical hyperexcitation followed by depressed cortical activity that had been separately noted in animal studies, led Milner 17 years later to speculate that the phenomenon of SCD might account for aura in migraine.[11]

Because aura is typically short, and occurs unpredictably, it has been difficult to study. Recently, functional MRI techniques that can measure second-to-second activation of the occipital cortex were used to study migraine attacks that were triggered by a visual stimulus. Headache, even in subjects who did not experience visual aura, was preceded by a wave of initial neuronal activation followed by suppression, which slowly propagated into the adjacent occipital cortex at a rate of 3 to 6 mm per min. The neuronal suppression was accompanied by vasodilation and tissue hyperoxygenation. This wave of altered neuronal activity, known as "spreading cortical depression," thus appears to be responsible for the neurologic events of aura and can trigger the vascular changes of migraine.[5]

Visual aura is associated with short-lived decreases in regional blood flow that start in the posterior areas of the brain; these changes migrate anteriorly over time. The amount of blood flow decline in patients with aura, however, is not enough to produce ischemic injury, and there is no evidence of any significant blood flow changes in migraine without aura. Rather than differences in blood flow, it is therefore more likely that there are fundamental differences between the physiology of cortical neurons and neuronal energy metabolism in patients who have migraine with aura compared with those who have migraine without aura and between both of these groups and normal controls.[12]

PATHOGENESIS OF SPREADING CORTICAL DEPRESSION

Some light has recently been shed on the mystery of how a brain event such as SCD, starting in an insensate part of the brain, is able to cause the pain of headache. Blood flow increases in the middle meningeal artery have been demonstrated after trauma-induced SCD. The expression of c-*fos*, a substance that is a surrogate marker of pain, was increased in lamina I and II in trigeminal nucleus caudalis, clearly demonstrating the link between head pain of migraine and SCD, the putative mechanism of aura.[13]

Nitric oxide (NO) may also mediate plasma protein extravasation (PPE). Four to 6 hours after infusion of nitroglycerin, patients with migraine (but not controls) developed a typical migraine headache.[14] This was caused by a delayed inflammatory response in the dura mater that is marked by increased expression of inducible nitric oxide synthase and upregulation of proinflammatory cytokines interleukin (IL)-1β and IL-6.[15] During migraine, NO metabolites (eg, nitrites/nitrates and secondary messengers of NO such as cyclic guanosine monophosphate [cGMP]) are increased in platelets.[16,17] Thus it seems inescapable that NO is intimately involved as a cause of PPE. Interestingly, nitroglycerin infusion provokes only headache, not aura, suggesting that NO is induced after, and not before, SCD. Furthermore, levels of platelet NO production are increased following stimulation with collagen and also vary with hormonal fluctuation.[18] This variability might, at least in part, underlie the increased susceptibility to migraine during certain portions of the men-

strual cycle. It might also explain why most menstrually-associated migraine occurs without aura.[19]

In addition to NO release, activation of the trigeminovascular system by spreading depression is theorized to cause release of various neuroinflammatory peptides, including calcitonin gene–related peptide (CGRP) and substance P (SP). Like NO, these substances promote leakage of plasma proteins from vessels into surrounding tissues, often referred to as PPE.[20] Electrical stimulation of the trigeminal ganglion in experimental animals causes release of these compounds, which can be blocked by many drugs that are effective antimigraine agents, such as triptans or indomethacin.[21,22] Levels of CGRP are elevated in the cranial circulation during attacks of migraine and normalize with successful treatment of migraine. Furthermore, CGRP infusions can precipitate migraine in some situations.[23]

The trigeminovascular pain pathway begins with transmission of impulses in the caudal brainstem and high cervical spinal cord. These impulses are conveyed by the quintothalamic tract to the thalamus, which processes vascular pain. Cranial blood vessels are innervated by the trigeminal system, whose unmyelinated nerve fibers come from the ophthalmic division of the fifth cranial nerve and upper cervical dorsal roots.[24] Localized within the nerves of the trigeminal system are neuropeptides, including CGRP, as well as neurokinin A and SP.[25] These neuropeptides are released from primary sensory nerve terminals that innervate the dural vessels, causing inflammation and dilation of the meningeal arteries, particularly those located within the dura mater. CGRP antagonists are in early trials for migraine treatment.

Finally, much interest has centered on the role of serotonin in the genesis of migraine. It has been known since the 1960s that circulating serotonin levels fall during a migraine attack and that infusions of serotonin could successfully abort an attack.[26] The advent of the new triptan drugs, which exert their effects through agonist activity at serotonin 1D and 1B receptors, has led to speculation that these agents may act by preventing the initial vasodilatory stimulus that activates perivascular sensory nerves. Serotonin receptors are found throughout the cranial circulation, on meningeal blood vessels, and to a lesser extent on vessels elsewhere. In addition, serotonin 1B and 1D receptors have been found in the trigeminal nucleus caudalis of the cat, in a distribution that correlates with locations where proteins are seen after pain-produced activation of neurons in the sagittal sinus.[27]

Very new work suggests that, over time, frequent migraine attacks can cause permanent changes in the brain that might alter pain perception and produce intractable headache. The periaqueductal gray (PAG) area in the brainstem is the center of a powerful descending analgesic network. MRI imaging has determined that iron accumulation occurs in the PAG and that these changes correlate with duration of migraine frequency, are not independent of the presence of aura, and do not correlate with patient age. Changes in the PAG may be attributable to iron-catalyzed, free-radical cell damage.[28] PET studies have shown that the PAG is hyperactive during migraine attacks, and there appears to be a genetic predisposition to hyperactivity in this system.[29,30] The ventrolateral subdivision of the PAG is of particular importance to the trigeminal nociceptive modulation.[31]

Thus, migraine is currently conceived of as a neurovascular phenomenon, in which neurologic events are fundamental and lead to reactive changes in vascular, sensory, and pain sensing pathways (Figure 3-1).

INFLUENCE OF STEROID HORMONES

Hormonal fluctuations associated with the normal menstrual cycle appear to affect susceptibility to migraine.[32] Estrogen is thought to be the sex steroid hormone that plays the most important role in modulating the phenotypic expression of migraine.[33,34] The influence of cycling ovarian steroids on the peptide neurotransmitter systems in the trigeminal ganglion has recently been studied. A marked increase in gene expression of neuropeptide Y (NPY) occurred during periods of falling estrogen levels and correlated with hormonal levels.[35] Because no changes in levels of CGRP occurred, it seems possible that sudden changes of NPY, precipitated by falling levels of estrogen, may modulate nociceptive or cerebrovascular responses seen with the menstrual cycle. The effect of estrogen cycling has been examined using transcranial magnetic stimulation (TMS) and, thus far, no differences have been noted in phosphene generation in relationship to the menstrual period.[36] Sex steroids are also known to

have important effects on brain development and function, beginning early in fetal development. It seems likely that these influences play an important, though poorly understood, role in determining female susceptibility to migraine.

SUMMARY

Migraine originates in the brain. Inherited hyperexcitability of neurons makes it easy for a variety of environmental and endogenous triggers to cause a depolarizing neuroelectric and metabolic event known as "spreading depression." This event activates the headache and associated features of the attack by mechanisms that remain to be determined but appear to involve either peripheral trigeminovascular or brainstem pathways, or both. Factors that increase or decrease neuronal excitability alter the threshold for the triggering of attacks. The influences of sex steroid hormones on brain structure, development, and function make women particularly vulnerable to migraine.[32]

REFERENCES

1. Honkasalo ML, Kaprio J, Winter T, et al. Migraine and concomitant symptoms among 8167 adult twin pairs. Headache 1995;35:70–8.

2. Nyholt DR, Lea RA, Goadsby PJ, et al. Familial typical migraine: linkage to chromosome 19p13 and evidence for genetic heterogeneity. Neurology 1998;50:1428–32.

3. Moskowitz MA. The visceral organ brain: implications for the pathophysiology of vascular head pain. Neurology 1991;41:182–6.

4. Cutrer FM, Sorensen AG, Weisskoff RM, et al. Perfusion-weighted imaging defects during spontaneous migrainous aura. Ann Neurol 1998;43:25–31.

5. Cao Y, Welch KMA, Aurora SK, Vikingstad EM. Functional MRI-BOLD of visually triggered headache and visual change in migraine sufferers. Arch Neurol 1999; 56:548–54.

6. May A, Kaube H, Buchel C, et al. Experimental cranial pain elicited by capsaicin: a PET study. Pain 1998;74: 61–6.

7. Aurora SK, Ahmad BK, Welch KMA, et al. Transcranial magnetic stimulation confirms hyperexcitability of occipital cortex in migraine. Neurology 1998;50:1111–4.

8. Welch KMA, D'Andrea G, Tepley N, et al. The concept of migraine as a state of central neuronal hyperexcitability. Neurol Clin 1990;8:817–28.

9. Mathew NT, Rapoport A, Saper J, et al. Efficacy of gabapentin in migraine prophylaxis. Headache 2001;41: 119–28.

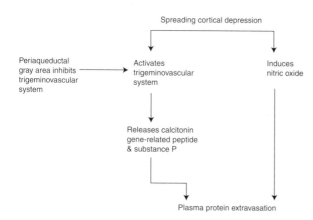

Figure 3-1 Spreading cortical depression triggers both neural and vascular changes important for migraine. Activity of the trigeminovascular system is inhibited by activation of the periaqueductal gray area.

10. Lashley KS. Patterns of cerebral integration indicated by the scotomas of migraine. Arch Neurol Psychiatr 1941; 46:331–9.

11. Milner P. Note on a possible correspondence between the scotomas of migraine and spreading depression of Leao. Electroencephalogr Clin Neurophysiol 1958;10:705.

12. Cutrer FM, O'Donnell AO, Sanchez del Rio M. Functional neuroimaging: enhanced understanding of migraine pathophysiology. Neurology 2000;55 Suppl 2: S36–45.

13. Bolay M, Reuter U, Dunn A, et al. Intrinsic brain activity triggers trigeminal meningeal afferents in a migraine model. Nat Med 2002;8:136–42.

14. Olesen J, Iversen HK, Thomsen LL. Nitric oxide supersensitivity: a possible molecular mechanism of migraine pain. Neuroreport 1993;4:1027–30.

15. Reuter U, Bolay H, Jansen-Olsen I, et al. Delayed inflammation in rat meninges: implications for migraine pathophysiology. Brain 2001;124:2490–502.

16. Stepien A, Chalimoniuk M. Level of nitric oxide-dependent cGMP in patients with migraine. Cephalalgia 1998;18:631–4.

17. Shimomura T, Murakami M, Kotani K, et al. Platelet nitric oxide metabolites in migraine. Cephalalgia 1999; 19:218–22.

18. Sarchielli P, Tognoloni M, Russo S, et al. Variations in the platelet arginine/nitric oxide pathway during the ovarian cycle in females affected by menstrual migraine. Cephalalgia 1996;16:468–75.

19. Stewart WF, Lipton RB, Chee E, et al. Menstrual cycle and headache in a population sample of migraineurs. Neurology 2000;55:1517–23.

20. Moskowitz MA, Macfarlane R. Neurovascular and molecular mechanisms in migraine headaches. Cerebrovasc Brain Metab Rev 1993;5:159–77.

21. Markowitz S, Saito K, Moskowitz MA. Neurogenically mediated leakage of plasma proteins occurs from blood vessels in dura mater but not brain. J Neurosc 1987;7: 4129–36.

22. Buzzi MG, Moskowitz MA. Evidence for 5-HT1B/1D receptors mediating the antimigraine effect of sumatriptan and dihydroergotamine. Cephalalgia 1991; 11:165–8.

23. Lassen L, Jacobsen V, Petersen P, et al. Human calcitonin gene-related peptide (hCGRP)-induced headache in migraineurs. Eur J Pharmacol 1998;5 Suppl 3:S63.

24. Silberstein SD, Lipton RB, Goadsby PJ. The pathophysiology of primary headache. In: Silberstein SD, Goadsby PJ, editors. Headache in clinical practice. Oxford (UK): Isis Medical Media, Ltd; 1998. p. 41–58.

25. Goadsby PJ, Edvinsson L, Ekman R. Vasoactive peptide release in the extracerebral circulation of humans during migraine headache. Ann Neurol 1990;28:183–7.

26. Goadsby PJ, Edvinsson L. Human in vivo evidence for trigeminovascular activation in cluster headache: neuropeptide changes and effects of acute attack therapies. Brain 1994;117:424–34.

27. Kaube H, Keay KA, Hoskin KL, et al. Expression of c-Fos-like immunoreactivity in the caudal medulla and upper cervical spinal cord following stimulation of the superior sagittal sinus in the cat. Brain Res 1993;629: 95–102.

28. Welch KMA, Nagesh V, Aurora SK, Gelman N. Periaqueductal gray matter dysfunction in migraine: cause or burden of illness. Headache 2001;41:629–37.

29. Bahra A, Matharu MS, Buchel C, et al. Brainstem activation specific to migraine headache. Lancet 2001; 357:1016–7.

30. Knight YE, Bartsch T, Kaube H, Goadsby PJ. P/Q-type calcium-channel blockade in the periaqueductal gray facilitates trigeminal nociception: a functional genetic link for migraine. J Neurosci 2002;22:1–6.

31. Knight YE, Goadsby PJ. The periaqueductal grey matter modulates trigeminovascular input: a role in migraine? Neuroscience 2001;106:793–800.

32. Silberstein SD, Merriam GR. Estrogens, progestins and headache. Neurology 1991;41:775–93.

33. Martin VT, Wenke S, Zoma W, et al. Does the headache phase of the menstrual cycle have an effect on headache? Headache 2002;42:438–9.

34. Sommerville BW. The role of estradiol withdrawal in the etiology of menstrual migraine. Neurology 1972;22: 355–65.

35. Berman N, Puri V, Cui L, et al. Trigeminal ganglion neuropeptides cycle with ovarian steroids in a model of menstrual migraine. Headache 2002;42:438.

36. Mulleners WM, Chronicle EP, Koehler PJ, Vredeveld JW. Longitudinal assessment of cortical excitability in women with menstrual migraine. Cephalalgia 2001;21: 392.

CHAPTER 4

Diagnosis of Common Headache Disorders

Loretta Mueller, DO, FACOFP

CASE

LW is a 45-year-old female teacher who began to have headaches at age 12 years. She describes the headaches as a severe, throbbing sensation, usually located over one temple but sometimes involving the entire side of her head. The location of the pain can change from side to side. In addition to the head pain, LW reports nausea, and increased pain with bending or walking during the headache. LW says that no one else in her family has migraine but does recall that her mother suffered from bad "sinus headaches." When LW started using oral contraceptives at age 18 years, her headache frequency increased to four per month, and she began to experience visual changes preceding some of her headaches. She describes these changes as a shimmering, slowly enlarging blind spot in her vision that lasts 15 to 30 minutes and then slowly fades away, to be followed by her typical head pain. Once a month or so, LW experiences brief, lancinating pains that she describes as "jolts." These last no more than a fraction of a second and can occur anywhere in her head.

When LW became pregnant, her headaches improved, and she used only occasional acetaminophen to control them. Two weeks postpartum, however, she developed a headache that was different from her previous episodes of pain. This headache was generalized, reached peak intensity in an hour, and by the time she consulted a physician, the headache had been present for 5 days. It was severe, continuous, throbbing pain with nausea, photophobia, pain with eye movements,

and episodes of "dimmed vision" lasting several seconds. Occasionally, she could hear a "whooshing" sound, like a heartbeat. Physical examination was normal except for possible papilledema.

LW began with migraine without aura but developed neurologic accompaniments to her headache when exposed to exogenous estrogen. Like many migraineurs, she also experiences idiopathic stabbing headache. Postpartum, LW developed signs and symptoms suggestive of a secondary headache due to cerebral venous thrombosis.

LW's history illustrates the diagnostic dilemmas faced every day in the clinic. Few patients complaining of headache offer up a classic "textbook" description of their headaches. Even in a single patient with a single headache disorder, headache presentation is rarely stereotyped but instead changes, occasionally dramatically, from headache to headache. Additionally, the characteristic features necessary to make a specific headache diagnosis may be unreported by the patient, masked by treatment, attributed to other disorders, or affected by other medications. Finally, even patients like LW, who have longstanding benign headache disorders, can develop secondary, dangerous forms of headache as well.

Even a passing familiarity with the diagnostic classification of the major benign headache disorders, however, makes it possible to recognize the patterns of common headaches and to distinguish worrisome from benign headaches.

KEY CHAPTER POINTS

- Diagnosis of the primary headache disorders is clinical, based on criteria developed by the International Headache Society (IHS). Migraine is the benign headache disorder that most commonly brings patients to medical attention.

- Specific "red flags" and danger signs aid recognition of secondary causes of headache. Some secondary causes of headache are unique to or more common in women than in men. These include the headache of preeclampsia, cerebral venous thrombosis, and benign intracranial hypertension.

- **Common diagnostic pitfalls in headache diagnosis can be recognized and avoided. Most patients who describe several different headache types turn out to have a single headache disorder with variable presentations. Tension-type, sinus, and temporomandibular headache disorders are vastly overdiagnosed.**

COMMON HEADACHE DISORDERS

Headache diagnosis is clinical; no "gold standard" tests or biologic markers exist. The 2003 IHS criteria for the primary headache disorders of migraine, tension-type, and cluster headaches are presented in Tables 4-1, 4-2, and 4-3, respectively. They describe the classic presentation of each headache type and enable researchers to study homogeneous populations of headache sufferers.

The IHS criteria broadly divide headache into "primary" and "secondary" headache disorders. The primary headache disorders are those in which the headache condition itself is the problem, and no underlying or dangerous cause for it can be identified. Secondary headaches, in contrast, are those attributable to an underlying condition such as infection, tumor, hemorrhage, or a disorder of the sinuses, eyes, ears, neck, or teeth. Most of the primary and secondary headache disorders are more common in women than in men (Table 4-4).

Two features of the IHS classification system are worth noting: 1) the older terms "classic" and "common" migraine have been replaced by the descriptive terms "migraine with aura" and "migraine without aura" and 2) the term "tension-type headache" (TTH)

Table 4-1 International Headache Society Diagnostic Criteria for Migraine

International Headache Society Diagnostic Criteria for Migraine Without Aura

A. At least five attacks fulfilling B–D

B. Headache attacks lasting 4–72 hours (untreated or unsuccessfully treated)

C. Headache has at least two of the following characteristics:
  - Unilateral location
  - Pulsating quality
  - Moderate or severe pain intensity
  - Aggravation caused by routine physical activity (eg, walking or climbing stairs)

D. During headache at least one of the following:
  - Nausea and/or vomiting
  - Photophobia and phonophobia

E. Not attributed to another disorder

International Headache Society Diagnostic Criteria for Typical Aura With Migraine Headaches

(Headache fulfills migraine without aura diagnosis)

A. At least two attacks fulfilling criteria B–D

B. Aura consisting of at least one of the following but no motor weakness:
  - Fully reversible visual symptoms including positive features (eg, flickering lights, spots, or lines) and/or negative features (ie, loss of vision)
  - Fully reversible sensory symptoms including positive features (ie, pins and needles) and/or negative features (ie, numbness)
  - Fully reversible dysphasic speech disturbance

C. At least two of the following:
  - Homonymous visual symptoms and/or unilateral sensory symptoms
  - At least one aura symptom develops gradually over ≥ 5 minutes and/or different aura symptoms occur in succession over ≥ 5 minutes
  - Each symptom lasts ≥ 5 and ≤ 60 minutes

D. Headache fulfilling criteria B–D for *Migraine Without Aura* begins during the aura or follows aura within 60 minutes

E. Not attributed to another disorder

Adapted from the International Classification of Headache Disorders.[34]

Table 4-2 International Headache Society Diagnostic Criteria for Tension-Type Headache

Episodic Tension-Type Headache

A. At least 10 previous headache episodes fulfilling criteria B–D listed below. If occurring < 1 day per month on average (< 12 days per year) classified as *infrequent episodic tension-type headache.* If occurring ≥ 1 but ≤ 15 days per month for at least 3 months (≥ 12 and < 180 days per year), classified as *frequent episodic tension-type headache*

B. Headache lasting from 30 minutes to 7 days

C. Headache has at least two of the following characteristics:
- Bilateral location
- Pressing/tightening (nonpulsating) quality
- Mild or moderate intensity
- Not aggravated by routine physical activity such as walking or climbing stairs

D. Both of the following:
- No nausea or vomiting (anorexia may occur)
- No more than one of photophobia or phonophobia

E. Not attributed to another disorder

Chronic Tension-Type Headache

A. Frequent headaches fulfilling criteria B-D listed below. Headaches must occur ≥ 15 days per month for > 3 months

B. Headache lasting from hours to continuous

C. Headache has at least two of the following characteristics:
- Bilateral location
- Pressing/tightening (nonpulsating) quality
- Mild or moderate intensity
- Not aggravated by routine physical activity such as walking or climbing stairs

D. Both of the following:
- No nausea or vomiting (anorexia may occur)
- No more than one of photophobia or phonophobia

Adapted from the International Classification of Headache Disorders.[34]

replaces older terms such as "tension headache" or "muscle contraction" headache. This is because neither muscle tension nor psychological tension is reliably associated with these moderate, nondescript headaches.

Migraine

Almost 90% of women presenting to a primary care practice with recurrent, disabling headaches will turn out to have migraine. Migraine should thus top the list of differential diagnoses in a woman whose chief complaint is headache.

Around 70% of migraineurs note a family history of headaches.[1] Environmental influences on migraine are also important; twin studies show only a 50% concordance rate for migraine in monozygotic twins. This suggests that environmental factors account for at least half of the variability in phenotypic expression of migraine.[2,3] Hormonal effects on brain structure, development, and function undoubtedly account for the fact that migraine genes are more frequently expressed in

women than in men, and that the disorder is generally more severe when it occurs in women.

Diagnosis

Certain features are highly characteristic of migraine, but none, other than head pain, is absolutely required for diagnosis or experienced by every migraineur or with every headache. A constellation of these signs and symptoms, however, is diagnostic of the disorder. Migraine is unilateral in 70% of patients, throbbing in 80%, moderate to severe in 70%, worsened with physical exertion in 76%, and associated with nausea in 36%, vomiting in 18%, photophobia in 66%, and phonophobia in 49% of patients (see Table 4-1).[4] Migraine often resolves after sleeping or vomiting. Children are more likely to experience bilateral head pain and to have prominent gastrointestinal symptoms, especially vomiting. When migraine is unilateral, it can vary from side to side from one headache to another or even within a single headache; 20% of sufferers have

Table 4-3 International Headache Society Diagnostic Criteria for Cluster Headache

A.   At least five attacks fulfilling criteria B–D

B.   Severe or very severe unilateral orbital, supraorbital, and/or temporal pain lasting 15–180 minutes if untreated

C.   Headache is accompanied by at least one of the following:
- Ipsilateral conjunctival injection and/or lacrimation
- Ipsilateral nasal congestion and/or rhinorrhea
- Ipsilateral eyelid edema
- Ipsilateral forehead and facial sweating
- Ipsilateral miosis and/or ptosis
- A sense of restlessness or agitation

D.   Attacks have a frequency from one every other day to eight per day

E.   Not attributed to another disorder

Adapted from the International Classification of Headache Disorders.[34]

"side-locked" headaches, always occurring on the same side.[5] This historic feature is worth noting when it is described because side-locked headaches are slightly more likely to be caused by underlying structural abnormalities such as nonruptured arteriovenous malformations (AVMs).[6]

The majority of migraineurs experience two to four attacks per month, but 10% have at least one migraine a week.[7] In a subset of patients, migraine evolves over time from an episodic to a daily pattern. This is often termed "chronic daily headache," and may include chronic migraine or chronic tension-type headache (headache ≥ 15 days per month) or medication overuse headache. Although the adult IHS criteria specify migraine duration in adults as 4 to 72 hours, pediatric migraine is recognized as shorter (1 to 72 hours), whereas menstrually-associated migraines may last for days. However, 40% of patients have attacks that last at least 24 hours.[7] Migraines that last longer than 72 hours are termed "status migrainosus."[8]

Eighty percent of migraineurs rate their migraine pain intensity as severe or extremely severe.[9] Over 90% of migraineurs report impairment of daily function during an attack, with over one-half requiring bedrest with some of their headaches. Nearly one-quarter of migraine patients say they have at some point required emergency room treatment for a migraine.[9,10]

Female migraineurs have more functional impairment and disability than men as well as a greater median attack rate, higher rate of aura, longer duration of attacks (71% versus 48% have an attack duration greater than 24 hours), greater gastrointestinal complaints (62% versus 47% have nausea), photophobia (84% versus 77%), phonophobia (79% versus 73%) and the need for bedrest (Table 4-5).[11–19] It is estimated that women migraineurs lose 5.6 days annually due to bedrest with headache versus 3.8 days annually for men.[20] Eighty percent of the estimated $1 billion (US)

direct cost spent annually for migraine in the United States and 80% of the $13 billion (US) annual US labor cost losses due to work absenteeism and reduced productivity are spent on female migraineurs.[20] Despite the disability associated with migraine, fewer than 50% of migraineurs in one survey had consulted a physician for headache management over the last year.[9]

Prodrome and Aura

Many patients with migraine experience disabling symptoms of various kinds both before and after the traditionally recognized aura and headache phases of a migraine.[21] Up to 60% of sufferers recognize premonitory symptoms of prodrome, which can occur hours or days before a migraine and may include yawning, changes in sleep quality, irritability, subtle difficulties with writing or communication, fluid retention, food cravings, fatigue, or, alternatively, experiencing a burst of energy and increased productivity, hours to a day before a headache. If prodromes are recognized, patients may be able to take preemptive steps to avoid a headache. At this early stage of the headache, simple well-tolerated measures are especially likely to be effective, and their use should be encouraged. These include the use of non-pharmacologic strategies such as biofeedback, relaxation, ingestion of caffeine, or avoidance of alcohol or other headache triggers. If medication is necessary during prodrome, clinical experience suggests that simple nonsteroidal anti-inflammatory drugs are useful; one study demonstrates the effectiveness of naratriptan used during prodrome.[22]

Postdromal symptoms occur after the severe pain and associated symptoms of migraine resolve and are described as a fatigued "hangover" feeling, frequently with mood changes, scalp tenderness, and residual mild head or neck pain similar to TTH. If treatment is desired, these symptoms respond well to nonsteroidal anti-inflammatory agents. Aggressive, early interven-

Table 4-4 Gender Distribution of Selected Headaches

Female Predominance	Male Predominance
Migraine (3:1)[12,111]	Cluster HA (2.1–6.7:1)[46,50]
• Aura without HA (2.5:1)[16]	Benign cough HA (4:1)[73]
Tension-type HA (5:4)[42]	Benign exertional HA (4:1)[72]
• Episodic TTH (1.2:1)[75]	HA associated with sexual activity (5.7:1)[79]
• Chronic TTH (2:1)[66]	SUNCT HA (2.3–4.3:1)[65–67]
Chronic daily HA (9:1)[83]	
Chronic paroxysmal hemicrania (2.4:1)[60]	
Hemicrania continua (5:1)[62]	
Idiopathic stabbing HA (6:1)[70,71]	
Post-traumatic HA (2:1)[112]	
Cervicogenic HA	
Idiopathic intracranial HTN (4.3–8:1)[113]	
Post-lumbar puncture HA	
Subarachnoid hemorrhage (10:1, > 70 years old)	
Meningioma (2:1)[114,115]	
Pituitary adenoma (1–3.2:1)[116,117]	
Temporal arteritis (2:1)[118]	

HA = headache; HTN = hypertension; SUNCT = short lasting, unilateral neuralgiform headache attacks with conjunctival injection, tearing, sweating, and rhinorrhea; TTH = tension-type headache.

tion in the headache attack, with the aim of complete rather than partial pain relief, may decrease the likelihood that postdromal symptoms will occur.

Unlike the vague constitutional symptoms of prodrome, approximately 30% of migraineurs experience a gradual onset of progressive, reversible focal neurologic signs just preceding or during migraine attacks. Of these, 10% experience auras with all headaches (migraine with aura), and 20% experience both migraine with and without aura.[23] Aura symptoms are most commonly visual, less commonly sensory or motor, and rarely auditory or olfactory.[24–27] Typically, symptoms develop gradually over several minutes and resolve in less than 1 hour. Prolonged auras last longer than 1 hour. Ninety-nine percent of auras are visual, often described as flashing lights in peripheral visual fields (photopsia), wavy or zigzag lines (fortification spectra), slowly enlarging blind spots, frequently edged with shimmering lights (scintillating scotoma), or loss of visual fields (homonymous hemianopia).[28] Sensory auras occur in 31% of those who experience aura. Typical features include tingling, paresthesias, and/or numbness that develop over several minutes and gradually "march" up one arm and into the face. Speech

disturbances occur with 18% of auras. Progressive unilateral paresis in the extremities and/or face occur with 6% of auras. Sensory and motor auras almost always occur in conjunction with visual auras.[28]

Typical migraine aura can be distinguished from cerebrovascular attacks by its slow progression, the occurrence of both positive and negative neurologic signs (ie, flashing lights with vision loss, tingling sensory change with numbness), a previous history of typical migraine attacks, and usual onset of headache following resolution of neurologic symptoms. First onset of aura, especially late onset (over 50 years of age), prolonged aura, aura without prior migraine history, or atypical aura may require further investigation. Auras may occur sporadically or only once in a migraineur's lifetime.

Auras may occur without an accompanying headache; this is termed typical or migraine aura without headache. Aura without headache commonly starts or increases in frequency during the perimenopausal years and is 2.5 times more common in women than in men.[16] This "flurry" of episodes of aura without headache that is seen in many migraineurs as they grow older has been termed "late-life migraine accompani-

Table 4-5 Migraine: Not an Equal Opportunity Disorder

	Women	Men
Annual days of bedrest due to migraine[20]	5.6	3.8
Duration of attack over 24 hours[119]	71%	48%
Photophobia[119]	84%	77%
Phonophobia[119]	79%	73%
Nausea[119]	62%	47%
Contribution to annual $1 billion (US) direct costs of migraine[20]	80%	20%
Contribution to lost labor and productivity costs due to migraine[20]	80%	20%

ments."[16,29] The diagnosis of aura without headache should be made cautiously, if at all, in patients who have no prior history of migraine because carotid artery disease, embolic phenomena, and retinal tears may mimic aura without headache.

Less common subtypes of migraine aura include migrainous infarcts, familial hemiplegic migraine, basilar migraine, ophthalmoplegic migraine, and retinal migraine. Familial hemiplegic migraine (FHM), which consists of headache in conjunction with a rare form of motor aura, is familial and has been linked to gene mutations on chromosomes 1 and 19.[30,31] FHM typically starts during childhood or adolescence. In addition to the typical motor auras found in this condition, visual, sensory, brainstem, and/or cerebellar disturbances may be present with symptoms that include unilateral weakness, aphasia, ataxia, confusion, and changes in consciousness, sometimes lasting for days or leaving residual deficits.[1] Differential diagnoses include stroke; mitochondrial myopathy, encephalopathy, lactic acidosis, and stroke-like episodes (MELAS); cerebral autosomal dominant arteriopathy with subcortical infarcts and leukoencephalopathy (CADASIL); and focal seizures. Although episodes occur infrequently, their dramatic presentation and often prolonged duration warrants a more aggressive preventive treatment approach and referral to a headache specialist.

Basilar-type migraine is most common in female adolescents and young adults, with a female to male prevalence ratio of 3:1. Its distinguishing characteristics include bilateral focal neurologic signs, vertigo, tinnitus, auditory disturbance, dysarthria, diplopia, ataxia, and/or changes in consciousness or confusion, presumably caused by neuronal depolarization originating in the brainstem or bilateral occipital lobes.[32,33] The name of the disorder has been changed from "basilar" to "basilar-type" migraine in the 2003 IHS criteria. This change is a prelude to the elimination of this disorder altogether, reflecting the lack of evidence that the syndrome has anything at all to do with the basilar artery. The differential diagnosis is lengthy and includes panic disorder with bilateral paresthesias, seizure disorder, vertebrobasilar ischemia, vascular malformation, posterior fossa lesion, or demyelinating disorder.[1]

Only a few cases of retinal migraine have been reported. It is a rare type of migraine with aura, characterized by repeated episodes of monocular visual disturbances or blindness occurring in temporal relation to the migraine attack and lasting less than 1 hour.[34] Ophthalmologic abnormalities such as vitreous or retinal hemorrhage, vascular malformation, tumor, coagulopathy, or an embolic phenomenon may cause similar symptoms.[31]

Migrainous infarction, previously termed "complicated migraine," is defined by the IHS criteria as one or more migrainous aura symptoms associated with neuroimaging confirmation of ischemic infarction. Important diagnostic requirements are that patients must have experienced similar auras in the past with their migraine attacks, the infarct episode occurred with a usual attack, and other potential causes of infarction are ruled out by diagnostic evaluation.[34] Although an increased relative risk of ischemic stroke has been found with migraine, especially in young women under 45 years of age (threefold risk in migraine without aura and sixfold risk in migraine with aura), true migraine infarction by current definition is rare.[35] Migrainous infarct is a diagnosis of exclusion, and the differential diagnosis includes atherosclerosis, stroke based on other risk factors (oral contraceptive use, hypertension, smoking, age over 35 years), vasoconstricting medications, rare disorders such as MELAS, CADASIL, arteritis, carotid or vertebral artery dissection, and coagulopathies.[1]

Migraine Triggers and Precipitants

Many environmental and endogenous events have been noted by migraineurs to increase the chance that attacks of migraine will occur. It is important to remember that, for most migraineurs, the possible triggers for migraine are many and varied. Thus, preoccupation with the idea "If I could just find the one thing that is causing my headaches and eliminate it, I would be better" should be discouraged as being unrealistic. Most triggers do not inevitably cause headache; rather, they make it more likely that a headache will occur. Precipitants may be additive or inconsistent and not always identifiable. Table 4-6 lists commonly mentioned migraine triggers.[19,36] Many female migraineurs note that the hormonal fluctuations associated with natural menstrual periods or use of oral contraceptives, fertility medications, or estrogen replacement therapy are especially likely to provoke migraine. Sixty percent of female migraineurs note more frequent migraines without aura over their menstrual period, termed "menstrually-associated migraine."[37] In a prospective 98-day diary study of 81 female migraineurs, peak elevated risk for migraine occurred on the first and second days of menstrual flow.[38] Approximately 7 to 14% of female migraineurs have headaches exclusively over their menses and at no other time of the month. Interestingly, menstrual-precipitated headache appears more likely to be migraine without aura. Migraine with aura does not appear to be as sensitive to hormonal fluctuations.[39,40]

Tension-Type Headache

Only 15% of TTH sufferers consult a physician for treatment, so although this is the most common type of headache in the population at large, it is less common than migraine as a medical complaint.[41] Like migraine, TTH is more common in women than in men.[42]

Definition

TTH is mild to moderate in intensity, with the pain usually described as a bilateral pressure sensation that is not generally worsened by exertion or associated with nausea, photophobia, or phonophobia (see Table 4-2). TTH can last from 30 minutes to 7 days.[34] Those occurring less than 15 days per month are termed "episodic tension-type headache." If headaches occur 15 days or more per month over a 3-month period, they are classified as "chronic tension-type headache" (CTTH). CTTH prevalence increases with chronological age, whereas episodic TTH prevalence decreases with advanced age.

The episodic form of TTH is further subdivided into those that are "associated with pericranial tenderness" or "not associated with pericranial tenderness." Pericranial muscle abnormalities include muscle tenderness on manual palpation or increased surface amplitude tracings on electromyography. However, muscle abnormalities are not unique to TTH. In fact, neck tenderness is extremely common in migraine and can also be seen with cervicogenic headaches and in headaches associated with other disorders, especially fibromyalgia. Ninety percent of fibromyalgia sufferers are women. The syndrome is defined by multiple tender areas throughout the body. Headaches, most with tension-type features, occur in 53% of fibromyalgia sufferers.[43] A progressive increase in the frequency or intensity of TTH should raise suspicion for secondary causes of headache such as tumor. The possibility of analgesic or caffeine overuse leading to medication-induced headache should also be considered.

Precipitants

Triggers of TTH are similar to those of migraine; this, along with other similarities between the two disorders, has led some experts to suggest that TTH is not a separate disorder but is simply one end of the migraine spectrum. Others continue to believe that the two disorders are distinct.[44] Hormonal fluctuations can trigger TTH but are generally not as prominent a trigger as they are in migraine. TTH incidence peaks during the first 2 days of menstrual flow.[38] The name "tension-type" is widely viewed as unsatisfactory because it

---

Table 4-6 Commonly Mentioned Triggers of Migraine

Psychological stress, particularly low-grade, chronic "hassles," and the period immediately after a stressful event (so-called "let-down" headaches are highly characteristic of migraine)

Changes in sleep regimens, including oversleeping, changes in time zones, or shift work

Skipping meals or dehydration

Certain foods (eg, caffeine, alcohol, aged cheeses, chocolate, monosodium glutamate, nitrates, raw onion, garlic, artificial sweeteners, nuts, seeds, dairy products)

Caffeine withdrawal

Physical exertion

Strong sensory experiences such as loud noise, bright sunlight, strong odors

Hormonal fluctuations, especially a drop in estrogen levels from a previously sustained high level

Medications for other conditions. Most notorious are nitrates and vasodilatory drugs such as sildenafil and nifedipine

Adapted from Mueller L.[36]

implies causation by psychological or muscle tension. In fact, elevated levels of muscle or psychological tension have not been convincingly demonstrated in TTH sufferers. However, stress (everyday hassles more so than a catastrophic stressor) is the most commonly mentioned trigger, noted in 80% of sufferers.[44] TTH studies have not found a greater number of stressors among TTH sufferers compared with non-headache controls but have found a heightened perception of stress and everyday hassles with less effective coping strategies such as self-criticism, lack of social supports, and avoidance.[37]

Cluster Headache

Cluster headache, afflicting an estimated 0.4% of the population, is rarer than TTH or migraine.[45] Unlike the primary headache disorders of migraine and TTH, cluster headache is more common in men. Because it is perceived as an affliction of men, the correct diagnosis may be delayed or missed in women. Age at first onset of episodic cluster headache shows a bimodal incidence peak in women. The first peak occurs in the second decade of life, and the second peak in the sixth decade of life.[46,47] The coincidence of the second peak with perimenopause suggests that hormonal fluctuations may play some role in the onset of the disorder. Like migraine and TTH, cluster headache occurs in both episodic and chronic forms. Mean age of onset for chronic cluster headache in women is higher than the mean age of onset for chronic cluster headache in men and for the onset of episodic cluster headache in women.[46] Recent evidence suggests that the prevalence of cluster headache in women is increasing, with male-to-female prevalence ratios in various studies ranging from as high as 6.7:1 to as low as 2.1:1.[48,49] This apparent increase in female prevalence has been variously attributed to changes in the social roles of women, such as larger numbers of women working outside the home, with consequent exposure to putative cluster triggers such as stress, shift work, and increased alcohol and tobacco consumption. Alternatively, it has been suggested that the recognition of cluster headache and increased accuracy of diagnosis in women is responsible for the changing prevalence ratios.[50] Interestingly, although cluster headache is more prevalent in Caucasians of both genders, the gender ratio is reversed among African-Americans with the disorder; more African-American women than men are diagnosed with cluster headache.[45,51]

Diagnosis

Cluster headache is a severe, short (15 to 180 minutes), and invariably unilateral head pain with associated autonomic features that may include conjunctival injection, lacrimation, nasal congestion, rhinorrhea, forehead and facial diaphoresis, miosis, ptosis, and eye-lid edema on the side ipsilateral to the head pain (see Table 4-3).[34] The quality of the pain is described as stabbing, burning, or a "hot poker" type of pain often localized to the area behind the eye; head pain is usually side-locked during a particular cluster cycle, although it may change sides from one cycle to the next.

Cluster headaches are more severe but much shorter than migraines and progress rapidly to peak intensity. Unlike migraineurs, who prefer to lie still with an attack, cluster patients are commonly agitated and physically restless. Migrainous features such as nausea, vomiting, photophobia, and phonophobia may occasionally occur but are less prominent than seen in migraine. Aura has been described with cluster headache but is not common. During an active cluster period, individual headache attacks occur from once every other day to eight times a day, often awakening the sufferer from sleep. Attacks frequently occur with regular periodicity, especially during periods of relaxation or 1 to 2 hours after sleep (during the first rapid eye movement period). The term "cluster" is used to describe the typical pattern of headache attacks, during which one to eight headaches will occur each day for weeks or months and then disappear completely during remission periods lasting months or years. Cycles that last longer than 1 year without remissions longer than 2 weeks are subtyped as chronic cluster headache. Episodic cluster headache, the most common subtype, lasts 7 days to 1 year with pain-free intervals lasting 2 weeks or more.

Fifteen percent of cluster sufferers have chronic cluster, with 10% diagnosed as primary chronic cluster, unremitting from first onset, and 5% diagnosed as secondary cluster, evolving from an episodic pattern.[52] Physical characteristics such as a "leonine" facial appearance and rough, "peau d'orange" skin have been suggested to be common in men with cluster headache, although the accuracy of this description is questionable.[53] Both genders of cluster sufferers are typically heavier users of tobacco, caffeine, and alcohol than the general population.[54,55]

Cluster attacks in women may be shorter in duration, less likely to be associated with sympathetically mediated autonomic symptoms (less miosis and ptosis), and more likely to display migrainous features (nausea and vomiting).[51,56] Women may be less likely to respond to typically used treatments for cluster headache, with lower reported response rates to abortive therapy such as oxygen and various preventive therapy combinations.[57]

Precipitants

Alcohol ingestion rapidly precipitates a cluster attack during an active headache cycle but can be used with impunity during remission periods. Otherwise, few of the common migraine triggers precipitate cluster attacks. The pressurization of airplane cabins is usually similar to that found at 8,000 feet above sea level; this may precipitate an attack and patients should be discouraged from flying during a cycle. Although many cluster patients are smokers, smoking cessation does not appear to alter the course of the disorder. Patients may have first onset or return of a cluster cycle after head trauma or an episode of sinusitis. Headache cycles may start at predictable times of the year, with a peak incidence several weeks before or after the shortest or longest day of the year (January and July) or during season changes with changing of daylight saving time (October and April).[58]

Trigeminal-Autonomic Cephalgias

The trigeminal-autonomic cephalgias (TACs) are so named for autonomic symptoms associated with headache. This headache category includes the diagnoses of cluster (see above): short-lasting, unilateral neuralgiform headache attacks with conjunctival injection, tearing, sweating, and rhinorrhea (SUNCT); long-lasting autonomic symptoms with associated hemicrania (LASH); chronic and episodic paroxysmal hemicrania; and hemicrania continua (HC).

Chronic and episodic paroxysmal hemicranias are described as severe burning or throbbing pain occurring unilaterally in the distribution of the first division of the trigeminal nerve and associated with autonomic features. The attack duration is longer than that in the SUNCT syndrome and shorter than seen in cluster, each lasting 2 to 45 minutes (average 5 to 10 minutes) and recurring over 5 times daily, with a reported attack frequency of up to 40 episodes daily (average 10 to 15 attacks daily).[59] Attacks are occasionally triggered by neck movement or occipital palpation. Remission periods of months to years may occur. These headaches are termed "episodic," whereas headaches without remission periods are termed "chronic," which, like cluster, can be chronic from the onset or have evolved from an episodic type. Chronic paroxysmal hemicrania (CPH) is more common than the episodic type and has a mean age of onset of 33 years and a female predominance of 2 to 1.[60] Most of these headaches respond dramatically to indomethacin treatment.[34]

Hemicrania continua, like the paroxysmal hemicranias, is responsive to treatment with indomethacin. Mean age at first onset is 35 years and the female to male ratio is 5:1.[61] Attacks are strictly unilateral without side shift, moderate to severe in intensity, and less commonly associated with migrainous characteristics, autonomic features (50%), or physical precipitants.[62] Autonomic features generally are mild compared with LASH and CPH and occur only during exacerbations of head pain. Headaches commonly resemble chronic tension-type except for unilaterality and occasional migrainous exacerbations or stabs similar to idiopathic stabbing headache.[63] Remitting forms of HC may occur, but headaches are typically continuous with fluctuations in intensity and exacerbations with characteristics of migraine (photophobia, phonophobia, nausea, and vomiting) and cluster (conjunctival injection, eye lacrimation, ptosis, and nasal congestion).

Another recently described indomethacin-responsive headache with autonomic features is an episodic headache disorder with LASH.[64] In a case report, unilateral autonomic features were prominent, preceding and outlasting the headache by hours. The headache features were migraine-like, occurring ipsilateral to the autonomic features, and lasting 1 to 3 days. Autonomic features and headache were responsive to indomethacin.

SUNCT syndrome is rare but has been reported in several case reviews. Suspicion for an organic etiology such as cerebellopontine angle tumor should be high. Mean age of first onset of SUNCT is 51 years, and it occurs 2.25 to 4.3 times more commonly in men.[65–67] The headache is described as moderate-to-severe stabbing, burning, neuralgic pain that occurs unilaterally in the distribution of the first division of the trigeminal nerve. Associated features include ipsilateral eye lacrimation, nasal congestion, and conjuctival injection. Attacks occur spontaneously or may be precipitated by a variety of stimuli, such as touching areas of the face, moving the neck or face, or chewing. Paroxysms of pain rapidly reach peak intensity and are brief (15 to 120 seconds). Attack frequency is 3 to 100 attacks per day with an average of 5 to 6 per hour.[68] Temporal patterns of attacks and varying remission periods lasting weeks to over a year have been reported.[69] Attacks rarely occur during sleep. SUNCT syndrome may be misdiagnosed as cluster headache, trigeminal neuralgia, CPH, or idiopathic stabbing headache.

Trigeminal neuralgia is not associated with autonomic features. The pain associated with CPH is longer in duration and responsive to indomethacin treatment.

Stabbing Headache or "Jabs and Jolts"

Idiopathic stabbing headaches are described as "jabs" or "jolts" that occur anywhere in the head and last a fraction of a second. Pain is usually felt in the distribution of the first division of the trigeminal nerve, and pain may recur several times a day without regularity. Lifetime prevalence is estimated at 2%, and it is more commonly found in migraineurs and has a female to male prevalence ratio of 6:1.[70,71] Idiopathic stabbing headache can be confused with SUNCT syndrome when most of the stabs of pain occur in the first division of the trigeminal nerve, but attacks are less frequent, moderate in intensity, and shorter in duration, lasting only a fraction of a second.[34] However, they are not associated with autonomic features and do not have a temporal pattern.

Cold Stimulus Headache

Cold stimulus headache is due to external cooling of the head or ingestion of cold food. Lifetime prevalence is 15%, and it is more common in migraineurs.[70] External cooling of the head typically produces a bilateral headache of variable intensity and duration. Ingestion of cold items such as ice cream may produce an intense brief headache in the midfrontal area lasting less than 5 minutes, previously termed "ice-cream headache."

Benign Cough Headache, Exertional Headache, and Headache Associated with Sexual Activity

Benign cough headache, with a lifetime prevalence of 1%, is a brief, sudden-onset, explosive, bilateral headache lasting a few seconds to a few minutes occurring after coughing, sneezing, straining, or weight lifting.[72] A duller headache lasting several hours may follow. A sudden onset of headache with weight training should prompt further investigation for cerebral aneurysm, Arnold-Chiari malformation, third ventricle tumor or cyst, AVM, posterior fossa tumor, cerebral aneurysm, carotid stenosis, or vertebrobasilar disease. Benign cough headache occurs more commonly in men, with a gender ratio of 4:1.[73] Mean age of onset is 55 years.

Benign exertional headache, with a 1% lifetime prevalence, is a bilateral, throbbing, nonexplosive headache with migrainous features that occurs during or after physical exercise and lasts 5 minutes to 24 hours. Exercising in hot weather or at high altitudes may precipitate the headache. Mean age of onset is the mid-twenties, earlier than benign cough headache, and the gender ratio is approximately 4:1 with a male predominance. Differential diagnosis includes subarachnoid hemorrhage (SAH), sinusitis, and tumor.[72] Anginal symptoms presenting as exertional headache have also been reported.[74]

Headache associated with sexual activity, previously termed "coital headache," is subdivided into dull, explosive, and postural types. All types occur in association with sexual activity and are bilateral at onset. The most worrisome is the "explosive type," which has characteristics of SAH that include sudden onset during the peak of orgasm. In fact, two studies found that 4.5% and 12% of patients with SAH experienced hemorrhage during orgasm, when elevations of blood pressure of up to 214/135 have been recorded.[75–77] Characteristics include severe, often throbbing or stabbing pain lasting 1 minute to 3 hours, with an average duration of 30 minutes.[78] The "dull type" is similar to TTH. The "postural type" is similar to a low cerebrospinal fluid (CSF) pressure headache, where headache intensifies with standing and eases with recumbency. Headaches associated with sexual activity are more commonly found in men (85%).[79] Lifetime prevalence in the general population has been reported at 1%.[70] Prognosis is variable, with approximately one-half of patients noting permanent remission after 6 months and the other 50% having sporadic recurrences.[80] Many also suffer with exertional headaches.[81]

Chronic Migraine

The term "chronic daily headache" (CDH) is defined as "persistent headache of at least 4 hours duration occurring at least 15 days per month."[82] The term "chronic migraine" has been introduced in the revised 2003 IHS classification; many patients previously considered to have CDH now meet criteria for chronic migraine. Five percent of the population has CDH, and the preponderance of sufferers are women (9% versus 1%).[83] Secondary causes for CDH should be sought before diagnosing primary CDH. One study found that 9.6% of patients with CDH who had a magnetic resonance venography imaging study of the brain had findings consistent with venous thrombosis, and one-half of these subjects did not have papilledema on physical examination.[84]

Various subtypes of CDH include new onset daily persistent headache (NDPH), CTTH, chronic migraine, formerly referred to as "transformed migraine" (TM), and HC.[85,86] NDPH is a daily or near-daily headache of abrupt onset, lasting at least 1 month, which is unremitting from its onset and is not a progression or transformation from previous migraine or TTH. Headaches may include characteristics of CTTH with or without migrainous features.[87] They may first occur after a viral illness or with no apparent cause. NDPHs are more common in adolescents or young adults and may be refractory to treatment early in their course. CTTH differs from NDPH in the context of CDH by evolving from episodic TTH and not having an abrupt onset.

Migraine occurring ≥ 15 days per month for at least 3 months, chronic migraine, is the most common CDH seen in a headache specialty practice and is frequently associated with medication misuse and rebound headache. The term transformed migraine includes chronic migraine and medication overuse headache. Patients begin with episodic migraines, which increase in frequency over time and become daily or near daily. Migrainous features such as nausea, photophobia, and phonophobia often become less prominent, but episodic full-blown migraine features will still occur.[87] Medication overuse may alter headache characteristics. If headaches remit after withdrawal of overused medication, they are termed "headache induced by substance use or exposure" (see section "Headache Associated with Substances or Their Withdrawal" below). HC headaches are discussed elsewhere (see section "Trigeminal-Autonomic Cephalgias" above).

The prevalence of these various subtypes of CDH vary, depending on whether a general population or headache center population is sampled. In a general population study in Spain, 4.7% suffered with CDH. Of this CDH population, 47.2% had CTTH, 50.6% had TM, 0.1% had NDPH, and 0% had HC. Only 17% of CDH subjects in this population study overused analgesics (31% of the TM subpopulation), in contrast to headache center populations reporting daily analgesic use in up to 87% of their TM patients.[83,88] Additionally, a greater proportion of patients with CDH at a headache center (80%) suffered with TM than CTTH (15%).[83]

NDPH accounted for 22% of total patients with CDH, meeting CDH criteria from first onset of headache in a study examining the course of CDH in a headache center population.[87] Seventy-eight percent of the total CDH population started with episodic headaches; 19% of these abruptly transitioned into CDH, and 81% gradually converted to CDH from their episodic pattern. The transition from episodic headache to CDH occurred over an average of 10 years. NDPH or abrupt transition to CDH from an episodic pattern was associated with conditions such as head, neck, or back injuries; flulike illness; sinusitis; medical illness; or surgical procedures in 61% of patients.[89] Headache characteristics did not differ between NDPH and abrupt transition to CDH from episodic headache except for more nausea in the latter group.

Primary CDHs that occur 15 days per month or more, but last less than 4 hours, include cluster headache, idiopathic stabbing headache, CPH, and hypnic headache.[90]

Hypnic headaches are nocturnal headaches commonly described as bilateral, mild to moderate in intensity, with occasional throbbing. They last only 5 to 60 minutes and are not associated with autonomic features. Hypnic headaches are more prevalent in women and the elderly.

SECONDARY CAUSES OF HEADACHE

Although most women with recurrent headaches who present to a primary care physician will prove to have migraine, secondary, potentially life-threatening headaches must be considered in the differential diagnosis, especially during pregnancy or postpartum. Although diagnostic and epidemiologic characteristics guide diagnosis, clinical judgment remains essential.

The diagnostic criteria for all of the primary headache disorders include the statement that "history, physical, and neurologic examination do not suggest a secondary headache, or, if they do suggest one, appropriate investigations have been done to rule out secondary headache."[34] In most cases, a comprehensive headache history is enough to rule out secondary headache types. Based on an extensive review of the evidence, the American Academy of Neurology (AAN) has issued a practice parameter stating that neuroimaging studies are not recommended in adults who have recurrent headaches that have not recently changed in character and that meet criteria for migraine and who have a normal neurologic examination.[91] In these cases, the likelihood of finding significant intracranial pathology on imaging studies is estimated at around 0.18%.[52]

Despite this recommendation, the American Migraine Study found that 37% of diagnosed migraineurs in the general population had at some point had a computed tomography (CT) scan of the head, 27% had undergone magnetic resonance imaging, 26% had received an electroencephalogram, and 44% had undergone blood work as part of their headache work-up.[9] Perhaps the extent of diagnostic work-up in these patients is understandable because not all ominous secondary headaches have specific characteristics and some may occasionally mimic primary headache disorders. However, at least some of this unnecessary testing could probably be avoided by greater familiarity with the criteria for diagnosis of the benign headache disorders, especially migraine, and an improved understanding of ominous or dangerous headache features (see Table 4-7).

An exhaustive discussion of all forms of secondary headache is beyond the scope of this chapter, but several of the secondary forms of headache are unique to, or more common in, women and will be reviewed in detail.

Arterial Hypertension

Arterial hypertension may present with headaches. Blood pressures must be high (greater than 220/120) or be associated with a rapid rise, as seen with an acute pressor response to an exogenous agent, preeclampsia, or eclampsia, to cause headache. Associated features of hypertensive encephalopathy include headache, nausea, vomiting, seizures, and decreased consciousness. Papilledema and retinal hemorrhages may be seen on examination. Eclampsia is associated with hypertension, edema, and proteinuria and seizures during pregnancy or shortly after delivery. Late postpartum eclampsia may occur up to 1 month after delivery, and 83% of patients experienced severe headache and/or visual changes mimicking migraine auras prior to seizures in one study.[92] Some studies have suggested that preeclampsia is more common in women with a history of migraine, but other studies do not support an elevated risk. Pheochromocytoma may also cause hypertensive headache associated with episodes of diaphoresis, palpitations, anxiety, and hypertension.

Low Cerebrospinal Fluid Pressure

Headache is the most common presenting manifestation of intracranial hypotension. Low CSF pressure

Table 4-7 Suspicious Headache Features and Differential Diagnoses

Late first onset of HA (> 50 years old) or systemic symptoms (myalgias, arthralgias, weight loss)

- Intracranial neoplasm (primary or metastatic)

- Temporal arteritis (polymyalgia rheumatica)

First and/or worst HA (versus recurrent pattern)

- Subarachnoid hemorrhage

Change in HA character (progressive increased frequency and/or severity over months or weeks or different from usual headache type)

- Intracranial neoplasm

Signs or symptoms of increased intracranial pressure (increased pain with coughing, straining, Valsalva maneuvers, pulsatile tinnitus, visual obscurations, papilledema, vision loss [enlarged blind spot], especially in obese young female)

- Idiopathic intracranial hypertension

- Cerebral venous sinus thrombosis

- Arnold-Chiari malformation

- Intracranial neoplasm

Rapid peak intensity of HA (especially with focal neurologic signs or changes in consciousness, with sexual activity or exertion, with hypertension or family history of aneurysm)

- Subarachnoid hemorrhage

- Cerebral venous sinus thrombosis

- Malignant hypertension

HA with fever and meningeal signs or occurring in those at risk of intracranial infection (immunosuppressed individuals)

- Meningitis

- Encephalitis

- Subarachnoid hemorrhage

HA after trauma

- Epidural or subdural hematoma

- Post-traumatic aneurysm

HA with endocrine disorders or visual loss (bitemporal hemianopia)

- Pituitary adenoma

HA refractory to treatment

- Idiopathic intracranial hypertension

- Sphenoid sinusitis

- Cerebral venous sinus thrombosis

Continued

Table 4-7 *Continued*

HA associated with abnormal neurologic findings (focal neurologic signs, seizures, cranial nerve palsies)

- Intracranial mass
    - Brain abscess
    - Neoplasm
    - Unruptured arteriovenous or venous malformation
- Lyme borreliosis
- Arterial hypertension (eclampsia)
- Cerebral venous sinus thrombosis
- CNS arteritis
- Carotid or vertebral artery dissection

CNS = central nervous system; HA = headache.

headache may be secondary to a lumbar puncture or CSF fistula after trauma or surgery or may occur for unknown reasons. Headache is characteristically bilateral, worsens within 15 minutes after standing, and is relieved within 30 minutes after recumbency. Valsalva's maneuvers such as coughing or straining exacerbate pain, which is frequently refractory to pharmacologic therapy.[93] Post-lumbar puncture headaches occur in 15 to 30% of patients, more commonly in younger females. Onset of headache may be minutes or up to 12 days postpuncture, and headache duration averages 2 to 14 days, sometimes months. Low CSF pressure headache should be considered in the differential diagnosis of headache occurring in women after epidural or spinal anesthesia is used for delivery or surgery.

Headaches Associated with Substances or Their Withdrawal

Women are more likely than men to experience CDH. In over 75% of cases, CDH results from the transformation of episodic to chronic migraine. Medication-induced or "rebound" headache is commonly associated with, and may cause, this transformation. The estimated prevalence of rebound headache in the general population is 1% but is very much higher in a headache specialty practice. The term "rebound" is used to describe the paradoxic worsening of headache frequency and severity that occurs from consistent use of acute care medications. There is no consensus about the types and amounts of medications required to produce this phenomenon. Generally, headaches occur almost daily and consist of a background TTH with intermittent, superimposed migrainous features or full-blown migraine attacks.[94] Patients usually cannot predict which headaches will become

severe and treat all headaches early for fear of exacerbation. The motivation of medication overuse for most is to remain functional for their daily duties. With continued overuse, acute care medications usually become less or ineffective, and prophylactic therapies are ineffective until the offending symptomatic medications are discontinued. Caffeinated beverages or combination medications containing caffeine, ergotamine, barbiturate, or opioid are the most common offenders, although "rebound" has been reported with nearly any acute care medication, even triptans.[95,96]

The 2003 IHS criteria specify that medication overuse headaches occur in people with preexisting primary headache, usually migraine or tension-type, who over use acute therapy.[34] Medication overuse headache occurs > 15 days per month in association with acute therapy 2 to 3 days per week for ≥ 3 months. Meaningful benefit is usually achieved after withdrawal of the misused medication.[97–99] Opioids and barbiturates should be withdrawn slowly to avoid withdrawal seizures. Withdrawal of the offending abortive medication or caffeinated beverages initially intensifies headaches, so-called "headaches from withdrawal of a substance after chronic use." This period may last several days to several months, and 80% of patients improve after withdrawal.[100] Headaches may also occur after withdrawal of acute use of a substance such as alcohol, also termed "hangover" headache.

Headache Associated with Endocrine Disorders

Endocrine disorders such as hypothyroidism, hyperthyroidism, or hyperparathyroidism are other causes of headaches. Hypothyroidism, more common in women, has been reported to cause a mild, non-throbbing, continous headache that most commonly starts 1 to 2 months after symptoms of hypothyroidism begin and is responsive to thyroid replacement hormone therapy.[101]

Neck Disorders Causing Headache

Hemicranial pain originating and referred from muscular, articular, osseous, neurogenic, or vascular structures in the neck is termed cervicogenic headache (CH). It is a syndrome, or final common pathway, to headache pain originating from the neck.[102] The head pain is most commonly described as non-throbbing, of moderate-to-severe intensity, with a tendency toward chronicity and refractoriness to pharmacologic measures. Vascular qualities such as nausea, phonophobia, or photophobia may be present but are usually less distinct than in migraine. Additional symptoms may include precipitation of headache with certain neck movements or awkward posturing, restricted range of motion of the cervical spine, and vague pain in the shoulder or arm ipsilateral to the headache pain.[34] Patients diagnosed with cervicogenic headache must demonstrate clinical, laboratory, or radiographic evidence of a cervical spine or neck disorder known to cause headache. Clinical signs must implicate the abnormality as a cause of headache or diagnostic blocks must relieve the pain. In addition, headache should resolve within 3 months of correction of the abnormality. Prevalence data varies widely (0.4 to 13.8%) depending on criteria used and populations examined.[103–105] CH is most likely seen in orthopedic and chronic pain practices.

CH, like post-traumatic headache or neck pain, is more commonly found in females. It is common to experience de novo CH after head trauma. In one study of 587 whiplash patients presenting for emergency room consultation, 222 experienced headaches of some type after 1 month.[106] Eight percent of these met criteria for de novo CH at 6 weeks. Only 3% still complained of CH after 1 year, suggesting that most post-traumatic CHs improve or resolve within 1 year. This may have therapeutic implications on the aggressiveness of therapy attempted before at least a year of conservative treatment.

COMMON MISDIAGNOSES OF HEADACHES

IHS criteria are not especially well suited for use in clinical practice because many patients do not meet these strict research standards for diagnosis, yet still have the disorder in question and will benefit from treatment.

Tension-Type Headache is Overdiagnosed

TTH is overdiagnosed; by definition, it is not a disabling or severe headache. Most patients with intermittent TTH self-treat using over-the-counter medications with good results. A patient whose headache is severe enough to consult a physician is unlikely to have TTH.

A recent study showed that over 80% of patients diagnosed as having TTH in fact have migraine on more careful evaluation. Thus, caution should be exercised in making a diagnosis of TTH.

Dental Disorders and Headache

Dental conditions such as cracked teeth, dental caries, abscesses, and temporomandibular joint (TMJ) dysfunction can cause headaches but more likely act as nonspecific triggers aggravating previously present primary headache conditions. TMJ disorders are rarely a sole etiology of headache and most commonly involve myofascial dysfunction from bruxism or malocclusion rather than a structural joint disorder. Diagnostic features of TMJ disease are decreased range of motion of the jaw, crepitus or clicking of the joint, tenderness over the area or in the ear, and tenderness to palpation.

Neck Pain Associated with Migraine

Neck pain in association with headache does not always indicate underlying structural neck pathology or CH. Neck pain is common in migraine. In a survey of 144 patients with migraine, 108 (75%) complained of associated neck pain. Migraine can begin with or be preceded by a sensation of tightness or tension in the neck; alternatively, neck pain may develop during the headache and last beyond it. Patients who complain of neck pain as part of their headache are commonly diagnosed as having tension headaches. Many undergo physical therapy or chiropractic manipulation, often with benefit. However, neck pain due to migraine resolves along with the headache when patients are treated with specific antimigraine medication.[107] Patients with migraine whose neck complaints resolve with migraine-specific therapy are unlikely to have associated cervical pathology.

Nose and Sinus Disorders are Uncommon Causes of Headache

Exacerbation of headaches may occur during allergy seasons in the spring and fall. Vasomotor rhinitis or allergic rhinitis causes inflammation and possibly temporary obstruction of the osteomeatal complex. Activation of trigeminal sensory afferent fibers from the sinuses due to altered barometric pressure with weather fronts (barosinusitis) may exacerbate primary headache disorders. Studies found that 50% of migraineurs reported headaches influenced by weather and 45% of patients reported sinus symptoms such as nasal congestion and rhinorrhea with their migraine.[108,109]

The American Migraine Study II found that 42% of patients who met criteria for a diagnosis of migraine reported that they had been diagnosed as having sinus headache by a physician. This confusion is understandable because the pain of migraine can be felt over the bridge of the nose, the cheeks, or the retroorbital area. However, facial pain or pressure in the absence of another major nasal symptom or sign does not constitute a suggestive history for sinusitis.

According to the American Academy of Otolaryngology-Head and Neck Surgery, headache is a minor factor in the diagnosis of sinusitis. Headache must also present with at least one of the following: nasal purulence on examination, nasal obstruction or blockage or discharge, or fever. True sinus-caused headache is rare and generally accompanies only severe cases of acute sinus inflammation. This should be easily recognizable because of associated signs and symptoms such as purulent nasal drainage and fever.

Headache as a feature of chronic sinus infection is not common. In fact, a recent evaluation of 24 patients with self-identified sinus headaches found that 23 (96%) satisfied criteria for migraine.[110] All of these patients had nasal congestion as part of their headache syndrome, which probably led them to attribute their symptoms to sinus problems. However, the "sinus" headaches in these patients were relieved with sumatriptan.

Also contributing to the confusion between migraine and sinus headache is the fact that over-the-counter sinus medications that contain vasoconstrictive decongestants or analgesics are sometimes effective in mild migraine attacks. This seeming response to "specific" medication reinforces in the patient's mind the idea that sinus problems are responsible for the headache. Furthermore, if antibiotics are used, when the migraine headache improves in a day or so, patients may attribute this to the drug rather than the natural history of migraine. Avoiding overdiagnosis of sinus headache is an important way of decreasing the inappropriate use of antibiotics.

Clinical data thus show that the vast majority of patients with self-described "sinus headache" actually have headaches meeting IHS criteria for migraine or migrainous headache. These patients also often experience symptoms such as sinus pain and pressure, nasal symptoms, and ocular symptoms that are not included in the IHS diagnostic criteria. Nasal or other symptoms commonly associated with "sinus headache" should prompt an evaluation of a headache patient for migraine. These symptoms should not inevitably trigger a diagnosis of "sinus headache" or exclude a diagnosis of migraine headache.

References

1. Solomon S. Migraine variants. Curr Pain Headache Rep 2001;5:165–9.

2. Ulrich V, Gervil M, Kyvik KO, et al. Evidence of a genetic factor in migraine with aura: a population-based Danish twin study. Ann Neurol 1999;45:242–6.

3. Ulrich V, Olesen J, Gervil M, Russell MB. Possible risk factors and precipitants for migraine with aura in discordant twin-pairs: a population-based study. Cephalalgia 2000;20:821–5.

4. Micieli G. Suffering in silence. In: Edmeads J, editor. Migraine: a brighter future. Worthing: Cambridge Medical Publications; 1993. p. 1–7.

5. Silberstein SD. Menstrual migraine. J Womens Health Gend Based Med 1999;8:919–31.

6. Meyer JS, Kawamura J. Cerebral vascular disease and headache. In: Diamond S, Dalessio DJ, editors. The practicing physician's approach to headache. 5th ed. Baltimore: Williams and Wilkins; 1992. p. 162–73.

7. Henry P, Michel P, Bouchat B, et al. A nationwide survey of migraine in France: prevalence and clinical features in adults. Cephalalgia 1992;12:229–37.

8. Winner P, Wasiewski W, Gladstein J, Linder S. Multicenter prospective evaluation of proposed pediatric migraine revisions to the IHS criteria. Headache 1997;37:545–8.

9. Lipton RB, Diamond S, Reed ML, et al. Migraine diagnosis and treatment: results from the American Migraine Study II. Headache 2001;41:638–45.

10. Lipton RB, Stewart WF. Migraine in the United States: a review of epidemiology and health care use. Neurology 1993;43 Suppl 3:S6–10.

11. Stewart WF, Linet M, Celentano D, et al. Age- and sex-specific incidence rates of migraine with and without visual aura. Am J Epidemiol 1991;134:1111–20.

12. Stang PE, Yanagihara T, Swanson JW, et al. Incidence of migraine headache: a population-based study in Olmsted County, Minnesota. Neurology 42;1983:1657–62.

13. Stewart WF, Lipton RB, Liberman J. Variation in migraine prevalence by race. Neurology 1996;47:52–9.

14. Stewart WF, Shechter A, Lipton RB. Migraine heterogeneity: disability, pain intensity, and attack frequency and duration. Neurology 1994;44 Suppl 4:S24–39.

15. Lipton RB, Stewart WF, Celentano DD, Reed ML. Undiagnosed migraine headaches: a comparison of symptom-based and reported physician diagnosis. Arch Intern Med 1992;152:1273–8.

16. Russell MB, Rasmussen BK, Thorvaldsen P, Olesen J. Prevalence and sex-ratio of subtypes of migraine. Int J Epidemiol 1995;24:612–8.

17. Rasmussen BK, Rigmor J, Schroll M, et al. Epidemiology of headache in a general population—a prevalence study. J Clin Epidemiol 1991;44:1147–57.

18. Weitzel KW, Strickland JM, Smith KM, Goode JV. Gender-specific issues in the treatment of migraine. J Gend Specif Med 2001;4:64–74.

19. Rasmussen BK, Olesen J. Migraine with aura and migraine without aura: an epidemiological study. Cephalalgia 1992;12:221–8.

20. Hu XH, Markson LE, Lipton RB, et al. Burden of migraine in the United States: disability and economic costs. Arch Intern Med 1999;159:813–8.

21. Silberstein SD, Young WB. Migraine aura and prodrome. Semin Neurol 1995;45:175.

22. Luciani R, Carter D, Mannix L, et al. Prevention of migraine during prodrome with naratriptan. Cephalalgia 2000;20:122–6.

23. MacGregor A. What is migraine? In: MacGregor A, editor. Managing migraine in primary care. Osney Mead (Oxford): Blackwell Science Ltd; 1999. p. 21–33.

24. Fuller GN, Guiloff RJ. Migrainous olfactory hallucinations. J Neurol Neurosurg Psychiatry 1987;50:1688–90.

25. Diamond S, Freitag FG, Prager J, Gandi S. Olfactory aura in migraine [letter]. N Engl J Med 1985;312:1390–1.

26. Schreiber AO, Calvert PC. Migrainous olfactory hallucinations. Headache 1986;26:513–4.

27. Rubin D, McAbee GN, Feldman-Winter LB. Auditory hallucinations associated with migraine. Headache 2002;42:646–8.

28. Russell MB, Olesen J. A nosographic analysis of migraine aura in a general population. Brain 1996;119:355–61.

29. Fisher CM. Late-life migraine accompaniments: further experience. Stroke 1986;17:1033–42.

30. Joutel A, Bousser MG, Biousse V, et al. A gene for familial hemiplegic migraine maps to chromosome 19. Nat Genet 1993;5:40–5.

31. Gardner K, Barmada MM, Ptacek LJ, et al. A new locus for hemiplegic migraine maps to chromosome 1q31. Neurology 1997;49:1231–8.

32. Sturzenegger MH, Meienberg O. Basilar artery migraine: a follow-up study of 82 cases. Headache 1985;25:408–15.

33. Bickerstaff ER. Migraine variants and complications. In: Blau JN, ed. Migraine: clinical and research aspects. Baltimore: Johns Hopkins University Press; 1987. p. 55–75.

34. The international classification of headache disorders. 2nd ed. Cephalalgia 2003. [In press]

35. Tzourio C, Tehindrazanarivelo A, Iglesias S, et al. Case-control study of migraine and risk of ischemic stroke in young women. BMJ 1995;310:830–3.

36. Mueller L. Tension-type, the forgotten headache. Postgrad Med 2002;111:25–50.

37. Granella F, Sances G, Zanferrari C, et al. Migraine without aura and reproductive life events: a clinical epidemiological study in 1300 women. Headache 1993; 33:385–9.

38. Stewart WF, Lipton RB, Chee E, et al. Menstrual cycle and headache in a population sample of migraineurs. Neurology 2000;28:1517–23.

39. Cupini LM, Matteis M, Troisi E, et al. Sex-hormone-related events in migrainous females. A clinical comparative study between migraine with aura and migraine without aura. Cephalalgia 1995;15:140–4.

40. Russell MB, Rasmussen BK, Fenger K, Olesen J. Migraine without aura and migraine with aura are distinct clinical entities: a study of four hundred and eighty-four male and female migraineurs from the general population. Cephalalgia 1996;16:239–45.

41. Mattsson P, Svardsudd K, Lundberg PO, Westerberg CE. The prevalence of migraine in women aged 40–74 years: a population-based study. Cephalalgia 2000;20:893–9.

42. Friedman AP, de Sola Pool N, von Storch TJ. Tension headache. JAMA 1953;151:174–7.

43. Silberstein SD, Lipton RB, Goadsby PJ, Smith RT. Tension-type headache: diagnosis and treatment. In: Silberstein SD, Lipton RB, Goadsby PJ, Smith RT, editors. Headache in primary care. Oxford: Isis Medical Media Ltd; 1999. p. 83–91.

44. Rasmussen BK. Migraine and tension-type headache in a general population: precipitating factors, female hormones, sleep pattern and relation to lifestyle. Pain 1993;53:65–72.

45. Kudrow L. Cluster headache: mechanisms and management. New York (NY): Oxford University Press; 1980.

46. Ekbom K, Svensson DA, Traff H, Waldenlind E. Age at onset and sex ratio in cluster headache: observations over three decades. Cephalalgia 2002;22:94–100.

47. Manzoni GC, Micieli G, Granella F, et al. Cluster headache: course over ten years in 189 patients. Cephalalgia 1991;11:169–74.

48. Dodick DW, Rozen TD, Goadsby PJ, Silberstein SD. Cluster headache. Cephalalgia 2000;20:787–803.

49. Manzoni GC. Male preponderance of cluster headache is progressively decreasing over the years. Headache 1997;37:588–9.

50. Manzoni GC. Gender ratio of cluster headache over the years: a possible role of changes in lifestyle. Cephalalgia 1998;18:138–42.

51. Rozen TD, Niknam R, Shechter AL, et al. Cluster headache in women: clinical characteristics and comparison to cluster headache in men [abstract]. Neurology 1999;52:A471.

52. Silberstein SD. Practice parameter evidence-based guidelines for migraine headache (an evidence-based review): report of the Quality Standards Subcommittee of the AAN. Neurology 2000;55:754–62.

53. Kudrow L. Cluster headache: diagnosis, management, and treatment. In: Dalessio DJ, Silberstein SD, editors. Wolff's headache and other head pain. 6th ed. Oxford: Oxford University Press; 1993. p. 171–97.

54. Levi R, Edman GV, Ekbom K, Waldenlind E. Episodic cluster headache II. High tobacco and alcohol consumption in males. Headache 1992;32:184–7.

55. Nappi G on behalf of the Italian Cooperative Study Group on the Epidemiology of Cluster Headache (ICECH). Case-control study on the epidemiology of cluster headache. I. Etiological factors and associated conditions. Neuroepidemiology 1995;14:123–7.

56. Manzoni GC, Micieli G, Granella F, et al. Cluster headache in women: clinical findings and relationship with reproductive life. Cephalalgia 1988;8:37–44.

57. Rozen TD, Niknam R, Shechter AL, et al. Gender differences in clinical characteristics and treatment response in cluster headache patients. Cephalalgia 1999;19:323.

58. Kudrow L. The cyclic relationship of natural illumination to cluster period frequency. Cephalalgia 1987;7:76–8.

59. Rapoport AM, Sheftell FD. Diagnosis and classification of headache disorders. In: Rapoport AM, Sheftell FD, editors. Headache disorders: a management guide for practitioners. Philadelphia: W.B. Saunders Company; 1996. p. 5–20.

60. Antonaci F, Sjaastad O. Chronic paroxysmal hemicrania (CPH): a review of clinical manifestations. Headache 1989;29:648–56.

61. Headaches provoked by exertional factors. In: Saper JR, Silberstein S, Gordon SD, et al, editors. Handbook of headache management. 2nd ed. Baltimore (MD): Williams and Wilkins; 1999. p. 238–48.

62. Pareja JA, Antonaci F, Vincent M. The hemicrania continua diagnosis. Cephalalgia 2001;21:940–6.

63. Silberstein SD, Lipton RB, Goadsby PJ, Smith RT. Chronic headache: diagnosis and treatment. In: Silberstein SD, Lipton RB, Goadsby PJ, Smith RT, editors. Headache in primary care. Oxford: Isis Medical Media Ltd; 1999. p. 93–104.

64. Rozen TD. LASH: a syndrome of long-lasting autonomic symptoms with hemicrania (a new indomethacin-responsive headache). Headache 2000;40:483–6.

65. Pareja JA, Sjaastad O. SUNCT syndrome. A clinical review. Headache 1997;37:195–202.

66. Pareja JA, Sjaastad O. SUNCT syndrome in the female. Headache 1994;34:217–20.

67. Goadsby PJ, Lipton RB. A review of paroxysmal hemicranias, SUNCT syndrome and other short-lasting headaches with autonomic feature, including new cases. Brain 1997;120:193–209.

68. Newman JC. Effective management of ice pick pains, SUNCT, and episodic and chronic paroxysmal hemicrania. Curr Pain Headache Rep 2001;5:292–9.

69. Lain AH, Caminero AB, Pareja JA. SUNCT syndrome, absence of refractory periods and modulation of attack duration by lengthening of the trigger stimuli. Cephalalgia 2000;20:671–3.

70. Rassmussen BK. Epidemiology of headache. Cephalalgia 1995;15:45–68.

71. Pareja JA, Ruiz J, Deisla C, et al. Idiopathic stabbing headache (jabs and jolts syndrome). Cephalalgia 1996; 16:93–6.

72. Wall M, Silberstein SD, Aiken RD. Headache associated with abnormalities in intracranial structure or function: high cerebrospinal fluid pressure headache and brain tumor. In: Silberstein SD, Lipton RB, Dalessio DJ, editors. Wolff's headache and other head pain. New York (NY): Oxford University Press; 2001. p. 393–416.

73. Rooke E. Benign exertional headache. Med Clin North Am 1968;52:801–8.

74. Grace A, Horgan J, Breathnach K, Staunton H. Anginal headache and its basis. Cephalalgia 1997;17:195–6.

75. Fisher CM. Headache in cerebrovascular disease. In: Vinken PJ, Bruyn GW, editors. Handbook of clinical neurology. Vol 5. Amsterdam: Elsevier; 1968. p. 124–6.

76. Lundberg PO, Osterman PO. The benign and malignant forms of orgasmic cephalgia. Headache 1974;14:164–5.

77. Littler WA, Honour AJ, Sleight P. Direct arterial pressure, heart rate, and electrocardiogram during human coitus. J Reprod Fertil 1974;40:321–31.

78. Silberstein SD, Lipton RB, Goadsby PJ, Smith RT. Headache associated with disease in the intracranial cavity. In: Silberstein SD, Lipton RB, Goadsby PJ, Smith RT, editors. Headache in primary care. Oxford: Isis Medical Media Ltd; 1999. p. 123–33.

79. Lance JW. Headaches related to sexual activity. J Neurol Neurosurg Psychiatry 1976;39:1226–30.

80. Ostergaard JR, Kraft M. Natural course of benign coital headache. BMJ 1992;305:1129.

81. Silbert PL, Edis RH, Stewart-Wynn EG, Gubbay SS. Benign vascular sexual headache and exertional

headache: interrelationships and long term prognosis. J Neurol Neurosurg Psychiatry 1991;54:417–21.

82. Silberstein SD, Lipton RB, Solomon S, Mathew NT. Classification of daily and near-daily headaches: proposed revisions to the IHS criteria. Headache 1994;34:1–7.

83. Castillo J, Munoz P, Guitera V, Pascual J. Epidemiology of chronic daily headache in the general population. Headache 1999;39:190–6.

84. Quattrone A, Bono F, Oliveri RL, et al. Cerebral venous thrombosis and isolated intracranial hypertension without papilledema in CDH. Neurology 2001;57:31–6.

85. Silberstein SD, Lipton RB. Chronic daily headache. Curr Opin Neurol 2000;133:277–83.

86. Silberstein SD, Lipton RB, Sliwinski M. Classification of daily and near-daily headaches: field trial of revised IHS criteria. Neurology 1996;47:871–5.

87. Silberstein SD, Lipton RB. Chronic daily headache, including transformed migraine, chronic tension-type headache, and medication overuse. In: Silberstein SD, Lipton RB, Dalessio DJ, editors. Wolff's headache and other head pain. New York (NY): Oxford University Press; 2001. p. 247–82.

88. Mathew NT. Chronic refractory headache. Neurology 1993;43 Suppl 3:S26–33.

89. Spierings ELH, Schroevers M, Honkoop PC, Sorbi M. Development of chronic daily headache: a clinical study. Headache 1998;38:529–33.

90. Raskin NH. The hypnic headache syndrome. Headache 1988;28:534–6.

91. Frishberg B. Evidence-based guidelines in the primary care setting: Neuroimaging in patients with nonacute headache. The American Academy of Neurology. Available at: http://www.aan.com (accessed October 7, 2003).

92. Lubarsky SL, Barton JR, Friedman SA, et al. Late postpartum eclampsia revisited. Obstet Gynecol 1994;83: 502–5.

93. Lay CL, Campbell JK, Mokri B. Low cerebrospinal fluid pressure headache. In: Goadsby P, Silberstein SD, editors. Blue books of practical neurology: headache. Boston: Butterworth-Heinemann; 1997. p. 355–68.

94. Mathew NT, Stubits E, Nigam MP. Transformation of episodic migraine into daily headache: analysis of factors. Headache 1982;22:66–8.

95. Wainscott G, Volans G, Wilkinson M. Ergotamine induced headaches. BMJ 1974;2:724.

96. Gaist D, Tsiropoulos I, Sindrup SH, et al. Inappropriate use of sumatriptan: population-based register and interview study. BMJ 1998;316:1352–3.

97. Diener H, Tfelt-Hansen P. Headache associated with chronic use of substances. In: Olesesn J, Tfelt-Hansen P, Welch K, editors. The headaches. 1st ed. New York (NY): Raven Press; 1993. p. 721–7.

98. Diener HC, Mathew NT. Drug-induced headache. In: Diener HC, editor. Drug treatment of migraine and other frequent headaches. Vol 17. Basel: Karger Press; 2000. p. 347–56.

99. Linton-Dahlof P, Linde M, Dahlof C. Withdrawal therapy improves chronic daily headache associated with long-term misuse of headache medication: a retrospective study. Cephalalgia 2000;20:658–62.

100. Rapoport AM, Sheftell FD. Pharmacologic treatment of migraine. In: Rapoport AM, Sheftell FD, editors. Headache disorders: a management guide for practitioners. Philadelphia (PA): W.B. Saunders Company; 1996. p. 77–98.

101. Moreau T, Manceau E, Giroud-Baleydier F, et al. Headache in hypothyroidism. Prevalence and outcome under thyroid hormone therapy. Cephalalgia 1998;18:687–9.

102. Antonaci F, Fredriksen TA, Sjaastad O. Cervicogenic headache: clinical presentation, diagnostic criteria, and differential diagnosis. Curr Pain Headache Rep 2001;5:387–92.

103. Sjaastad O, Fredriksen TA, Pfaffenrath V. Cervicogenic headache: diagnostic criteria. Headache 1990;30:725–6.

104. D'Amico D, Leone M, Bussone G. Side-locked unilaterality and pain localization in long-lasting headaches: migraine, tension-type headache, and cervicogenic headache. Headache 1994;34:526–30.

105. Pfaffenrath V, Kaube H. Diagnostics of cervicogenic headache. Funct Neurol 1990;5:159–64.

106. Drottning P, Staff PH, Sjaastad O. Cervicogenic headache (CEH) after whiplash injury. Cephalalgia 2002;22:165–71.

107. Kaniecki RG, Totten J. Cervicalgia in migraine: prevalence, clinical characteristics, and response to treatment [abstract]. Cephalalgia 2001;21:296–7.

108. Raskin NH. Headache. 2nd ed. New York (NY): Churchill Livingstone; 1998.

109. Barbanti P, Fabbrini G, Pesare M, et al. Unilateral cranial autonomic symptoms in migraine. Cephalalgia. 2002; 22:256–9.

110. Schreiber CP, Cady RK, Billings C. Subjects with self-described 'sinus' headache meet HIS diagnostic criteria for migraine [abstract]. Cephalalgia 2001;21:298.

111. Stewart WF, Lipton RB, Celentano DD, Reed ML. Prevalence of migraine headache in the United States. Relation to age, race, and other sociodemographic factors. JAMA 1992;267:64–9.

112. Silberstein SD, Lipton RB, Goadsby PJ, Smith RT. Post-traumatic headache. In: Silberstein SD, Lipton RB, Goadsby PJ, Smith RT, editors. Headache in primary care. Oxford: Isis Medical Media Ltd; 1999. p. 117–22.

113. Durcan FJ, Corbett JJ, Wall M. The incidence of pseudotumor cerebri: population studies in Iowa and Louisiana. Arch Neurol 1988;45:875–7.

114. Forsyth PA, Posner JB. Headache in patients with brain tumors. A study of 111 patients. Neurology 1993;43: 1678–83.

115. Black PM. Brain tumors. Part 1 and 2. N Engl J Med 1991;324:1471–6, 1555–64.

116. Hosokawa M, Asano A, Itioka O, et al. Pituitary adenoma and headache. Jpn J Headache 1987;14:59–63.

117. Yokoyama S, Mamitsuka K, Tokimura H, Asakura T. Headache in pituitary adenoma cases. J Jpn Soc Study Chron Pain 1994;13:79–82.

118. Diamond S. Acute headache. Differential diagnosis and management of the three types. Postgrad Med 1992;3: 21–30.

119. Stewart WF, Lipton RB, Dimon D. Work-related disability: results from the American Migraine Study. Cephalalgia 1996;16:231–8.

CHAPTER 5

Evaluation of the Woman with Headache

Beau K. Nakamoto, MD, and Kathleen B. Digre, MD

CASE

AS is a 32-year-old woman who has a history of periodic migraine, as did her mother. Over the previous 2 months, she had developed daily headaches that were different from her typical intermittent headaches. These were described as an aching sensation behind her eyes and in the neck and upper back. She also heard a "wooshing noise" in her head, especially at night when it was quiet. On occasion, she had bilateral visual dimming. Headaches seemed worse in the morning and improved as the day went on. She also had an increased number of her typical migraines.

On examination, she had normal blood pressure; her general examination was only notable for a weight of 240 pounds with a height of 63 inches. Neurologic examination revealed bilateral swelling of the optic discs but was otherwise normal. A magnetic resonance scan of the head showed an empty sella but was otherwise normal. Lumbar puncture revealed an elevated opening pressure of 340 mm H_2O. The diagnosis of idiopathic intracranial pressure was made, and the patient was placed on the diuretic acetazolamide to reduce spinal fluid formation.

This case illustrates just one of the complexities involved in the evaluation of patients with headache, regardless of gender. Recognizing dangerous or secondary causes of headache and distinguishing them from new onset or changing primary headache disorders such as migraine, can be a challenge. Although the patient in this case had a long-standing history of obvious migraine, the changing character of her headaches and the presence of symptoms such as visual changes that cannot be ascribed to migraine suggested the need for further evaluation. In this case, diagnostic evaluation revealed idiopathic intracranial hypertension, a common cause of secondary headache in obese women. This chapter outlines a systematic approach to evaluation of the patient with headache with the goal of distinguishing benign from worrisome causes of headache.

KEY CHAPTER POINTS

- **History is consistently more important than physical examination in headache diagnosis.**
- **Disability evaluation provides important diagnostic and treatment information.**
- **Diagnostic testing is infrequently useful in headache diagnosis.**
- **Some primary and secondary headache disorders are more common in women; a few occur only in women.**

HISTORY TAKING VERSUS PHYSICAL EXAMINATION IN DIAGNOSIS

History Taking

Headache is among many medical disorders in which the historic information and description of the headache obtained from the patient is of principal importance. Certain historic information is essential for diagnosis of one of the common primary headache disorders (which remain entirely *clinical* diagnoses, without confirmatory laboratory, imaging, or examination findings) but is also needed to correctly assess the probability of one of the rare but important secondary causes of headache.

Table 5-1 summarizes five important features of the headache history. First, a family history of benign, recurrent headache should be sought because several of the primary headache disorders (migraine and tension-type headache) are familial.[1-4] It is helpful to inquire about "headache" in general, rather than ask a specific question about "migraine," for example. Many women who deny having a family member with migraine will nonetheless report relatives with "sinus" or "sick" headaches—in all likelihood migraine.

A second historic feature that is important to determine is the natural history of a typical, severe attack. Does the patient have premonitory or prodromal symptoms that alert her to impending headaches, such as fatigue, yawning, or exuberance? Has the patient ever had aura or other neurologic accompaniments to a headache, even if they do not occur with every headache? Does the headache begin abruptly or develop gradually? Is it unilateral or bilateral, and what part of the head hurts? Ask the patient to describe the character of the pain; be ready with a list of adjectives to help patients with this task. For example, you might ask them whether the pain is steady, sharp, pounding, throbbing, squeezing, aching, or burning. How long does the headache last if it is untreated or if treatment is not successful? Are there any associated features? Nausea, vomiting, photophobia, phonophobia, worsening with activity, tearing, rhinorrhea, conjunctival injection, facial sweating, and eyelid edema will often be spontaneously described by patients without prompting and are very useful in narrowing the diagnostic focus. Finally, information about factors that aggravate or relieve the headache, such as rest, hormonal fluctuations, stress, or alcohol ingestion, is helpful.

Third, scrutinize the history of headache itself. Is this a woman's first headache, or has she had others? Did the headache problem begin in childhood, puberty, adulthood, or coincide with pregnancy or head trauma? What medical evaluation, if any, has occurred, and what was the outcome?

Fourth, a careful medical history is important, especially information about comorbid medical or psychiatric disorders that might influence treatment choices. The list of medical conditions that can cause or exacerbate headache is endless. Conditions that are common in women and deserve special consideration include endocrine abnormalities, especially hypothyroidism, hematologic disturbances such as iron-deficiency anemia, and collagen vascular diseases such as systemic lupus erythematosus. Affective disorders such as depression are no longer thought to cause headache, but they are more common in patients who have migraine and when present can complicate management.

Finally, a careful history of medication or other treatments is essential. What medications has the patient taken for the acute attack? Be sure to ask about over-the-counter medications and gauge the frequency of use for acute care medications because analgesic-induced rebound headache is common and easily missed without this history. Has the patient used medication for nausea? What medications has the patient tried to prevent headaches? What non-pharmacologic treatments or lifestyle changes has she made? A special inquiry about the use of herbs, supplements, and vitamins is particularly important because, as with over-the-counter medications, patients often do not report such treatment without prompting.

Physical Examination Supplements the History

As a general rule, the examination should include measurement of blood pressure, heart rate, weight, height, cardiac auscultation, examination of the muscles of the head, neck, and temporomandibular joint, and evaluation of the patient's demeanor and thought processes. During the neurologic examination, attention must be given to the optic discs to ensure that there is no disc swelling, which may suggest a secondary cause of headache. The neurologic examination is usually normal in most patients with primary headaches and can even be normal in those with secondary headache disorders.

A few words about the details of a "headache examination" are in order. This evaluation should include observing the posture of the individual—is the neck straight rather than slightly curved, as is normal? Straightening may indicate a postural component to the headache or suggest that the headache has lead to an abnormal head posture. In either case, physical therapy and neck exercises may be helpful. Palpate the temporomandibular joint—is the patient able open her mouth three fingerbreadths? Most patients with true temporomandibular joint disease do not complain of headache but will describe pain with talking or chewing. However, in headache-prone individuals, temporomandibular joint disease may aggravate the existing headache disorder. [5] Compress the superficial temporal arteries. If this maneuver relieves the headache, there may be a vascular component to the headache. Compress the insertions of the trapezius muscle and frontalis muscle; some patients with tension-type headache will experience relief with this maneuver. Palpate the scalp. Individuals with frequent migraine may experience tenderness around the head during a headache, and some develop unremitting sensitivity that may indicate allodynia, a situation in which, probably as a result of central sensitization from repeated attacks of migraine, normally nonpainful stimuli cause discomfort. Such patients may report that it "hurts to brush my hair."

Some "red flags" in the headache history should alert the examiner to the possibility of a secondary cause of headache. Table 5-2 summarizes historic features that warrant further evaluation for the presence of a dangerous underlying cause of headache. Sudden onset of a severe headache, particularly if the headache is described as "the worst" headache a patient has ever had, is always worrisome. Although "thunderclap" or "crash" headache can be a primary headache disorder, the possibility of a warning bleed or subarachnoid hemorrhage must be ruled out, generally with a plain

Table 5-1 The Headache History

History is the single most important clue to the diagnosis of any headache condition because the examination is often normal. Five features of the history are especially important:

1. Family history. Determine if the patient is genetically headache prone.
    - Ask if the patient's mother, father, sister, or brother ever had a headache. "Sinus headache" is usually recurrent migraine.
    - Is there a family history of depression, bipolar, or anxiety disorders?

2. The attack history. Because many people have more than one kind of headache, it is important to query the events of each headache type.
    - Is this a new headache or an old headache? New headaches need to be closely scrutinized for features that may signal a secondary cause.
    - Are there warning signals that precede the headache onset (eg, fatigue and yawning)? Auras are frequently neurologic symptoms occurring before an attack (eg, visual spots, lights, wavy lines, sparks, flashes, zigzag lines, heat wave sensations, numbness, weakness, and vertigo).
    - Where is the headache located (unilateral or bilateral, holocranial, hemicranial, temporal, parietal, retroorbital, or supraorbital)?
    - How frequently does it occur (daily, weekly, monthly, or rarely)?
    - How long does it last (hours, days, or weeks)?
    - What type of pain is it (throbbing, dull aching, stabbing, or burning)?
    - When does it occur (morning or night, does it awaken her from sleep)?
    - How does it come on (suddenly or gradually)?
    - What are the associated symptoms (nausea, vomiting, photophobia, phonophobia, tearing, rhinorrhea, conjunctival injection, facial sweating, or eyelid edema)?
    - Are there precipitating factors (diet, stress, menstruation)?
    - What factors relieve the headache (bedrest, dark and quiet room, vomiting, ice or heat packs, pacing, or medications)?
    - What are aggravating factors (movement, lack of sleep, sunlight, position changes, driving, or stress)?
    - How does it leave (suddenly or gradually)?

3. The history of the headache itself. What has happened to the headache over time?
    - Was there car sickness or night terrors as a child? These are frequently associated with migraines.
    - Was there episodic nausea or abdominal pain as a child? Abdominal headache are another kind of migraine in children.
    - When did the headache start? Adolescence is a frequent starting point.
    - Were there any milestones in life when the headaches got worse? Life-stressors (eg, marriage, death of a relative, college, new baby, moving) all can make underlying headaches worse.
    - Have the headaches changed over time?

4. Past medical and psychiatric history. Both can affect diagnosis or prognosis
    - Medical considerations: COPD, thyroid disease (40% have headache), hypertension, anemia
    - Psychiatric comorbidities: abuse (sexual, physical, or other), depression, anxiety
    - Social history: smoking, alcohol, caffeine intake, or drugs

5. Treatment history and response
    - Prescription medications[142]
        - Vasodilators (nitroglycerin, isosorbide dinitrate); these can aggravate headaches, especially migraine
        - Antihypertensives (reserpine, captopril, atenolol, metoprolol, prazosin, minoxidil); some are used to treat migraine while others may aggravate it
        - Nonsteroidal anti-inflammatory drugs (indomethacin, diclofenac, piroxicam)
        - H_2 receptor antagonists (cimetidine, ranitidine)
        - Calcium channel blockers (nifedipine, verapamil)

Continued

Table 5-1 *Continued*

- Hormonal preparations (contraceptives, danazol, estrogens, clomiphene)
- Antibiotics (griseofulvin, trimethoprim-sulfamethoxazole)
- Nonprescription medications
  - Over-the-counter caffeine preparations combined with aspirin or acetaminophen can cause rebound headache (eg, Anacin, Excedrin).
  - Medications with sympathomimetic effects (eg, pseudoephedrine) may increase headaches.
  - Drug abuse (eg, cocaine, amphetamine)
  - Herbal preparations (ginseng, feverfew, St. John's Wort)

COPD = chronic obstructive pulmonary disease.

computed tomographic (CT) scan of the head, followed by lumbar puncture if the CT scan is normal. Table 5-3 lists the differential diagnosis of a "thunder-clap" headache.

New-onset headaches require thoughtful evaluation. In most cases, especially in younger women whose history is consistent with a primary headache disorder and whose examination is normal, such evaluation can take the form of empiric treatment and careful follow-up. The passage of time and response to standard headache treatment will prove reassuring in almost all cases. A few secondary headache disorders should be considered in this population, especially idiopathic intracranial hypertension. Space occupying lesions, congenital malformations (eg, Arnold-Chiari malfor-mation), vascular malformations, venous occlusive disease, and vasculitis are much less common but should be considered in patients who do not respond as expected to treatment.

In contrast, new-onset headache in women over 50 years of age is cause for more concern, and should lead to a more extensive evaluation. Diagnoses that merit special scrutiny in this age group include giant cell (temporal) arteritis, brain tumors, and vascular disease.

New-onset headache in pregnancy may be due to any of the disorders that cause headache in nonpregnant women, but causes of headache specific to pregnancy must also be assessed. Table 5-4 lists the differential diagnosis of a new headache in pregnancy. Of these, the headache of preeclampsia is especially important to identify.

Table 5-2 Red Flags in a Woman with Headache

Unusually severe headache of sudden onset (ie, "worst headache of my life")

Unexplainable worsening of previously existing headaches

Dramatic or unusual change in character of the typical prodrome of the headache

Headaches awakening the patient in the middle of the night (provided it is not a cluster headache)

Headaches much worse when recumbent or with coughing, sneezing, or Valsalva's maneuver

New-onset headaches at an older age (> 50 years) without a positive family history

New headache in a patient with cancer or known HIV

Headache associated with systemic illness (eg, fever, chills, rash, stiffness of neck)

Any abnormal neurologic finding—including the presence of papilledema

Focal deficits that do not disappear after the headache is over

HIV = human immunodeficiency virus.

DISABILITY EVALUATION

Affective disorders such as depression and anxiety are more common in patients with migraine than in the general population but are not the cause of migraine.[6–8] Rather, both disorders appear to result from underlying abnormalities in the central nervous system. The stereotyped view of the patient with headache, especially the migraineur, as a neurotic or complaining woman is slowly disappearing as evidence emerges about the biologic causes of primary headache and the resultant disability and impaired quality of life it causes.[9] Many patients who meet diagnostic criteria for migraine report that they have never received such a diagnosis from a healthcare professional.[10] This is important because more than 80% of undiagnosed migraineurs experience some degree of disability with their headaches and would presumably benefit from recognition and treatment.[11] Furthermore, migraines in women are reported to be more severe and longer lasting than those in males, causing more bedrest and missed days of school or work.[12] Accurate measures of migraine-caused disability are especially important in women because they allow identification of those who would benefit from treatment and provide a way of monitoring treatment effectiveness.

Table 5-3 Causes of a Thunderclap Headache

Primary Headache	Secondary Headache
Benign exertional headache	Subarachnoid hemorrhage
Cluster headache	Intracranial hemorrhage
Orgasmic headache	Pituitary apoplexy
	Cervical disc herniation
	Intracranial hypotension
	Intracranial hypertension
	Vasculitis
	Internal carotid artery dissection
	Cerebral venous thrombosis
	Hydrocephalus
	Colloid cyst of the third ventricle
	Meningitis
	Glaucoma

Table 5-4 Differential Diagnosis of Secondary Headache in Pregnancy

Intracranial hemorrhage
    Subarachnoid hemorrhage
    Arteriovenous malformation

Severe preeclampsia/eclampsia

Stroke (carotid or vertebral artery dissection)

Cerebral venous thrombosis

Intracranial hypertension (eg, IIH)

Brain tumor
    Meningioma
    Pituitary adenoma
    Metastatic choriocarcinoma
    Acoustic neuroma

Two scoring systems that quickly assess disability associated with a headache are the Migraine Inventory Disability Assessment Score (MIDAS) and the Headache Impact Test (HIT). Versions of both MIDAS and HIT are given in Tables 5-5 and 5-6.

As evident from Table 5-5, MIDAS sums the number of productive days lost due to headaches in two settings: the workplace and the home. These two settings are most important in the 20- to 50-year-old age group where migraines are most prevalent.[13] The composite score represents the disability caused by the headaches. The two additional questions A and B are not scored but provide clinically relevant information (ie, headache frequency and intensity) to the physician regarding headaches that can be used to evaluate the severity of the headache, appropriate treatment for the headache, and overall response to therapy. A recent study found that the majority of physicians (89%) found MIDAS easy to use, and there was a high correlation (mean correlation coefficient = 0.69) between the MIDAS score and the patients' pain, disability, and need for treatment.[14] Furthermore, prior studies show high test-retest reliability (ie, measure of the reproducibility of results when the test is administered to the same person twice)[15,16] and validity (ie, correlation between the test measure and a gold standard measure, in this case a 90-day daily headache diary covering topics similar to those found on MIDAS) of the overall MIDAS score.[17] Therefore, MIDAS provides physi-

cians with a clinically useful, easy to use means of assessing disability from migraines and also has the advantage of being reliable and valid enough to use in research protocols.

HIT also was designed with the purpose of assessing what impact the headache had on a patient's life but was designed for greater accessibility. HIT can be found on the Internet at <www.headachetest.com> and <www.amihealthy.com>. There is also a paper-based version known as HIT-6. HIT has high test-retest reliability, but the validity of MIDAS is superior to HIT.[18,19]

HIT differs from MIDAS in a number of ways. First, HIT combines headache intensity and frequency along with questions regarding disability in the computation of its composite score. As a result, the composite score is based on different measures and cannot be expressed in intuitive units (eg, days). This limits its practical utility. Second, calculation of the composite score involves several steps including multiplication and addition, limiting its ease of use.

Nonetheless, both MIDAS and HIT-6 have the benefit of being a self-administered test to evaluate the impact of headache on a woman's daily life. Both scales are reliable and validated and widely used and distributed. Ultimately, these tools will facilitate communication between physicians and patients about their headaches in addition to providing a measure of response to therapeutic interventions.

DIAGNOSTIC TESTING

Neuroimaging is unnecessary for most patients with a chief complaint of headache.[20,21] The chance of finding intracranial pathology in a patient with an isolated complaint of headache and a normal neurologic exam-

Table 5-5 MIDAS: Migraine Inventory Disability Assessment Score

1. In the last 3 months, how many days of work or school have you missed?

2. In the last 3 months, how many days has your productivity been reduced by one-half?

3. In the last 3 months, how many days have you been unable to do household chores?

4. In the last 3 months, how many days has your ability to do household chores been reduced by one-half?

5. In the last 3 months, how many days have you missed family or social occasions?

A. In the last 3 months, how many days did you have a headache?

B. On a scale of 0 to 10, on average, how painful are your headaches?

Scoring (based on total number of days from questions 1 to 5, ignore A and B)

MIDAS Score	MIDAS Grade	Definition
0 to 5	I	Little or no disability
6 to 10	II	Mild disability
11 to 20	III	Moderate disability
21+	IV	Severe disability

Adapted from Midas. Do you suffer from headaches? Available at http//www.midas-migraine.net (accessed November 8, 2003).

ination is extremely low (0.3 to 0.4%),[21] and routine CT or magnetic resonance imaging (MRI) for all migraineurs is thus not cost effective.[22,23] Scans done to "reassure" the patient about the absence of serious disease may not prove helpful if minor abnormalities (such as the white-matter changes discussed below) are found. Although they have no clinical or treatment implications, such findings often paradoxically increase, rather than decrease, patient anxiety about an underlying serious cause of headache. However, whenever there is a "red flag" in the history, or an abnormality on examination, imaging should be considered.

Although CT is excellent as a quick screen for acute intracranial hemorrhage or trauma, MRI is the preferred imaging test for a number of reasons. The sellar region, posterior fossa, and the cervical medullary junction are better characterized with MRI. In addition, focal neurologic deficits due to an acute stroke can be detected with MRI diffusion sequences. If suspicion exists of venous sinus or arterial disease, magnetic resonance venography (MRV) and magnetic resonance angiography (MRA) are very helpful. Third, MRI costs almost the same as CT.[21]

White-matter changes on MRI are common in migraineurs, and have been reported in 6 to 46% of this population. Although these white-matter changes are more common in women, this is most likely because migraine is more common in women.[24–28] The white-matter changes are nonspecific hyperintensities seen on T2-weighted imaging sequences, located in the subcortical, deep, or periventricular white matter, and with a preference for the frontoparietal lobes.[29–31] Confluent lesions are unusual.[30,32] These changes are more commonly seen in basilar migraine or migraines with aura,[30] although similar changes have been seen in tension headaches as well.[33] The cause and significance of these changes is controversial. It is possible that ischemic mechanisms are involved. Interpreting these lesions as evidence of a demyelinative disease such as multiple sclerosis should be approached with caution,[32,34] especially since similar lesions occur in almost 27% of normal 20- to 40-year-olds.[35]

Special consideration should be paid to evaluation of headache in a pregnant woman (Table 5-7). In general, most diagnostic tests and procedures are safe to the mother and developing fetus. The US Food and Drug Administration reports that all MRI below 4T pose a nonsignificant risk.[36] Gadolinium contrast used in MRI does cross the placental barrier, but no adverse effects to the fetus have been noted. Although no consensus exists on the matter, a reasonable recommendation is to "avoid exposure of the embryo or fetus to high magnetic fields in the first or second trimesters of pregnancy unless absolutely indicated…gadolinium injection (as well as CT contrast) should be avoided during pregnancy unless considered to be absolutely necessary for patient care."[37] As for CT, imaging of the head, cervical spine, and thoracic spine exposes the uterus to minimal amounts of radiation, but imaging of the lumbar region results in sizeable exposure. Although the iodinated contrast used does not cross the placenta, fluoroscopic angiograms potentially deliver relatively large doses of radiation to the uterus, unless abdominal shielding can be provided.[37]

PRIMARY HEADACHE DISORDERS

At least 20% of women in the United States meet criteria for the diagnosis of migraine.[38] Even this figure, though, may underestimate the prevalence of the disorder. Although the International Headache Society criteria for migraine are invaluable for studies and clinical trials, they may not identify migraine in individuals who fulfill only some of the criteria. For example, a woman with a bilateral frontal headache of moderate to severe intensity with photophobia (and no phonophobia) whose headache worsens when she takes a walk almost certainly has migraine but does not meet the strict research definition of migraine because of the absence of significant nausea or vomiting and phonophobia.

Table 5-6 Headache Impact Test (HIT-6)

Questions	Never (6 points each)	Rarely (8 points each)	Sometimes (10 points each)	Very Often (11 points each)	Always (13 points each)
When you have headaches, how often is the pain severe?					
How often do headaches limit your ability to do usual daily activities including household work, work, school, or social activities?					
When you have a headache, how often do you wish you could lie down?					
In the past 4 weeks, how often have you felt too tired to do work or daily activities because of your headache?					
In the past 4 weeks, how often have you felt fed up or irritated because of your headaches?					
In the past 4 weeks, how often did headaches limit your ability to concentrate on work or daily activities?					

To score, add points for answers in columns 1 to 5. Scoring: (36 to 78 range)

< 50	Headaches are not having a major impact on your life.
50 to 55	Headaches have some impact on your life.
56 to 59	Headaches have a substantial impact on your life.
> 59	Headaches are having a very severe impact on your life.

Table 5-7 Evaluating Headache in Pregnancy

Test	Risk to Mother	Risk to Fetus	Contraindications
MRI			
With diffusion	None	None known; FDA risk category C	Metal, cardiac pacemaker, otologic implant
With perfusion	None	Same as above	Same as above
With gadolinium	None	Same as above	Same as above
MRA	None	Same as above	Same as above
CT			
Without contrast	None	Minimal*	None
With contrast	None	Minimal*	Dye allergy
SPECT	None	Minimal (< 0.5 rad)	None
Angiography	Minimal	Minimal*	Dye allergy
Ultrasound			
Carotid/vertebral	None	None	None
TCD	None	None	None
Echocardiogram			
TTE	None	None	None
TEE	None	None	None
Lumbar puncture	None	None	Incipient herniation; mass lesion
EEG	None	None	None
Visual fields	None	None	None
Dilated funduscopy	None	None with punctual occlusion	Incipient glaucoma
Fluorescein angiogram[143,144]	None	None; FDA risk category C	Minimal allergies
Indocyanine green angiogram[145]	None	None; FDA risk category C	Minimal allergies

Adapted from Digre KB, Varner MW, Skalabrin E, Belfort M. Diagnosis and management of cerebrovascular disorders in pregnancy. In: Adams HP, editor. Handbook of cerebrovascular diseases. New York, (NY): Marcel-Dekker, 2003. [In press]

CT = computed tomography; EEG = electroencephalography; FDA = Food and Drug Administration; MRA = magnetic resonance angiography; MRI = magnetic resonance imaging; SPECT = single photon emission computed tomography; TCD = transcranial Doppler; TEE = transesophageal echocardiogram; TTE = transthoracic echocardiogram.
*Abdominal shielding.

Patients who do not fulfill a textbook description of migraine, especially those in whom some commonly expected features such as nausea are missing, are often diagnosed with tension-type headache. This is compounded by the fact that individuals with migraine are more prone to other headache types (eg, tension-type headache), and it is common for individuals with a history of migraine to have more than one type of headache. A review of primary headache disorders is covered elsewhere in this book (see Chapter 4, "Diagnosis of Common Headache Disorders").

SECONDARY HEADACHE DISORDERS

Many secondary causes of headache are more common in women. See Table 5-8 for a comparison between men and women of neurologic disorders that frequently present with headache. Although discussion of all of these disorders is beyond the scope of this chapter, a few deserve special mention.

Aneurysmal Subarachnoid Hemorrhage

The incidence of subarachnoid hemorrhage is about 6 cases per 100,000 patient-years. Although there are a

Table 5-8 Comparison of Neurologic Diseases that Cause Headache in Men and Women

	Women (%)	Men (%)
Aneurysmal SAH	65	35[40]
AVM	45	55[146]
Stroke		
CVT	56	44[147]
Arterial		
Carotid dissection	47	53[148]
Vertebral dissection	57	43[148]
Vasculitis		
TA	80	20[149]
Takayasu's	86	14[62]
PAN	36	62[62]
SLE	83	17[62]
RA	71	29[150]
Wegener's	36	64[62]
Behcet's	34	66[62]
Meningitis		
Viral (enterovirus)	40	60[151]
Bacterial	40	60[152]
Fungal	33	67[153]
IIH	84	16[154]
Low pressure headaches	75	25[112]
Tumors		
Meningioma	60	40[155]
Pituitary adenoma	67	33[133]
Glioma (high grade)	40	60[156]
Other		
Pituitary apoplexy	33	67[138]
Chiari malformation	57	43[157]

AVM = arteriovenous malformation; CVT = cerebral venous thrombosis; IIH = idiopathic intracranial hypertension; PAN = polyarteritis nodosa; RA = rheumatoid arthritis; SAH = subarachnoid hemorrhage; SLE = systemic lupus erythematosus; TA = temporal arteritis.

number of causes of subarachnoid hemorrhage, ruptured aneurysms are most frequent.[39] Aneurysmal subarachnoid hemorrhages are more common in women than in men.[40] Case fatality rates associated with aneurysmal subarachnoid hemorrhage range from 32 to 67%,[41] and although approximately two-thirds of survivors achieve some form of independence, a majority (approximately 90%) of women have some restriction in lifestyle.[42] On initial presentation, 23 to 50% of patients with subarachnoid hemorrhage are given an incorrect diagnosis,[43–46] and up to 17% receive a misdiagnosis of a primary headache disorder.[44]

The classic presentation of a subarachnoid hemorrhage (ie, a uniquely severe, rapid onset "worst headache of their lives" associated with neck stiffness, alteration of consciousness, and an abnormal neurologic examination) is difficult to miss. Nonetheless, deviations from the classic presentation can be misdiagnosed as a migraine, tension-type, or sinus-related headache.[43–47] The characteristics of headache secondary to subarachnoid hemorrhages are highly variable. The headache can be localized or generalized, continuous, or resolve spontaneously or with nonnarcotic analgesics. Eight percent of the headaches are mild rather than severe.[48,49] It is difficult to distinguish the headache of aneurysmal subarachnoid hemorrhage from other primary headache disorders based solely on the presence of explosive onset or vomiting because this is often the presentation of benign thunderclap headache.[50] Associated abnormalities on the neurologic examination (eg, nuchal rigidity, altered consciousness, papilledema, retinal or subhyaloid hemorrhages, cranial nerve palsies, nystagmus, or focal signs) are helpful clues to the correct diagnosis when present. However, 12% of patients with subarachnoid hemorrhage present with the "worst headache" of their lives yet have a normal neurologic examination (Figure 5-1).[51,52]

Therefore, given the variability of headache characteristics and the fact that a normal neurologic examination can be present in aneurysmal subarachnoid hemorrhages, all patients with a thunderclap headache

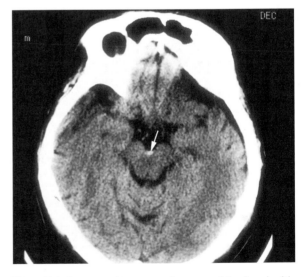

Figure 5-1 Computed tomography scan of the head without contrast demonstrating a sentinel subarachnoid bleed (*arrow*) from an aneurysm. The patient presented with a thunderclap headache and a normal neurologic examination.

(ie, very rapid onset of a severe and unusual headache, often described as "worst headache of their life") should be evaluated with a noncontrast CT scan of the head. If the CT scan is normal and there continues to be a clinical suspicion for subarachnoid hemorrhage, lumbar puncture should be performed. Most consider the presence of xanthochromia as the primary criteria for the diagnosis of subarachnoid hemorrhage. However, it is important to keep in mind that the supernatant fluid remains clear for at least 2 and up to 12 hours after the initial aneurysmal bleed.[53] Diagnosis is further clouded when bloody cerebrospinal fluid (CSF) is obtained; the "three-tube method" (ie, looking for decreasing erythrocyte counts in three successive tubes of CSF) is not entirely reliable.[54,55] Therefore, one should not hesitate to proceed with further invasive or noninvasive imaging techniques such as MRA, CT angiography, or conventional arterial digital subtraction angiography if the diagnosis is unclear. MRA has been reported to demonstrate 95% of aneurysms previously shown by digital subtraction angiography, allowing resolution of aneurysms as small as 3 mm.[56–58] CT angiography has been reported to have a sensitivity and specificity of about 98% with the ability to detect aneurysms up to 1.53 mm in diameter.[59] Nonetheless, despite the improvement in these noninvasive methods, digital subtraction angiography remains the gold standard.

Vasculitis

Temporal Arteritis

Temporal arteritis is an inflammatory condition of the cranial arteries. It is uncommon before the age of 50 years. The headache is usually bitemporal, with severe temporal artery and scalp tenderness. The headache is not always in the temporal region. In fact, a review of biopsy-proven cases of temporal arteritis showed that the headache was as likely to occur in the front, back, and vertex area. Furthermore, the pain characteristics also were not helpful.[60] Other associated symptoms and signs include jaw claudication, fever, weight loss, diplopia, and polyarthralgia rheumatica. Jaw claudication and diplopia are two historic clues that are highly specific for temporal arteritis. Furthermore, beading or prominence of the temporal artery, and temporal artery tenderness on physical examination increase the likelihood of the disorder.[61] Laboratory examination may reveal anemia or elevated erythrocyte sedimentation rate (ESR) or C-reactive protein (CRP). Diagnosis is by superficial temporal artery biopsy. Immediate steroid therapy is the mainstay of therapy. Recognition of temporal arteritis is important because untreated it can lead to blindness from arteritic involvement of the cilioretinal arteries, central retinal artery, or ophthalmic artery. This means that in any older individual with new onset of headache, a search for an elevated ESR or CRP is necessary.

Systemic Lupus Erythematosus

Systemic lupus erythematosus (SLE) is an autoimmune disorder resulting from the production of antibodies directed against one or more components of cell nuclei. Peak incidence occurs between the ages of 15 and 40 years, with a female-to-male ratio of about 5:1, affecting as many as 1 in 1,000 young women.[62,63] SLE presents with a wide constellation of signs and symptoms, including rash, arthritis, pleuritis, pericarditis, seizures, cognitive dysfunction, and psychosis. Diagnosis is based on a constellation of clinical signs and laboratory findings (Table 5-9). Antinuclear antibodies are a relatively sensitive screen for SLE (95%),[64] though antibodies to native or double-stranded deoxyribonucleic acid (DNA) and anti-Smith screening are tests specific for diagnosis.

Neuroimaging should be considered in patients with SLE who develop focal neurologic signs, seizures, or mental status changes because central nervous system (CNS) involvement can occur in up to two-thirds of SLE patients.[65,66] Patients with focal neurologic disease are more likely to have abnormalities shown on MRI than those with nonfocal disease (73% versus 39%, respectively).[67] Arterial or venous infarction, which occurs in up to 20% of patients with SLE[68,69] secondary to a hypercoagulable state from antiphospholipid antibodies or emboli from Libman-Sacks endocarditis, can be easily detected with diffusion-weighted MRI. MRI is more sensitive than CT and is preferred over CT when considering CNS lupus.[70] Other findings that often present on MRI include 1) nonspecific multifocal areas of increased signal in both gray and white matter on T2-weighted sequences that occasionally enhance,[71,72] 2) periventricular lesions indistinguishable from multiple sclerosis,[73] 3) intracranial calcifications in the basal ganglia, thalami, dentate nuclei, cerebellar white matter, or cerebral cortex,[74,75] and 4) global atrophy.[71,72]

Headache is a common symptom in patients with SLE, with a lifetime prevalence of 34 to 39% and 23 to 27% for migrainous and non-migrainous headaches, respectively.[76–78] Migraine with aura tends to be more common than migraine without aura.[76,78] The non-migrainous headaches are usually tension-type.[79,80] A majority of headaches (66 to 73%) appear following the onset of other SLE manifestations.[80,81] The frequency and severity of headaches do not correlate with disease activity, the presence of CNS involvement, or the severity of Raynaud's phenomenon.[78,79] Nonetheless, it is reasonable to consider ruling out SLE in any young female patient with migraine and Raynaud's phenomenon.

Antiphospholipid antibodies (eg, anticardiolipin and lupus anticoagulant antibodies) have a high prevalence in SLE.[82–84] There are numerous cases of migraine-like headaches occurring in association with

Table 5-9 Diagnostic Criteria for Systemic Lupus Erythematosus*

1. Malar rash

2. Discoid rash

3. Photosensitivity

4. Oral or nasopharyngeal ulcers

5. Nonerosive arthritis

6. Serositis

   Pleuritis, or

   Pericarditis

7. Renal disorder

   Persistent proteinuria greater than 0.5 g/day or
      greater than 3+ if quantitation not performed, or

   Cellular casts (red cell, hemoglobin, granular,
      tubular, or mixed)

8. Neurologic disorder

   Seizures, or

   Psychosis

9. Hematologic disorder

   Hemolytic anemia, or

   Lymphopenia ($< 1,500/mm^3$), or

   Thrombocytopenia ($< 100,000/mm^3$)

10. Immunologic disorder

    Positive lupus erythematosus cell preparation, or

    Anti-DNA antibodies, or

    Anti-Sm antibodies, or

    Chronic (> 6 months) false-positive serologic test
       for syphilis

11. Antinuclear antibody

Adapted from Tan EM et al.[158]

DNA = deoxyribonucleic acid; Sm = Smith.

*Diagnosis can be made if any four or more of the 11 criteria are present serially or simultaneously during any interval of observation.

antiphospholid antibodies,[85–94] but there are also other studies that do not suggest that such headaches are any more frequent in patients with such antibodies.[76,79,95,96] Migraines associated with antiphospholipid antibodies may occur in association with other neurologic or systemic complications. This suggests that the elevated antiphospholipid antibodies are related to an underlying disorder such as SLE and that the association with migraines may be coincidental.

Takayasu's Arteritis

Takayasu's arteritis is a rare, chronic vasculitis of the aorta and its branches. Young Asian women are most commonly affected, presenting in the second or third decade of life, seldom with onset after 40 years of age. Constitutional symptoms (eg, fever, night sweats, malaise, weight loss, arthralgia, and myalgias) are present in only 20% of patients at onset.[97] Over weeks to months, subsequent symptoms of arterial insufficiency develop (eg, extremity claudication, angina pectoris, exertional dyspnea, amaurosis, dizziness, and diplopia). Headache is the most common neurologic manifestation (present in 55%), followed by transient ischemic attacks, cerebral infarction, hypertensive encephalopathy, lacunar infarct, seizure, paraplegia, watershed infarct, cerebral hemorrhage, the "moyamoya" phenomenon, and confusion, in order of frequency.[98] Although temporal arteritis can have a similar presentation, with headaches and signs of limb ischemia occurring in 10 to 15% of cases,[99,100] the age of the patient can be used as a differentiating factor between these two diseases. On physical examination, hypertension, retinopathy, carotid bruit, brachial blood pressure asymmetry, or diminished peripheral pulses may be present, although it is not uncommon for these signs to be absent at onset.[97] Laboratory abnormalities include normochromic anemia and azotemia. ESR is elevated in 72% of cases.[97] Chest radiograph may reveal widening of the thoracic aorta. Electrocardiogram may reveal evidence of ischemia. Angiogram is the gold standard for diagnosis, showing smooth tapered stenosis. The subclavian artery is most commonly affected; the carotid artery is involved in over 50%.[97,101] Steroids are the mainstay of treatment, although other immunosuppressive agents such as cyclophosphamide, azathioprine, and methotrexate have been tried in refractory cases. Arterial insufficiency can be managed surgically with angioplasty or stenting.

Idiopathic Intracranial Hypertension

Idiopathic intracranial hypertension (IIH) is a condition of women of childbearing years. The incidence is 10 to 20 in 100,000 in obese women. This means that IIH is as common in obese women as multiple sclerosis is in the general population.[102] Headache is the most common symptom in women with this disorder, occurring in over 90% of individuals. The diagnosis is made by fulfilling the modified Dandy criteria: 1) signs and symptoms of increased intracranial pressure, 2) elevated intracranial pressure (usually greater than 250 mm H_2O) on lumbar puncture with normal CSF indices, and 3) normal imaging studies (usually MRI and MRV) to exclude other causes of increased pressure, including venous thrombosis. Characteristic MRI findings of increased intracranial pressure are shown in Figure 5-2. MRV is also important because dural venous thrombosis is the major differential consideration in this disorder and can present with symptoms and signs identical to IIH.[103]

The headache characteristics of IIH traditionally were thought to resemble migraine.[104,105] However, more recently, IIH has also been found to present with chronic daily headache in about 14% of individuals.[106] Therefore, if an obese woman presents with daily, incapacitating headaches, one should consider IIH as a possible diagnosis. Making the diagnosis is important because the quality of life for women with this disorder is poor as compared with normal weight or obese controls,[107] and treatment of the headache associated with IIH with a migraine preventative and a diuretic such as acetazolamide is often effective.[108] The presence of visual symptoms (eg, transient visual obscurations), auditory symptoms (eg, pulsatile tinnitus, whooshing noises in the head), and diplopia may help to differentiate the IIH headache from other primary headache disorders.[109]

IIH is not a benign disorder. Twenty-five percent of individuals have permanent significant loss of visual function. Although visual acuity may be maintained until late stages of the illness, visual field loss is significant. Therefore, all women with IIH should be referred for visual function testing by a neuro-ophthlamologist.[110]

Intracranial Hypotension

Intracranial hypotension also causes headache. Although the characteristic headache is one that improves when lying down and worsens when the sufferer is upright, some individuals can present with chronic daily headache. A plea has been made to call this "CSF hypovolemia" rather than intracranial hypotension[111] because the headache and other features may not correlate with low CSF pressure but rather with low CSF volume.

CSF hypovolemic headache occurs in two settings. The first is a post-lumbar puncture headache, which occurs in 15 to 30% of individuals after a spinal tap.[112] Post-lumbar puncture headaches are more prevalent and more severe in women and are more likely to be accompanied by nausea than are those that occur in men.[113] CSF hypovolemic headaches also occur as a result of spontaneous intracranial hypotension. The cause may be as innocuous as fly-fishing or yoga but, more frequently, a jarring injury or no antecedent cause is found.

Hypovolemic headache may be generalized or focal. Other neurologic symptoms may also be present, including vertigo, nausea, neck stiffness, imbalance, diplopia, and facial numbness. The diagnosis is made in several ways. Imaging may identify the classic findings of low-pressure headache including cerebellar tonsillar

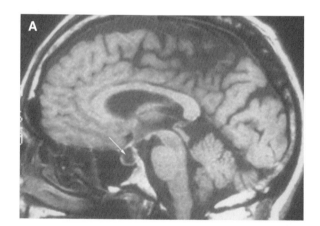

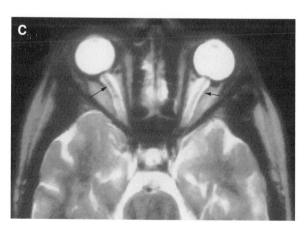

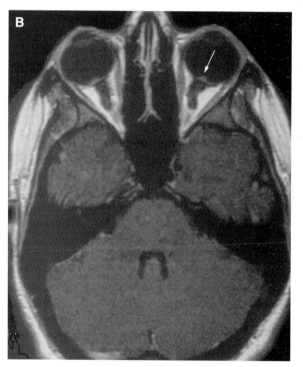

Figure 5-2 MRI findings of idiopathic intracranial hypertension are shown in these sagittal T1-weighted (*A*), axial T1-weighted (*B*), and axial T2-weighted (*C*) images. *A* demonstrates an empty sella (*arrow*). Intraocular protrusion of the optic nerve (*arrow*) and tortuosity of the orbital optic nerve are demonstrated in *B*. Distension of the perioptic subarachnoid space is seen in *C* (*arrows*).

herniation, engorgement of the pituitary gland, sagging of the hindbrain, and meningeal enhancement after gadolinium infusion. Figure 5-3 shows typical findings on MRI of intracranial hypotension. CSF examination may reveal low pressure and a mild leukocytosis. Recognition of this headache type is crucial because treatment with blood patches or directed closure of the site of a CSF leak is usually curative. If a blinded blood patch is unsuccessful, a systematic search for a CSF leak is necessary. Methods to diagnose these include an MRI of the thoracic > lumbar > cervical spine looking for Tarlov cysts. A CT myelogram is frequently necessary from the cervical to lumbar-sacral area. Finally, radionuclide cisternography has been helpful in some cases.[114]

Headache in Pregnancy

The most common type of headache in pregnancy is a preexisting primary headache disorder, especially migraine. Although new-onset migraine during pregnancy does occur,[115,116] the diagnosis of migraine should be made with caution because of the increased risk of some serious secondary forms of headache in pregnancy. Headache evaluation in the pregnant woman is much the same as that in a nonpregnant woman, with heightened alertness for the following secondary headaches as outlined in Table 5-4.

Cerebral Venous Thrombosis

Cerebral venous thrombosis (CVT) used to be thought of as the most common cause of stroke in pregnancy. However, it is more frequent in the postpartum period.

The two most common presenting symptoms in CVT are headache and seizures. Hemiplegia, papilledema, coma, and obtundation occur less frequently. CVT is frequently associated with infection, hypercoagulable states, and hyperviscosity syndromes (eg, sickle cell disease, dehydration). The diagnosis is made by appropriate imaging studies, usually MRI and MRV. These studies are very good at diagnosing all three types of CVT: dural venous thrombosis, cortical vein thrombosis, and internal cerebral vein thrombosis. The headache associated with CVT may not provide many clues as to its cause. Other symptoms of increased intracranial pressure should be sought, including pulsatile tinnitus, transient visual obscurations, seizures, and obtundation.

Treatment is aimed at correction of the underlying condition (eg, infection, hypercoagulability). Anticoagulation with heparin is indicated. The headache may improve with the anticoagulant therapy.[117]

Eclampsia and Severe Preeclampsia

Eclampsia and severe preeclampsia are pregnancy-specific disorders. Preeclampsia (also known as toxemia) is a syndrome characterized by the initial onset of proteinuria (> 300 mg/24 hr) and hypertension (> 140/90 mm Hg) in late pregnancy. Preeclampsia is a common complication of pregnancy, occurring in about 50 of 100,000 deliveries.[118] The neurologic manifestations include headache, visual changes (including scotoma), confusion or obtundation, and possible stroke. The International Headache Society classifies preeclampsia and eclampsia together, requiring the

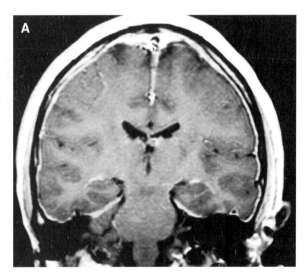

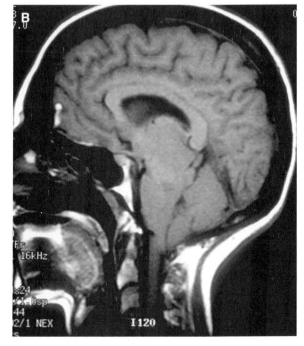

Figure 5-3 Magnetic resonance imaging findings seen in intracranial hypotension. *A,* Coronal T1-weighted contrast-enhanced image demonstrating diffuse pachymeningeal enhancement. *B,* Sagittal T1-weighted image demonstrating flattening of the pons and descent of the cerebellar tonsils.

presence of headache during pregnancy, edema or proteinuria, and elevated blood pressure.[119] Headache can be the initial symptom, occurring before other objective manifestations of the disorder; the headache may be mistakenly attributed to migraine with aura based on the visual symptoms such as spots and lights that can occur. The headache correlates with the rise in blood pressure and usually disappears within 7 days after blood pressure reduction or termination of pregnancy. Occurrence of preeclampsia and eclampsia has been reported in the puerperal period.[120]

Laboratory evaluation may reveal a hemolytic anemia, elevated liver enzymes, and low platelets (HELLP syndrome). Scotomas associated with severe preeclampsia or eclampsia can be plotted by a neuro-ophthalmologist using a special tool known as an Amsler grid. Positive grids correlate with the probability of positive imaging findings on MRI.[121] MRI can demonstrate curvilinear T2-weighted signals in the parietal-occipital junction. Figure 5-4 shows MRI findings of severe preeclampsia. Although the preceding evaluation can assist with diagnosis, severe preeclampsia or eclampsia is a clinical diagnosis. Definitive treatment is delivery of the fetus, the benefits of which must be weighed against an increased chance of adverse outcome for the baby associated with premature delivery. Magnesium sulfate treatment has been shown to be superior to anticonvulsant and antihypertensive use in several well-controlled studies.[122,123]

NEOPLASMS

Meningioma

Meningiomas are benign tumors arising from the meningeal covering of the brain and spinal cord. Meningioma is the most common benign brain tumor and constitutes 20% of all intracranial tumors. In women, the annual incidence ranges from 2 to 7 in 100,000 people. Incidence increases with age and peaks in the seventh decade. The reason for the female predilection is unknown. Risk factors include ionizing radiation and head trauma. There is also an increased incidence in patients with breast cancer.[124,125] Meningiomas are usually slow growing and present with a variety of symptoms (eg, headache, seizures, focal deficits, cranial neuropathies, and visual field defects) depending on where they are located. Common locations include the convexity of the brain, sphenoid wing, olfactory groove, and the suprasellar or petrosal region, and intraorbital.[125] Parasagittal meningiomas are common and must be considered in the differential diagnosis of a slowly progressive spastic paraplegia. Also, thorough funduscopy is important to exclude a Foster Kennedy syndrome (ie, ipsilateral optic atrophy and contralateral papilledema) secondary to a large optic nerve meningioma.

Special attention must be given to meningiomas in the pregnant patient because these tumors can enlarge during pregnancy allowing previously clinically silent lesions to become significant.[126–128] It is hypothesized that increased blood volume during pregnancy or the influence of sex hormones (eg, progesterone, androgen, and estrogen) may account for this phenomenon.[129–131] Enlarging meningiomas can cause focal signs (eg, hemisensory loss or weakness, aphasia, or visual field defects) or seizures (eg, focal or generalized). Although meningiomas are focal lesions, depending on the size and location, diffuse signs of increased intracranial pressure (eg, headache, nausea, vomiting, or diplopia) may also be produced. The nausea and vomiting of increased intracranial pressure may be confused with morning sickness; remember that the latter is usually limited to the first trimester and subsequently improves. MRI with contrast is appropriate if enlargement of a previously asymptomatic meningioma is suspected. Treatment of meningiomas is surgical but is often delayed until after delivery unless life-threatening or the neurologic deficit is severe.

Pituitary Adenoma

Pituitary adenomas are benign epithelial tumors originating from cells of the adenohypophysis. They comprise 10 to 20% of all intracranial tumors[125] but can be found in up to 10% of the normal population.[132] Pituitary adenomas are classified according to size (ie, macroadenomas are ≥ 1 cm; microadenomas are < 1 cm) and the hormones they produce (ie, prolactin, growth hormone (GH), adrenocorticotropic hormone, follicular stimulating hormone, and luteinizing hormone—listed in order of decreasing frequency). Thirty percent of pituitary adenomas are nonsecretory. Prolactin-secreting tumors are the most common. Prolactin- and GH-secreting adenomas are more common in women. Seventy percent of cases present between 30 and 50 years of age, with a small minority (2 to 7%) presenting at < 20 years of age.[133] Presentation varies depending on the size of the tumor and the hormone secreted. The most common syndrome is hyperprolactinemia. In women, common complaints include galactorrhea, amenorrhea, and infertility. If the tumor enlarges, the optic nerve, chiasm, or track can be compressed, resulting in a variety of visual field defects including bitemporal hemianopia (most common), homonymous hemianopia, or a monocular field defect. Headaches associated with pituitary adenomas are primarily the result of mass effect and are usually nonspecific but characteristically occur at the vertex.[125] There have also been reports of cluster-like headache associated with pituitary adenoma, possibly as a result of extension near the cavernous sinus.[134–136] In one case report, these cluster-like headaches resolved with surgical removal of the pituitary adenoma.[134] The evaluation

A

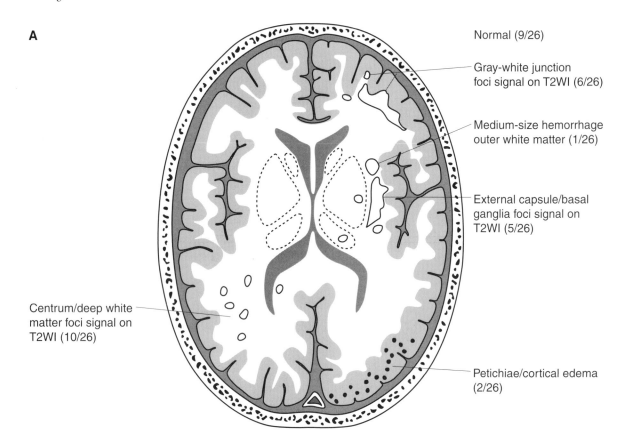

Normal (9/26)

Gray-white junction foci signal on T2WI (6/26)

Medium-size hemorrhage outer white matter (1/26)

External capsule/basal ganglia foci signal on T2WI (5/26)

Centrum/deep white matter foci signal on T2WI (10/26)

Petichiae/cortical edema (2/26)

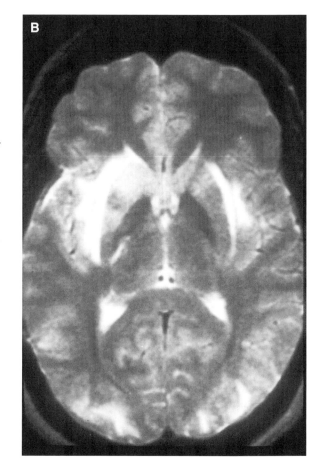

Figure 5-4 *A*, Magnetic resonance imaging findings in the basal ganglia of 26 severe preeclamptic or eclamptic patients. Adapted from Digre et al[121]. T2-weighted image abnormalities in the occipital lobe are seen in *B*. T2WI = T2-weighted image.

of a pituitary adenoma is a multidisciplinary effort consisting of referral to a neuroendocrinologist, neurosurgeon, and ophthalmologist. Treatment can consist of medical treatment with dopamine agonists, surgical excision, or a combination of both. The desire for future fertility in women may influence treatment decisions.

During pregnancy, pituitary adenomas can enlarge and become clinically significant, resulting in neurologic symptoms.[137] Although rare, pituitary apoplexy (ie, pituitary infarction or hemorrhage) also must be considered in women presenting with a thunderclap headache. In addition to headache, associated signs can include hypotension, sudden loss of vision, cranial nerve palsies, meningismus, and altered level of consciousness. CT of the head with and without contrast will show the lesion in 50% of cases, and if clinical suspicion is high, a contrast MRI is indicated. Xanthochromia can be seen on lumbar puncture in 40 to 67% of cases, but the CSF can be clear if the hemorrhage is confined to the gland.[138] Treatment for severe cases includes steroids and surgical decompression of the sella.

Metastatic Choriocarcinoma

Choriocarcinomas are rare germ cell tumors that develop from trophoblastic tissue after an abortion or ectopic, molar, or term pregnancy. The incidence in North America is 1 in 40,000 to 70,000 pregnancies.[139] Cerebral metastases are common, occurring in 14 to 28% of cases,[140] usually presenting with the subacute onset of focal signs. Infarction or parenchymal hemorrhage can occur if there is invasion into the blood vessels. Elevated beta human chorionic gonadotropin (HCG) is helpful in the diagnosis. Treatment includes combination chemotherapy and cranial radiation; prognosis is improved with early diagnosis.[141] Therefore, although rare, metastatic choriocarcinoma should be considered in any pregnant female with headache and focal signs or hemorrhage on imaging studies.

REFERENCES

1. Stewart WF, Staffa J, Lipton RB, et al. Familial risk of migraine: a population-based study. Ann Neurol 1997; 41:166–72.

2. Russell MB, Olesen J. Increased familial risk and evidence of genetic factor in migraine. BMJ 1995;311:541–4.

3. Gardner K. The genetic basis of migraine: how much do we know? Can J Neurol Sci 1999;26 Suppl 3:S37–43.

4. Russell MB. Genetic epidemiology of migraine and cluster headache. Cephalalgia 1997;17:683–701.

5. Graff-Radford SB. Oromandibular disorders and headache. A critical appraisal. Neurol Clin 1990;8:929–45.

6. Breslau N, Davis GC, Schultz LR, et al. Migraine, physical health and psychiatric disorder: a prospective epidemiologic study in young adults. J Psychiatr Res 1993; 27:211–21.

7. Breslau N, Davis GC, Schultz LR, Peterson EL. Joint 1994 Wolff Award Presentation. Migraine and major depression: a longitudinal study. Headache 1994;34:387–93.

8. Merikangas KR, Angst J, Isler H. Migraine and psychopathology. Results of the Zurich cohort study of young adults. Arch Gen Psychiatry 1990;47:849–53.

9. Rains JC, Penzien DB, Martin VT. Migraine and women's health. J Am Med Womens Assoc 2002;57:73–8.

10. Lipton RB, Diamond S, Reed M, et al. Migraine diagnosis and treatment: results from the American Migraine Study II. Headache 2001;41:638–45.

11. Lipton RB, Stewart WF, Celentano DD, et al. Undiagnosed migraine headaches: a comparison of symptom-based and reported physician diagnosis. Arch Intern Med 1992;152:1273–8.

12. Hu XH, Markson LE, Lipton RB, et al. Burden of migraine in the United States: disability and economic costs. Arch Intern Med 1999;159:813–8.

13. Stewart WF, Lipton RB, Dawson AJ, et al. Development and testing of the Migraine Disability Assessment (MIDAS) Questionnaire to assess headache-related disability. Neurology 2001;56(6 Suppl 1):S20–8.

14. Lipton RB, Stewart WF, Sawyer J, et al. Clinical utility of an instrument assessing migraine disability: the Migraine Disability Assessment (MIDAS) questionnaire. Headache 2001;41:854–61.

15. Stewart WF, Lipton RB, Whyte J, et al. An international study to assess reliability of the Migraine Disability Assessment (MIDAS) score. Neurology 1999;53:988–94.

16. Stewart WF, Lipton RB, Kolodner K, et al. Reliability of the Migraine Disability Assessment Score in a population-based sample of headache sufferers. Cephalalgia 1999;19:107–14; discussion 74.

17. Stewart WF, Lipton RB, Kolodner K, et al. Validity of the Migraine Disability Assessment (MIDAS) Score in comparison to a diary-based measure in a population sample of migraine sufferers. Pain 2000;88:41–52.

18. Stewart WF, Lipton RB, Simon D, et al. Reliability of an illness severity measure for headache in a population sample of migraine sufferers. Cephalalgia 1998;18: 44–51.

19. Stewart WF, Lipton RB, Simon D, et al. Validity of an illness severity measure for headache in a population sample of migraine sufferers. Pain 1999;79:291–301.

20. Consensus conference: computed tomographic scanning of the brain. JAMA 1982;247:1955–8.

21. Frishberg BM. The utility of neuroimaging in the evaluation of headache in patients with normal neurologic examinations. Neurology 1994;44:1191–7.

22. Weingarten S, Kleinman M, Elperin L, et al. The effectiveness of cerebral imaging in the diagnosis of chronic headache. Arch Intern Med 1992;152:2457–62.

23. Akpek S, Arac M, Atilla S, et al. Cost-effectiveness of computed tomography in the evaluation of patients with headache. Headache 1995;35:228–30.

24. Cooney BS, Grossman RI, Farber RE, et al. Frequency of magnetic resonance imaging abnormalities in patients with migraine. Headache 1996;36:616–21.

25. Osborn RE, Alder DC, Mitchell CS. MR imaging of the brain in patients with migraine headaches. AJNR Am J Neuroradiol 1991;12:521–4.

26. Soges LJ, Cacayovin ED, Petro GR, et al. Migraine: evaluation by MR. AJNR Am J Neuroradiol 1988;9:425–9.

27. Jacome DE, Leborgne J. MRI studies in basilar artery migraine. Headache 1990;30:88–90.

28. Kaplan RD, Solomon GD, Diamond S, et al. The role of MRI in the evaluation of a migraine population: preliminary data. Headache 1987;27:315–8.

29. Robbins L, Friedman H. MRI in migraineurs. Headache 1992;32:507–8.

30. Fazekas F, Koch M, Schmidt R, et al. The prevalence of cerebral damage varies with migraine type: a MRI study. Headache 1992;32:287–91.

31. Igarashi H, Sakai F, Kan S, et al. Magnetic resonance imaging of the brain in patients with migraine. Cephalalgia 1991;11:69–74.

32. Ferbert A, Busse D, Thron A. Microinfarction in classic migraine? A study with magnetic resonance imaging findings. Stroke 1991;22:1010–4.

33. De Benedittis G, Lorenzetti A, Sina C, et al. Magnetic resonance imaging in migraine and tension-type headache. Headache 1995;35:264–8.

34. Ziegler DK, Batnitzky S, Barter R, et al. Magnetic resonance image abnormality in migraine with aura. Cephalalgia 1991;11:147–50.

35. Horikoshi T, Yagi S, Fukamachi A. Incidental high-intensity foci in white matter on T2-weighted magnetic resonance imaging. Frequency and clinical significance in symptom-free adults. Neuroradiology 1993;35:151–5.

36. Schenck JF. Safety of strong, static magnetic fields. J Magn Reson Imaging 2000;12:2–19.

37. Schwartz RB. Neuroradiographic imaging: techniques and safety considerations. Adv Neurol 2002;90:1–8.

38. Rasmussen BK. Epidemiology of headache. Cephalalgia 1995;15:45–68.

39. van Gijn J, Rinkel GJ. Subarachnoid haemorrhage: diagnosis, causes and management. Brain 2001;124 (Pt 2):249–78.

40. Longstreth WT Jr, Nelson LM, Koepsell TD, et al. Clinical course of spontaneous subarachnoid hemorrhage: a population-based study in King County, Washington. Neurology 1993;43:712–8.

41. Hop JW, Rinkel GJ, Algra A, et al. Case-fatality rates and functional outcome after subarachnoid hemorrhage: a systematic review. Stroke 1997;28:660–4.

42. Hop JW, Rinkel GJ, Algra A, et al. Quality of life in patients and partners after aneurysmal subarachnoid hemorrhage. Stroke 1998;29:798–804.

43. Mayer PL, Awad IA, Todor R, et al. Misdiagnosis of symptomatic cerebral aneurysm. Prevalence and correlation with outcome at four institutions. Stroke 1996; 27:1558–63.

44. Kassell NF, Kongable GL, Torner JC, et al. Delay in referral of patients with ruptured aneurysms to neurosurgical attention. Stroke 1985;16:587–90.

45. Adams HP Jr, Jergenson DD, Kassell NF, et al. Pitfalls in the recognition of subarachnoid hemorrhage. JAMA 1980;244:794–6.

46. Neil-Dwyer G, Lang D. 'Brain attack'—aneurysmal subarachnoid haemorrhage: death due to delayed diagnosis. J R Coll Physicians Lond 1997;31:49–52.

47. Schievink WI, van der Werf DJ, Hageman LM, et al. Referral pattern of patients with aneurysmal subarachnoid hemorrhage. Surg Neurol 1988;29:367–71.

48. Weir B. Headaches from aneurysms. Cephalalgia 1994; 14:79–87.

49. Seymour JJ, Moscati RM, Jehle DV. Response of headaches to nonnarcotic analgesics resulting in missed intracranial hemorrhage. Am J Emerg Med 1995;13: 43–5.

50. Linn FH, Rinkel GJ, Algra A, et al. Headache characteristics in subarachnoid haemorrhage and benign thunderclap headache. J Neurol Neurosurg Psychiatry 1998; 65:791–3.

51. Morgenstern LB, Luna-Gonzales H, Huber JC Jr, et al. Worst headache and subarachnoid hemorrhage: prospective, modern computed tomography and spinal fluid analysis. Ann Emerg Med 1998;32(3 Pt 1):297–304.

52. Linn FH, Wijdicks EF, van der Graaf Y, et al. Prospective study of sentinel headache in aneurysmal subarachnoid haemorrhage. Lancet 1994;344:590–3.

53. Walton JN. Subarachnoid haemorrhage. Edinburgh: Livingstone; 1956. p. 1–297.

54. Vermeulen M. Subarachnoid haemorrhage: diagnosis and treatment. J Neurol 1996;243:496–501.

55. Buruma OJ, Janson HL, Den Bergh FA, et al. Blood-stained cerebrospinal fluid: traumatic puncture or haemorrhage? J Neurol Neurosurg Psychiatry 1981;44: 144–7.

56. Sevick RJ, Tsuruda JS, Schmalbrock P. Three-dimensional time-of-flight MR angiography in the evaluation of cerebral aneurysms. J Comput Assist Tomogr 1990;14: 874–81.

57. Pernicone JR, Siebert JE, Potchen EJ, et al. Three-dimensional phase-contrast MR angiography in the head and neck: preliminary report. AJNR Am J Neuroradiol 1990; 11:457–66.

58. Ross JS, Masaryk TJ, Modic MT, et al. Intracranial aneurysms: evaluation by MR angiography. AJR Am J Roentgenol 1990;155:159–65.

59. Kato Y, Katada K, Haya Kawa M, et al. Can 3D-CTA surpass DSA in diagnosis of cerebral aneurysm? Acta Neurochir (Wien) 2001;143:245–50.

60. Solomon S, Cappa KG. The headache of temporal arteritis. J Am Geriatr Soc 1987;35:163–5.

61. Smetana GW, Shmerling RH. Does this patient have temporal arteritis? JAMA 2002;287:92–101.

62. Klippel JH, Weyand CM, Crofford LJ, et al. Primer on the rheumatic diseases. 12th ed. Atlanta (GA): Arthritis Foundation; 2001. p. xiii, 700.

63. Mills JA. Systemic lupus erythematosus. N Engl J Med 1994;330:1871–9.

64. Hochberg MC. Systemic lupus erythematosus. Rheum Dis Clin North Am 1990;16:617–39.

65. West SG, Emlen W, Wener MH, et al. Neuropsychiatric lupus erythematosus: a 10-year prospective study on the value of diagnostic tests. Am J Med 1995;99:153–63.

66. Ferro JM. Vasculitis of the central nervous system. J Neurol 1998;245:766–76.

67. Stimmler MM, Coletti PM, Quismorio FP Jr. Magnetic resonance imaging of the brain in neuropsychiatric systemic lupus erythematosus. Semin Arthritis Rheum 1993;22:335–49.

68. Futrell N, Millikan C. Frequency, etiology, and prevention of stroke in patients with systemic lupus erythematosus. Stroke 1989;20:583–91.

69. Kitagawa Y, Gotoh F, Koto A, et al. Stroke in systemic lupus erythematosus. Stroke 1990;21:1533–9.

70. Sibbitt WL Jr, Sibbitt R, Griffey RH, et al. Magnetic resonance and computed tomographic imaging in the evaluation of acute neuropsychiatric disease in systemic lupus erythematosus. Ann Rheum Dis 1989;48:1014–22.

71. Tanabe J, Weiner MW. MRI-MRS of the brain in systemic lupus erythematosus. How do we use it to understand causes of clinical signs? Ann N Y Acad Sci 1997;823:169–84.

72. Osborn AG. Diagnostic neuroradiology. St. Louis (MO): Mosby; 1994. xvii, 936.

73. Miller DH, Ormerod IE, Gibson A, et al. MR brain scanning in patients with vasculitis: differentiation from multiple sclerosis. Neuroradiology 1987;29:226–31.

74. Yamamoto K, Noga Ki H, Takase Y, et al. Systemic lupus erythematosus associated with marked intracranial calcification. AJNR Am J Neuroradiol 1992;13:1340–2.

75. Daud AB, Nuruddin RN. Solitary paraventricular calcification in cerebral lupus erythematosus: a report of two cases. Neuroradiology 1988;30:84–5.

76. Markus HS, Hopkinson N. Migraine and headache in systemic lupus erythematosus and their relationship with antibodies against phospholipids. J Neurol 1992;239:39–42.

77. Glanz BI, Venkatesan A, Schur PH, et al. Prevalence of migraine in patients with systemic lupus erythematosus. Headache 2001;41:285–9.

78. Isenberg DA, Meyrick-Thomas D, Snaith ML, et al. A study of migraine in systemic lupus erythematosus. Ann Rheum Dis 1982;41:30–2.

79. Sfikakis PP, Mitsikostas DD, Manoussakis MN, et al. Headache in systemic lupus erythematosus: a controlled study. Br J Rheumatol 1998;37:300–3.

80. Vazquez-Cruz J, Traboulssi H, Rodriguez-De la Serna A, et al. A prospective study of chronic or recurrent headache in systemic lupus erythematosus. Headache 1990;30:232–5.

81. Anzola GP, Dalla Volta G, Balestrieri G. Headache in patients with systemic lupus erythematosus: clinical and telethermographic findings. Arch Neurol 1988;45:1061–2.

82. Merkel PA, Chang Y, Pierangeli SS, et al. The prevalence and clinical associations of anticardiolipin antibodies in a large inception cohort of patients with connective tissue diseases. Am J Med 1996;101:576–83.

83. Cervera R, Khamashta MA, Font J, et al. Systemic lupus erythematosus: clinical and immunologic patterns of disease expression in a cohort of 1,000 patients. The European Working Party on Systemic Lupus Erythematosus. Medicine (Baltimore) 1993;72:113–24.

84. Love PE, Santoro SA. Antiphospholipid antibodies: anticardiolipin and the lupus anticoagulant in systemic lupus erythematosus (SLE) and in non-SLE disorders. Prevalence and clinical significance. Ann Intern Med 1990;112:682–98.

85. Hogan MJ, Brunet DG, Ford PM, et al. Lupus anticoagulant, antiphospholipid antibodies and migraine. Can J Neurol Sci 1988;15:420–5.

86. Brandt KD, Lessell S. Migrainous phenomena in systemic lupus erythematosus. Arthritis Rheum 1978;21:7–16.

87. Brandt KD, Lessell S, Cohen AS. Cerebral disorders of vision in systemic lupus erythematosus. Ann Intern Med 1975;83:163–9.

88. Landi G, Calloni MV, Grazia Sabbadinni M, et al. Recurrent ischemic attacks in two young adults with lupus anticoagulant. Stroke 1983;14:377–9.

89. Harris EN, Gharavi AE, Asherson RA, et al. Cerebral infarction in systemic lupus: association with anticardiolipin antibodies. Clin Exp Rheumatol 1984;2:47–51.

90. Levine SR, Welch KM. The spectrum of neurologic disease associated with antiphospholipid antibodies. Lupus anticoagulants and anticardiolipin antibodies. Arch Neurol 1987;44:876–83.

91. Levine SR, Joseph R, D'Andrea G, et al. Migraine and the lupus anticoagulant. Case reports and review of the literature. Cephalalgia 1987;7:93–9.

92. Mackworth-Young CG, Loizou S, Walport MJ. Primary antiphospholipid syndrome: features of patients with raised anticardiolipin antibodies and no other disorder. Ann Rheum Dis 1989;48:362–7.

93. Shuaib A, Barklay L, Lee MA, et al. Migraine and antiphospholipid antibodies. Headache 1989;29:42–5.

94. Asherson RA, Khamashta MA, Gil A, et al. Cerebrovascular disease and antiphospholipid antibodies in systemic lupus erythematosus, lupus-like disease, and the primary antiphospholipid syndrome. Am J Med 1989; 86:391–9.

95. Montalban J, Cervera R, Font J, et al. Lack of association between anticardiolipin antibodies and migraine in systemic lupus erythematosus. Neurology 1992;42(3Pt1): 681–2.

96. Hering R, Coutuner EG, Steiner TJ, et al. Anticardiolipin antibodies in migraine. Cephalalgia 1991;11:19–21.

97. Kerr GS, Hallahan CW, Giovdano J, et al. Takayasu arteritis. Ann Intern Med 1994;120:919–29.

98. Wang JZ. [Neurological manifestation of Takayasu's arteritis]. Zhonghua Shen Jing Jing Shen Ke Za Zhi 1992;25:369–71, 385–6.

99. Cherin P, De Gennes C, Beltry O, et al. Ischemic Vernet's syndrome in giant cell arteritis: first two cases. Am J Med 1992;93:349–52.

100. Klein RG, Hunder GG, Stanson AW, et al. Large artery involvement in giant cell (temporal) arteritis. Ann Intern Med 1975;83:806–12.

101. Ishikawa K. Natural history and classification of occlusive thromboaortopathy (Takayasu's disease). Circulation 1978;57:27–35.

102. Durcan FJ, Corbett JJ, Wall M. The incidence of pseudotumor cerebri. Population studies in Iowa and Louisiana. Arch Neurol 1988;45:875–7.

103. Biousse V, Ameri A, Bousser MG. Isolated intracranial hypertension as the only sign of cerebral venous thrombosis. Neurology 1999;53:1537–42.

104. Wall M. Idiopathic intracranial hypertension. Neurol Clin 1991;9:73–95.

105. Digre KB. Idiopathic intracranial hypertension headache. Curr Pain Headache Rep 2002;6:217–25.

106. Mathew NT, Ravishankar K, Sanin LC. Coexistence of migraine and idiopathic intracranial hypertension without papilledema. Neurology 1996;46:1226–30.

107. Kleinschmidt JJ, Digre KB, Hanover R. Idiopathic intracranial hypertension: relationship to depression, anxiety, and quality of life. Neurology 2000;54:319–24.

108. Wang SJ, Silberstein SD, Patterson S, et al. Idiopathic intracranial hypertension without papilledema: a case-control study in a headache center. Neurology 1998;51: 245–9.

109. Giuseffi V, Wall M, Siegel PZ, et al. Symptoms and disease associations in idiopathic intracranial hypertension (pseudotumor cerebri): a case-control study. Neurology 1991;41(2Pt1):239–44.

110. Digre KB. Not so benign intracranial hypertension. BMJ 2003;326:613–4.

111. Mokri B. Spontaneous cerebrospinal fluid leaks: from intracranial hypotension to cerebrospinal fluid hypovolemia—evolution of a concept. Mayo Clin Proc 1999; 74:1113–23.

112. Khurana RK. Intracranial hypotension. Semin Neurol 1996;16:5–10.

113. Vilming ST, Kloster R, Sandvik L. The importance of sex, age, needle size, height and body mass index in post-lumbar puncture headache. Cephalalgia 2001;21:738–43.

114. Christoforidis GA, Menta BA, Landi JL, et al. Spontaneous intracranial hypotension: report of four cases and review of the literature. Neuroradiology 1998;40:636–43.

115. Maggioni F, Alessi C, Maggino T, et al. Headache during pregnancy. Cephalalgia 1997;17:765–9.

116. Sibai BM, McCubbin JH, Anderson GD, et al. Eclampsia. I. Observations from 67 recent cases. Obstet Gynecol 1981;58:609–13.

117. Bousser MG. Cerebral venous thrombosis: diagnosis and management. J Neurol 2000;247:252–8.

118. ACOG practice bulletin. Diagnosis and management of preeclampsia and eclampsia. Number 33, January 2002. American College of Obstetricians and Gynecologists. Int J Gynaecol Obstet 2002;77:67–75.

119. Classification Committee of the International Headache Society. Classification and diagnostic criteria for headache disorders, cranial neuralgias and facial pain. Cephalalgia 1988;8 Suppl 7:1–96.

120. Landy SH, Donovan T. Pre-eclampsia and eclampsia headache: classification recommendation. Cephalalgia 1999;19:67–9.

121. Digre KB, Varner MW, Osborn AG, et al. Cranial magnetic resonance imaging in severe preeclampsia vs eclampsia. Arch Neurol 1993;50:399–406.

122. The Eclampsia Trial Collaborative Group. Which anticonvulsant for women with eclampsia? Evidence from the Collaborative Eclampsia Trial. Lancet 1995;345: 1455–63.

123. The Magpie Trial Collaborative Group. Do women with pre-eclampsia, and their babies, benefit from magnesium sulphate? The Magpie Trial: a randomised placebo-controlled trial. Lancet 2002;359:1877–90.

124. Longstreth WT Jr, Dennis LK, McGuire VM, et al. Epidemiology of intracranial meningioma. Cancer 1993; 72:639–48.

125. Black PM. Benign brain tumors. Meningiomas, pituitary tumors, and acoustic neuromas. Neurol Clin 1995;13: 927–52.

126. Fox MW, Harms RW, Davis DH. Selected neurologic complications of pregnancy. Mayo Clin Proc 1990;65:1595–618.

127. Wan WL, Geller JL, Feldon SE, et al. Visual loss caused by rapidly progressive intracranial meningiomas during pregnancy. Ophthalmology 1990;97:18–21.

128. DeGrood RM, Beemer WH, Fenner DE, et al. A large meningioma presenting as a neurologic emergency in late pregnancy. Obstet Gynecol 1987;69(3 Pt 2):439–40.

129. Poisson M, Pertuiset BF, Hauw JJ, et al. Steroid hormone receptors in human meningiomas, gliomas and brain metastases. J Neurooncol 1983;1:179–89.

130. Moguilewsky M, Pertuiset BF, Verzat C, et al. Cytosolic and nuclear sex steroid receptors in meningioma. Clin Neuropharmacol 1984;7:375–81.

131. Carroll RS, Zhang J, Black PM. Expression of estrogen receptors alpha and beta in human meningiomas. J Neurooncol 1999;42:109–16.

132. Hall WA, Luciano MG, Doppman JL, et al. Pituitary magnetic resonance imaging in normal human volunteers: occult adenomas in the general population. Ann Intern Med 1994;120:817–20.

133. Faglia G. Epidemiology and pathogenesis of pituitary adenomas. Acta Endocrinol (Copenh) 1993;129 Suppl 1:1–5.

134. Milos P, Havelius U, Hindfelt B. Clusterlike headache in a patient with a pituitary adenoma. With a review of the literature. Headache 1996;36:184–8.

135. Tfelt-Hansen P, Paulson OB, Krabbe AA. Invasive adenoma of the pituitary gland and chronic migrainous neuralgia. A rare coincidence or a causal relationship? Cephalalgia 1982;2:25–8.

136. Greve E, Mai J. Cluster headache-like headaches: a symptomatic feature? A report of three patients with intracranial pathologic findings. Cephalalgia 1988;8:79–82.

137. Magyar DM, Marshall JR. Pituitary tumors and pregnancy. Am J Obstet Gynecol 1978;132:739–51.

138. Bills DC, Meyer FB, Laws ER, et al. A retrospective analysis of pituitary apoplexy. Neurosurgery 1993;33:602–8; discussion 608–9.

139. Bracken MB, Brinton LA, Hayashi K. Epidemiology of hydatidiform mole and choriocarcinoma. Epidemiol Rev 1984;6:52–75.

140. Olive DL, Lurain JR, Brewer JI. Choriocarcinoma associated with term gestation. Am J Obstet Gynecol 1984; 148:711–6.

141. Seckl MJ, Newlands ES. Treatment of gestational trophoblastic disease. Gen Diagn Pathol 1997;143:159–71.

142. Solomon GD. Concomitant medical disease and headache. Med Clin North Am 1991;75:631–9.

143. Greenberg F, Lewis RA. Safety of fluorescein angiography during pregnancy. Am J Ophthalmol 1990;110: 323–5.

144. Halperin LS, Olk RJ, Soubrane G, et al. Safety of fluorescein angiography during pregnancy. Am J Ophthalmol 1990;109:563–6.

145. Fineman MS, Maguire JI, Fineman SW, et al. Safety of indocyanine green angiography during pregnancy: a survey of the retina, macula, and vitreous societies. Arch Ophthalmol 2001;119:353–5.

146. Hofmeister C, Stapf C, Hartmann A, et al. Demographic, morphological, and clinical characteristics of 1289 patients with brain arteriovenous malformation. Stroke 2000;31:1307–10.

147. Ameri A, Bousser MG. Cerebral venous thrombosis. Neurol Clin 1992;10:87–111.

148. Saver JL, Easton JD. Dissections and trauma of cevicocerebral arteries. In: Barnett HJM, Mohr JP, Stein BM, Yatsu FM, editors. Stroke: pathophysiology, diagnosis, and management. 3rd ed. Philadelphia: WB Saunders; 1998. p. 770.

149. Salvarani C, Cantini F, Boiardi L, et al. Polymyalgia rheumatica and giant-cell arteritis. N Engl J Med 2002; 347:261–71.

150. Lee DM, Weinblatt ME. Rheumatoid arthritis. Lancet 2001;358:903–11.

151. Rotbart HA. Viral meningitis. Semin Neurol 2000;20: 277–92.

152. Hussein AS, Shafran SD. Acute bacterial meningitis in adults. A 12-year review. Medicine (Baltimore) 2000;79: 360–8.

153. Davis LE. Fungal infections of the central nervous system. Neurol Clin 1999;17:761–81.

154. Digre KB, Corbett JJ. Pseudotumor cerebri in men. Arch Neurol 1988;45:866–72.

155. DeAngelis LM. Brain tumors. N Engl J Med 2001;344: 114–23.

156. Wen PY, Fine HA, Black PM, et al. High-grade astrocytomas. Neurol Clin 1995;13:875–900.

157. Levy WJ, Mason L, Hahn JF. Chiari malformation presenting in adults: a surgical experience in 127 cases. Neurosurgery 1983;12:377–90.

158. Tan EM, Cohen AS, Fries JF, et al. The 1982 revised criteria for the classification of systemic lupus erythematosus. Arthritis Rheum 1982;25:1271–7.

CHAPTER 6

Acute Treatment of Migraine Attacks

Richard G. Wenzel, PharmD, and Merle L. Diamond, MD, FACEP

> **CASE**
>
> BP is a 23-year-old woman with a 4-year history of self-described "tension headaches" that have escalated in frequency and severity and now occur at least once every 2 weeks. When her headaches first started, she usually tried to sleep them off or used over-the-counter agents that were effective "if I got it early." She is now concerned about the escalating frequency of headaches and her increasingly poor response to medications. Nausea accompanies her more severe headaches and, although she has never missed work or school, she says "I just force myself to function, and as soon as I get home I go to a dark room to sleep." BP has never been diagnosed with migraine and has never used a prescription medication for her headaches. Her physical and neurologic examinations, as well as routine laboratory tests, are normal.
>
> A paradox of migraine treatment is that, despite the availability of new and highly effective medications for the disorder,[1] most patients with migraine have not been diagnosed. Of those who have received a diagnosis and are offered treatment, fully one-third are still prescribed a butalbital-containing product.[2] Overuse or misuse of barbiturate-containing combination medications prescribed for migraine treatment is a significant cause of worsening headache and dependence syndromes among patients with
>
> headache. For some patients, these drugs may create the expectation that migraine medication should make them feel "good" as opposed to being pain-free and able to function.
>
> Consumption of over-the-counter (OTC) agents has remained constant, with six of ten migraine sufferers using OTC products to the exclusion of other drugs.[3] Despite this use, the majority of migraineurs experience disability with attacks (inability to perform work, school, or household tasks); it is important to remember that OTC products have not been demonstrated to be effective for disabling attacks.[4] Use of emergency department (ED) services is rising, with 24% of sufferers visiting an ED within the last 90 days.[3] In 1989, only 18% of migraine patients had been to the ED within the last 3 months.
>
> Clearly, clinical practice patterns lag behind improved knowledge about "best-practice" treatment of migraine attacks. This chapter focuses on effective management of the individual migraine attack, with an emphasis on preserving the patient's ability to function. Because most patients with migraine will have multiple attacks over a lifetime, the safety and adverse event profiles of drugs used for abortive treatment of migraine are examined with an eye towards their benefit-to-harm ratio in the context of chronic use.

KEY CHAPTER POINTS

- **Evidence-based guidelines for acute migraine therapy emphasize the use of migraine-specific medications for patients with disabling attacks. Treatment goals include rapid, complete relief of pain and associated symptoms, ideally without impairment of functional ability.**
- **Augmentation strategies, including dose escalation, combination therapy, early interven-**

tion, non-pharmacologic techniques, and preventive medications can be used for patients whose response to abortive therapy is inconsistent or suboptimal.

- **"Rescue therapy" when first-line treatment fails will prove necessary for almost all migraineurs; this can involve the use of injectable triptans, rectal suppositories, or opioid medications.**

- Overuse of acute headache medications can lead to paradoxical worsening of headache. Medication withdrawal is often necessary to restore response to other forms of treatment.

ACUTE MIGRAINE GUIDELINES AND THERAPY

Evidence-based guidelines for the treatment of migraine were released in 2000 by the United States Headache Consortium.[5] The guidelines identified goals for acute migraine treatment. These are to 1) rapidly and consistently relieve attacks without pain recurrence; 2) reduce the need for "rescue" medications; 3) minimize adverse effects; 4) restore patients' ability to function; and 5) optimize patient self-care. The guidelines advocate individualizing therapy, based on an evaluation of attack frequency, severity, associated symptoms, and a complete medication history.

For individuals consistently enduring disabling attacks, the guidelines concluded that the following medications have the most impressive clinical trial evidence of efficacy: triptans, dihydroergotamine (DHE), butorphanol, and acetaminophen with codeine. A warning was issued for the two opioid agents that their use should be limited to 2 or fewer days per week, owing to an increased risk of medication-induced headaches because of too-frequent consumption. For patients who routinely experience nondisabling attacks (the minority of migraine sufferers), the following agents were identified by the guidelines as demonstrating efficiency in controlled trials: ibuprofen; naproxen sodium; tolfenamic acid; aspirin; and a combination product of acetaminophen, aspirin, and caffeine (AAC).

In general, the use of treatments that have been rigorously evaluated is preferred over those that have limited evidence for their effectiveness. However, the number of drugs that have been carefully studied for acute treatment of migraine is surprisingly small; some patients may not respond to, do not tolerate, or have medical contraindications to the use of the drugs recommended by the guidelines. In these cases, the use of medications that have been less rigorously tested but that are clinically useful is defensible.

STRATIFIED CARE

The Consortium treatment guidelines recommend matching medication potency with disease severity, a treatment strategy often referred to as "stratified care." Thus, migraine-specific agents are recommended as initial treatment for sufferers who consistently experience moderate-to-severe attacks or disability.

A number of methods are available to help clinicians measure migraine-induced disability.[6] Impact-based recognition uses a validated tool like the Migraine Disability Assessment questionnaire (MIDAS), which measures 3 month's worth of migraine-related loss of function in work, school, and household domains. Another validated option is the Headache Impact Test (HIT), which provides a "snapshot" of the current impact of migraine on the ability of the patient to perform daily activities. These tools, which express impact on numeric scales easily understood by patients, can be employed at the initial appointment and serve as guides to treatment. Additionally, serial measures can illustrate improvement, or lack of improvement, from treatment. The objective scores provided by these instruments are often useful in discussing treatment needs with insurers or other third parties who have limited understanding of migraine but are generally familiar with disease-impact scores.

Pattern-based recognition requires patients to maintain headache journals or diaries over time, typically a minimum of 1 to 2 months. In these diaries, the patients record such variables as when attacks occur, their severity, what identifiable precipitating factors occurred, and how the headache responded to treatment. Diaries are valuable because, in addition to providing a prospective record of headache, they foster patient involvement in care, an important component of treatment of any chronic illness. A sample headache diary can be found in Appendix 8-B, "Headache Diary" in Chapter 8 "Other Approaches to Headache Management."

In contrast to stratified care, step care involves initially giving a nonspecific medication, such as OTC analgesics, regardless of the patient's current frequency or severity of attacks.[7] Patients then escalate through a series of drugs, either within or between episodes, until acceptable relief is attained or the attack resolves of its own accord. Despite the lack of scientific validation of this treatment strategy, low patient satisfaction with the method, and poor results in clinical practice, step care for migraine remains common. Most headache experts believe that step care should be reserved for the minority of patients who have consistently mild attacks. Almost by definition, patients who seek medical consultation for migraine do so because of significant disability or pain and are thus unlikely to benefit from step care. The therapeutic failures that result from its use are demoralizing to patients, delay effective therapy, foster medication overuse, and may cause frustrated patients to lapse from care. Furthermore, stratified care has been shown in prospective, controlled clinical trials to be superior to step care as a treatment approach in individuals with moderate-to-severe attacks. Recent research concluded that patients with MIDAS grade III or IV disability experienced statistically and clinically greater acute attack relief over the span of six attacks with zolmitriptan as initial therapy compared with aspirin and metoclopramide combination therapy.[7]

In addition to the type of medication used, the timing of medication administration during an individual attack can also influence efficacy.[8] A typical migraine attack can be arbitrarily divided into five phases, as illustrated in Figure 6-1. These consist of prodrome, aura, early headache, late headache, and postdrome.

Prodrome is a premonition, normally unaccompanied by specific symptoms, suggesting that a migraine attack will occur in the near future—typically within a few hours. Not all migraineurs consistently experience prodrome. However, for those who do, and whose premonitions are generally accurate, the possibility of drug administration during the prodrome phase is appealing. Administration at such an early phase might significantly increase the chance that an attack can be preempted or aborted in its very early stages.

Aura consistently occurs in only 15% of migraineurs and involves manifestations of focal and reversible brain dysfunction. Aura, too, represents an opportunity to treat at the initial stages of an attack.

Early headache is marked by onset and then escalation of pain and/or associated symptoms. If untreated, or unsuccessfully treated, early headache frequently evolves into late headache, when pain and associated symptoms reach peak intensity. Historically, late headache is the phase in which most patients use medication or seek treatment in an ED because this is the point when patients are convinced that the headache is "real." Recent evidence suggests, however, that late headache represents a firmly established attack that is less likely to respond to treatment. Patients who reach late headache are rarely able to avoid functional impairment; thus, their lives and those of the people around them (eg, family members and co-workers) are disrupted. During postdrome, the headache pain and symptoms have resolved but nonpainful symptoms, such as fatigue, may persist. Treatment at this stage can improve return to function.

Not all patients experience this textbook evolution of headache from prodrome to postdrome; some awaken with well-established late headache or have headaches that develop rapidly. Those who do have headaches that progress gradually, though, may benefit from phase-specific treatment. For example, simple analgesics such as ibuprofen, naproxen sodium, tolfenamic acid, aspirin, or an AAC combination product may provide good relief if used during prodrome, aura, or postdrome.[8] A recent small study ($n = 20$) showed that naratriptan 2.5 mg, administered when patients "knew headache was inevitable," prevented the occurrence of headache in 60% of patients and reduced the severity of headaches that did occur.[9] Prodrome is also the period during which non-pharmacologic techniques such as biofeedback, deep breathing, exercise, cold packs, or meditation are most likely to be effective. Even when not effective on their own, these strategies should be continued. They cost nothing, have no

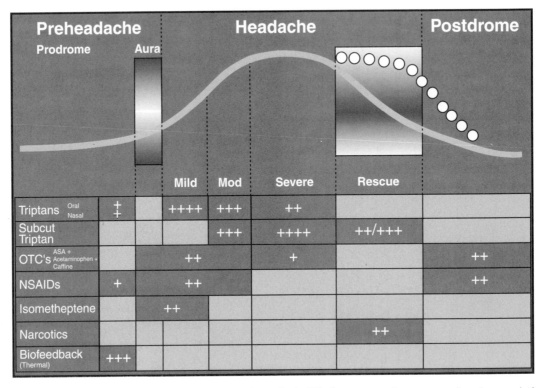

Figure 6-1 Therapeutic phases of migraine. Adapted from Cady RK. Focus on primary care: female population with migraine. Obstet Gynecol Survey 1999;54 Suppl:S7–13. ASA = acetylsalicylic acid; mod = moderate; NSAID = nonsteroidal anti-inflammatory drug; OTC = over the counter; subcut = subcutaneous; + = expected level of efficiency.

adverse effects, and may enhance the efficacy of any medication that is used.

Migraine-specific drugs, such as triptans, work well for early headache, whereas rescue agents are more likely to be necessary in late headache or when oral migraine-specific drugs fail to provide relief. Because many patients delay taking medication until the late headache phase has started, adequate education is needed so that patients will know that chances of success are increased if they treat their headache at the first universally recognizable phase—early headache.

MIGRAINE-SPECIFIC MEDICATIONS

Triptans

The seven triptans available in the United States are sumatriptan, zolmitriptan, rizatriptan, naratriptan, almotriptan, frovatriptan, and eletriptan. Recommended doses are contained in Table 6-1. Unlike ergotamine, which has effects at multiple adrenergic, dopaminergic, and other serotonin receptors, the triptans are selective agonists at serotonin-1 (5-HT-1) B/D receptors.[10] This activity inhibits the release of vasoactive peptides, thus reducing sterile neurogenic perivascular inflammation, reversing cranial vessel vasodilation that can occur during attacks, and causing inhibition of nociception within the brainstem.

Compared with placebo, triptans have been demonstrated to provide clinically significant relief of the pain, disability, and associated symptoms (nausea, vomiting, photophobia, and phonophobia) of migraine attacks. Few well-designed, head-to-head controlled trials have been conducted. Despite their diverse kinetic properties, the oral triptans have similar therapeutic effects. The "superiority" of one particular triptan compared to another remains a matter of debate. A recent meta-analysis[11] of 53 triptan trials did not deem one agent as the treatment of choice, instead concluding that "at marketed doses, all oral triptans were effective and well-tolerated," and that "finding the best therapy may involve trial and error: if the first triptan fails one may successfully switch to another." In clinical practice, a patient should try a particular triptan for two headache attacks; if response is not optimal, another may be tried.

The 2-hour "headache response" (severe or moderate pain reduced to mild or no pain) to the oral triptans ranges from 40 to 70%, whereas 2-hour "pain-free" response varies from 20 to 40%. Recurrence of headache within 24 hours after initial relief ranges from 9 to 34%.[12]

Non-efficacy-related factors, including dosage, formulation, and formulary status, are arguably stronger differentiating features of the triptans than efficacy. Sumatriptan can be prescribed subcutaneously or intranasally, allowing for a more rapid onset of action compared to oral administration, typically within 10 to 60 minutes. Injectable sumatriptan has provided a headache response in up to 80% of attacks, although adverse effects and a recurrence of headache within 24 hours are slightly higher compared with oral triptans. The headache response of intranasal sumatriptan is comparable to oral tablets, albeit with quicker onset. Nonoral formulations are well suited for patients whose attacks typically reach a severe state rapidly (60 minutes or less), for instances when patients awake with a severe migraine, and/or for attacks accompanied with nausea and/or vomiting. A prefilled subcutaneous autoinjector and single-use nasal spray apparatus facilitate quick, uncomplicated administration, although patients prescribed either of these devices need education regarding the proper dexterity technique.

Zolmitriptan was the second triptan to be introduced in the US. It is available in oral, orally dissolving tablet, and nasal spray formulations. A recent pooled data analysis showed both oral formulations to have onset of action as early as 30 minutes after treatment in some patients[13]; zolmitriptan nasal spray appears to have higher nasopharyngeal absorption (30%) than other nasal sprays. This represents an advantage in producing early plasma levels of the drug. Whether this translates into an improved nasal spray is unclear. Head-to-head trials will be required to assess the possibility.[14] In one study, zolmitriptan nasal spray produced detectable plasma levels in all subjects 5 minutes after dosing, compared with only one-third of patients receiving oral tablets who had measurable plasma levels 10 minutes after dosing.[15]

Despite the quicker onset and greater response of nonoral preparations, migraine patients prefer medications administered by mouth. Oral rizatriptan has the shortest time to maximum concentration, although whether this translates into a clinically meaningful advantage is not clear. Both rizatriptan and zolmitriptan are available in an orally dissolving tablet (ODT) that can be simply placed onto the tongue or inside the cheek and which provides convenience that many patients value. Although rare, some patients cannot swallow conventional tablets yet still prefer an oral formulation. ODTs are a good choice for them. These formulations are not as fast-acting as swallowed tablets, although patients may perceive them to be. Naratriptan has a slower onset of action compared with other triptans, although for some patients this will be offset by the advantage of a lower rate of adverse effects and headache recurrence; this medication is best reserved for patients whose attacks reach peak intensity slowly (typically 4 hours or more) or patients with significant adverse effects to other triptans.

Almotriptan is well tolerated, with efficacy comparable to that of the other oral triptans. It is widely available on formularies, an important prescribing con-

Table 6-1 Recommended Doses of Triptans

	Usual Oral Dose (mg)	Maximum Daily Dose (mg/day)	2-Hour Headache Response*	2-Hour Pain-Free[†]	Metabolism	Time to Peak Concentration (Hours)
Sumatriptan (Imitrex®)	100	300	57 to 60	27 to 30	MAO	2 to 3
Rizatriptan (Maxalt®)	10	30/15[‡]	67 to 69	37 to 41	MAO-A	1 to 1.5
Zolmitriptan (Zomig®)	5	10	60 to 65	30 to 35	N-desmethyl metabolite, CYP1A2	1.5 to 2
Almotriptan (Axert®)	12.5	25	57 to 65	32 to 39	CYP3A4 and 2D6	1.5 to 2
Frovatriptan (Frova®)	2.5	7.5	38 to 41	N/A	CYP1A2	2 to 3
Naratriptan (Amerge®)	2.5	5	47 to 51	20 to 24	CYP enzymes	2 to 3
Eletriptan (Relpax®)	40	80	65 to 68	30 to 35	CYP3A4	1 to 1.5

Adapted from Ferrari MD et al[11]; Dodick DW et al[12]; Diamond SD, Moore KL[25]; Miles CB.[26]

CYP = cytochrome P-450; MAO = monoamine oxidase.

*Absolute percentages of patients with headache response at 2 hours.

[†]Absolute percentages of patients pain-free at 2 hours.

[‡]Maximum daily dose when used concomitantly with propranolol.

sideration in many cases. Frovatriptan, like naratriptan, has a slower onset of action and lower headache response rate at 2 hours; like naratriptan, it is probably best reserved for patients with slow-onset headaches. The long half-life of this drug differentiates it from the other triptans; the clinical situation in which that represents an advantage may be menstrual migraine. Its use in this setting is discussed in Chapter 10, "Menstrual Migraine."

Serious adverse effects from the triptans are uncommon, especially if these drugs are used near the beginning of an attack. The most frequent adverse events include paresthesias, flushing, pain at the injection site, and chest pain or neck symptoms that occasionally resemble angina. The etiology of these chest symptoms remains unclear; in almost all cases, they are not felt to be cardiac in origin. Nonetheless, because the triptans do cause a small degree of coronary artery constriction, they should not be prescribed for patients known to have cardiovascular disease or those with multiple cardiac risk factors. Fortunately, the highest prevalence of migraine is in women between 25 and 45 years of age, a subgroup of the general population at very low risk of coronary artery disease. Among patients with some identifiable cardiac risk factors such as family history, obesity, smoking, lack of exercise, and postmenopausal status, contraindications need to be determined on an individual basis.[16] Extensive postmarketing data for the triptans does not demonstrate an unusual rate of cardiac events, despite extensive global use. As of December 1998, a total of 236 million migraine attacks in 9 million people worldwide had been treated with sumatriptan, with only 451 significant cardiac events regarded as possibly attributable to the drug.[17] In a prospective study involving approximately 12,000 patients using injectable sumatriptan, no drug-related deaths or significant cardiovascular morbidity was observed.[18] No evidence exists that one triptan is safer or more dangerous than another; thus, a patient who is not a candidate for one triptan based on cardiac risk is not a candidate for any other, either. In addition, such patients should not be given ergotamine compounds because coronary constriction caused by ergots is more pronounced and longer lasting than that seen with the triptans. Triptan-induced rebound headache has been reported but seems less common and less difficult to treat than rebound headaches associated with other compounds.

Ergots

In the United States, ergotamine alone is available only in sublingual preparations of 1 or 2 mg. In combination with caffeine, it is available as a rectal suppository. An ergot derivative, dihydroergotamine (DHE), can be administered parenterally (intravenous, intramuscular, or subcutaneous) or intranasally. These agents have similar but broader pharmacologic activity than the triptans. Both are indicated for moderate-to-severe acute migraine attacks and provide an alternative to triptans. Clinical experience suggests that DHE offers advantages of improved efficacy, lower headache recurrence, and lower likelihood of headache induction with repetitive use over ergotamine.

The American Academy of Neurology has endorsed the use of repetitive, scheduled doses of intravenous DHE 1 mg per dose, a total of 3 mg per day, for up to 7 days, as effective and safe for the treatment of intractable headache episodes.[19] The most commonly used protocol is DHE 0.5 to 1 mg given intravenously every 8 hours for a total of nine doses, typically in an inpatient setting where blood pressure and other parameters can be monitored. Intravenous DHE is especially useful in the ED for patients presenting with extremely severe attacks unresponsive to other agents and/or with status migrainosus (attack of greater than 72 hours). When DHE is administered parenterally, pretreatment with an antiemetic agent such as metoclopramide is warranted. It may also be prudent to obtain an electrocardiogram, especially in patients with any cardiac risk factors.

Patients can administer DHE at work using the nasal spray that is available, or can even be taught self-injection if necessary. Such self-administration can eliminate the need to seek help in a physician's office or the ED. Patients prescribed either of these options must be properly educated and have sufficient dexterity to manipulate the syringe or nasal administration device. The recommended nasal dose is a total of four sprays, one spray in each nostril, which is then repeated in 15 minutes. For those who fail to obtain adequate relief, an additional spray in each nostril can be administered at 2 hours, bringing the total to six sprays in 24 hours. Because of its long duration of action, DHE is also an option for predictable migraine situations such as menstrual migraine.

Another drawback of the ergots, in addition to the fact that they cause more frequent adverse effects compared with triptans, is that all ergot-derived medications are absolutely contraindicated during pregnancy. Women of childbearing age who are prescribed these agents for home use must use adequate contraception. Ergots should not be used within 24 hours of a triptan, and, like triptans, should be avoided in individuals with cardiac disease.

Ergotamine was the most widely used migraine agent until the introduction of the triptans. Clinical experience suggests that it is associated with a risk of over-consumption, leading to a daily headache pattern widely referred to as "rebound" headache. Therefore, clear limits of use must be established in any patient prescribed ergotamine. The usual dose is 1 to 2 mg at the onset of an attack, then 1 mg every 30 minutes to a maximum of 6 mg in total per attack, 10 mg in total per week. Ideally, episodes of use should be separated by 3 or 4 treatment-free days. In certain situations, such as a predictable migraine occurring with menstruation and at no other times of the month, these limits can be expanded to 3 to 5 consecutive days per month. Prescription of a limited number of tablets can help avoid overuse syndromes. Patients who begin to overuse the agent will be prompted, by the need for a refill, to contact the physician, who can intervene to prevent overuse.

Isometheptene

Isometheptene is another mild vasoconstrictor agent that was widely used prior to the introduction of the triptans but is less often selected today. It contains a combination of acetaminophen, isometheptene, and dichloralphenazone. Clinical experience suggests that this drug works well for patients with mild, nondisabling migraine episodes. Many patients report that the brand name drug Midrin® provides faster and more reliable relief than generic formulations. The usual dosage is two capsules at the onset of headache, followed by one capsule every hour as needed, up to a daily total of five capsules. Again, limits on use should be established to prevent the development of overuse syndromes.

Nonsteroidal Anti-inflammatory Drugs

Nonsteroidal anti-inflammatory drugs (NSAIDs) work well when used early in an attack. Inhibition of prostaglandin synthesis prevents neurogenically mediated inflammation in the trigeminovascular system. The drugs may also affect serotonin neurotransmission and modulate vasoconstriction. The NSAIDs inhibit inflammation through their effects on chemotaxis, phagocytosis, kinin generation, and lysosomal enzyme release. Those NSAIDs that have demonstrated efficacy in migraine abortive therapy include naproxen sodium, aspirin, flurbiprofen, etodolac, mefenamic acid, diclofenac sodium, and ibuprofen.

NSAID therapy is associated with gastrointestinal symptoms, including nausea, abdominal distress, dyspepsia, diarrhea, dizziness, and tinnitus. Because of the risk of gastrointestinal bleeding, these agents should not be used in patients with history of peptic ulcer disease. The NSAIDs are also contraindicated in patients with renal dysfunction. Patients who do not obtain adequate relief with NSAIDs are prone to overuse them in a desperate attempt to obtain relief. They are at significant risk of serious morbidity over a lifetime of such excessive use, and such situations clearly warrant attempts to introduce more effective and specific migraine treatment.

Antidopaminergic Drugs

In the emergency setting, the phenothiazines—chlorpromazine and prochlorperazine—have been effective in migraine acute therapy.[20] The dopaminergic and adrenergic effects of these agents have been cited as the reason for their efficacy. These agents are especially useful for their beneficial effects on nausea, although the sedation they provide may facilitate resolution of the attack through sleep as well.

Lidocaine

Intranasal lidocaine is also effective for migraine acute therapy, with headache improvement reported in slightly over one-half of patients.[21] Because it is cumbersome to administer, and lasts for only 1 to 2 hours, this treatment is not widely used. However, it is a useful strategy for some patients who cannot safely use any other treatment, or those who have extremely severe attacks and need 1 or 2 hours of respite while awaiting the onset of action of a more effective drug. One-half to 1 mL of 4% lidocaine solution is placed in a dropper and dripped slowly into the nostril on the painful side over a period of several minutes. The patient lies supine on a flat surface, with the neck extended back at a 45-degree angle and turned toward the side of administration. Both nostrils can be treated if the headache is bilateral. Side effects include allergic reactions, numbing of the throat with subsequent difficulty swallowing (temporary), and sore throat.

AUGMENTATION STRATEGIES

The response of a particular patient to a particular triptan is not predictable. When prescribed a triptan (or any other acute medication), patients should be instructed to treat at least two attacks. At that point, if results are disappointing, a different agent should be tried. Lack of response to one triptan does not mean that another will be ineffective. If oral triptans are inconsistently effective, various augmentation strategies can be considered. These include early use of the triptan before the headache has a chance to establish itself, combination therapy using a triptan and an anti-inflammatory medication, or switching to a more effective formulation such as nasal spray or injection. Triptan administration during the early headache phase improves efficacy while leading to fewer adverse effects.[22] Dosing should be reviewed as well. Although occasional patients do well with low or intermediate doses of medication, many prefer or even require the use of higher doses. For example, dosing studies show 35 to 60% of patients prefer 100 mg sumatriptan, with only 10 to 25% preferring 25 mg.[23,24]

Regardless of which agent is selected, use of a prokinetic or antiemetic drug may improve absorption and lessen associated symptoms. Nausea and vomiting, in particular, can be as disabling as the headache itself.

RESCUE THERAPY

No medication works for every attack. In some cases, failure of first-line therapy can be attributed to failure to treat at an early stage of the attack, rapid development of nausea or vomiting that precludes use of the typical first-line drug, or use of an inadequate dose. In late phase headache, the therapeutic goal changes from reversing the attack to providing adequate pain relief; this late phase, second-line treatment is often termed "rescue" therapy.

Essentially, all patients should have a rescue strategy, even if a frequent need for such treatment is not anticipated. In general, nonoral therapy is preferred, to decrease the chance that nausea or vomiting will interfere with its effect and force a trip to the ED. The following rescue choices are recommended based on guidelines and clinical experience.[25]

Injectable NSAIDs

Parenteral ketorolac 30 to 60 mg has a rapid onset of action and bypasses the gastrointestinal tract, an advantage in patients with nausea. Preloaded syringes are available by prescription and can be used as home-based rescue therapy by reliable, trained patients. Individuals able to tolerate oral formulations can be given an NSAID by mouth, preferably with longer duration of activity to reduce the possibility of headache recurrence in those who respond. In addition to oral and parenteral formulations, indomethacin can be compounded as a 50 mg rectal suppository. Table 6-2 lists the doses of some long-acting NSAIDs appropriate for use as rescue therapy.

Neuroleptics

Neuroleptic agents are extremely useful for rescue therapy. The choices include parenteral or rectal chlorpromazine 25 to 50 mg, parenteral or rectal prochlorperazine 10 mg, parenteral haloperidol 1 to 5 mg, parenteral droperidol 0.625 to 2.5 mg, and parenteral mesoridazine 10 to 25 mg. Their beneficial effects likely result from their antinausea properties, sedative actions, and dopaminergic and adrenergic actions. Drowsiness is common, and patients should be observed prior to release home after treatment. If used in the home setting, patients should be advised to avoid driving or other mentally demanding activities. Some neuroleptic agents, particularly haloperidol, may cause extrapyramidal adverse effects that can be treated with diphenhydramine, benztropine, or benzodiazepines. Phenothiazine suppositories are an excellent choice for home-administered rescue therapy. They are easily used, treat associated symptoms such as vomiting, and have a wide margin of safety.

Antihistamines

Increased plasma histamine levels during migraine attacks have been reported, perhaps contributing to an inflammatory response and pain. Antihistamines, including parenteral preparations of diphenhydramine 25 to 50 mg or hydroxyzine 25 to 50 mg can be useful for migraine patients. These agents are also beneficial for mild-to-moderate anxiety—a frequent occurrence in acutely distressed patients. Sedation normally accompanies antihistamine use, especially when given parenterally. Common dosages of neuroleptics and antihistamines for use in headache therapy are listed in Table 6-3.

Valproic Acid

Valproic acid, 300 to 1,000 mg, given by intravenous push or rapid intravenous infusion (5 to 10 minutes) has shown efficacy in open-label, uncontrolled trials of migraine treatment. Valproic acid is a particularly attractive choice for patients who cannot use other medications as a result of cardiac disease. Additionally, adverse effects to valproic acid are infrequent and benign. Because valproic acid is teratogenic, a pregnancy test should be considered before it is used in women of childbearing potential. Use of this treatment is limited to medical settings.

Steroids

Steroids, including parenteral dexamethasone 6 to 8 mg, or methylprednisolone 250 to 500 mg, can be used for rescue therapy. An oral steroid "burst" of dexamethasone 1.5 mg twice daily for 2 days, then 0.75 mg

Table 6-2 Doses of Long-Lasting Nonsteroidal Anti-inflammatory Drugs for Rescue Therapy

Drug	Dosing Range (mg/dose)	Maximum (mg/day)	Route	Frequency
Indomethacin	25 to 50	200	Oral/IV/Rectal	Two to three times daily
Nabumetone	500 to 1,000	2,000	Oral	One to two times daily
Ketoprofen extended-release	100 to 200	300	Oral	One to two times daily
Oxaprozin	600 to 1,200	1,800	Oral	Once daily
Piroxicam	10 to 20	20	Oral	Once daily

IV = intravenous.

Table 6-3 Neuroleptics and Antihistamines

Drug	Dosing Range (mg/dose)	Route	Frequency
Droperidol	1.25 to 2.5	IM/IV	Up to every 6 hours*
Haloperidol	1 to 5	IM	Up to every 6 hours
Chlorpromazine	10 to 15	IM/IV	Up to every 6 hours
Olanzapine	5 to 10	PO	Up to every 6 hours†
Hydroxyzine	25 to 50	IM	Up to every 6 hours
Diphenhydramine	50 to 100	IM/IV	Up to every 6 hours

IM = intramuscular; IV = intravenous; PO = by mouth.
*Has black-box warning from Food and Drug Administration due to prolonged Q-T interval.
†A parenteral formulation may soon be available.

twice daily for 1 day, then 0.75 mg daily for 2 days is one regimen that can be used on an outpatient basis. Long-term use of steroids places patients at risk of a variety of adverse effects, including serious complications such as osteonecrosis. Therefore, steroid use should be limited.

Magnesium

Magnesium deficiency has been reported to contribute to migraine. Magnesium 500 to 1,000 mg given intravenously has been shown, in small studies, to provide migraine attack relief. The exact mechanism of action is unclear. Magnesium is well tolerated but must be given intravenously to be effective for an acute attack. This limits its use to hospital or clinic settings.

Opioids

Although their use for first-line treatment of migraine is strongly discouraged by most headache experts, opioids are appropriate choices for rescue treatment of migraine. Their use in patients with active substance problems or those with a risk of such problems should be limited and strictly monitored. Criteria for prescribing opioids are listed in Table 6-4. Clinicians can select from butorphanol, codeine, morphine, methadone, and hydromorphone, among others, all of which are available in multiple dosages and formulations. As a result of their relative safety in pregnancy, opioids are often recommended as first-line choices for treatment in pregnant women suffering with an intractable attack.[26]

Emergency Department Treatment of Migraine

Self-administration of rescue agents is preferable; many of the options described above can be used by reliable patients at home, decreasing the need to seek help in a healthcare facility. Occasional trips to the ED are not cause for alarm, but frequent visits suggest a patient might benefit from comprehensive specialty evaluation of the headache problem. Other indications for specialty consultation include regular use of acute therapies more than 2 days per week, attacks that in the patient's opinion regularly disrupt their lives, and lack of relief from adequate trials of medications for attacks. If attacks are severe enough to lead to an ED visit, multimodal therapy is usually recommended to avoid treatment failure and the need for re-treatment within a short period of time. Once the possibility of a secondary headache has been ruled out, patients in the ED for migraine should be considered for treatment with vigorous intravenous hydration. Use of a specific antimigraine agent such as DHE or injectable sumatriptan ideally should be given with an antidopaminergic antiemetic that will decrease nausea or vomiting and allow for the beneficial effects of sedation and sleep to help with headache resolution. The use of steroids should also be considered, especially for long duration attacks. If opioids are used, an adequate dose should be given, along with an antiemetic. Although widely used, meperidine is not the opioid of choice for migraine, owing to its active metabolites and excitatory effects on the central nervous system.

Table 6-4 Criteria for Prescribing Narcotics

The patient reports identical previous migraine headaches, AND

During the migraine, the sufferer is in moderate-to-severe distress, AND

The patient has no history of substance abuse, AND

At least one of the following applies:
- in the past, the patient consistently has not obtained relief from triptans/ergots
- in the past, the patient has not obtained relief from non-narcotic agents
- the patient has used the maximum amount of their usual acute agents yet the headache persists or recurs
- the usual migraine acute medications are contraindicated

Adapted from Diamond S et al.[27]

References

1. Cady RK, Schreiber C, Farmer K. Primary headache: a convergence hypothesis. Headache 2002;42:204–16.

2. Wenzel RG, Sarvis CA. Do butalbital-containing products have a role in the management of migraine? Pharmacotherapy 2002;22:1029–35.

3. Lipton RB, Diamond S, Reed M, et al. Migraine diagnosis and treatment: results from the American Migraine Study II. Headache 2001;41:638–45.

4. Wenzel RG, Sarvis CA, Krause ML. Over-the-counter medications for acute migraine attacks: literature review and recommendations. Pharmacotherapy 2003;23:494–505.

5. Silberstein SD. Practice parameter: evidence-based guidelines for migraine headache. Neurology 2000;55:754–62.

6. Sheftell FD, Tepper SJ. New paradigms in the recognition and acute treatment of migraine. Headache 2002;42:58–69.

7. Lipton RB, Stewart WF, Stone AM, et al. Stratified care versus step care strategies for migraine. JAMA 2000;284:2599–605.

8. Cady R. Advances in migraine treatment: the era of the triptans. Part 2. Richmond (VA): Medical College of Virginia; 1999.

9. Luciani R, Carter D, Mannix L, et al. Prevention of migraine during prodrome with naratriptan. Cephalalgia 2000;20:122–6.

10. Goadsby PJ, Lipton RB, Ferrari MD. Migraine: current understanding and treatment. N Engl J Med 2002;346:257–70.

11. Ferrari MD, Roon KI, Lipton RB, Goabsby PJ. Oral triptans in acute migraine treatments: a meta-analysis of 53 trials. Lancet 2001;358:1668–75.

12. Dodick DW, Silberstein S, Dahlöf CG. Is there a preferred triptan? Headache 2002;42:1–7.

13. Ward T, Dowson A, Charlesworth B, et al. Thirty-minute efficacy of Zolmitriptan oral formulations is the treatment of moderate to severe migraine: results of a pooled data analysis. Poster presentation "The Practicing Physician's Approach to the Difficult Migraine Patient," 2003 July; Orlando (FL), USA.

14. Charlesworth BR. Zolmitriptan nasal spray 5 mg shows rapid absorption and consistent pharmacokinetics that translate into fast, reliable efficacy in the treatment of migraine. Poster presentation "The Practicing Physician's Approach to the Difficult Migraine Patient," 2003 July; Orlando (FL): USA.

15. Yates R, Nairn K, Dixon R, Seaber E. Preliminary studies of the pharmacokinetics and tolerability of Zolmitriptan nasal spray in healthy volunteers. J Clin Pharmacol 2002;42:1237–43.

16. Young WB, Mannix L, Adelman JU, Shechter AL. Cardiac risk factors and the use of triptans: a survey study. Headache 2000;40:587–91.

17. Welch KMA, Mathew NT, Stone P, et al. Tolerability of sumatriptan: clinical trials and post-marketing experience. Cephalalgia 2000;20:687–95.

18. O'Quinn S, Davis RL, Gutterman DL, et al. Prospective large-scale study of the tolerability of subcutaneous sumatriptan injection for acute treatment of migraine. Cephalalgia 1999;19:223–31.

19. American Academy of Neurology. Practice parameter: appropriate use of ergotamine tartrate and dihydroergotamine in the treatment of migraine and status migrainosus. Neurology 1995;45:585–7.

20. Jones J, Pack S, Chun E. Intramuscular prochlorperazine versus metoclopramide as single-agent therapy for the treatment of acute migraine. Am J Emerg Med 1996;14:262–4.

21. Maizels M, Scott B, Cohen W, Chen W. Intranasal lidocaine for treatment of migraine: a randomized, double-blind, controlled trial. JAMA 1996;276:319–21.

22. Cady RK, Sheftell F, Lipton RB, et al. Effect of early intervention with sumatriptan on migraine pain: retrospective analyses of data from three clinical trials. Clin Ther 2000;22:1035–48.

23. Dowson AJ, Ashford EA, Prendergast S, et al. Patient-selected dosing in a six-month open-label study evaluating oral sumatriptan in the acute treatment of migraine. Int J Clin Pract Suppl 1999;105:25–33.

24. Salonen R, Ashford EA, Gibbs M, Hassani H. Patient preference for oral sumatriptan 25 mg, 50 mg, or 100 mg in the acute treatment of migraine: a double-blind, randomized, crossover study. Sumatriptan Tablets S2CM11 study group. Int J Clin Pract Suppl 1999;105:16–24.

25. Diamond SD, Moore KL. Headache of the month: a 38-year-old woman with intractable migraine. Consultant 1999;39:2313–23.

26. Miles CB. Treatment of migraine during pregnancy and lactation. S D Med J 1995;48:373–7.

27. Diamond S, Diamond ML, Silberstein S, Winner P. Advances in migraine management: the roles of acute, prophylactic, and rescue medications. Headache Q 2001;12:183–94.

CHAPTER 7

Preventive Therapy of Migraine

Lisa K. Mannix, MD

CASE

KM, a 28-year-old woman with a history of episodic migraine since her teenage years, seeks consultation about headaches that interfere with her work and family activities. She has been having three to five migraine attacks monthly for the past 6 months. She uses abortive treatment consisting of both an injectable triptan and an oral nonsteroidal anti-inflammatory drug (NSAID); this regimen provides modest and inconsistent relief of her headaches. Ineffectively treated headaches can continue for 2 days. KM works full time as a medical librarian and estimates that she misses 1 to 2 days of work a month due to headache. Her only daily medication is a multivitamin. In the past, she took amitriptyline for migraine prevention but stopped it due to weight gain. Her brother suffers from migraine and responded well to treatment with divalproex sodium. KM had some postpartum depression following the birth of her daughter 18 months earlier. Review of systems revealed occasional gastrointestinal symptoms, mostly constipation. KM and her husband

would like to have another child the following year. Her physical and neurologic examinations are normal, with a blood pressure of 108/64 and heart rate of 60 beats per minute. A magnetic resonance imaging scan of the brain performed 1 year ago was normal.

For many women with headache, treatment must be aimed at prevention of attacks as well as acute treatment of individual headaches. Alterations in daily habits and routines and other non-medication interventions, such as biofeedback, are frequently beneficial in reducing headache frequency. However, some women, especially those with severe headaches, will require pharmacologic intervention to augment (not replace) these non-pharmacologic treatment strategies. Evidence-based guidelines exist for migraine treatment but may need to be modified depending on a woman's individual circumstances. This chapter presents practical information on choosing and using headache preventive medications in female headache patients.

KEY CHAPTER POINTS

- Women who have frequent, disabling attacks of headache that are not well controlled with acute treatment may benefit from prophylactic treatment to decrease headache frequency and severity.
- Prophylactic treatment includes both pharmacologic and non-pharmacologic treatment. Incorporating non-pharmacologic treatment strategies is especially important for women who must avoid pharmacologic treatment while attempting pregnancy and during pregnancy and lactation.

- Evidence-based guidelines for prophylactic treatment of headache have been developed by the US Headache Consortium. Effective preventive drugs may work through a variety of mechanisms. The choice of prophylactic therapy should be based on a combined assessment of its effectiveness, safety, and tolerability profile and the woman's comorbid medical disorders and preferences for treatment.
- General principles of prophylactic treatment include starting with a low dose of drug, increasing slowly, and allowing an adequate period of time to judge benefit, usually 2 to 3 months. The optimal duration of prophylactic

treatment has not been determined and must be decided on an individual basis.

• Headache presentation and the choice and doses of medications used for treatment may all be different in women than in men. Oral contraceptives may affect headaches and interact with certain prophylactic medications.

PROPHYLACTIC THERAPY FOR TREATMENT OF HEADACHE

Although some standardized questionnaires, such as the migraine disability assessment (MIDAS) or headache impact test (HIT) (see Chapter 5, "Evaluation of the Woman with Headache" Tables 5-5 and 5-6), have been developed to measure the impact of headache and predict treatment needs, neither these nor other tools can replace clinical judgment about when prophylactic therapy should be considered for individual women with headache.[1] Decisions about who will benefit from prophylactic headache treatment should take into account the following factors:

• Headache frequency. Patients with two or more headaches a week, even if they are well managed with abortive medication, are at risk of developing medication overuse syndromes; prophylaxis should be carefully considered.

• Medical contraindication to the use of abortive therapy. Patients with cardiovascular disease who must avoid triptans, for example, may find their need for such medications reduced or eliminated by prophylactic therapy.

• Patient compliance with acute therapy. Some patients are unable to use abortive medications early in an attack or compulsively overuse acute medication in anticipation of attacks. Successful prophylactic therapy is one way of minimizing the impact of these behaviors.

• Tolerability of acute therapy. Most acute headache medicines are well tolerated. For those patients with side effects, however, prophylactic treatment will decrease the frequency with which they must use acute medication and cope with adverse events. Although unproven, there is a strong clinical impression that prophylactic therapy may also improve responsiveness to acute therapy, allowing for the use of lower doses or less potent classes of medication, with a corresponding reduction in side effects.

• Cost of acute therapy. If effective in headache treatment, prophylactic therapy will generally reduce the need for, and hence the cost of, acute medication.

• Patient preference. Patients with very severe or disabling headaches, especially those with an inconsistent response to acute therapy, may prefer the security of prophylaxis even if they have relatively few headaches.

• Uncommon migraine conditions. Many experts recommend prophylaxis for women with hemiplegic or basilar migraine, migraine with prolonged aura, or a history of migrainous infarction.[2]

In KM's case, she is experiencing frequent, disabling migraine attacks that have not been consistently controlled with aggressive attempts at abortive therapy. Prophylaxis of her headaches should be strongly considered.

NON-PHARMACOLOGIC PROPHYLAXIS

Although prophylactic treatment of headache is often thought of as inevitably involving medication, reasonable non-pharmacologic strategies are enormously helpful and should be emphasized for every patient. These strategies are thoroughly reviewed in Chapter 8, "Other Approaches to Headache Management," and should be viewed as the foundation of prophylactic treatment for every patient, even those who require additional treatment with medication. Regular use of non-pharmacologic treatment strategies can augment the effectiveness of medications and exert a medication-sparing effect, even if it does not eliminate the need for medication. Women who are attempting pregnancy or who are pregnant or lactating are often highly motivated to minimize or avoid pharmacologic treatment; others have a philosophical preference to avoid medication, which should be respected.

GUIDELINES FOR MIGRAINE TREATMENT

The US Headache Consortium has developed evidence-based guidelines for migraine treatment, including pharmacologic preventive therapy.[3,4] In clinical practice, many medications, in addition to those recommended by the guidelines, are used successfully. Some of the newer acute headache drugs have rapid onset of action, consistent effectiveness, and excellent safety profiles, making it more and more possible to successfully treat more migraineurs with acute medications alone. Many patients prefer to avoid the use of daily medication, if at all possible. Consequently, practitioners are faced with increasingly difficult decisions about whether to prescribe acute care treatment only or to also use preventive medications. The goals of migraine preventive therapy are to reduce attack frequency, severity, and duration; improve responsiveness to treatment of acute attacks; and improve function and reduce disability.[2] In clinical trials, the most efficacious medications reduce headache frequency by 50 to 80%.[5] Therefore, most migraine patients on preventive pharmacologic agents will continue to have headaches requiring acute treatment.

COMMON CLASSES AND MODE OF ACTION OF MIGRAINE PREVENTIVE DRUGS

Beta-Blockers

Beta-blockers are the most widely used class of prophylactic migraine medication. Their exact mechanism of action in migraine is unknown. These drugs block beta-receptors in vascular smooth muscle to prevent arterial dilation and inhibit catecholamine-induced platelet aggregation, platelet adhesiveness, and prostaglandin production.[6] Beta-blockers without intrinsic sympathomimetic effect (propranolol, timolol, atenolol, nadolol, and metoprolol) have all been shown to produce approximately a 50% reduction in headache frequency in 60 to 80% of cases.[7,8] Those beta-blockers with intrinsic sympathomimetic activity (acebutolol, alprenolol, oxprenolol, and pindolol) are not effective migraine preventive agents. Only propranolol and timolol have Food and Drug Administration (FDA) approval for the indication of migraine.

As propranolol, timolol, atenolol, nadolol, and metoprolol are thought to be equally effective, selection among them depends on adverse effects, ease of administration, and cost. Propranolol is the most frequently used of these agents for migraine, but because of its high lipid solubility, it may more frequently cause side effects such as depression, nightmares, and lethargy. Cardioselective agents such as metoprolol and atenolol may be used with caution in asthmatic patients. Female athletes may not be able to tolerate the bradycardia and decreased exercise tolerance. Beta-blockers should not be discontinued abruptly due to rebound tachycardia. Many experts prefer to avoid beta-blockers in patients who have migraine with aura, based on case reports suggesting that cerebral ischemia might be worsened by these drugs; recent research suggests this may only be necessary when a clear stroke risk other than migraine is present.[9]

Propranolol is commonly initiated at a dose of 20 mg PO bid and titrated to 40 mg bid. The dose can be gradually increased to 160 mg and as high as 360 mg/day. Because of side effects, few patients are able to tolerate higher dose levels. If propranolol is not tolerated, consider switching to metoprolol 100 mg, ½ tablet PO bid. The dose can be increased to 100 mg bid. Women may require smaller doses of this agent than do men. Women have 100% higher maximal concentrations and systemic exposure of metoprolol metabolites compared with men, even after adjusting for body weight. This results in a greater reduction in heart rate and systolic blood pressure in women exposed to the drug.[10] Although both propranolol and metoprolol have short half-lives, in migraine prophylaxis, bid dosing is sufficient rather than the recommended tid or qid. Timolol doses range from 20 to 60 mg/day, given in divided doses. Nadolol and atenolol have the longest plasma half-lives, permitting once-a-

day dosing that may improve compliance. Propranolol likewise has a long-acting (LA) preparation (up to 160 mg/day), also permitting once-a-day dosing following initial titration with short-acting propranolol. Atenolol, usually begun at a dose of 25 mg daily and increased as tolerated to 100 mg daily, and nadolol, used at doses ranging from 10 to 120 mg daily, come in scored tablets that permit more flexible dosing than long-acting propranolol.

Calcium Channel Antagonists

Calcium channel antagonists (CCAs) are the prophylactic treatment of choice for cluster headache but are also frequently used for migraine prevention, in spite of contradictory evidence regarding their efficacy for this indication. Their popularity for migraine may reflect not so much their efficacy as the fact that they are generally well tolerated, with few dangerous side effects. Previously, their antimigraine efficacy has been attributed to their protective effects during anoxia or their ability to block intracranial vasoconstriction.[7,11] However, certain CCAs (verapamil, nifedipine) display moderate affinity for the 5-hydroxytryptamine-2 ($5-HT_2$) receptor and may work through that mechanism.[12] Verapamil is the CCA most frequently used for headache prevention, but it appears to be modestly effective in preventing migraine.[13,14] Side effects include constipation and peripheral edema. Verapamil is extensively metabolized by the hepatic cytochrome P-450 (CYP) system. In women, verapamil oral clearance is lower than that in men, indicating a higher bioavailability of verapamil in women, which may in turn result in higher systemic exposures. Clinically, women may have a greater compensatory increase in heart rate in response to the reduction of blood pressure with CCAs. Via the baroreflex response, this may prevent even further blood pressure decreases in women relative to men.[10] Because these differences are mediated primarily through body mass, dose should be based on lean body mass.[15]

Verapamil may be started at a dose of 80 or 120 mg bid and increased if necessary to 640 mg/day in two to three divided doses. At higher doses, electrocardiograms can be performed to monitor cardiac conduction delays that can occur. Eight weeks may be needed to see maximal benefit. Verapamil sustained-release preparations (240 mg/day) may be given in once-per-day dosing but at twice the cost and with less consistent absorption than the standard preparation.

Amlodipine (up to 10 mg/day) seems to be an effective migraine preventive medication.[16] It causes less constipation than verapamil but more peripheral edema. Diltiazem and nifedipine are not commonly used in migraine treatment. Evidence is lacking to support the use of nifedipine in headache treatment, and it may in fact precipitate headaches in many migraine patients because of its rapid vasodilatory action.[17,18]

The CCA flunarizine, widely used for prophylaxis of migraine in Europe, is unavailable in the United States.[19] Nicardipine was effective in one small placebo study (20 mg bid) and in one open-label study.[20,21] There is preliminary evidence that nimodipine is effective for migraine prevention, but it is prohibitively expensive.[22,23]

Other Antihypertensives

Studies in the 1970s, using the alpha-2 agonist clonidine, demonstrated minimal efficacy in migraine prevention.[24] This medication is now not commonly used in long-term treatment. It may be beneficial for adjunctive short-term treatment of withdrawal syndromes associated with discontinuation of overused analgesics, especially opioids.[25] In a small study, the angiotensin-converting enzyme inhibitor lisinopril was shown to be effective in migraine prevention.[26] The angiotensin receptor-blocker candesartan, at a dose of 16 mg PO once daily, has also recently been shown to be beneficial in migraine prophylaxis.[27] Further research on these drugs will establish more clearly their role in headache treatment. In the meantime, it is worth remembering that drugs that act on the renin-angiotensin system are associated with severe fetal and neonatal morbidity and mortality when used during the second and third trimesters of pregnancy.

Antidepressants

In general, antidepressants modulate 5-HT$_2$ receptor density. Antidepressants downregulate both the 5-HT$_2$ and adrenergic receptors. All antidepressants, regardless of class, lower the density and the functional activity of 5-HT$_2$ receptors.[28] The tricyclic antidepressant (TCA) amitriptyline is the most studied antidepressant drug and has good efficacy in headache prophylaxis.[29,30] Amitriptyline is effective for migraine, tension-type headaches, and chronic daily headaches.[31] Its clinical efficacy is particularly interesting because it is a potent blocker of 5-HT uptake, and it is also an antagonist of multiple neurotransmitter receptors. Either its 5-HT$_2$ receptor antagonism or its ability to block 5-HT uptake may account for its prophylactic antimigraine efficacy. Increasing 5-HT levels, via uptake blockade, may have a mild analgesic effect in humans.[32] The prophylactic effect of amitriptyline is independent of its antidepressant actions. Its antiheadache effect is achieved at a lower dose than that required for maximal antidepressant benefit.[33,34] The effect of amitriptyline in promoting sleep is frequently an important additional benefit.

Amitriptyline is best started at 10 or 12.5 mg (½ of a 25 mg tablet), given in the evening, and titrated up as tolerated to not more than 100 mg daily. Amitriptyline is usually well tolerated in the small doses required to treat headaches. Initial drowsiness decreases with time and is dose-related. Dry mouth and weight gain are common side effects and may not be well tolerated.

Doxepin has an efficacy and adverse effect profile similar to amitriptyline. Doxepin is a very potent 5-HT$_2$ blocker. It too can be given once per day in a nightly dose to promote sleep. The dose recommendations are similar to those of amitriptyline, with the caveat that because it comes as a capsule rather than a tablet, dosing is less flexible than with amitriptyline.

The timing of an evening TCA dose must be individually adjusted to maximize sleep and minimize morning drowsiness. If daytime sedation continues with amitriptyline or doxepin, then switching to imipramine is recommended. Imipramine is less sedating, has fewer anticholinergic effects, and clinically seems less likely to cause weight gain than amitriptyline. Dosing is similar to that for amitriptyline. Imipramine plasma protein binding is lower in women than in men, but the clinical significance of this is unclear.[10] Nortriptyline is also an effective antimigraine medication that has fewer anticholinergic side effects and is less sedating than amitriptyline. Again, because it comes in capsule form only, dosing is less flexible than with amitriptyline or imipramine. An initial dose of 10 mg may be gradually increased to 50 to 75 mg qhs as tolerated.

If daytime sedation remains a problem, protriptyline may be a good choice. It is nonsedating and may cause less weight gain than other antidepressants. Protriptyline should be started with a low daytime dose (5 mg) and gradually increased using the 10 mg tablets. Protriptyline can cause significant dry mouth. Desipramine is another relatively nonsedating antidepressant that also has fewer anticholinergic side effects than amitriptyline; unfortunately, it has not been well studied in migraine, so its effects, if any, in migraine are based on speculation rather than fact. Other side effects of TCAs include tremors, confusion, tachycardia, palpitations, constipation, blurred vision, and urinary retention. Antidepressant therapy can precipitate mania in bipolar patients and may reduce seizure threshold.[9]

A monoamine oxidase inhibitor (MAOI), such as phenelzine at 30 to 90 mg daily in divided doses, can be an effective antimigraine medication when other medications have failed.[35] There is evidence that MAOI efficacy may relate to its ability to increase levels of endogenous 5-HT. However, patients on MAOIs must follow a rigid diet that avoids tyramine-containing foods such as alcohol and cheddar cheese, in addition to avoiding concomitant use of certain medications, including meperidine and sympathomimetics. Inadvertent consumption of these contraindicated drugs or foods can cause fatal hypertensive crisis. Other common side effects include insomnia, orthostatic hypotension, edema, and weight gain. MAOIs can be combined carefully with some medications, whereas others, such as the triptans, must be avoided. With newer, more convenient-to-use preventives, the MAOIs are now infrequently used.

The selective serotonin reuptake inhibitors (SSRIs) fluoxetine, sertraline, paroxetine, and citalopram are widely used in headache treatment, despite extensive evidence that they are less effective than many other classes of medications, including TCAs, for treating headaches. Several studies have suggested a possible benefit of fluoxetine in migraine.[36–39] Saper and colleagues, in a double-blind study, found fluoxetine ineffective in the treatment of migraine.[40] However, the dose and length of treatment in this study may have been suboptimal. S-Fluoxetine, an isomer of the racemic fluoxetine mixture currently available, has also been studied for migraine prophylaxis, with marginally positive results.[41] Certainly, fluoxetine and other SSRIs may be of value in the management of chronic daily headache and migraine that are comorbid with depression.[40] Start fluoxetine dosing at 10 mg daily in the morning and increase as needed to 60 mg.

A small study suggests the efficacy of fluvoxamine, another SSRI, in reducing migraine frequency.[42] Fluvoxamine plasma concentrations are 70 to 100% higher in women than in men. Although there appears to be no relationship between concentration and antidepressant effect, the higher concentrations could increase adverse events such as drug interactions.[10] Other SSRIs have little evidence-based support for efficacy in migraine prevention.

Although TCAs are effective in treating headaches at lower doses than required for their antidepressant effect, the opposite may be true of the SSRIs. Strong clinical impressions exist that usual to high doses of SSRI are required for effective headache prophylaxis. Side effects include nausea, nervousness, insomnia, and nightmares. Adverse effects that are especially bothersome to women include weight gain and sexual dysfunction. Although SSRIs are effective antidepressant medications and somewhat better tolerated than TCAs, their unproved efficacy as antimigraine medications should limit their use as monotherapy in migraine preventive treatment. However, SSRIs can be combined with other more effective migraine preventives for improved headache control and management of comorbid depression and anxiety.

Although it has weak, if any, effects on headache, the antidepressant trazodone may have a role in headache treatment as a highly sedating sleep medication without anticholinergic side effects. Venlafaxine extended-release is a well-tolerated novel antidepressant for which there is some evidence that it reduces the frequency of migraine and tension-type headaches.[43] This medication is a 5-HT reuptake inhibitor at lower doses (less than 100 mg) and at higher doses also inhibits norepinephrine (NE) reuptake. Doses for headache prevention range from 37.5 to 300 mg daily. In addition to side effects similar to those of SSRIs, some patients will have blood pressure increases while on venlafaxine. Other antidepressant medications that have been used in headache treatment include nefazodone, which inhibits 5-HT reuptake and is a $5-HT_2$ receptor antagonist. One small, open-label study suggests the benefit of nefazodone for chronic daily headache, especially in patients with comorbid depression.[44] Mirtazapine disinhibits both 5-HT and NE neurotransmission via binding with presynaptic alpha-2 receptors. However, it is also antagonistic for $5-HT_2$, $5-HT_3$, and histamine (H_1), which may contribute to its unfavorable side effect profile, with prominent sedation and weight gain. There is one case report of the successful use of mirtazapine in migraine prevention.[45] Bupropion, an NE and dopamine (DA) reuptake inhibitor, has not been systematically studied in headache prevention, although there are anecdotal reports of benefit in a variety of headache types.[46,47] However, its dopaminergic activity may play a role in migraine pathophysiology. It is also beneficial for smoking cessation and can be valuable in helping patients with headache to stop smoking. Other advantages of bupropion include the low incidence of side effects such as weight gain or sexual dysfunction.

Although antipsychotic medications, such as the phenothiazines, are used in the acute treatment of migraine, they have not been thoroughly studied for migraine prevention. Atypical antipsychotics, such as olanzapine, may be useful in the management of chronic daily headache.[48] Weight gain and sedation are common side effects with these medications.

Antiepileptic Drugs

Antiepileptic drugs (AEDs) may affect migraine through multiple mechanisms, not all of which are fully understood.

Valproate or divalproex sodium is the AED most studied in migraine and has been found to be effective in reducing the frequency of migraine headaches compared to placebo.[49–51] Valproate interacts with the central 5-HT system and reduces the firing rate of midbrain serotonergic neurons. In addition, valproate blocks the development of neurogenic inflammation by enhancing peripheral γ-aminobutyric acid (GABA) activity at the GABA A receptor. Finally, valproate-induced increased central activation of GABA A activity may enhance central antinociception.[52–54]

Doses of divalproex sodium should start at 125 mg or 250 mg once or twice a day and be titrated up to 1,000 to 1,500 mg daily in divided doses. Although nausea, tremor, cognitive impairment, and sedation are common complaints among seizure patients on divalproex sodium, weight gain and hair loss are more common side effects in the headache population. The extended-release formulation offers more convenient once-daily dosing and is reported to be associated with fewer side effects.[51] This formulation is initiated at 500 mg nightly and increased after 1 week to 1,000 mg nightly.

Although valproate does not affect estrogen levels, it can cause elevations of androgens.[55] Women with epilepsy taking valproate are at increased risk of polycystic ovary syndrome. However, women with epilepsy, in general, are more likely to have polycystic-appearing ovaries, a condition not known to occur at higher-than-normal rates in women with migraine.[55] Valproate is associated with neural tube defects in infants of women with epilepsy taking the drug during pregnancy. The neural tube forms very early in pregnancy, thus providing little opportunity for women who become unexpectedly pregnant to discontinue the drug in a timely fashion. Because of this very serious side effect, extreme caution should be exercised in prescribing valproate to any woman with migraine who is of childbearing potential, and it should generally not be considered a first-line prophylactic drug in this population.

Valproate can cause rare idiosyncratic reactions such as pancreatitis or hepatitis. Rarely, thrombocytopenia, pancytopenia, and bleeding disorders can occur with valproate. Baseline blood tests (liver chemistry and complete blood count) are suggested, but continuous laboratory monitoring of the adult headache patient on valproate monotherapy is not indicated, as clinical monitoring is safe, appropriate, and cost-effective.[52,56,57] Moreover, valproate serum levels do not correlate with headache control and are not necessary for that reason.[52] Caution should be used when administering valproate with barbiturate-containing analgesics, as idiosyncratic severe sedation and coma can occur.[9]

Gabapentin increases brain GABA levels in humans and may work by mechanisms similar to divalproex sodium. Gabapentin is modestly effective as migraine prophylaxis as well as in the treatment of trigeminal neuralgia, postherpetic pain, and peripheral neuralgia.[58] Doses of 1,800 to 2,400 mg divided tid and higher may be necessary for migraine prevention. Gabapentin is typically well tolerated, with drowsiness and dizziness being the most common complaints. Shifting the higher doses toward evening may help decrease the effect of drowsiness.

Topiramate is an AED that is increasingly used for migraine prevention. One small controlled trial and several open-label studies have shown the benefit of topiramate in migraine prevention.[59–61] In a large US study, the optimal dosing regimen was 100 mg per day. Topiramate may also be beneficial in the treatment of cluster headache and chronic daily headache.[62–64]

Topiramate should be started at low doses, generally 15 or 25 mg once at bedtime, and increased slowly to a target dose of 100 mg daily, usually given in divided doses. Some patients experience cognitive side effects. Paresthesias are also common in migraine sufferers taking topiramate, and patients must be informed that the drug increases the risk of renal stone formation and has been associated with rare cases of glaucoma. In contrast to nearly all other headache preventive drugs, topiramate appears to cause weight loss. This side effect is highly desirable for large numbers of patients and is probably as important as the drug's efficacy in driving prescriptions for this drug.

Lamotrigine blocks voltage-sensitive sodium channels, leading to the inhibition of neuronal release of glutamate. Glutamate is a neuroexcitatory amino acid that may play a role in the development of cortical spreading depression, which is a proposed mechanism of migraine aura. Lamotrigine has been effective in reducing the frequency of migraine aura but has little effect on the headache phase of migraine.[65–67] Thus, this drug appears to have an important role as one of the few effective treatments for patients in whom aura, and not headache, is the target of treatment. The initial dose of 25 mg daily can be slowly increased to 100 to 200 mg. Slow titration can decrease the risk of developing rash. Other newer anticonvulsants, including tiagabine (mean dose 4 to 16 mg/day), levetiracetam (250 mg titrating up to 1,000 to 1,500 mg twice daily), and zonisamide (100 to 600 mg daily), are also being investigated as migraine prophylaxis.[68] Older AEDs such as phenytoin, carbamazepine, and clonazepam are not effective in headache prophylaxis.[2]

Serotonergic Agents

Methysergide, 2 mg tid, can be an effective antimigraine medication when other agents have failed. It is an effective preventive medication in migraine and cluster headaches.[69,70] It is a semisynthetic ergot alkaloid that has antagonistic action at the 5-HT$_2$ receptor and the ability to block neurogenic inflammation. Retroperitoneal and retropleural fibrosis have been associated with long-term methysergide use. Therefore, a 3- to 4-week "drug holiday" should be taken every 6 months. Methysergide's side effects include nausea, diarrhea, abdominal pain, dizziness, drowsiness, hallucinations, and leg pain or restlessness. This medication is less commonly used now because certain acute treatment medications (eg, triptans, ergots) must be avoided when using these ergot alkaloid preventive medications. The US manufacturer of this drug has recently discontinued its production, and patients requiring its use may be forced to obtain the drug from Canadian or European sources.

Other serotonin antagonists, such as cyproheptadine, have also been reported to be effective in migraine prophylaxis.[71] These drugs are potent 5-HT$_2$ receptor antagonists. Cyproheptadine, also used as an antihistamine, 4 to 8 mg nightly, is helpful for migraine prevention and inducing sleep. Due to weight gain, this medication is poorly tolerated in adults but can be useful in underweight children with allergy symptoms. Pizotifen and lisuride, serotonin antagonists that are not available in the United States, have also demonstrated benefit in headache prevention.[2]

Nonsteroidal Anti-inflammatory Drugs

The beneficial effects of NSAIDs in headache prophylaxis may be due to the inhibition of inflammation, decreased formation of prostaglandins, and impairment of platelet aggregation.[6] Several studies provide indirect evidence of the effectiveness of aspirin in migraine prophylaxis. The American (male) Physicians' Health Study and a study of British male doctors demonstrated 20 to 30% fewer migraines in the aspirin-treated groups.[72,73] Doses were 325 mg every other day and 500 mg daily in the two studies, respectively. However, the aspirin benefit was small and not statistically significant in a group of women migraineurs in the Women's Health Study.[74] Other studies of aspirin for migraine prophylaxis have been equivocal.[2] Naproxen sodium has the most evidence among the NSAIDs to support its use in migraine prevention, particularly the short-term prevention of anticipated menstrual attacks of migraine.[75–78] Ketoprofen, mefenamic acid, and flurbiprofen have also demonstrated benefit in headache prevention.[79–81] Other NSAIDs that have not been proven effective include fenoprofen, indomethacin, and nabumetone.[2] Gastrointestinal (GI) side effects such as nausea, vomiting, gastritis, and blood in the stool are common with extended use of NSAIDs. Furthermore, acute therapy with NSAIDs must be used cautiously if the patient is also using daily preventive NSAIDs. The COX-2 inhibitor rofecoxib appeared in one study to be modestly useful in migraine prevention[82]; these drugs may have a better GI tolerability profile than conventional nonselective NSAIDs.

Other Agents

Tizanidine, an antispasticity agent, is an alpha-2 adrenergic agonist that inhibits the release of NE at the level of the spinal cord and brain, with central muscle relaxant and antinociceptive effects. Tizanidine has been shown to be of benefit in chronic tension-type headache.[83] An open-label and a double-blind placebo-controlled trial demonstrated the benefit of tizanidine in the treatment of chronic daily headache.[84,85] Doses start at 1 to 2 mg nightly and are titrated as tolerated up to 24 mg daily in divided doses. Side effects include weakness, sedation, hypotension, and liver enzyme elevations, which are reversible on drug discontinuation. Patients whose headaches are associated with muscle

pain and spasm may be candidates for tizanidine. Baclofen, which is also an antispasticity agent, has been used to treat trigeminal neuralgia and has been studied in open-label fashion for migraine and for cluster headache prevention.[86,87] Many patients do not tolerate the sedation and weakness associated with baclofen.

Magnesium (Mg) has been studied as a migraine prophylactic agent based on the evidence of Mg abnormalities in some migraineurs and the role that Mg is theorized to play in migraine pathophysiology and gating of N-methyl-D-aspartate (NMDA) receptors. Low Mg levels have been demonstrated in blood, blood cells, saliva, and cerebrospinal fluid in migraineurs, both ictally and interictally.[88] Reduced intracellular concentration of Mg in the cortex of migraine subjects was reported and is consistent with the role of Mg in neuronal hyperexcitability.[89,90] Animal and human studies have shown that low Mg levels induce cerebral arterial vasospasm; potentiate the contractile response of blood vessels to vasoactive substances such as serotonin; enhance the sensitivity of NMDA receptors to glutamate, thus inducing epileptiform discharges and cortical spreading depression; increase thrombin-induced platelet aggregation leading to serotonin release; and may be proinflammatory.[88]

One study using trimagnesium dicitrate, 600 mg (24 mmol) daily, demonstrated reduced headache frequency.[88] However, another study using magnesium-L-aspartate-hydrochloride-trihydrate, 486 mg (20 mmol), failed to show benefit over placebo.[91] The dosage and formulation of Mg used in these two studies may explain the differences in outcome. Magnesium pyrrolidone carboxylic acid three times daily perimenstrually (total daily amount of Mg equal to 360 mg) reduced the number of days with headache and also improved premenstrual complaints.[92] The most common side effect is diarrhea, which can often be minimized by reducing the dose of Mg.

Riboflavin (vitamin B$_2$) is an important precursor molecule for energy metabolism; because abnormalities of mitochondrial energy metabolism may play a role in migraine pathophysiology, this substance has been used for the treatment of migraine. In an open pilot study and subsequent randomized controlled trial, high-dose riboflavin (400 mg daily) decreased headache frequency with few side effects.[93,94] Side effects are minimal and the cost of treatment is low.

Herbal products such as feverfew have become popular with patients. There are several proposed mechanisms for feverfew's prophylactic usefulness in migraine, including inhibitory effect on the release of 5-HT from blood platelets and anti-inflammatory activity. However, strong scientific evidence for efficacy is lacking.[95–97] In one study, capsules taken orally once daily, containing the equivalent of 2.19 μmol (standard deviation 0.63) of the active ingredient parthenolide from feverfew grown in the investigator's laboratory and prepared under standard conditions, did reduce migraine frequency and severity.[98] In another poorly designed study, patients previously taking feverfew were assigned to placebo or two capsules daily, which contained 25 mg each of powdered, freeze-dried feverfew leaves. Those continuing on feverfew had no change in headache frequency or severity, whereas those who changed to placebo had increased headache frequency and severity.[99] A recent double-blind, randomized, placebo-controlled dose-response study of feverfew failed to show a significant migraine prophylactic effect in general. However, a small subgroup of patients with more frequent attacks (at least four per month) experienced a clinically significant reduction in attack frequency.[100] Mouth sores are a side effect with feverfew. The main criticism of feverfew as a migraine preventive therapy is the lack of standardization in product preparations because herbal products are not subject to FDA regulations.

Other commonly touted herbal or "natural" supplements do not have proven efficacy in migraine prevention. Patients should be cautioned that "natural" does not necessarily mean "safe." As patients may not report supplement use, it is prudent to always inquire directly about the use of such products and to counsel patients appropriately regarding possible interactions with prescription or over-the-counter medications.[101]

Botulinum toxin A is a neurotoxin used in the treatment of strabismus, blepharospasm, dystonia, facial wrinkles and hyperfunctional lines, and other disorders of muscle contraction. The primary mechanism of action is chemodenervation by the inhibition of vesicular release of acetylcholine at the neuromuscular junction, resulting in temporary muscle paresis or paralysis. The exact mechanism of botulinum toxin A in migraine prevention is unknown. An initial open-label study suggested that botulinum toxin A may be beneficial for acute and prophylactic migraine treatment.[102] One double-blind study examined the efficacy and safety of botulinum toxin A for the prevention of moderate to severe migraine, injecting doses of 0, 25, or 75 units symmetrically into glabella, frontalis, and temporalis muscles.[103] The 25-unit dose resulted in a significant reduction in migraine frequency and associated symptoms during the 90 days following injection and was superior to the 75 unit dose with regard to the main efficacy endpoints.[103] Botulinum toxin A is well tolerated, with no serious adverse events. Bruising at the injection site and transient ptosis can occur. The prolonged duration of the botulinum effect, 2 to 4 months, eliminates concerns regarding compliance with daily pharmacologic agents. Furthermore, there are no systemic effects such as weight gain, sedation, or cognitive impairment as there are with other preventive medications. However, the cost of botulinum can be high, and it is not uniformly covered by prescription insurance.

CHOICE OF PREVENTIVE THERAPY

The prophylactic medications considered by the US Headache Consortium guidelines to be first-line treatment for various headaches have similar efficacy but very different safety and tolerability profiles (Table 7-1). Some common side effects of these drugs, such as weight gain or teratogenic potential, are especially unappealing to female patients. Other drugs have side effects that can be used to advantage in certain women; for example, the sedation associated with TCAs may be useful in a patient who has difficulty with sleep. Some women may hesitate

Table 7-1 Safety and Tolerability Issues with Migraine Prophylaxis of Particular Importance to Women

Adverse Effect	Drugs More Likely to Cause Adverse Effect	Drugs Less Likely to Cause Adverse Effect
Teratogenesis	AEDs, *especially* VPA (associated with neural tube defects), ARBs, and ACE inhibitors	Beta-blockers, TCAs
Weight gain	TCAs, VPA, GBP, beta-blockers, many SSRIs	CCAs, TPM, bupropion
Fatigue	TCAs, beta-blockers, many SSRIs, AEDs, tizanidine	
Nightmares	Beta-blockers, SSRIs	
Cognitive impairment	AEDs	
Hair loss	VPA	
Sexual dysfunction	SSRIs, TCAs	
Orthostatic hypotension	Beta-blockers, TCAs, tizanidine	
Constipation	CCA, TCAs	Magnesium, riboflavin

ACE inhibitor = angiotensin-converting enzyme inhibitor; AED = antiepileptic drug; ARB = angiotensin receptor blocker; CCA = calcium channel antagonist; GBP = gabapentin; SSRI = selective serotonin reuptake inhibitor; TCA = tricyclic antidepressant; TPM = topiramate; VPA = valproate.

to use sedating medications, however, even at bedtime, especially if they must care for children or be alert for other important reasons.

For most women, the possibility of weight gain is the single most unacceptable side effect of headache prophylaxis. Unfortunately, weight gain occurs commonly with many of the typically used migraine prophylactic agents. A recent study highlighted the importance of this problem.[104] The weight of patients begun on five commonly used migraine prophylactic drugs was monitored over 9 months. Patients on fluoxetine gained an average of 5 pounds, whereas those on nortriptyline and divalproex gained on average 3 pounds. Patients on riboflavin did not, on average, gain or lose weight. Topiramate use was associated with an average 10-pound weight loss.

The increasingly recognized serious health consequences of even mild weight gain, coupled with the high prevalence of eating disorders in women, make it especially desirable to avoid the use of medications that cause weight gain when suitable alternatives exist. Additionally, it is important to recognize that medications can contribute to weight gain either directly, by increasing appetite or decreasing activity levels, or indirectly, as in cases where an increase in body weight may reflect the improvement of migraine and consequent return of appetite.[105] For this reason, regular aerobic exercise should be encouraged for all headache patients, not just those taking a pharmacologic agent that may contribute to weight gain.

Most headache preventive medications were designed to treat other medical disorders and were discovered by serendipity to benefit migraine or other headache disorders. The fact that most drugs used for prevention of headache have beneficial effects on other conditions can sometimes be exploited to the patient's advantage. Frequently, comorbid or co-occurring illness will be the deciding factor in selecting migraine preventive medications (Table 7-2). For example, a patient with both depression and migraine may find both conditions improved with the use of antidepressant therapy. In the same manner, however, coexisting conditions can also limit the use of certain drugs. A woman with asthma should not be given a beta-blocker for migraine prevention because safer alternatives exist.

Comorbid disorders are those that occur together more frequently than would be predicted by chance. Migraine, depression, and anxiety are examples of comorbid disorders. Other conditions occur together by chance, and these are referred to as coexisting or co-occurring disorders. Many of these disorders are especially common in women (Table 7-3) and must often be taken into account in selecting headache treatment.

Patient preference and lifestyle are also important factors in choosing preventive therapy. A competitive athlete is unlikely to tolerate the hypotension and bradycardia associated with a beta-blocker. A surgeon with aura once a month may be willing to take daily preventive medication in an effort to avoid the possibility of unpredictable visual impairment interfering with her work. The changing nature of women's lives also affects what kind of treatment is acceptable. As women increasingly work outside the home, they often retain the primary responsibility for household and social duties within the home. Women, more than men, report that headaches impact relationships with family and others.[106] Women also report more concern than do men about the effect of pain on their lives and on interference with activities, and this has been shown to prompt more rapid medical consultation about headache.[107] The value that women place on avoiding a disruption of social and emotional ties may influence a woman's decision to start a preventive medication sooner rather than later, in order to minimize the impact of headache on her life.

The choice of preventive therapy for our case patient, KM, cannot be based on efficacy alone. Because KM had weight gain with amitriptyline in the past, it will be especially important to avoid treatment choices associated with a high likelihood of weight gain. Because of her tendency toward constipation, medications aggravating that condition should also be avoided. If KM has residual symptoms of depression, an antidepressant medication, probably an SSRI, may be beneficial for the treatment of both depression and migraine, although the scientific evidence for headache benefit with this class of drugs is not as strong as that for other classes of medication. KM has relatively low blood pressure and heart rate and may have difficulty tolerating any lowering of these caused by the use of an antihypertensive agent. Clinically, it is often noted that a beneficial response of one family member to a particular class of medications may predict good response in other family members. Since KM's brother had responded to treatment with an AED, she may have a higher likelihood of headache improvement with this class of medication. Plans for conception will limit the use of valproate.

PRINCIPLES OF PROPHYLACTIC TREATMENT

The following principles are useful in prophylactic therapy:

- Start low, go slow, taper off
- Use the lowest effective dose
- Once-daily dosing is preferable
- Maximize the dose before determining ineffectiveness
- Allow at least 4 to 8 weeks for efficacy
- Limit frequent analgesic use (rebound), which can interfere with prophylaxis

Begin with a low dose of the chosen drug and increase slowly until clinical benefits are achieved in the absence of adverse events or until further dose escalations are limited by adverse events. Aim for the lowest effective dose associated with tolerable side effects. Compliance and convenience are improved with the use of once-daily dosing; some preventive agents typically given in divided doses for other conditions can be successfully used as single doses in migraine treatment (eg, certain beta-blockers or AEDs). Be certain that the dose has been maximized and adequate time for effect has been achieved before determining that the agent is or is not useful.

Up to 80% of chronic daily headache sufferers are overusing analgesics. This can lead to analgesic-induced headache, also called "medication overuse headache" or "rebound headache." Acute and preventive medications are less likely to be effective in a patient overusing analgesics, such as those containing acetaminophen, butalbital, or caffeine. For best results from a prophylactic regimen, therefore, it is essential that patients who are overusing abortive medications discontinue the offending drug. Thereafter, the goal of management is to avoid further analgesic overuse, which would again interfere with preventive therapy.

The optimal duration of headache prophylaxis has not been scientifically established. In predictable situations, prophylaxis may be used for a short term; for example, perimenstrually or when planning high-elevation trips. Otherwise, preventive medication is taken daily even in the absence of headache, and decisions about when to discontinue use are individualized. Most experts believe that to provide an adequate trial of the medication, daily prophylaxis should be maintained for a minimum of 2 or 3 months, allowing time for the patient to adjust to the medication and possible side effects and to determine whether any effects on headache are due to the drug or simply to the natural waxing and waning of headache that occurs over time. The best preventive results seen in clinical trials have generally occurred in the third month of therapy.

In stable patients with prolonged preventive medication use, occasional attempts can be made to taper and discontinue the drugs. However, if headache frequency increases, the medication should be titrated back to the lowest effective dose. Of great interest is the fact that the headache preventive effects of some drugs may last beyond the duration of actual drug treatment, a so-called "carry-over" effect.[108] Our case patient, KM, should allow at least 1 month to determine the initial effect and any adverse events associated with preventive therapy. Thereafter, she may continue preventive treatment for 3 or more months to assess the benefits and drawbacks of the drug. She may need to taper and discontinue the therapy when she plans to become pregnant.

Although monotherapy is desirable, a single agent may not provide adequate headache reduction and some patients require a combination of preventive medications. Co-pharmacy, as used in other chronic conditions such as diabetes and hypertension, can also be applied to headache management. The combination of a TCA and SSRI can be beneficial in reducing headache frequency and intensity as well as effectively treating depression. Caution is necessary to avoid high TCA blood levels with this combination. Of course, certain drug combinations, such as MAOIs and SSRIs, should be avoided. Moreover, proper selection of acute medications is necessary with certain preventive medications. Acute therapy with vasoconstrictive agents, including the triptans or ergots, should not be used in patients taking certain daily preventive medications such as methysergide. Many acute and preventive medications for migraine act on the serotonergic system. Prescribing physicians should be alert to signs or symptoms of serotonin syndrome, with features such as mental status and behavioral changes, tremor, hyperreflexia, motor weakness, fever, chills, or other autonomic symptoms. Despite the frequency with which combinations and high doses of serotonergic drugs are used, however, the development of serious serotonin syndrome appears to be clinically rare.[109] At the time of this writing, only six cases of serotonin syndrome complicating migraine therapy have been reported—three cases with subcutaneous sumatriptan and three cases within intravenous dihydroergotamine.[110]

EFFECT OF ORAL CONTRACEPTIVES ON MIGRAINE PROPHYLACTIC THERAPY

What family planning and contraception issues must be taken into account when prescribing headache prophylaxis?

Both tension-type and migraine headaches are more common in women than in men, with peak prevalence between the ages of 25 and 55 years. Therefore, many women with headaches requiring prophylactic treatment will be of childbearing potential. Discussions about family planning and contraception should take place early in treatment. Optimization of non-pharmacologic treatment methods before pregnancy is attempted is especially helpful. Although it may be ideal for a woman to discontinue all medications prior to conception, this is not always possible for some severely affected patients. If pharmacologic prophylaxis of headaches is felt to be necessary despite pregnancy, it is important to discuss with the patient and her partner the potential risks of treatment and to select a medication with the least adverse effects on the fetus.

Women of childbearing potential should be on adequate contraception before starting migraine preventive medication. Combination oral contraceptives (OCs) are a popular and effective form of birth control. However, evidence regarding the effects of OCs on

Table 7-2 Commonly Used Migraine Preventive Medications with Special Attention to Therapeutic Advantages and Disadvantages of Importance to Women

Mechanism/Class	Selected Medication(s)	Therapeutic Advantages	Side Effects and Contraindications
Beta-blockers	Propranolol, timolol, atenolol, nadolol, metoprolol	Minimizes symptoms of performance anxiety, mitral valve prolapse, hypertension, angina	Raynaud's, fatigue, orthostatic hypotension, bradycardia, decreased exercise tolerance, nightmares, depression, weight gain. Avoid in asthma, congestive heart failure, insulin-dependent diabetes
Calcium channel antagonists	Verapamil	Raynaud's, hypertension	Constipation, orthostatic hypotension, fatigue
Antidepressants			
TCA	Amitriptyline, doxepin, imipramine, nortriptyline	Depression, insomnia, fibromyalgia, underweight	Fatigue, weight gain, constipation, sedation; lower seizure threshold. Caution in bipolar disorder, heart block
	Protriptyline, desipramine	Less sedating; may cause less weight gain than other TCAs	Dry mouth, constipation, lower seizure threshold, some weight gain. Caution in bipolar disorder, heart block
MAOI	Phenelzine	Treatment-resistant migraine, refractory depression	Insomnia, orthostatic hypotension, edema, weight gain, limited acute therapy with serotonin agonists, hypertensive crisis with tyramine-containing foods and certain medications
SSRI	Fluoxetine, sertraline, paroxetine, citalopram, fluvoxamine	Anxiety/depression, obsessive compulsive disorder, eating disorder, fibromyalgia	Fatigue, sexual dysfunction, weight gain, nightmares. Caution in bipolar disorder
Dopaminergic antidepressant	Bupropion	Depression, smoking cessation, weight loss	Anxiety, insomnia, lower seizure threshold
AED	Divalproex sodium	Mood stabilization, seizure disorder, bipolar, no interaction with OC	Neural tube deflects with 1st trimester pregnancy exposure, weight gain, hair loss, increased androgen levels, cognitive impairment. Avoid in liver or pancreatic disorders
	Gabapentin	Few drug interactions, postherpetic neuralgia, peripheral neuropathy, fibromyalgia, seizure disorder, no interaction with OC	Fatigue, compliance with multiple daily doses
	Topiramate	Mood stabilization, weight loss, peripheral neuropathy, seizure disorder	Weight loss, interference with estrogen OC at daily doses > 200 mg; cognitive impairment; paresthesias; renal calculi

Continued

Table 7-2 *Continued*

Category	Drug	Indication	Side effects/cautions
Serotonin antagonists	Methysergide	Resistant migraine	Weight gain, retroperitoneal and retropleural fibrosis requiring drug holidays, limited acute therapy with serotonin agonists
	Cyproheptadine	Insomnia, allergy symptoms, underweight	Weight gain, sedation
NSAID	Naproxen sodium	Dysmenorrhea, arthritis	GI upset/bleeding, limited acute medication (NSAID) use, possible rebound headache. Caution in renal disorder
	COX-2 inhibitors	Dysmenorrhea, improved GI tolerability, arthritis	GI upset/bleeding, limited acute medication (NSAID) use, possible rebound headache. Caution in renal disorder
	Aspirin	Secondary stroke and myocardial infarction prophylaxis, arthritis	GI upset/bleeding, limited acute medication (NSAID) use, possible rebound headache. Caution in renal disorder
Antispasticity	Tizanidine	Muscle relaxation, fibromyalgia, insomnia	Sedation, hypotension
Elemental supplement	Magnesium	Premenstrual symptoms	Diarrhea
Vitamin supplement	Riboflavin (vitamin B$_2$)	Dietary supplementation	Diarrhea
Herbal supplement	Feverfew	Nonprescription	Drug not regulated by Food and Drug Administration for consistency or safety, possible drug interactions
Toxin	Botulinum toxin A	Cosmetic/hyperfunctional facial lines, compliance, few adverse effects	Cost
Hormone	Estrogen-containing OC	Contraception, amenorrhea (continuous dosing), dysmenorrhea, vasomotor symptoms, bone protection, acne	Stroke risk, cancer risk, weight gain, drug interactions

AED = antiepileptic drug; GI = gastrointestinal; MAOI = monoamine oxidase inhibitor; NSAID = nonsteroidal anti-inflammatory drug; OC = oral contraceptive; SSRI = selective serotonin reuptake inhibitor; TCA = tricyclic antidepressant.

Table 7-3 Migraine Comorbid and Co-occurring Disorders

Cardiovascular

Hypertension

Mitral valve prolapse

Raynaud's phenomenon

Stroke

Psychiatric

Depression

Anxiety

Bipolar disorder

Eating disorders

• Anorexia/bulimia

• Obesity

Neurologic

Seizure disorder

Gastrointestinal

Gastric ulcers

Irritable bowel syndrome

Pulmonary

Smoking

Asthma

Allergies

Endocrine

Menstrual abnormalities

Hypothyroidism

Chronic pain

Fibromyalgia

Chronic fatigue syndrome

headache is conflicting, and, clinically, it appears that some women note headache worsening, whereas others have no change or even improvement in their headaches.[111] Each woman should monitor headaches closely when starting or changing an OC. One small crossover study of no treatment compared with a combination OC (norgestrel 0.5 mg + ethinyl estradiol 0.005 mg), dosed for 3 weeks followed by 1 week without treatment each month for 2 months, showed no benefit of the OC in the prevention of migraine but also no worsening of the disorder with treatment.[112] However, most women use OCs for contraception, not headache control. When selecting an OC for a woman with migraine, it is probably best to choose a low-dose monophasic estrogen and progestin combi-

nation to minimize hormonal fluctuations throughout the month.[113]

The use of OC has been controversial in women with migraine. This dates back to the relatively high risk of thrombotic events and stroke associated with higher-dose (50 µg) estrogen pills. These risks are lower with the current low-dose estrogen combination and progesterone-only pills.[114–116] In general, the risk of stroke in women with migraine, especially migraine with aura, is approximately two to three times higher than in women without migraine.[117] However, the baseline risk of stroke in women under the age of 45 years is very low and any increase as a result of OCs is minimal. Concomitant use of OCs by patients with high blood pressure or those who smoke appears to cause a synergistic increase in the risk of ischemic stroke associated with migraine, although no differences in increased risk were observed between migraine with aura and migraine without aura.[118,119] Caution should thus be used when prescribing OCs to women with migraine who have cardiac or cerebrovascular risk factors, and lifestyle modification should be encouraged. The current consensus is that for most women with migraine (without or with typical aura), low-dose OC use is safe.[120] The slight increased stroke risk may be offset by the reduction of the risks of unplanned pregnancy.

The effects of other medications used for headache on the efficacy of OCs must also be considered. OC failure rates are very low, but they do depend on patient compliance, as well as drug interactions that may interfere with the metabolism of contraceptive hormones. Although the effect of the menstrual cycle on central nervous system disorders such as migraine, depression, and epilepsy is well characterized, the influence of fluctuating endogenous hormones on pharmacologic agents used to treat these disorders is not well understood. Female sex hormones are metabolized by hepatic CYP isoenzymes. Some medications commonly used in headache treatment, especially certain AEDs, may interfere with estrogen levels.[121] Research on the effects of AEDs in women with epilepsy may apply to the use of these drugs in women with migraine. In women with epilepsy, AEDs can induce, inhibit, or have no effect on the hepatic CYP enzyme system. Inducers of these enzymes, including phenytoin, carbamazepine, phenobarbital, and primidone, decrease estrogen levels up to 40%.[122] Topiramate also induces hepatic enzymes but does not significantly lower estrogen levels at daily topiramate doses of 200 mg or less (higher doses of this agent are not commonly used to treat headaches).[123,124] By increasing the hepatic metabolism of synthetic estrogens, these enzyme-inducing pharmacologic agents decrease estrogen levels, possibly resulting in failure of the contraceptive to block ovulation. The most serious consequence of this is unplanned pregnancy, although breakthrough bleeding can also occur. It is important to remember that contraceptive failure can occur in the absence of breakthrough bleeding.[122]

Valproate inhibits hepatic enzyme activity, so it does not affect estrogen levels and therefore does not interfere with OC efficacy.[55] Gabapentin and lamotrigine are neutral with respect to the hepatic enzyme system and, therefore, also do not interfere with OC efficacy.

A survey of neurologists and obstetricians found that although most of them treat women of childbearing age who have epilepsy, few were aware of the effects of the six most common AEDs on OCs.[122] Although studies of patients using AED have been conducted mostly in women with epilepsy, the findings and recommendations are likely applicable to women with migraine who use AED for migraine prevention.[55,122] Folic acid supplementation (0.4 mg/day) should be recommended to all women of childbearing potential to reduce the risk of neural tube defects. Some AEDs interfere with folic acid metabolism, possibly requiring even higher supplemental folic acid doses.[125] Long-term AED use may reduce bone density, thus consideration should be given to the use of calcium and vitamin D supplements in patients using these agents for long-term headache prophylaxis.[126]

Our case patient, KM, should be on adequate contraception prior to and while taking preventive pharmacologic agents. If she chooses to use OCs, she should be made aware of possible changes in her headaches and the slightly increased risk of stroke. KM should be advised of the possible interactions of OCs and AEDs, as well as the teratogenetic potential of certain preventive medications, should contraception fail.

GENDER DIFFERENCES IN CHOICE OF PROPHYLACTIC THERAPIES FOR MIGRAINE

The burden of benign headache, especially migraine, including duration of disability and frequency of attacks, is greater in women than in men.[127] Therefore, women may need different treatment approaches—higher quantities of medications, longer duration on therapy, and co-pharmacy. Underrepresentation of women in clinical trials has been less of a problem in headache studies than in studies of other disorders. The percentage of women in clinical trials of migraine preventive medications ranges from 42 to 100%.[128] However, migraine clinical trials have generally not been stratified by gender or attempted to evaluate gender-specific differences in response. Studying gender differences in treatment is complicated by sufficient sample size, statistical power, and optimal study design that excludes confounders such as age, race, menstrual cycle, or co-medications.[15] Although not studied in headache populations, several pharmacologic agents used in headache prevention, including lamotrigine

and venlafaxine, have been evaluated for gender differences, with none found.[15]

A woman's age is also an important consideration in deciding on migraine preventive therapy. Older women continue to have a higher prevalence of migraine than men of the same age.[127] Elderly women take more medications than younger women and elderly men, metabolize medications more slowly than younger adults, may need a lower effective dose than is commercially available, represent the majority of seniors, and have the lowest body weight of any group.[129] Elderly women are also at higher risk than younger women of complications secondary to medication side effects or interactions—these complications can have serious medical consequences for the patient. For example, a headache medication that causes dizziness can lead to a fall, with the resultant fracture of an osteoporotic hip. In addition to the current concerns regarding long-term estrogen replacement, hormone replacement therapy (HRT) can have implications on headache frequency and severity as well as lead to drug interactions with the hepatic enzyme system. Older women may also have poorer access to prescription medications due to high drug costs and poor prescription coverage.

Gender differences exist in the pharmacokinetics and pharmacodynamics of some pharmacologic agents. Although investigation of these differences has not been addressed specifically in the migraine population, some findings may have relevance to preventive medication use in women with migraine. Pharmacokinetics is the activity of the drug in the body over time, including absorption, distribution, localization in tissues, biotransformation, and excretion. Pharmacodynamics is the biochemical and physiologic effects of drugs and the mechanisms of their actions.[130]

Gender differences in pharmacokinetics occur through several mechanisms. First, absorption rate and duration do not demonstrate significant differences despite the fact that women secrete less gastric acid and have slower gastric emptying, which may be exacerbated by or linked to estrogen and progesterone. It is unknown if gender differences occur in the gastrointestinal CYP system as in the hepatic CYP system. Second, oral bioavailability differs due to intestinal and hepatic metabolic enzymes. Third, drug distribution is affected by body weight, body composition, physiologic changes during the menstrual cycle, and plasma protein binding secondary to hormonal characteristics. Finally, drug elimination gender differences are due to metabolic CYP enzyme system differences.[15] Gender differences are evident in the CYP system where women have higher activity of some isoenzymes (CYP 2D6) and lower activity of others (CYP 1A2).[10] Women have higher hepatic clearance for substrates of CYP 3A (erythromycin, verapamil) than men, which may be related to lower hepatic P-glycoprotein activity in women.[10]

Other physiologic factors resulting in gender-related pharmacokinetic differences may be related to the fact that women have

- generally lower body weight and organ size,
- higher percentage of body fat,
- lower glomerular filtration rate, and
- different gastric motility.[10]

Gender differences in pharmacodynamics are more difficult to determine, are more complex, and may be influenced by various factors simultaneously.[15] Despite these differences, for the majority of investigated drugs in the past few years, no or very minor gender differences have been detected in pharmacokinetics or pharmacodynamics.[15] Gender differences in pharmacokinetics generally seem to be subtle and of questionable clinical relevance.[10] Many of the differences disappear after correction for gender-specific size and weight differences. Therefore, dosing based on body weight or body surface area is likely to minimize the concern about gender differences in drug effects.[15] It is useful to remember that drug metabolism is also affected by such things as cigarette smoking, alcohol consumption, endogenous sex steroids (eg, the menstrual cycle), and other drugs.[131] This underscores the importance of emphasis on an overall healthy lifestyle for women with migraine.

Provider prescribing habits also reflect some gender differences. For example, women as a group are more likely than men to receive prescriptions for psychotropic drugs such as anxiolytics and antidepressants. Antidepressant use in women was positively predicted by the diagnosis of musculoskeletal conditions.[132] In addition, women are frequently prescribed antidepressants for unexplained symptoms such as headache.[133] Biologic, social, and behavioral factors may influence doctors to prescribe different types of medications to men and women.[134] Interestingly, in one study using case vignettes, the gender of the prescribing physician, and not patient gender or race, affected the prescription of pain medications, suggesting that male and female physicians may react differently to gender or racial cues.[135]

There may also be gender differences in adverse effects of medications. Women have traditionally been underrepresented in dose ranging studies and are more likely than men to use other medications such as OC and HRT, which may affect adverse events.[129] Women may be at higher risk of side effects with some antihypertensives and drugs with potential for causing cardiac arrhythmias (such as the TCAs).[129] Dosing of these classes of medications may therefore need to be adjusted to reduce potential adverse events in women. Adverse drug reactions, particularly cutaneous responses, are more likely in women than in men, possibly because of a higher incidence of immunologic diseases in women.[136] Drug reactions may also occur more often in women because they use more medications than men, including hormonal preparations, and over-the-counter products and supplements.[136] The higher use of medications in general may reflect women's more frequent access to providers and differential prescribing by practitioners.

REFERENCES

1. Dowson AJ. Assessing the impact of migraine. Curr Med Res Opin 2001;17:298–309.

2. Ramadan NM, Silberstein SD, Freitag FG, et al. Evidenced-based guidelines for migraine headache in the primary care setting: pharmacological management for prevention of migraine. Available at: http//www.aan.com/public/practiceguidelines/05.pdf (accessed June 28, 2001).

3. Silberstein S. Practice parameter: evidence-based guidelines for migraine headache (an evidence-based review): report of the Quality Standards Subcommittee of the American Academy of Neurology. Neurology 2000;55:754–62.

4. Snow V, Weiss K, Wall EM, Mottur-Pilson C. Pharmacologic management of acute attacks of migraine and prevention of migraine headache. Ann Intern Med 2002;137:840–9.

5. Ramadan N, Schultz L, Gilkey S. Migraine prophylactic drugs: proof of efficacy, utilization, and cost. Cephalalgia 1997;17:73–80.

6. Solomon GD. Pharmacology and use of headache medications. Cleve Clin J Med 1990;57:627–35.

7. Andersson KE, Vinge E. Beta-adrenoceptor blockers and calcium antagonists in the prophylaxis and treatment of migraine. Drugs 1990;39:355–73.

8. Limmroth V, Michel MC. The prevention of migraine: a critical review with special emphasis on beta-adrenoceptor blockers. Br J Clin Pharmacol 2001;52:237–43.

9. Silberstein SD, Goadsby PJ. Migraine: preventive treatment. Cephalalgia 2002;22:491–512.

10. Meibohm B, Beierle I, Derendorf H. How important are gender differences in pharmacokinetics? Clin Pharmacokinet 2002;41:329–42.

11. Peroutka SJ. The pharmacology of calcium channel antagonists: a novel class of anti-migraine agents? Headache 1983;23:278–83.

12. Peroutka SJ. Antimigraine drug interactions with serotonin receptor subtypes in human brain. Ann Neurol 1988;23:500–4.

13. Markley HG, Cheronis JC, Piepho RW. Verapamil in prophylactic therapy of migraine. Neurology 1984;34:973–6.

14. Solomon GD, Steel JG, Spaccavento LJ. Verapamil prophylaxis of migraine: a double-blind, placebo-controlled study. JAMA 1983;250:2500–2.

15. Beierle I, Meibohm B, Derendorf H. Gender differences in pharmacokinetics and pharmacodynamics. Int J Clin Pharmacol Ther 1999;37:529–47.

16. Dandapani BK, Hanson MR. Amlodipine for migraine prophylaxis. Headache 1998;38:624–6.

17. McArthur JC, Marek K, Pestronk A, et al. Nifedipine in the prophylaxis of classic migraine: a crossover, double-masked, placebo-controlled study of headache frequency and side effects. Neurology 1989;39:284–6.

18. Shukla R, Garg RK, Nag D, Ahuja RC. Nifedipine in migraine and tension headache: a randomised double blind crossover study. J Assoc Physicians India 1995; 43:770–2.

19. Amery WK, Caers LI, Aerts TJ. Flunarizine, a calcium entry blocker in migraine prophylaxis. Headache 1985;25:249–54.

20. Leandri M, Rigardo S, Schizzi R, Parodi CI. Migraine treatment with nicardipine. Cephalalgia 1990;10:111–6.

21. Romeu Bes J. Nicardipine in the prevention of migraine headaches. Clin Ther 1992;14:672–7.

22. Gelmers HJ. Nimodipine, a new calcium antagonist, in the prophylactic treatment of migraine. Headache 1983;23:106–9.

23. Havanka-Kanniainen H, Hokkanen E, Myllyla VV. Efficacy of nimodipine in the prophylaxis of migraine. Cephalalgia 1985;5:39–43.

24. Kallanranta T, Hakkarainen H, Hokkanen E, Tuovinen T. Clonidine in migraine prophylaxis. Headache 1977;17:169–72.

25. Bredfeldt RC, Sutherland JE, Kruse JE. Efficacy of transdermal clonidine for headache prophylaxis and reduction of narcotic use in migraine patients. A randomized crossover trial. J Fam Pract 1989;29:153–6; discussion 157–8.

26. Schrader H, Stovner LJ, Helde G, et al. Prophylactic treatment of migraine with angiotensin converting enzyme inhibitor (lisinopril): randomised, placebo controlled, crossover study. BMJ 2001;322:19–22.

27. Tronvik E, Stovner LJ, Helde G, et al. Prophylactic treatment of migraine with an angiotensin II receptor blocker: a randomized controlled trial. JAMA 2003;289:65–9.

28. Silberstein SD. Preventive treatment of migraine: an overview. Cephalalgia 1997;17:67–72.

29. Ziegler DK, Hurwitz A, Hassanein RS, et al. Migraine prophylaxis. A comparison of propranolol and amitriptyline. Arch Neurol 1987;44:486–9.

30. Gomersall JD, Stuart A. Amitriptyline in migraine prophylaxis. Changes in pattern of attacks during a controlled clinical trial. J Neurol Neurosurg Psychiatry 1973; 36:684–90.

31. Tomkins GE, Jackson JL, O'Malley PG, et al. Treatment of chronic headache with antidepressants: a meta-analysis. Am J Med 2001;111:54–63.

32. Peroutka SJ. The pharmacology of current anti-migraine drugs. Headache 1990;30:5–11; discussion 24–28.

33. Couch JR, Ziegler DK, Hassanein R. Amitriptyline in the prophylaxis of migraine. Effectiveness and relationship of antimigraine and antidepressant effects. Neurology 1976;26:121–7.

34. Couch JR, Hassanein RS. Migraine and depression: effect of amitriptyline prophylaxis. Trans Am Neurol Assoc 1976;101:234–7.

35. Anthony M, Lance JW. Monoamine oxidase inhibition in the treatment of migraine. Arch Neurol 1969;21:263–8.

36. Adly C, Straumanis J, Chesson A. Fluoxetine prophylaxis of migraine. Headache 1992;32:101–4.

37. d'Amato CC, Pizza V, Marmolo T, et al. Fluoxetine for migraine prophylaxis: a double-blind trial. Headache 1999;39:716–9.

38. Oguzhanoglu A, Sahiner T, Kurt T, Akalin O. Use of amitriptyline and fluoxetine in prophylaxis of migraine and tension-type headaches. Cephalalgia 1999;19:531–2.

39. Saper JR, Silberstein SD, Lake AE III, Winters ME. Fluoxetine and migraine: comparison of double-blind trials. Headache 1995;35:233.

40. Saper JR, Silberstein SD, Lake AE III, Winters ME. Double-blind trial of fluoxetine: chronic daily headache and migraine. Headache 1994;34:497–502.

41. Steiner TJ, Ahmed F, Findley LJ, et al. S-fluoxetine in the prophylaxis of migraine: a phase II double-blind randomized placebo-controlled study. Cephalalgia 1998;18:283–6.

42. Bank J. A comparative study of amitriptyline and fluvoxamine in migraine prophylaxis. Headache 1994;34: 476–8.

43. Adelman LC, Adelman JU, Von Seggern R, Mannix LK. Venlafaxine extended release (XR) for the prophylaxis of migraine and tension-type headache: a retrospective study in a clinical setting. Headache 2000;40:572–80.

44. Saper JR, Lake AE, Tepper SJ. Nefazodone for chronic daily headache prophylaxis: an open-label study. Headache 2001;41:465–74.

45. Brannon GE, Rolland PD, Gary JM. Use of mirtazapine as prophylactic treatment for migraine headache. Psychosomatics 2000;41:153–4.

46. Goodman JF. Treatment of headache with bupropion. Headache 1997;37:256.

47. Pinsker W. Potentially safe and effective new treatment for migraine? Headache 1993;33:163.

48. Silberstein SD, Peres MF, Hopkins MM, et al. Olanzapine in the treatment of refractory migraine and chronic daily headache. Headache 2002;42:515–8.

49. Mathew NT, Saper JR, Silberstein SD, et al. Migraine prophylaxis with divalproex. Arch Neurol 1995;52:281–6.

50. Klapper J. Divalproex sodium in migraine prophylaxis: a dose-controlled study. Cephalalgia 1997;17:103–8.

51. Freitag FG, Collins SD, Carlson HA, et al. A randomized trial of divalproex sodium extended-release tablets in migraine prophylaxis. Neurology 2002;58:1652–9.

52. Silberstein SD, Wilmore LJ. Divalproex sodium: migraine treatment and monitoring. Headache 1996;36:239–42.

53. Cutrer FM, Limmroth V, Moskowitz MA. Possible mechanisms of valproate in migraine prophylaxis. Cephalalgia 1997;17:93–100.

54. Rothrock JF. Clinical studies of valproate for migraine prophylaxis. Cephalalgia 1997;17:81–3.

55. Morrell MJ, Flynn KL, Seale CG, et al. Reproductive dysfunction in women with epilepsy: antiepileptic drug effects on sex-steroid hormones. CNS Spectrums 2001;6:771–86.

56. Silberstein SD. Divalproex sodium in headache: literature review and clinical guidelines. Headache 1996;36:547–55.

57. Schulman EA, Silberstein SD. Symptomatic and prophylactic treatment of migraine and tension-type headache. Neurology 1992;42:16–21.

58. Mathew NT, Rapoport A, Saper J, et al. Efficacy of gabapentin in migraine prophylaxis. Headache 2001;41:119–28.

59. Storey JR, Calder CS, Hart DE, Potter DL. Topiramate in migraine prevention: a double-blind, placebo-controlled study. Headache 2001;41:968–75.

60. Young WB, Hopkins MM, Shechter AL, Silberstein SD. Topiramate: a case series study in migraine prophylaxis. Cephalalgia 2002;22:659–63.

61. Mathew NT. Antiepileptic drugs in migraine prevention. Headache 2001;41 Suppl 1:S18–24.

62. Wheeler SD, Carrazana EJ. Topiramate-treated cluster headache. Neurology 1999;53:234–6.

63. Forderreuther S, Mayer M, Straube A. Treatment of cluster headache with topiramate: effects and side-effects in five patients. Cephalalgia 2002;22:186–9.

64. Mathew NT, Kailasam J, Meadors L. Prophylaxis of migraine, transformed migraine, and cluster headache with topiramate. Headache 2002;42:796–803.

65. D'Andrea G, Granella F, Cadaldini M, Manzoni GC. Effectiveness of lamotrigine in the prophylaxis of migraine with aura: an open pilot study. Cephalalgia 1999;19:64–6.

66. Lampl C, Buzath A, Klinger D, Neumann K. Lamotrigine in the prophylactic treatment of migraine aura – a pilot study. Cephalalgia 1999;19:58–63.

67. Steiner TJ, Findley LJ, Yuen AW. Lamotrigine versus placebo in the prophylaxis of migraine with and without aura. Cephalalgia 1997;17:109–12.

68. Krymchantowski AV, Bigal ME, Moreira PF. New and emerging prophylactic agents for migraine. CNS Drugs 2002;16:611–34.

69. Silberstein SD. Methysergide. Cephalalgia 1998;18:421–35.

70. Dodick DW, Capobianco DJ. Treatment and management of cluster headache. Curr Pain Headache Rep 2001;5:83–91.

71. Mylecharane EJ. 5-HT2 receptor antagonists and migraine therapy. J Neurol 1991;238 Suppl 1:S45–52.

72. Buring JE, Peto R, Hennekens CH. Low-dose aspirin for migraine prophylaxis. JAMA 1990;264:1711–3.

73. Peto R, Gray R, Collins R, et al. Randomised trial of prophylactic daily aspirin in British male doctors. BMJ 1988;296:313–6.

74. Bensenor IM, Cook NR, Lee IM, et al. Low-dose aspirin for migraine prophylaxis in women. Cephalalgia 2001;21:175–83.

75. Bellavance AJ, Meloche JP. A comparative study of naproxen sodium, pizotyline and placebo in migraine prophylaxis. Headache 1990;30:710–5.

76. Lindegaard KF, Ovrelid L, Sjaastad O. Naproxen in the prevention of migraine attacks. A double-blind placebo-controlled cross-over study. Headache 1980;20:96–8.

77. Welch KM, Ellis DJ, Keenan PA. Successful migraine prophylaxis with naproxen sodium. Neurology 1985;35:1304–10.

78. Ziegler DK, Ellis DJ. Naproxen in prophylaxis of migraine. Arch Neurol 1985;42:582–4.

79. Stensrud P, Sjaastad O. Clinical trial of a new anti-bradykinin, anti-inflammatory drug, ketoprofen (19.583 r.p.) in migraine prophylaxis. Headache 1974;14:96–100.

80. Johnson RH, Hornabrook RW, Lambie DG. Comparison of mefenamic acid and propranolol with placebo in migraine prophylaxis. Acta Neurol Scand 1986;73:490–2.

81. Solomon GD, Kunkel RS. Flurbiprofen in the prophylaxis of migraine. Cleve Clin J Med 1993;60:43–8.

82. Mannix LK, Von Seggern RL, Adelman, JU. Rofecoxib for prevention of menstrual migraine: an open-label trial. Neurology 2003;60 Suppl 1:A405–6.

83. Fogelholm R, Murros K. Tizanidine in chronic tension-type headache: a placebo controlled double-blind cross-over study. Headache 1992;32:509–13.

84. Saper JR, Winner PK, Lake AE III. An open-label dose-titration study of the efficacy and tolerability of tizanidine hydrochloride tablets in the prophylaxis of chronic daily headache. Headache 2001;41:357–68.

85. Saper JR, Lake AE III, Cantrell DT, et al. Chronic daily headache prophylaxis with tizanidine: a double-blind, placebo-controlled, multicenter outcome study. Headache 2002;42:470–82.

86. Hering-Hanit R. Baclofen for prevention of migraine. Cephalalgia 1999;19:589–91.

87. Hering-Hanit R, Gadoth N. The use of baclofen in cluster headache. Curr Pain Headache Rep 2001;5:79–82.

88. Peikert A, Wilimzig C, Kohne-Volland R. Prophylaxis of migraine with oral magnesium: results from a prospective, multi-center, placebo-controlled and double-blind randomized study. Cephalalgia 1996;16:257–63.

89. Ramadan NM, Halvorson H, Vande-Linde A, et al. Low brain magnesium in migraine. Headache 1989;29:416–9.

90. Welch KM, D'Andrea G, Tepley N, et al. The concept of migraine as a state of central neuronal hyperexcitability. Neurol Clin 1990;8:817–28.

91. Pfaffenrath V, Wessely P, Meyer C, et al. Magnesium in the prophylaxis of migraine—a double-blind placebo-controlled study. Cephalalgia 1996;16:436–40.

92. Facchinetti F, Sances G, Borella P, et al. Magnesium prophylaxis of menstrual migraine: effects on intracellular magnesium. Headache 1991;31:298–301.

93. Schoenen J, Lenaerts M, Bastings E. High-dose riboflavin as a prophylactic treatment of migraine: results of an open pilot study. Cephalalgia 1994;14:328–9.

94. Schoenen J, Jacquy J, Lenaerts M. Effectiveness of high-dose riboflavin in migraine prophylaxis. A randomized controlled trial. Neurology 1998;50:466–70.

95. Vogler BK, Pittler MH, Ernst E. Feverfew as a preventive treatment for migraine: a systematic review. Cephalalgia 1998;18:704–8.

96. Ernst E, Pittler MH. The efficacy and safety of feverfew (*Tanacetum parthenium* L.): an update of a systematic review. Public Health Nutr 2000;3:509–14.

97. Pittler MH, Vogler BK, Ernst E. Feverfew for preventing migraine. Cochrane Database Syst Rev 2000:CD002286.

98. Murphy JJ, Heptinstall S, Mitchell JR. Randomised double-blind placebo-controlled trial of feverfew in migraine prevention. Lancet 1988;2:189–92.

99. Johnson ES, Kadam NP, Hylands DM, Hylands PJ. Efficacy of feverfew as prophylactic treatment of migraine. BMJ 1985;291:569–73.

100. Pfaffenrath V, Diener HC, Fischer M, et al. The efficacy and safety of *Tanacetum parthenium* (feverfew) in migraine prophylaxis – a double-blind, multicentre, randomized placebo-controlled dose-response study. Cephalalgia 2002;22:523–32.

101. Miller LG. Herbal medicinals: selected clinical considerations focusing on known or potential drug-herb interactions. Arch Intern Med 1998;158:2200–11.

102. Binder WJ, Brin MF, Blitzer A, et al. Botulinum toxin type A (BOTOX) for treatment of migraine headaches: an open-label study. Otolaryngol Head Neck Surg 2000;123:669–76.

103. Silberstein S, Mathew N, Saper J, Jenkins S. Botulinum toxin type A as a migraine preventive treatment. For the BOTOX Migraine Clinical Research Group. Headache 2000;40:445–50.

104. Loewinger LE, Young WB. Headache preventives: effect on weight. Neurology 2002;58 Suppl 3:A286.

105. Pijl H, Meinders AE. Bodyweight change as an adverse effect of drug treatment. Mechanisms and management. Drug Saf 1996;14:329–42.

106. Kryst S, Scherl E. A population-based survey of the social and personal impact of headache. Headache 1994; 34:344–50.

107. Vallerand AH, Polomano RC. The relationship of gender to pain. Pain Manag Nurs 2000;1:8–15.

108. Rothrock JF, Mendizabal JE. An analysis of the "carry-over effect" following successful short-term treatment of transformed migraine with divalproex sodium. Headache 2000;40:17–9.

109. Blier P, Bergeron R. The safety of concomitant use of sumatriptan and antidepressant treatments. J Clin Psychopharmacol 1995;15:106–9.

110. Mathew NT, Tietjen GE, Lucker C. Serotonin syndrome complicating migraine pharmacotherapy. Cephalalgia 1996;16:323–7.

111. Silberstein S, Merriam G. Sex hormones and headaches. J Pain Symptom Manage 1993;8:98–114.

112. Ryan RE. A controlled study of the effect of oral contraceptives on migraine. Headache 1978;17:250–1.

113. Mannix LK, Calhoun AH. Menstrual migraine: designing a treatment strategy. Female Patient 2001;26:46–51.

114. Lidegaard O. Oral contraception and risk of cerebral thromboembolic attack: results of a case-control study. BMJ 1993;306:956–63.

115. Petitti D, Sidney S, Bernstein A, et al. Stroke in users of low-dose oral contraceptives. N Engl J Med 1996;335:8–15.

116. Ischaemic stroke and combined oral contraceptives: results of an international, multicentre, case-control study. WHO Collaborative Study of Cardiovascular Disease and Steroid Hormone Contraception. Lancet 1996;348:498–505.

117. Lidegaard O. Oral contraceptives, pregnancy, and the risk of cerebral thromboembolism: the influence of diabetes, hypertension, migraine, and previous thrombotic disease. Br J Obstet Gynaecol 1995;102:153–9.

118. Chang CL, Donaghy M, Poulter N. Migraine and stroke in young women: case-control study. The World Health Organisation Collaborative Study of Cardiovascular Disease and Steroid Hormone Contraception. BMJ 1999;318:13–8.

119. Tzourio C, Tehindrazanarivelo A, Iglesias S, et al. Case-control study of migraine and risk of ischaemic stroke in young women. BMJ 1995;310:830–3.

120. Bousser MG, Conard J, Kittner S, et al. Recommendations on the risk of ischaemic stroke associated with use of combined oral contraceptives and hormone replacement therapy in women with migraine. The International Headache Society Task Force on Combined Oral Contraceptives and Hormone Replacement Therapy. Cephalalgia 2000;20:155–6.

121. Schwartz JB. Gender-specific therapy: medication-related concerns and issues regarding HRT in women. J Gend Specif Med 2000;3:27–30.

122. Krauss GL, Brandt J, Campbell M, et al. Antiepileptic medication and oral contraceptive interactions: a national survey of neurologists and obstetricians. Neurology 1996;46:1534–9.

123. Rosenfeld WE, Doose DR, Walker SA, Nayak RK. Effect of topiramate on the pharmacokinetics of an oral contraceptive containing norethindrone and ethinyl estradiol in patients with epilepsy. Epilepsia 1997;38:317–23.

124. Doose D, Jacobs D, Squires L, et al. Oral contraceptive-AED interactions: no effect of topiramate as monotherapy at clinically effective doses of 200 mg or less. Epilepsia 2002;43:205.

125. El-Sayed YY. Obstetric and gynecologic care of women with epilepsy. Epilepsia 1998;39 Suppl 8:S17–25.

126. Farhat G, Yamout B, Mikati MA, et al. Effect of antiepileptic drugs on bone density in ambulatory patients. Neurology 2002;58:1348–53.

127. Lipton RB, Stewart WF, Diamond S, et al. Prevalence and burden of migraine in the United States: data from the American Migraine Study II. Headache 2001;41:646–57.

128. Evidence report: drug treatments for the prevention of migraine. 1998. Available at: http://clinpol.mc.duke.edu/Pubs/Publications/Drug_Manuscript.pdf (accessed October 24, 2002).

129. Cohen JS. Do standard doses of frequently prescribed drugs cause preventable adverse effects in women? J Am Med Wom Assoc 2002;57:105–10; 114.

130. Berg MJ. Drugs, vitamins, and gender. J Gend Specif Med 1998;1:10–1.

131. Tanaka E. Gender-related differences in pharmacokinetics and their clinical significance. J Clin Pharm Ther 1999;24:339–46.

132. Simoni-Wastila L. Gender and psychotropic drug use. Med Care 1998;36:88–94.

133. O'Malley PG, Jackson JL, Santoro J, et al. Antidepressant therapy for unexplained symptoms and symptom syndromes. J Fam Pract 1999;48:980–90.

134. Sayer GP, Britt H. Sex differences in prescribed medications: another case of discrimination in general practice. Soc Sci Med 1997;45:1581–7.

135. Weisse CS, Sorum PC, Sanders KN, Syat BL. Do gender and race affect decisions about pain management? J Gen Intern Med 2001;16:211–7.

136. Rademaker M. Do women have more adverse drug reactions? Am J Clin Dermatol 2001;2:349–51.

CHAPTER 8

Other Approaches to Migraine Management

Kathleen Farmer, PsyD, and Roger Cady, MD

> ## CASE
>
> SK is a 38-year-old woman with predictable migraine attacks that usually occur 3 days before her menstrual period begins. For these, she takes a triptan and is generally able to function. However, she also experiences less predictable headache attacks at other times of the month, sometimes during business trips or important social events. These headaches often catch her unprepared, either without medication or in a situation where she is unable to treat the headache immediately. In those cases, her medication is sometimes ineffective and she is forced to bed, unable to do what she has planned. During her last pregnancy, SK was advised to avoid medication of any kind to treat her headaches. She felt helpless and discouraged by her inability to control the pain associated with her severe attacks of migraine.
>
> SK is typical of most migraine patients; even those who respond well to medications will inevitably experience headaches for which those treatments are unavailable, contraindicated, or ineffective. Non-pharmacologic methods of headache management will therefore be valuable for essentially every patient with migraine. Non-pharmacologic methods of headache management include the use of self-management techniques such as biofeedback and cognitive techniques. This chapter will review these as well as other complementary headache treatments such as acupuncture, physical therapy, and herbal and vitamin supplementation. Large segments of the population are interested in or prefer complementary rather than traditional medical methods, and physicians need to understand and value this as evidence of a desire to become responsible and accountable.[1] In this changing atmosphere, the physician becomes a consultant and a monitor of treatment progress and an expert on the pharmacologic treatment of disorders. The physician must also recognize that self-management techniques are useful adjuncts to medical interventions.

KEY CHAPTER POINTS

- Self-management strategies and techniques give patients a sense of control over headache and reduce disability. A headache diary and identification and manipulation of risk and protective factors are two important components of an effective self-management strategy for headache.
- Biofeedback-assisted relaxation and cognitive-behavioral methods are specific headache treatments that are especially useful when reliance on medication is undesirable.
- Herbs, vitamins, mineral supplements, and other physical treatments are of great interest to many headache patients. The evidence base for these approaches varies greatly in quality, but few are likely to be harmful. Several strategies can be recommended to patients.

SELF-MANAGEMENT STRATEGIES AND TECHNIQUES IN HEADACHE MANAGEMENT

The Case for Self-Management Techniques

The primary headache disorders are conditions of long duration, in which treatment of individual attacks generally occurs without direct medical supervision. Reliance on healthcare professionals for advice about how to manage every attack is neither practical nor possible. Patients who have developed a repertoire of self-management strategies are better equipped to deal effectively with attacks that do not respond to treatment or those in which medication use is not possible. The belief that migraine is manageable and the certainty that if one approach fails, another will be effective in resolving the pain, are important goals of self-management strategies.

Self-management involves two components. The first is development of a treatment strategy for the acute attack, ideally a collaborative plan designed by both the physician and the patient; this may or may not involve the use of medication. The second part involves patient efforts to regulate the migraine threshold. This threshold can be thought of as the balance between demands on the central nervous system and the physiologic resources available to meet these demands. If demands outweigh available resources, a migraine is likely to result. If the external demands and stresses are identified, usually through keeping a headache diary, protective behaviors can be used to reduce or control them; in this way, some headache attacks may be prevented. With practice, most migraineurs can learn to identify and modulate bodily processes involved in migraine and reduce the reaction of the nervous system to painful stimuli. Successful use of self-management strategies decreases the anxiety that many patients experience as a result of wondering when the next attack will occur and allows patients to gain confidence about their ability to cope with and control headaches. Over a lifetime, this can substantially reduce the disability associated with headache.

All patients with recurrent headache benefit from self-management techniques, but they are especially important for patients who need or want to minimize reliance on medication. These groups include children, patients with two or more headaches a week, and women who are pregnant, lactating, or attempting pregnancy. Still other patients have medical contraindications to, or an inability to tolerate, migraine-specific medications.[2]

Self-management involves a number of strategies. These include learning about migraine and what it means to be a migraineur; techniques such as biofeedback and cognitive approaches (discussed separately in the next section); and keeping a diary to aid in identification of headache patterns, treatment response, and recognition of risk factors for headache.

Education

Beliefs about migraine are often based as much on bias or myth as on fact.[3] Women who have struggled for years with disabling headaches may be convinced that headache reflects a defect in character, a psychiatric problem, or a serious underlying medical condition.

Learning About Migraine

It is helpful to discuss migraine as a genetically-based biochemical disorder for which the patient is not to blame. A migraineur is born with a highly sensitive nervous system that predisposes her to develop migraine attacks in response to internal or external environmental stimuli.[4–7] In infancy, there may be colic; in childhood, there may be episodes of vomiting, dizziness, or abdominal pain. Eventually, car and motion sickness may develop.[8] Patients are reassured to learn that there is much they can do to help control attacks of headache, even if they cannot be entirely eliminated. A treatment agreement (Appendix 8-A), to establish mutual treatment expectations and guidelines, is especially useful for patients with chronic or complex headache problems.

Many patients benefit from a view of migraine as a neurologic process that is often predictable, culminating when uninterrupted in a severe headache with accompaniments of nausea, vomiting, photophobia, phonophobia, and cognitive impairment. Many women can trace progression through the typical phases of an attack (prodrome, aura, headache, resolution, and postdrome); recognition that headache is only the third of five segments encourages attention to methods of terminating the process before it results in headache and progressive disability.

How can patients recognize that a migraine is on the way? Common symptoms that indicate the "unbalanced" nervous system of prodrome include irritability, yawning, restlessness, lethargy, mood swings, slow thinking, and food cravings. After identifying her own typical premonitory symptoms, a woman can plan to intervene early in the headache process, perhaps with activities such as biofeedback, relaxation, deep breathing, a bubble bath, yoga, or a walk or jog in the woods. These diversionary tactics are frequently, although not always, successful in aborting a migraine attack, and knowledge that this is possible improves the sense of control. If the attack progresses despite early intervention, medication use, ideally at a mild stage of pain, is appropriate.

Diary

A headache diary (Appendix 8-B) may identify habits that stimulate an already sensitive nervous system or otherwise lower the threshold for a headache attack. Caffeine, for example, in coffee, soft drinks, chocolate, and tea, intensifies the reactivity of the nervous system. Used sparingly in small amounts, it is useful in treating headache, but when used regularly, caffeine withdrawal (not caffeine itself) can precipitate headache. Nicotine may have the same effect in some people. Alcohol is a vasodilator that can trigger headache attacks in susceptible patients. Reasonable recommendations for patients with frequent headache include limiting daily caffeine intake to two 6 to 8 oz servings before 3 pm; limiting alcohol to two drinks per day (or none in patients for whom it is a potent headache trigger); and smoking cessation.

The diary may identify other factors associated with headache, such as changes in barometric pressure, hormonal fluctuations, or periods of emotional "letdown" that are characteristic of migraine. Other individual, idiosyncratic risk factors for headache may be identified by the diary as well. Diaries also serve as an objective record of migraine frequency and medication response, especially important for making treatment decisions.

Serotonin levels in the brain decrease during migraine, suggesting that "serotonin-enhancing" activities might be useful protective strategies for migraineurs.[9] Such activities might include 20 or so minutes of strenuous physical exercise, a massage, affection or sexual activity, or the use of biofeedback or relaxation techniques.[10] Migraineurs also benefit from stability and routine, such as regular meals, avoiding missed meals, and consistent sleep and wake times, even on weekends or during vacation.

There are positive aspects to having such a highly sensitive nervous system. Migraineurs are often conscientious, vigilant to surroundings, and achievement-oriented, with a strong desire to please and a belief that hard work will pay off.[11] The list of highly successful migraineurs is lengthy, and includes writers such as Joan Didion and Lewis Carroll, statesmen such as Thomas Jefferson, scientists such as Charles Darwin, and even athletes such as Kareem Abdul Jabar.

BIOFEEDBACK-ASSISTED RELAXATION TECHNIQUES FOR HEADACHE CONTROL

Biofeedback is a process that increases voluntary control of physiologic functions that are ordinarily involuntary. Modification of these processes can alter susceptibility to headache through a variety of mechanisms.[12] Finger temperature, for example, is a good proxy measure of vigilance and stress. The average finger temperature is 85°F, but decreases as levels of emotional or physical stress increase. Chronically low finger temperature (below 80°F) may reflect persistent activation of the sympathetic nervous system and difficulty attaining a state of complete relaxation. Biofeedback trains the nervous system to minimize or shut out stressful external stimuli and directs attention instead to returning the body to homeostasis, often through the use of calming, relaxing music or visualization techniques. As this occurs, the finger temperature rises. Other forms of biofeedback use the electromyogram (EMG) for muscular tension or the electroencephalogram (EEG) for brain wave readings to gauge relaxation. A description of each type follows.

Generally, there are three types of biofeedback: thermal (temperature), muscular (EMG), and brain wave (EEG). Thermal and EMG biofeedback have evidence of efficacy in headache treatment. A combination of relaxation training and thermal biofeedback produces 33 to 37% improvement in headache activity, and this improvement is maintained over long periods of time.[1] Evidence-based guidelines for the use of biofeedback have been developed, based on a meta-analysis of studies that followed rigorous scientific design. Unfortunately, since the advent of the triptans in the 1990s, little research has been conducted on biofeedback, relaxation, or other nonpharmacologic treatment approaches to disabling headaches. Of the 355 behavioral and physical treatment articles identified over the past 30 years, only 39 studies met the criteria for inclusion in the meta-analysis. Of these, only 18 reported data that allowed comparison across studies using effect-size estimates. The evidence-based treatment guidelines for biofeedback were based on five studies that occurred from 1978 to 1985. The effectiveness of thermal biofeedback plus relaxation training was based on 10 studies that occurred from 1978 to 1991. Despite this dearth of recent empiric studies, the guidelines concluded that relaxation training, thermal biofeedback combined with relaxation training, EMG biofeedback, and cognitive-behavioral therapy have grade A evidence for usefulness, meaning that the quality of evidence was based on multiple well-designed randomized clinical trials, was directly relevant to the recommendation, and yielded a consistent pattern of findings.

Temperature biofeedback (Table 8-1) is by far the most practical for patients who do not desire or cannot access professional training. A simple, inexpensive finger thermometer allows the patient to practice at home whenever time permits. (Finger thermometers can be

Table 8-1 Sample Instructions for Temperature Biofeedback

Twice a day, for 10 minutes or longer, do the following:

- Tape a finger thermometer on the index finger.
- Measure finger temperature during a period of relaxation.
- Breathe slowly, deeply, from the abdomen.
- Focus on an idea or symbol, such as a star, a color, or a pleasant scene, as a way to clear other thoughts from the mind.
- Listen to an audiotape to relax body and mind (Appendix 8-C).

The goal of this treatment is to learn to warm your finger temperature to 96°F. This helps you to gain control over the cardiovascular effects of stress and tension. When practiced regularly, this may interrupt some of the early stages of headache that can be triggered by stress or tension. You can obtain an inexpensive temperature biofeedback audiotape with finger thermometer from Primary Care Network (through their Web site at http://www.primarycarenet.org or by calling 1-800-769-7565).

ordered from Echo, Inc through their Web site at http://www.echoinc.to or by phone at 937-322-4972 or 800-834-2463). In contrast, EMG and EEG biofeedback require sophisticated machinery and office visits for training.

EMG biofeedback may be especially effective, however, for patients who identify muscle tension as a frequent precipitant for or accompaniment to migraine attacks. Patients with tension-type, cervicogenic, and other headaches benefit as well. EMG biofeedback has been demonstrated to produce a 40% improvement in the headache severity index.

EEG biofeedback is employed infrequently for headache sufferers and is usually reserved for those with chronic headaches refractory to other types of interventions. No research on this biofeedback method met criteria for inclusion in the evidence-based guidelines cited earlier. Called "theta training," EEG biofeedback trains individuals to move from the beta brain wave characteristic in states of focused attention to the alpha frequency and finally into theta frequencies characteristic of relaxation. This is theorized to calm the nervous system with a subsequent beneficial effect on disabling headaches.[13]

Locating a biofeedback practitioner can be a challenge. The Association for Applied Psychophysiology and Biofeedback (AAPB; accessible at http://www.aapb.org) is the professional organization for those certified to conduct biofeedback training and can provide information; however, many psychologists practice biofeedback therapy without being certified or belonging to this organization. A list of practitioners can also be found at the Web site of the Biofeedback Certification Institute of America (BCIA; accessible at http://www.bcia.org/directory/membership.cfm).

COGNITIVE-BEHAVIORAL TECHNIQUES FOR HEADACHE CONTROL

Coping Skills

Many migraineurs, especially women, are exquisitely sensitive to the feelings and emotional needs of those around them; often, they feel responsible for another's distress or apathy. Cognitive techniques can help the female migraineur avoid putting the needs of others first and her own last. The coping skills that headache sufferers generally find most useful include cognitive restructuring, assertiveness training, and identifying goals.

Cognitive Restructuring

Negative self-talk is an automatic, private conversation that goes on inside a person's mind in response to an outside event. Often, these negative evaluations occur automatically, without a great deal of conscious thought or consideration. These thoughts may include cognitions such as "I can't do anything right"; "I am bad, fat,

stupid, ugly, not good"; "There is something wrong with me"; "When anything goes wrong, it's my fault." Under guidance from a psychologist or counselor, the individual identifies negative self-talk and rehearses changing the disparaging remarks to positive affirmations such as "I forgive myself for being imperfect"; "I am good"; "I am me"; "I deserve health and harmony." Replacing automatic negative cognitions often results in remarkable improvements in attitude and the ability to cope with headache and other stressful life events.[13]

Assertiveness Training

At times, replacing negative self-talk with affirmations is resisted by people who feel they are lying or that they do not deserve health or harmony. These people may feel that they do not deserve to have their own opinion or life. In interpersonal situations, they fear that saying "no" to the needs of others will cause rejection or abandonment. Such patients often benefit from formal assertiveness training.[14]

Assertiveness training involves a step-by-step process: 1) identify when a behavior is being asked that you do not want to do, which is usually signaled by feelings of guilt, anxiety, ignorance, or dread; 2) practice saying "no" in unimportant situations, such as in a supermarket; 3) say "no" to those who will be understanding, such as a friend; and 4) say "no" to the person who demands that you do something you do not want to do.

Once assertive behavior is learned, the woman should establish her own goals rather than rely on others to dictate behavior. Goals should be written down and divided into a time frame, such as within 1 week, 1 month, 6 months, 1 year, and 5 years.

OTHER MIGRAINE TREATMENTS

Vitamins, Minerals, Herbs

Riboflavin

A daily dose of 400 mg of riboflavin has been shown in a double-blind, placebo-controlled study to decrease the frequency of migraine. Riboflavin is a cofactor in mitochondrial energy reactions, and it is theorized that riboflavin supplementation may prevent exhaustion of mitochondrial energy stores and lessen the vulnerability of neurons to changes that provoke migraine.[15]

Magnesium

Magnesium (500 to 750 mg/day) has been reported to alleviate symptoms associated with premenstrual syndrome, including headache.[16–18]

Magnesium relaxes smooth muscle and affects the function of N-methyl-D-aspartate receptors in the brain. Eighty-three percent of migraineurs unresponsive to triptan treatment were found to have low levels of serum ionized magnesium. Treatment with intravenous administration of magnesium over a 2-week period returned ionized magnesium to a normal level. Over the next 6 months, while using oral magnesium supplements, two-thirds of migraine attacks were responsive to triptan treatment.[19]

Feverfew

Feverfew is an herb of the Chrysanthemum family and has been used for centuries in Europe to prevent disabling headaches. It is increasingly popular in the United States. Chemically, the active ingredient in feverfew has aspirin-like effects. A systematic review of clinical trials indicated a trend toward efficacy of feverfew over placebo, but the trials included in the review were of varying quality. A recent trial of high quality evaluated three doses of a highly purified extract of *Tanacetum parthenium* and placebo for migraine prevention. No dose-response curve was observed, and no statistical difference was demonstrated between any of the doses and placebo. However, a subset of patients with more frequent headache attacks seemed to benefit, leading the researchers to suggest that further study is needed.[20] In summary, the benefit of feverfew has not been clearly established, but there is little evidence that it is harmful. Because the strength and potency of the herb vary depending on the source and methods of manufacture, patients wishing to try it should be instructed to choose a single brand of feverfew and follow the instructions on the package regarding dosing, typically one capsule three to four times per day for 1 month.[21,22]

Butterbur Extract (Petasites hybridus)

Butterbur extract is another herbal remedy promoted for the treatment of headache. Three studies have investigated its daily use for the prevention of headache and all suggest modest efficacy.[23–25]

The active components of Butterbur extract, petasin and isopetasin, appear to inhibit leukotriene synthesis and thus exert an anti-inflammatory effect. Questions have been raised, however, about possible contamination of this herb with carcinogenic substances, suggesting that caution should be exercised in any recommendations for its use pending higher-quality studies on this aspect of treatment.

Transcutaneous Electrical Nerve Stimulation

Transcutaneous electrical nerve stimulation (TENS) uses a Food and Drug Administration–approved device that stimulates the skin with small electrical pulses. It is theorized that these pulses compete with pain sensations from the muscles for attention by the brain and interfere with brain appreciation of painful signals, thus lessening pain.

A TENS device looks like a beeper and clips onto a belt or pocket. Wires connect the power source with electrodes that are affixed by adhesives to the skin over the painful area. The electrical pulse is adjustable by controls on the device. TENS treatment is safe but requires prescription by a physician. Although in clinical practice it seems effective for patients who have a prominent muscular component to their headache pain, no controlled studies exist.[26]

Transcranial Electrical Stimulation

Transcranial electrical stimulation uses a device that produces special electrical frequencies designed for safe application to the head. There is preliminary evidence that it might be useful for some patients with headaches.[27] It has been suggested that transcranial stimulation enhances the release of neurochemicals such as serotonin from nerve cells.

With this form of treatment, electrodes are placed on the head, usually above the ears. A very small electrical current is applied and adjusted by controls on the device. The control is advanced until the individual feels a slight twinge, then turned down slightly until there is no sensation of electrical current.

Manual Methods

Evidence-based headache guidelines report that few studies exist to support the efficacy of acupuncture in headache treatment; there is no methodologically rigorous research that measured the usefulness of other manual methods. Clinically, however, many patients report muscle pain and tenderness as precipitants or accompaniments of attacks. Pain is especially common in the neck, shoulders, and upper back. Evaluation by a physical therapist may reveal rotation of the spine or pelvis that can be treated through physical therapy, and some patients report improvement in headaches in association with this type of treatment. Poor posture or maladaptive breathing habits that may aggravate headache can be corrected by one or two physical therapy sessions. In general, treatments that require active patient involvement are more likely to foster a sense of control over headache than are passive therapies such as massage or ultrasound.

Acupuncture and Acupressure

In acupuncture, fine metal needles are placed into specific channels (meridians) running through the body. Traditionally, this is believed to manipulate energy called "Chi." Modern studies suggest that acupuncture, when effective, may work through endogenous endorphin systems.[28,29] Often stimulated with mild electricity, the needles are left in place for 20 to 30 minutes, and a series of treatments is usually needed.

Acupressure techniques apply pressure rather than a needle to acupuncture points. Firm pressure applied to selected areas for several minutes is reported by many patients to provide headache relief. The most effective points are 1) between the thumb and index finger, 2) where the septum of the nose joins the forehead, 3) at the tender point between the eye and ear, and 4) above the ear at the hairline on the same side as the headache.

Manipulative Procedures

Manipulative procedures involve movement of joints or muscles in an effort to relieve tension and promote normal joint mechanics. Manipulative techniques sometimes used by headache patients include osteopathic procedures, performed by a doctor of osteopathy; chiropractic techniques, performed by a chiropractor; and muscle manipulation, performed by a physical therapist or a myofascial therapist. Specific techniques include Rolfing, Alexander, and Feldenkrais. The skill of the practitioner appears central to the success of these approaches. No good quality evidence exists that these procedures are useful for the treatment of headache, but most are unlikely to be harmful. An exception are techniques that involve cervical spine manipulation, which appear to be an independent risk factor for stroke. Chiropractic manipulation appears to raise the risk of vertebral artery dissection and stroke or transient ischemic attack approximately sixfold.[30] For many patients with headache, this risk will not be worth the benefits of treatment.

REFERENCES

1. Astin JA. Why patients use alternative medicine: results of a national study. JAMA 1998;279:1548–53.

2. Campbell JK, Penzien DB, Wall EM. Evidence-based guidelines for migraine headaches: behavioral and physical treatments. Neurology 2000;54:1553. Available at: http://www.aan.com (accessed January 2003).

3. Cady R, Farmer K. Headache free. New York (NY): Bantam Books; 1996. p. 1–6.

4. Wang W, Timsit-Bertheir M, Schoenen J. Intensity dependence of auditory evoked potentials is pronounced in migraine: an indication of cortical potentiation and low serotonergic neuro-transmissions. Neurology 1996;46:1404–9.

5. Aurora SK, Ahmad BK, Welch KM, et al. Transcranial magnetic stimulation confirms hyperexcitability of occipital cortex in migraine. Neurology 1998;50:1111–4.

6. Afra J, Masica A, Gerard P, et al. Interictal cortical excitability in migraine: a study using transcranial magnetic stimulation of motor and visual cortices. Ann Neurol 1998;44:209–15.

7. Hargreaves RJ, Shepheard SL. Pathophysiology of migraine—new insights. Can J Neurol Sci 1999;26 Suppl 3:S12–9.

8. Headache Classification Committee of the International Headache Society. Classification and diagnostic criteria for headache disorders, cranial neuralgias, and facial pain. Cephalalgia 1988;8 Suppl 7:1–96.

9. Goadsby PJ, Lipton RB, Ferrari MD. Migraine—current understanding and treatment. N Engl J Med 2002; 346:257–70.

10. Mathew RC, Ho BT, Kralik P, Claghorn JL. Biochemical basis for biofeedback treatment of migraine: a hypothesis. Headache 1979;19:290–3.

11. Primary Care Network. The migraineur's guide to migraine. Springfield (MO): Primary Care Network; 1998. p. 17–8. Available at: http://www.headachecare.com (accessed January 2003).

12. Farmer K. Biofeedback and headache. In: Cady RK, Fox AW, editors. Treating the headache patient. New York (NY): Marcel Dekker; 1995. p. 287–303.

13. Beck AT, Rush AJ, Shaw BF, Emery G. Cognitive therapy of depression. New York (NY): Guilford Press; 1979. p. 142–66.

14. Smith MJ. When I say no, I feel guilty. New York (NY): Bantam Books; 1975.

15. Schoenen J, Jacquy J, Lenaerts M. Effectiveness of high-dose riboflavin in migraine prophylaxis: a randomized controlled trial. Neurology 1998;50:466–70.

16. Peikert A, Wilimzig C, Kohne-Volland R. Prophylaxis of migraine with oral magnesium: results from a prospective, multi-center, placebo-controlled and double-blind randomized study. Cephalalgia 1996;16:257–63.

17. Pfaffenrath V, Wessely P, Meyer C, et al. Magnesium in the prophylaxis of migraine—a double-blind, placebo-controlled study. Cephalalgia 1996;16:436–40.

18. Facchinetti F, Sances G, Borella P, et al. Magnesium prophylaxis of menstrual migraine: effects on intracellular magnesium. Headache 1991;31:298–301.

19. Cady RK, Farmer KU. Effect of magnesium on responsiveness of migraineurs to a 5-HT-1 agonist (sumatriptan). Presentation at American Academy of Neurology Annual Meeting; 1998; Minneapolis (MN).

20. Pfaffenrath V, Diener HC, Fischer M, et al. The efficacy and safety of *Tanacetum parthenium* (feverfew) in migraine prophylaxis—a double blind, multicentre, randomized placebo-controlled dose-response study. Cephalalgia 2002;22:523–32.

21. Johnson ES, Kadam NP, Hylands DM, Hylands PJ. Efficacy of feverfew as prophylactic treatment of migraine. BMJ 1985;291:569–73.

22. Murphy JJ, Heptinstall S, Mitchell JR. Randomized double-blind placebo-controlled trial of feverfew in migraine prevention. Lancet 1998;2:189–92.

23. Gruia F. Zur biologischen Schmerzbekampfung. Erfahrungsheilkunde 1986;35:396–401.

24. Seeger P. Die therapeutischen Qualitarten von Petisites officianalis der Pestwurz. Erfahrungsheilkunde 1983; 32:6–12.

25. Steier L. Petadolex—ein Spasmoanalgeticum und die muscularen Kopfschmerzen. Dtsch Z Biol Zahnmed 1990;6:114–6.

26. Solomon S, Guglielmo KM. Treatment of headache by transcutaneous electrical stimulation. Headache 1985; 25:12–5.

27. Solomon S, Elkind A, Freitag F, et al. Safety and effectiveness of cranial electrotherapy in the treatment of tension headache. Headache 1989;29:445–50.

28. Lenhard L, Waite PM. Acupuncture in the prophylactic treatment of migraine headaches: pilot study. N Z Med J 1983;96:663–6.

29. Vincent CA. A controlled trial of the treatment of migraine by acupuncture. Clin J Pain 1989;5:305–12.

30. Smith WS, Johnston SC, Skalabrin EJ, et al. Spinal manipulative therapy is an independent risk factor for vertebral artery dissection. Neurology 2003;60:1424–8.

APPENDIX 8-A

CONTRACT

This contract is an agreement between _____ and

physician _____ concerning the use of medication.

Medications may perpetuate a headache pattern. If discontinued suddenly, a severe headache, called an "analgesic rebound headache," may result.

Headaches that are maintained by medication cannot resolve until the offending medication is stopped. Often, medicine used to prevent headache will not work if short-acting treatments are being overused. The only solution to this difficult problem is to discontinue the problem medication. Even though this is not easy, it is necessary to stop the daily headache pattern. The remaining headaches are usually intermittent and more treatable.

The following process is recommended to lessen the frequency of the daily headache:

1. Take the medication as prescribed, with the understanding that the daily headache medication will be discontinued in 2 weeks.
2. At the 2-week mark, discontinue all of the daily headache medication.
3. Expect that there may be physical symptoms of discomfort (nausea, muscle twitches) as well as mood changes (irritability and depression).
4. Realize that these symptoms will be worse for a day or two after the medication is discontinued but should then improve.
5. Report symptoms that are especially upsetting.
6. Learn and practice biofeedback at least twice a day, more frequently if the symptoms are bothersome.
7. Keep your appointments with the physician and other medical staff.
8. Daily headache medication can alter neuroreceptors. The regeneration of the cells of neuroreceptors may take up to 3 months. You will begin to feel better and should have fewer headaches in approximately 2 weeks after you stop the daily headache medication.
9. During the next 3 months, eat regularly scheduled meals, maintain a regular sleep schedule, and exercise vigorously for 30 minutes at least five times per week.

Signed_____   Date _____

Witness_____   Date _____

Reproduced with permission from Cady RK, Farmer KU. Self-management of migraine. Center for Medical Education; 2002. Available at: http://www.primarycarenet.org (accessed January 2003).

APPENDIX 8-B

HEADACHE DIARY

Y = Yes; N = No

Date	Medication	Pain Relief	Relief Fast Enough	Mood Changes	Return of Functions	Side Effects	Relief of Functions	Satisfactory Sleep	Feeling in Control

ASSESSMENT: CHANGES TO IMPROVE HEADACHE MANAGEMENT

Medication	Sleep	Stress	Biofeedback	Worries	Events	Other Comments

Reproduced with permission from Farmer K. Biofeedback and headache. In: Cady RK, Fox AW, editors. Treating the headache patient. New York (NY): Marcel Dekker; 1995. p. 287–303.

APPENDIX 8-C

BALANCING THE BODY FOR HEALTH

The following is an example of relaxation through visualization that patients may record in their own voice. The recording can then be played back and the relaxation process practiced on a regular basis.

INTRODUCTION

Migraine sufferers are born with a highly sensitive nervous system. They are attuned to the demands of the environment. Often, they put themselves last. The following process is a way to bolster the nervous system and to begin putting one's health first, before expectations, duties, or responsibilities.

The following process helps the body relax and clears the mind of troubling or repetitive thoughts. During this procedure, you will realize that what you think and how you react are a matter of choice. To reach this level of freedom from daily worries, you will need to practice twice a day, 10 minutes each time. In a week or two, your nervous system will be retrained to respond with calm observation rather than by the fight-

or-flight reaction that our body does automatically when we feel threatened.

RELAXATION PROCESS

Get comfortable. Sit in your favorite chair; prop up your feet. Unfold your arms and legs. Tell yourself you will not fall asleep. This exercise is to reprogram the nervous system, not to help you sleep. But after gaining control over your nervous system, you can use the same process for sleep as well.

Take a deep breath and slowly let it out. And take another deep cleansing breath and slowly let go. Two deep cleansing breaths are a sign to your body that it is time to relax, it is time to let go. It is time to stop all thoughts, worries, problems, and concerns, and go on a journey inward—a journey inward for knowledge and understanding.

Get in tune with your breathing as you breathe in peace, comfort, and relaxation and breathe out all negativity. Collect tension and breathe it out. Collect anger and breathe it out. Collect fear and breathe it out. Collect all negativity and breathe it out. Breathe slowly, as slow as you can breathe. Focus on the movement of oxygen filling your lungs. Your lungs hold onto the oxygen, feeding the cells of the body with pure clear oxygen, and carbon dioxide is being emptied from your lungs.

The rhythm of breathing is slow, very slow. You breathe in to the count of four, hold the breath to the count of four, and exhale to the count of eight. Breathe in, two, three, four; hold the breath, two, three, four; and breathe out, two, three, four, five, six, seven, eight.

As you breathe slowly, you sense your body slowing down, floating, secure, warm, at peace. With each breath, you can feel and sense and see yourself go deeper and deeper into relaxation as you become lighter and lighter. One breath at a time; one breath after the other. With each breath, you feel twice as relaxed as you did the breath before.

Focus on your pulse. Your heart beats the rhythm of your life. Your pulses take up the beat, the unique frequency of your life force. The pulse reverberates through your body and into the atmosphere around your body. Listen to the pulse in your neck. The pulse is slow and regular, echoing the beat of your heart. Pay attention to the pulse in the elbow joint, strong and smooth. Switch to the pulse in your wrist, rhythmic and reflective of the beat of your heart, which sets up the music of your life. Go down to the pulse behind your knee. This pulse is more distant from the heart but is strong and definite just the same. Go on to the pulse in your ankle, beating powerfully as an echo of the heartbeat.

After adjusting your pulses to a slow, calm, regular pace, inventory the muscles of your body. Is there tension anywhere? If so, choose one muscle and redirect the blood supply to that area. Feel that muscle warm, soften, and relax. You can imagine that you are breathing through that muscle. With each breath, the muscle relaxes a little more.

All the self-healing qualities of the body are contained within the blood supply. By redirecting the blood to a muscle that is tight, you are beginning the process of healing from the inside out. Imagine the blood encircling the muscle and bathing the muscle with the healing ingredients of the blood. The healing properties are absorbed into the muscle. The muscle begins to heal from the inside out. The muscle no longer has to hold itself together, waiting in readiness for action. The muscle can relax. Relaxation is as important for healing as readiness is for survival. There is a time for relaxing and there is a time for acting. For now, the healing property of relaxing is the requirement for the muscle so it will be ready to act if necessary.

The breathing is slow and regular; the pulses are strong and smooth; the muscles are relaxed and healthy. The body is at peace and content. But the mind may still be going 100 miles an hour.

We can think of only one thing at a time. Imagine a symbol, a scene, a color, or your favorite place. Picture an eagle or the beach or a soothing blue color or a special swimming hole. By putting one thing in your mind, all other thoughts, worries, problems, and concerns are pushed out. The thoughts may return like the wind that goes through the trees of a forest. But focus once again on the symbol or scene. Eventually, with practice, you will be able to exclude unwanted thoughts and focus on ideas you want to think about.

Affirmations too are a way to calm the mind. Everyday in every way, I'm getting better and better. I am lovable. I am worthwhile. I deserve health and harmony. Putting positive thoughts in the mind pushes out negativity. Some people believe that by imagining the worst, they are prepared to cope with disasters. But in truth, by imagining the worst, your body is in a fearful state of alert that wears down energy, positive attitude, and hope. By focusing on the positive, the body will have the resources to deal with whatever arises. I forgive myself for being imperfect.

The body is relaxed. The mind is positive. Imagine that you are standing underneath a waterfall of golden healing energy. The energy cascades over your head, face, and jaws, swirls around your neck and shoulders, and covers your body from your head to your toes with golden healing energy. This energy goes around, around, and around your body, forming a cocoon, an invisible shield of protection from demands of the environment. This shield protects from all negativity. Negativity bounces off of this shield, and inside, you are light, bright, safe, warm, and secure.

The golden healing energy sinks into your body through the pores of your skin and fills your body from your head to your toes with lightness, brightness, and warmth. The golden healing energy fills every single cell of your body, unleashing the healing potential of each cell. The healing potential from each cell joins to enhance the healing capabilities of the entire body. As the body fills with light, you can sense the balance within the body between the healthy side and the unhealthy side of self. By directing the golden healing energy, the unhealthy side of the self can be pushed from the body, allowing the healthy side to be the guide for the body and mind.

The healthy side balances the unhealthy side, much like a teeter-totter. By practicing this relaxation process twice a day, you stay in touch with your healthy side. When you become too busy to take care of your health, the seesaw moves in favor of the unhealthy side. This process of relaxation allows you to balance body and mind and to recognize when you need more exercise, more water, or more sleep; when you need to pay more attention to yourself or your family. This process is a way to communicate with the healthy side of yourself.

Everyday in every way, I'm getting better and better. Slowly, at your own pace, you may return to your normal level of awareness, feeling refreshed, alert, and calm.

Reproduced with permission from Farmer K. Balancing the system for health [audiotape]. Springfield (MO): Primary Care Network, 1998.

CHAPTER 9

Migraine in Female Children and Adolescents

Dawn A. Marcus, MD, and Elizabeth Loder, MD, FACP

CASE

HM is a 16-year-old girl who began having headaches at age 13 years. Her older brother used to come home from elementary school with sick headaches, but these resolved when he became a teenager. HM's mother was therefore surprised when HM started having headaches after becoming a teenager, about 6 months after the onset of her menstrual periods.

When HM's headache episodes begin, she becomes pale, turns off the television, and retreats to a darkened room. She describes a squeezing, pressure pain on both sides of the head, which usually resolves in about 3 hours. Drinking a cola or going to sleep can help relieve the headache. HM's doctor explained that migraines are typically unilateral, lasting over 4 hours. In addition, although HM's behavior suggests sensitivity to noise and light, she does not report photophobia or phonophobia to the doctor. Therefore, the doctor diagnosed "stress" headaches related to adolescence.

This case illustrates some important features of headache in children and adolescents. The primary headache disorders, especially migraine, occur in children more commonly than is recognized and may be undertreated. Headache diagnosis in the pediatric population can be challenging because of differences in headache presentation between children and adults and because it can be difficult to elicit the historic features necessary to make a specific headache diagnosis. Understandably, parental and medical attention are often focused on excluding ominous causes of headache; identification of potentially treatable "benign" forms of headache is not always emphasized. Early recognition and treatment of children experiencing headache-related disability, however, is important to minimize future functional impairment, maladaptive coping, and medication-use strategies.

KEY CHAPTER POINTS

- **The prevalence of headache in girls is higher than is commonly recognized; the most common disabling primary headache in girls is migraine, which peaks in incidence at the time of menarche.**
- **Childhood periodic syndromes related to migraine are important to recognize.**
- **Historic features and examination help distinguish between recurrent benign headache and ominous causes of headache.**
- **Headache-related disability in children and adolescents can be significant.**
- **Treatments for childhood and adolescent migraine are similar to those for adult migraine.**

PREVALENCE OF PRIMARY HEADACHE IN FEMALE CHILDREN

Primary headache is common in children, although often unrecognized unless children are directly questioned about headache. Many children assume that having headaches is a normal part of life, especially when they have family members who also report headaches. The prevalence of headache increases over the childhood years, peaking between ages 12 to 15 years (Figure 9-1).[1–6] Headache was identified in only 19.5% of 4,405 5-year-old children, with frequent headache occurring in only 3.6%.[3] A large cross-sectional survey of 5,562 older children (mean age 10 years) identified recurrent headache in 49%.[6]

As with adult headaches, there are important gender differences identified in pediatric headaches.

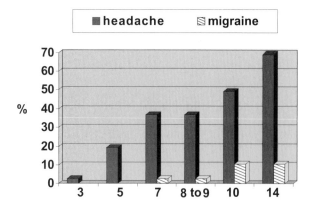

Figure 9-1 Prevalence of headache and migraine during childhood. Data adapted from the following sources: age 3: Zuckerman B et al[2]; age 5: Sillanpää M et al[3]; age 7: Sillanpää M[1]; ages 8 to 9: Metsähonkala L et al[4]; age 10: Özge A et al[6]; age 14: Sillanpää M.[1]

Sillanpää prospectively followed approximately 300 school-age children and questioned them about headache at ages 7 and 14 years.[1] At age 7, boys reported more frequent headache than girls. At age 14, girls were reporting more frequent headache than boys. A larger sample of 4,000 Finnish students confirmed a higher headache prevalence in girls (71%) than in boys (65%).[7]

Frequent headache was identified in 248 (7%) of 3,509 Greek schoolchildren (ages 4 to 15 years).[8] Of these, 219 met the International Headache Society (IHS) diagnostic criteria for migraine. Overall, girls were more likely to have migraine than boys (7% vs 5%; $p < .05$); however, female predominance in age distribution was not evident until age 10 years (Figure 9-2). A population-based survey of 2,165 Scottish schoolchildren similarly identified migraine as the most common type of chronic headache in children, with migraine occurring in 11% of children aged 5 to 15 years and

tension-type headache in only 1%.[9] The peak prevalence of migraine occurred at age 12 years. A similar evaluation of 1,445 adolescent students in Palermo, Italy, identified migraine within the previous year in 28% of boys and 20% of girls.[10]

In early childhood, migraine affects both boys and girls equally, with a prevalence of 4 to 5% for all children between ages 7 and 10 years. Boys begin to experience migraine earlier than girls, with a peak age of onset of headache in boys at 5 years and in girls at 12 years.[11] The onset of migraine in girls is closely linked to menarche, explaining the peak incidence in girls at 12 years. Dalsgaard-Nielsen showed that girls are more likely to begin having migraine during the same year as their menarche than at any other age.[11] Once girls begin to develop migraine, their prevalence is greater than that in boys. After age 11 years, girls are more likely to experience migraine than boys. This increased prevalence of migraine in girls continues through all remaining age ranges. As with HM and her brother, migraine also typically persists for more years in girls than in boys. By age 25 years, migraine will resolve for 33% of men and 15% of women who reported childhood migraine.[12] Therefore, headache begins later in females but persists for longer periods of time than in males.

These studies show that recurring primary headache, especially migraine, is common in children and adolescents. School-age children who are missing school or other activities, or napping during the day, should be questioned about headache. In addition, questions about headache should be a routine part of the pediatric screening for girls at or around the time of menarche.

CHILDHOOD PERIODIC SYNDROMES RELATED TO MIGRAINE

Several recurring, paroxysmal disorders of childhood are believed to be migraine equivalents, including cyclic vomiting or abdominal pain, benign paroxysmal vertigo, benign paroxysmal torticollis, and acute confusional state. Al-Twaijri and Shevell recorded the presence of migraine equivalents in 5,848 pediatric patients, of whom 1,106 were diagnosed with migraine.[13] Abdominal migraine was diagnosed in 20 patients, benign paroxysmal vertigo in 41, benign paroxysmal torticollis in 11, and acute confusional state in 5.

Sillanpää and colleagues noted a relationship between headache frequency and the prevalence of abdominal pain.[3] Risk of stomachache in 5 year olds with headache was almost 9 times greater in children reporting infrequent headache and 14 times greater in children with frequent headache compared with headache-free children. Recurrent abdominal pain shares epidemiologic features with migraine, with increasing prevalence during childhood and no gender

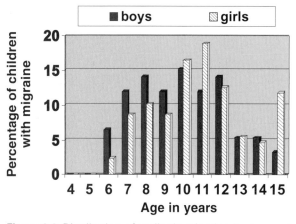

Figure 9-2 Distribution of pediatric migraine by age and gender. Adapted from Mavromichalis I et al.[8]

preference in early childhood but a female predominance after adolescence. Recurrent abdominal pain was identified in 2.9% of boys versus 2.2% of girls aged 5 to 8 years[14] but was in 36% of boys versus 45% of girls aged 11 to 12 years.[15] Campo and colleagues evaluated 28 patients with recurrent abdominal pain and matched controls during adolescence and again in adulthood, about 11 years later.[16] Migraine (36% vs 14%) but not headache in general (54% vs 43%) was more likely to be described in patients with recurrent abdominal pain than in controls. In addition, antimigraine therapy, including propranolol, cyproheptadine, and biofeedback, is beneficial for treating recurrent abdominal pain.[17,18]

Abu-Arafeh and Russell compared a randomly selected sample of 45 children with paroxysmal vertigo to 159 children with migraine and 159 controls.[19] Mean age of onset of paroxysmal vertigo was 11 years. In children with paroxysmal vertigo, migraine was also diagnosed in 24% and abdominal migraine/cyclic vomiting in 6%. Children with paroxysmal vertigo reported similar attack triggers to migraineurs (stress, fatigue, lack of sleep, skipping meals, weather, and bright lights), as well as similar somatic symptoms (pallor, gastrointestinal distress, and intolerance to noises and lights). A family history of migraine in at least one first-degree relative was reported for 42% of children with paroxysmal vertigo, 47% with migraine, and 18% of controls.

Benign paroxysmal torticollis typically affects infants and very young children, with the frequency of episodes decreasing with age.[20,21] Episodes of head tilt, vomiting, and ataxia may last hours to days. Benign paroxysmal torticollis generally resolves during the preschool years. As with migraine, benign paroxysmal torticollis more commonly affects girls.[22]

Acute confusional state is a rare migraine equivalent and must be differentiated from other causes of acute delirium.[23,24] Episodes typically last for minutes to hours. As with other migraine equivalents, acute confusional state tends to resolve in early childhood and be replaced with migraine headache episodes.[25]

Electroencephalography can be helpful in differentiating seizure from migraine in children with paroxysmal disorders. Radiographic studies of the head and neck should be routinely performed in children with paroxysmal torticollis. Migraine equivalents should be considered in pediatric patients with recurrent disorders who have completed negative medical evaluations, particularly when a strong family history of migraine is present.

EXAMINATION FOR HEADACHES IN ADOLESCENTS

Medical and neurologic examinations, as well as the temporal pattern and headache characteristics, help exclude ominous causes of headache. In children presenting with acute headache, infectious etiologies, like viral illness and sinusitis, are common and should be considered.[26] Imaging studies of the head are generally normal for chronic headache, as well as most causes of acute headache, and are best reserved for children who have experienced traumatic or progressive headache, have a history of neurologic illness (such as hydrocephalus), or have an abnormal neurologic examination.[27] As in adult populations, children who experience a significant change in chronic headache pattern, chronic progressive headaches, or failure to respond to standard therapy may also need additional medical and neurologic evaluations, including an imaging study.

The IHS first-edition criteria for the diagnosis of migraine were often difficult to apply to children. As described for HM, childhood headache is generally bilateral and often more brief than the 4 hours required for a migraine diagnosis.[9,28] Duration of migraine attacks was less than 2 hours in 19% of 196 child and adolescent migraine patients.[29] In addition, children and adolescents are less likely to describe their pain as throbbing or report sensitivity to noises and lights.[29]

The new second-edition IHS criteria provide more practically relevant standards for the diagnosis of pediatric migraine. Pediatric migraine criteria were changed to recognize the typically shorter pediatric headache duration of 1 to 72 hours and frequent presentation with bilateral pain. In addition, photophobia and phonophobia may now be inferred in children. Occipital headaches should be regarded with caution because of increased risk of posterior fossa lesions in pediatric populations.

As noted in the second IHS diagnostic edition, children often fail to verbally express migrainous features, such as sensitivities to noises and lights. Metsähonkala and colleagues interviewed children with headache and then evaluated prospective headache diaries from this same population.[30] A number of migrainous headache features that were not endorsed at the initial interview were recorded for the first time in diaries for the majority of children. This included aura (46%), vomiting (50%), nausea (31%), unilateral location (38%), throbbing quality (29%), photophobia (11%), and phonophobia (11%). Thus, the use of diaries that instructed children to focus on certain symptoms improved the description of those headaches as migraine. The authors postulated that, unlike adults, children have not had enough medical education about associated symptoms, and practice observing their headaches, to retrospectively provide accurate headache descriptions. In addition, the majority of children who had been diagnosed with migraine at interview were rediagnosed as having a second type of headache as well after their diaries were reviewed. This study highlights the importance of prospectively collecting headache diaries in adolescents prior to establishing firm diagnoses.

Stafstrom and colleagues demonstrated the usefulness of using headache drawings for migraine diagnosis by asking 226 children consulting for headache to draw a picture of how their headaches made them feel.[31] Each child received an independent headache diagnosis based on the drawing alone, as well as a diagnosis based on standard clinical evaluation. Headache drawings were very effective in representing migraine features, with a diagnostic sensitivity of 93%, specificity of 83%, and positive predictive value of 87%.

Headache evaluation should also seek psychosocial stressors, such as school, family, or relationship problems. One study identified significant personal stressors (family separation, moving, death) occurring within 12 months of headache onset in 73% of adolescents.[32] Migraine occurs more often in children reporting unhappiness, fear of failure at school, or fear of a teacher.[33] Depressive symptoms are identified on clinical interview in 86% of teenagers with daily headache.[34] In addition, being the victim of bullying is associated with frequent headache episodes in children between the ages of 7.5 and 10 years.[35]

HEADACHE-RELATED DISABILITY IN CHILDREN AND ADOLESCENTS

Headache is a frequently disabling complaint for adolescents. A recent survey of US high schools reported weekly headache in over 20% of adolescents, with daily headache reported for 11% of girls and 3.5% of boys.[36] Children with headache lose an average of 7.8 days per school year, compared to 3.7 days lost per year for children without headaches.[9] Frequent school absenteeism is a significant stressor, resulting in losses of academic performance, social interaction with peers, and self-esteem. These factors, themselves, often aggravate pain perception. Low self-esteem and depressive symptoms are premorbid predictors of adolescent headache in girls.[2] The longer school absence is maintained, the more difficult it is for children to return to school because of failure to maintain academic work and fear of isolation from peers on their return to school. Treatment begins with resuming a regular routine. Good school participation must be the top priority. School is important for social and emotional development, in addition to intellectual development. Homebound education cannot equal the experience of the classroom.

Psychosocial impact is not insignificant in pediatric headache sufferers. A comparison of 127 children and adolescents with headache and 83 controls identified clinically relevant emotional and behavioral problems in one-third of headache sufferers versus one-tenth of controls.[37] Quality-of-life measures for physical, social, emotional, and school functioning are also significantly reduced in children with migraine.[38]

Validated self-administered questionnaires may be clinically useful for identifying headache-related impact and disability. Hershey and colleagues developed and validated the PedMIDAS questionnaire, a 6-question assessment tool of migraine-related disability for children and adolescents.[39] The PedsQL 4.0, a validated instrument to measure health-related quality of life, has also been used in child and adolescent migraineurs.[40] Information about the PedsQL can be accessed at http://www.pedsql.org. These questionnaires can provide valuable information when assessing headache impact at baseline and following treatment.

TREATMENTS FOR CHILDHOOD AND ADOLESCENT MIGRAINE

The same type of acute care and preventive medications used in adults are often effective in older children and adolescents. Medication dosage, however, must be adjusted in children and small teenagers. Although many standard adult migraine therapies have been used clinically in pediatric patients, few studies have directly evaluated efficacy, tolerability, and safety in a pediatric population (Table 9-1).

Acute care management can often be very effective with analgesics, such as ibuprofen taken with a caffeinated beverage or an isometheptene compound. Interestingly, Lewis and colleagues showed a superior response to ibuprofen in boys compared with girls.[41] A similar superiority of analgesic response to ibuprofen has been demonstrated in adult males.[42] Migraine-specific therapies, such as the triptans, are used when simple or combination analgesics fail. Several studies have reported safe, tolerated, and effective relief with triptans in children and adolescents.[43-47] Orally disintegrating triptans may be particularly desirable in pediatric patients.

Amitriptyline, cyproheptadine, and propranolol are effective and tolerated preventive therapies in pediatric headache patients.[48,49] Selective serotonin reuptake inhibitors may also be useful in adolescents because of less sedative effects. Other preventive therapies have also demonstrated efficacy, safety, and tolerability in pediatric populations (see Table 9-1).[50-52]

Non-pharmacologic treatments, such as relaxation and biofeedback, are extremely effective in pediatric populations.[53-55] Sartory and colleagues showed superior response in pediatric migraineurs (ages 8 to 16 years) treated with stress management combined with relaxation or biofeedback in comparison with metoprolol.[55] Relaxation and biofeedback are most effective when patients receive instruction from trained personnel. A minimal-contact approach requires only a few supervised training sessions, followed by regular at-home practice. Psychologists, nurses, and physical therapists are often trained to teach pain management techniques. The use of self-help books and relaxation tapes without professional training is usually not effective. In addition, lifestyle modification, such as regular

Table 9-1 Treatment of Pediatric Migraine

Treatment	Ages Tested (Years)	Reference
Acute medication		
Ibuprofen	6–12	Lewis DW et al (2002)[41]
Sumatriptan injection	6–18	Linder SL (1996)[43]
Sumatriptan nasal spray	5–12	Wolf SM et al (2000)[44]
Sumatriptan tablets	5–12	Hershey AD et al (2001)[45]
Zolmitriptan tablet	12–17	Linder SL and Dowson AJ (2000)[46]
Rizatriptan tablet	12–17	Winner P et al (2002)[47]
Preventive medication		
Amitriptyline	mean 12 ± 3	Hershey AD et al (2000)[48]
Trazodone	7–18	Battistella PA et al (1993)[50]
Valproate	8–17	Serdaroglu G et al (2002)[51]
Topiramate	< 19	Hershey AD et al (2002)[52]
Non-pharmacologic treatment		
Biofeedback	7–17	Hermann C et al (1997)[53] and Scharff L et al (2002)[54]

eating and sleeping habits, avoidance of caffeinated beverages and alcohol, and regular exercise, are also beneficial preventive headache measures.[56] Acupuncture was effective in one small study with pediatric migraine; however, additional studies are needed before acupuncture can be widely recommended.[57]

Summary

Primary headache, especially migraine, occurs commonly in girls. Headache prevalence increases over childhood, peaking during the year of menarche. Menarche and the onset of cycling hormonal levels are postulated to trigger latent central nervous system vulnerabilities to headache. HM's story of headaches beginning 6 months after menarche, in a girl predisposed to migraine because of the family history in her brother, is typical. Routine evaluation of menstruating females for the occurrence of troublesome, recurring headaches may lead to early intervention and reduction of long-term, headache-related disability.

Headache in girls may be more likely to go unrecognized and untreated than headache in women. Migraine, in particular, is often underdiagnosed in children because many of the hallmark features of adult migraine (unilateral pain, longer duration of headache, and verbalized sensitivity to noises and lights) are not reported by children with migraine. Modifications to the IHS diagnostic criteria for pediatric migraine should improve recognition and identification of this important syndrome.

References

1. Sillanpää M. Changes in the prevalence of migraine and other headaches during the first seven school years. Headache 1983;23:15–9.

2. Zuckerman B, Stevenson J, Bailey V. Stomachaches and headaches in a community sample of preschool children. Pediatrics 1987;79:677–82.

3. Sillanpää M, Piekkala P, Kero P. Prevalence of headache at preschool age in an unselected child population. Cephalalgia 1991;11:239–42.

4. Metsähonkala L, Sillanpää M, Tuominen J. Social environment and headache in 8- to 9-year-old children: a follow-up study. Headache 1998;38:222–8.

5. Bohnen AM, van Suijlekom-Smit LA, Passchier J, van der Wouden JC. Pain in children and adolescents: a common experience. Pain 2000;87:51–8.

6. Özge A, Bugdayci R, Sasmaz T, et al. The sensitivity and specificity of the case definition criteria in diagnosis of headache: a school-based epidemiological study of 5562 children in Mersin. Cephalalgia 2003;23:138–45.

7. Sillanpää M, Piekkala P. Prevalence of migraine and other headaches in early puberty. Scand J Prim Health Care 1984;2:27–32.

8. Mavromichalis I, Anagnostopoulos D, Metaxas N, Papanastassiou E. Prevalence of migraine in schoolchildren and some clinical comparisons between migraine with and without aura. Headache 1999;39:728–36.

9. Abu-Arafeh I, Russell G. Prevalence of headache and migraine in schoolchildren. BMJ 1994;309:765–9.

10. Raieli V, Raimondo D, Cammalleri R, Camarda R. Migraine headaches in adolescents: a student population-based study in Monreale. Cephalalgia 1995;15:5–12.

11. Dalsgaard-Nielsen T. Some aspects of the epidemiology of migraine in Denmark. Headache 1970;10:14–23.

12. Bille B. A 40-year follow-up of school children with migraine. Cephalalgia 1997;17:488–91.

13. Al-Twaijri WA, Shevell MI. Pediatric migraine equivalents: occurrence and clinical features in practice. Pediatr Neurol 2002;26:365–8.

14. Bode G, Brenner H, Adler G, Rothenbacher D. Recurrent abdominal pain in children. Evidence from a population-based study that social and familial factors play a major role but not *Helicobacter pylori* infection. J Psychosom Res 2003;54:417–21.

15. Boey CM, Yao SB. An epidemiological survey of recurrent abdominal pain in a rural Malay school. J Paediatr Child Health 1999;35:303–5.

16. Campo JV, Di Lorenzo C, Chiappetta L, et al. Adult outcomes of pediatric recurrent abdominal pain: do they just grow out of it? Pediatrics 2001;108:e1.

17. Russell G, Abu-Arafeh I, Symon DN. Abdominal migraine: evidence for existence and treatment options. Paediatr Drugs 2002;4:1–8.

18. Weydert JA, Ball TM, Davis MF. Systemic review of treatments for recurrent abdominal pain. Pediatrics 2003;111:e1–11.

19. Abu-Arafeh I, Russell G. Paroxysmal vertigo as a migraine equivalent in children: a population-based study. Cephalalgia 1995;15:22–5.

20. Del Cuore F. Benign paroxysmal torticollis in childhood. Pediatr Med Chir 1997;19:69–70.

21. Balslev T, Falrup M, Ostergaard JR, Haslam RH. Benign paroxysmal torticollis. Recurrent involuntary twisting of the head in infants and young children. Ugeskr Laeger 1998;160:5365–7.

22. Hanukoglu A, Somekh E, Fried D. Benign paroxysmal torticollis in infancy. Clin Pediatr (Phila) 1984;23:272–4.

23. Amit R. Acute confusional state in childhood. Childs Nerv Syst 1998;4:255–8.

24. D'Cruz OF, Walsh DJ. Acute confusional migraine: case series and review of literature. Wis Med J 1992;91:130–1.

25. Ehyai A, Fenichel GM. The natural history of acute confusional migraine. Arch Neurol 1978;35:368–9.

26. Burton LJ, Quinn B, Pratt-Cheney JL, Pourani M. Headache etiology in a pediatric emergency department. Pediatr Emerg Care 1997;13:1–4.

27. Kan L, Nagelberg J, Maytal J. Headaches in a pediatric emergency department: etiology, imaging, and treatment. Headache 2000;40:25–9.

28. Winner P, Putnam G, Saiers J, et al. Demographic and migraine characteristics of adolescent patients: the Glaxo Wellcome adolescent clinical trials database. Headache 2000;40:438.

29. Wöber-Bingöl C, Wöber C, Karwautz A, et al. Diagnosis of headache in childhood and adolescence: a study of 437 patients. Cephalalgia 1995;15:13–21.

30. Metsähonkala L, Sillanpää M, Tuominen J. Headache diary in the diagnosis of childhood migraine. Headache 1997;37:240–4.

31. Stafstrom CE, Rostasy K, Minster A. The usefulness of children's drawings in the diagnosis of headache. Pediatrics 2002;109:460–72.

32. Kaiser RS, Primavera JP. Failure to mourn as a possible contributory factor to headache onset in adolescence. Headache 1993;33:69–72.

33. Anttila P, Metsähonkala L, Helenius H, Sillanpää M. Predisposing and provoking factors in childhood headache. Headache 2000;40:351–6.

34. Kaiser R. Depression in adolescent headache patients. Headache 1992;32:340–4.

35. Williams K, Chambers M, Logan S, Robinson D. Association of common health symptoms with bullying in primary school children. BMJ 1996;313:17–9.

36. Rhee H. Prevalence and predictors of headaches in US adolescents. Headache 2000;40:528–38.

37. Just U, Oelkers R, Bender S, et al. Emotional and behavioural problems in children and adolescents with primary headache. Cephalalgia 2003;23:206–13.

38. Powers SW, Patton SR, Hommel KA, Hershey AD. Quality of life in childhood migraines: clinical impact and comparison to other chronic illnesses. Pediatrics 2003;112:e1–5.

39. Hershey AD, Powers SW, Vockell AL, et al. PedMIDAS: development of a questionnaire to assess disability of migraines in children. Neurology 2001;57:2034–9.

40. Powers SW, Patton SR, Hommel KA, et al. Quality of life in pediatric migraine: age-related effects using PedsQL 4.0. Headache 2003;43:549.

41. Lewis DW, Kellstein D, Dahl G, et al. Children's ibuprofen suspension for the acute treatment of pediatric migraine. Headache 2002;42:780–6.

42. Walker JS, Carmody JJ. Experimental pain in healthy human subjects: gender differences in nociception and in response to ibuprofen. Anesth Analg 1998;86:1257–62.

43. Linder SL. Subcutaneous sumatriptan in the clinical setting: the first 50 consecutive patients with acute migraine in a pediatric neurology office practice. Headache 1996;36:419–22.

44. Wolf SM, Raynes H, Selman JE, Newman LC. A retrospective chart review of sumatriptan nasal spray (SNS) as an acute treatment of migraine in children. Headache 2000;40:438.

45. Hershey AD, Powers SW, LeCates S, Bentti AL. Effectiveness of nasal sumatriptan in 5- to 12-year-old children. Headache 2001;41:693–7.

46. Linder SL, Dowson AJ. Zolmitriptan provides effective migraine relief in adolescents. Int J Clin Pract 2000;54:466–9.

47. Winner P, Lewis D, Visser WH, et al. Rizatriptan 5 mg for the acute treatment of migraine in adolescents: a randomized, double-blind, placebo-controlled study. Headache 2002;42:49–55.

48. Hershey AD, Powers SW, Bentti A, Degrauw T. Effectiveness of amitriptyline in the prophylactic management of childhood headache. Headache 2000;40:539–49.

49. Diamond S, Lewis DW. Prophylactic treatment of pediatric migraine. Headache 2003;43:550.

50. Battistella PA, Ruffilli R, Cernetti R, et al. A placebo-controlled crossover trial using trazodone in pediatric migraine. Headache 1993;33:36–9.

51. Serdaroglu G, Erhan E, Tekgul H, et al. Sodium valproate prophylaxis in childhood migraine. Headache 2002;42:819–22.

52. Hershey AD, Powers SW, Vockell AB, et al. Effectiveness of topiramate in the prevention of childhood headaches. Headache 2002;42:810–8.

53. Hermann C, Blanchard EB, Flor H. Biofeedback treatment for pediatric migraine: prediction of treatment outcome. J Consult Clin Psychol 1997;65:611–6.

54. Scharff L, Marcus D, Masek BJ. A controlled study of minimal-contact thermal biofeedback in children with migraine. J Pediatr Psychol 2002;27:109–19.

55. Sartory G, Muller B, Metsch J, Pothmann R. A comparison of psychological and pharmacological treatment of pediatric migraine. Behav Res Ther 1998;36:1155–70.

56. Millichap JG, Yee MM. The diet factor in pediatric and adolescent migraine. Pediatr Neurol 2003;28:9–15.

57. Kemper KJ, Sarah R, Silver-Highfield E, et al. On pins and needles? Pediatric pain patients' experience with acupuncture. Pediatrics 2000;105:941–7.

CHAPTER 10

Menstrual Migraine

Elizabeth Loder, MD, FACP, and E. Anne MacGregor, MBBS, MFFP, DIPM

CASE

AR, a 38-year-old woman, reports a history of migraine since her teenage years. She notes that headaches are especially likely to occur in conjunction with her menstrual periods, although she acknowledges that other triggers, such as lack of sleep, emotional stress, and overexertion, can also produce headaches. Because her menstrual periods are so predictably associated with headache, she would like to know what can be done to decrease or eliminate these menstrually-associated migraine attacks (Table 10-1).

As this case illustrates, hormonal factors commonly influence the course of migraine. Rarely, though, are they the only trigger for headache. Because migraine is so common in women of childbearing age, it is important to understand the relationship between hormones and migraine.

KEY CHAPTER POINTS

- Hormonal fluctuation, especially changes in estrogen levels, is an important trigger of headache in many, but not all, women with migraine. Hormonal fluctuations have little effect on tension-type and cluster headache.

- Women with menstrual exacerbation of headache generally do not have hormonal abnormalities; rather, headaches are triggered by an abnormal central nervous system (CNS) response to changing hormonal levels. Tests of hormone levels are rarely useful in evaluating these headaches. Diagnosis is clinical, based on headache history and diary information.

- Standard migraine therapies work well for menstrually-triggered migraine attacks and are the mainstay of treatment.

- For the small subset of women for whom acute therapy alone does not suffice, and whose menstrual periods and associated headaches are predictable, preemptive treatment of the expected headache with scheduled perimenstrual use of a number of agents can be helpful. The best evidence is for regimens of estradiol 1.5 mg gel, estradiol 100 µg patches, or naproxen sodium 550 mg PO bid. Recent studies suggest that perimenstrual prophylaxis with triptans may be effective.

- A variety of treatments have been suggested for refractory menstrual migraine, but the quality of evidence for their use is generally poor.

EFFECT OF HORMONAL FLUCTUATIONS

Almost one-half of women with migraine notice that headache attacks are more likely to occur around menstrual periods; most of these women have attacks at other times of the month also. The term "menstrually-related migraine" is commonly used to describe this pattern of headaches. A much smaller percentage of women with migraine (less than 10%) report headaches that occur exclusively with menstruation and at no other time of the month, a pattern often referred to as "true" or "pure" menstrual migraine.[1] Although some migraine episodes undoubtedly occur with the menstrual period by coincidence alone, diary cards kept for a minimum of three menstrual cycles are necessary to confirm a causal relationship.

A series of experiments in the early 1970s suggested that falling estrogen levels, particularly an abrupt drop following a period of sustained high levels, are responsible for menstrual triggering of migraine (Figure 10-1).[2,3] Changes in progesterone levels, in contrast, did

Table 10-1 Management of Suspected Menstrual Migraine

First Visit

History and examination

Investigations (if indicated)

Provide acute therapy

Diaries

Discuss hormonal and nonhormonal predisposing factors and triggers

If taking combined oral contraceptives (COCs):

- Migraine without aura only in pill-free interval (PFI): confirm with diaries and consider three to four consecutive packets (reducing PFI to four to five per year) or continuous COC use
- Migraine with aura: change to progestogen-only or nonhormonal contraception
- Worsening migraine since starting COCs: consider change to progestogen-only or nonhormonal contraception

Second Visit (usually after three menstrual cycles)

Review efficacy of acute therapy and change as necessary

Identify symptoms suggestive of perimenopause

- Irregular periods
- Hot flushes/night sweats

Review diaries

- Nonmenstrual migraine
  - Consider standard prophylaxis if acute therapy alone inadequate
- Menstrually-related migraine
  - Consider anovulant hormonal contraceptives if contraception also required
  - Consider hormone replacement therapy if symptoms suggestive of perimenopause
- Menstrual migraine
  - Consider specific perimenstrual prophylaxis if periods regular and if acute therapy alone inadequate
  - Consider anovulant hormonal contraception if periods irregular and/or contraception also required
  - Consider hormone replacement therapy if symptoms suggestive of perimenopause

Follow-Up Visits

Review efficacy of acute therapy and change as necessary

Identify symptoms suggestive of perimenopause

Review diaries

Consider prophylaxis as indicated by symptoms and diaries

---

not seem to provoke headache.[4] Several other studies support this "estrogen withdrawal" theory. One study showed that the extent of decline from peak to trough estrogen was greater in all of the migraineurs than in the women in the control group who did not have migraine.[5] The authors concluded that variation in hormonal activity may be a potentially relevant factor in all women with migraine, with factors additional to the hormonal environment being responsible for the difference between subgroups of women with migraine linked or not linked to menstruation. Another investi-gator studied postmenopausal women challenged with estrogen, confirming that, in some of these women, a drop in serum estrogen could precipitate migraine, and that a period of estrogen priming was a necessary pre-requisite.[6] The estrogen withdrawal theory also explains why migraine is more likely to occur during the week of taking the placebo pill in traditional oral contraceptive regimens and during the estrogen-free period of older, interrupted estrogen replacement therapy regimens.

The chronologic association of migraine attacks with the menses as reported by authors and researchers

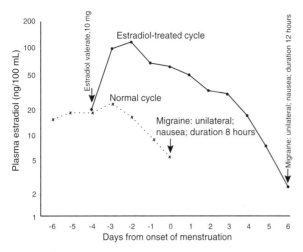

Figure 10-1 Migraine following estrogen withdrawal. Adapted from Somerville BW.[2]

has varied widely, ranging from headaches occurring as early as ovulation to those occurring as late as 9 days after the onset of the menstrual flow.

Most experts suggest that, to be plausibly attributed to menstruation, a migraine attack should correlate with the perimenstrual drop in estrogen levels, falling within −2 or −3 days to +3 or +4 days from the onset of the menstrual flow (day 1).[7] A large, population-based diary study of the relationship between menstruation and migraine supports this position, showing that excess risk of a migraine attack is largely confined to the first 2 days of bleeding.[8]

MacGregor and colleagues analyzed data collected from women attending the City of London Migraine Clinic and found a marked increase in migraine between 2 days before the onset of menses and the first 3 days of the menses.[1] The authors proposed that menstrual migraine be defined as "migraine attacks that regularly occur on or between days −2 and +3 of the menstrual cycle and at no other time" and that menstrually-related migraine be defined as "migraine attacks which occur throughout the cycle but which regularly increase in frequency on or between days −2 and +3 of the menstrual cycle." All menstrual and menstrually-related migraine attacks in this study were without aura, although women in the latter category had migraine attacks with aura at other times. These disorders are to be distinguished from premenstrual migraine, which is typically associated with the premenstrual syndrome, occurring from 2 to 7 days before the onset of menses.

Estrogen withdrawal is rarely the only trigger for migraine in women who have menstrual migraine. Why it is a prominent trigger for some women and not for others remains unexplained, as does the clinical observation that menstrually-provoked migraine may increase in prevalence and severity in the perimenopausal years. Regulation of the menstrual cycle is complex with ovarian steroids playing a limited role in the overall control. It is likely that the chemical alteration more directly responsible for migraine is the effect of the changing hormonal environment on other biochemical and metabolic pathways, rather than a direct effect of sex hormones (Figure 10-2). Hence it is unlikely that estrogen withdrawal is responsible for all menstrual migraine attacks in all women; other mechanisms may also be relevant, perhaps leading to a final common pathway.

TESTS OF HORMONE LEVELS

From a clinical perspective, and in counseling patients, it is important to understand that there is no evidence that hormonal levels are abnormal in women with migraine; what is abnormal is the response of the migraine-prone CNS to falling estrogen levels.[9] Although patients frequently request them, tests of hormone levels or other endocrinologic evaluation are unlikely to prove helpful in the evaluation and treatment of menstrually-related headaches.

DIAGNOSIS

A patient history of migraine occurring in relation to the menstrual cycle should be corroborated by prospective headache diaries. Because headaches commonly wax and wane and are influenced by many factors other than the menstrual cycle, it is best to ask the patient to record menstrual periods, headache frequency, and severity for at least 3 months.[10] Headache occurring

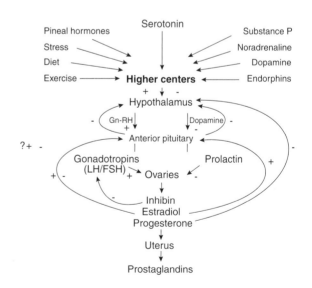

Figure 10-2 The hypothalamic-pituitary-ovarian axis. +/− = positive and negative feedback control; FSH = follicle stimulating hormone; Gn-RH = gonadotropin-releasing hormone; LH = luteinizing hormone. Reproduced with permission from MacGregor EA. Menstruation, sex hormones and migraine. Neurol Clin 1997;15:125–41.

within −2 to +3 days of the onset of menstrual flow (counting the first day of bleeding as day 1) in two out of three menstrual cycles is reasonable evidence of a clinically important link that might be exploited for therapeutic benefit. Several months of diary information also provide information about the timing of headaches that helps in planning treatment; in some women the headaches will begin with the onset of the menstrual flow, whereas in others they will begin several days before the onset of menses.

STANDARD MIGRAINE THERAPIES

If headache diaries establish a clear link between the menstrual cycle and migraine attacks, a treatment plan can be formulated (see Table 10-1). Benign and easily implemented strategies should be tried first, with complex or less well-studied therapies saved for patients who do not respond to first-line measures. The commonly held view that menstrual headaches are invariably more difficult to treat than nonmenstrual attacks is supported by some clinical studies but not by large population-based studies.[8,11] However, no account is made for intraindividual differences in attacks; within-patient analyses would be more clinically relevant. Because the majority of attacks, both menstrual and nonmenstrual, respond well to standard abortive therapy, the use of perimenstrual prophylaxis of headache will be needed in only a subset of patients (see Table 10-1).

Diet and Lifestyle

Some reasonable and easily implemented changes in daily habits and routines can decrease the likelihood of migraine attacks for many patients. Even when such measures are incompletely effective used alone, they should be continued because they may augment the effectiveness of other treatments. Women who know they are more susceptible to migraine around their menstrual periods should take extra care to avoid exposure to potential triggers during this time of heightened susceptibility. Dietary triggers for which there is reasonable evidence to support avoidance include alcohol and excessive caffeine consumption (because of headache from subsequent caffeine withdrawal). The strength of currently available evidence about dietary triggers does not justify other, more intrusive attempts at dietary manipulation. Regular and adequate amounts of sleep, avoidance of excessive stress or tension, and regular meals are all beneficial in generic migraine; by implication, these things are all the more important for women with an enhanced perimenstrual vulnerability to migraine. Biofeedback-assisted relaxation training has been shown to be helpful in migraine and is useful both in modifying acute attacks and in preventing future attacks.[12] This is a particularly attractive therapeutic option for women of childbearing age, because it does not involve the use of systemically

acting drugs. However, biofeedback by itself generally only reduces, but does not eliminate, the need for medication use.

Pharmacologic Treatment: Acute Therapy

General Considerations

The majority of patients with menstrual and menstrually-related migraine will do well with acute therapy only. Retrospective analyses of many clinical trial databases suggest that acute migraine agents work equally well for menstrual and nonmenstrual migraine attacks; few prospective trials of within-patient analyses in women with menstrual migraine have been undertaken and more study is needed. The results from one small prospective study of sumatriptan, which included women with menstrually-related migraine, suggested that menstrual attacks are less responsive to treatment than nonmenstrual attacks (Figure 10-3).[13] Factors that enhance the likelihood of successful acute therapy for other migraine episodes apply equally to menstrual attacks. These include the use of an appropriate medication, an adequate dose of the medication, the medication at a mild stage of the attack (rather than waiting until the attack is moderate to severe), and appropriate treatment of associated symptoms (for example, nausea or vomiting).

In general, nonsedating, disease-specific agents such as the triptans are highly preferred for first-line therapy in this generally young, otherwise healthy patient population. Women with menstrual and menstrually-related migraine are generally in a period of their lives in which they are likely to be employed, caring for young children, and responsible for additional family and household duties. The risk posed by nonspecific therapies of sedation or dependence is especially unwelcome in such a population. Migraine is a recurrent disorder, and the use of sedating or habit-forming medications such as barbiturate-containing medications may increase the chance of disability as

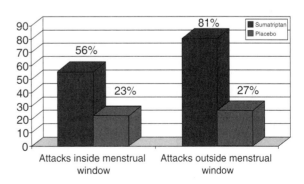

Figure 10-3 Efficacy of sumatriptan at 4 hours post-treatment in menstrually-associated migraine versus non-menstrual attacks. Adapted from Gross MLP et al.[13]

a result of treatment rather than the disorder itself. Nonspecific therapies, especially those containing barbiturates or caffeine, are frequently associated with medication overuse or rebound headache if used inappropriately.

Because they cause constriction of coronary arteries, triptans and ergotamine compounds are recommended for use only in patients who do not have evidence of or risk factors for coronary artery disease. The coronary constriction caused by ergot compounds is longer and more pronounced than that associated with triptans, making ergots a relatively less desirable choice than the triptans for most circumstances.[14] However, the longer duration of action of ergots compared with triptans has the theoretic advantage of less recurrence in longer-duration menstrual attacks. Fortunately, most patients with menstrual and menstrually-related migraine are relatively young and usually have few or no risk factors for coronary artery disease.

Nonsteroidal and Other Over-the-Counter Medications

Nonsteroidal and other over-the-counter medications work by interfering with the formation of prostaglandins that may play a role in menstrual headache as well as other menstrually-associated symptoms such as dysmenorrhea. In some cases, dosages that have been studied and shown to be effective in headache may be higher than those recommended on the label of the over-the-counter medication. Caffeine-containing products may be slightly more effective than preparations not containing caffeine but are also more likely to cause worsening headache when overused.[15] Other nonsteroidal anti-inflammatory drugs (NSAIDs) and caffeine-containing simple analgesics, in addition to those mentioned above, are also likely to be effective for the treatment of migraine attacks associated with menstruation. Acetaminophen alone seems less effective than drugs containing NSAIDs. Most women whose menstrual headaches are severe enough to seek medical attention are likely to have tried over-the-counter drugs without adequate benefit or will be found to be overusing them. Over-the-counter drugs are appropriate agents only for the treatment of mild to moderate headache, provided patients get adequate benefit and do not overuse them. If patients do not obtain at least 80% relief of headache for 4 to 6 hours, or need to use the medications continuously for 2 or more days around the menstrual period, prescription medications should be considered. A combination of acetaminophen, aspirin, and caffeine has been shown to be equally effective in treating menstrual and nonmenstrual headaches (61% of patients with menstruation-associated headaches obtained headache relief at 2 hours, compared with 58% of patients with non-menstruation-associated headaches).[16]

Nonspecific Prescription Medications for Migraine

Many products in common use in the United States contain short-acting barbiturates in combination with either acetaminophen or aspirin. Most, but not all, also contain 40 mg of caffeine per tablet. Because these are older medications, studies that meet modern standards of proof of efficacy are lacking. However, these drugs are widely perceived to be effective for mild to moderate headache. There is no evidence that these preparations are more effective than other analgesic medications; none is approved by the Food and Drug Administration (FDA) for the treatment of migraine headache. Barbiturate-containing drugs are not widely prescribed in Europe, where many of them are not even commercially available.

Barbiturate-containing compounds have proved highly prone to abuse and overuse in patients with headache; dependence syndromes among patients with problematic headaches are frequent and are difficult to treat.[15] Of even greater concern is recent evidence that use of these compounds is associated with a higher likelihood of progression from episodic to chronic daily headache. For all of these reasons, barbiturate-containing drugs are poor choices for treatment of migraine in the majority of patients.

Triptan Medications

Review of the large databases generated in clinical trials suggest that all of the commercially available triptans work as well for migraine attacks that occur with menstruation as they do for attacks at other times of the month. This is true for eletriptan, frovatriptan, naratriptan, rizatriptan, sumatriptan, and zolmitriptan.[17–22] However, these analyses did not involve women who identified themselves as having menstrual migraine and were not prospective studies.

One small, prospective, placebo-controlled study with sumatriptan suggested less efficacy for menstrual versus nonmenstrual attacks in women identified with menstrually-related migraine.[13] Naratriptan's longer half-life has led some to suggest that it may reduce recurrence; this is controversial, and lower recurrence rates must be interpreted in light of its lower efficacy rates.[23]

Zolmitriptan has been prospectively studied for acute treatment use in a large population of women identified as having menstrual migraine. In an intensity-based dosing regimen using zolmitriptan, 579 women with menstrually-associated migraine occurring in at least two or three prior menstrual cycles were randomized to zolmitriptan or placebo treatment.[22] They treated one attack per menstrual period for 3 months. Treatment was intensity based, with mild migraine headaches treated with one-half of a zolmitriptan 2.5 mg tablet, moderate with 2.5 mg, and severe with 5 mg (two 2.5 mg tablets) or placebo. One thousand two hundred thirty-two migraine attacks were treated, of which 48% demonstrated a 2-hour response to zolmitriptan versus a 27% response to placebo ($p < .001$). Treatment with zolmitriptan was more effective than placebo in achieving a response as early as 30 minutes (18% vs 14%; $p < .05$) and at 1 hour (33% vs 23%; $p < .01$). This prospective, placebo-controlled study provides evidence of the efficacy of zolmitriptan in the treatment of menstrually-associated migraine and demonstrated the early effectiveness of a triptan in a subgroup of attacks that have been generally regarded as difficult to treat.

PERIMENSTRUAL PROPHYLAXIS OR PRE-EMPTION

The predictability of menstrually-occurring migraine attacks in women with regular menstrual cycles makes it possible to preempt those attacks through the use of scheduled doses of prophylactic agents. Depending on the putative mechanism of action, perimenstrual treatment can be started from 1 week to 48 hours before the expected onset of migraine and continued into the menstrual period, if necessary.[24] In practice, this amounts to a 5- to 14-day course of prophylaxis. This short-term scheduled prophylaxis of anticipated attacks is sometimes referred to as "mini-prophylaxis."

Perimenstrual Estrogen Supplementation

On the basis that menstrual migraine has been associated with estrogen withdrawal in the late luteal phase of the menstrual cycle, trials have been undertaken using estrogen supplementation with percutaneous gel and transdermal patches to maintain estradiol levels until endogenous levels naturally rise in the first part of the subsequent cycle.

Percutaneous Estrogen Supplements

De Lignières and colleagues studied 18 women with strictly defined menstrual migraine who completed a double-blind, placebo-controlled crossover trial using 1.5 mg estradiol gel (which allows a mean estradiol plasma level of 80 pg/mL to be reached) or placebo daily for 7 days during three consecutive cycles.[25] Treatment was started 48 hours before the earliest expected onset of migraine. Only eight menstrual attacks occurred during the 26 estrogen-treated cycles (30.8%) compared with 26 attacks during the 27 placebo cycles (96.3%). Further, attacks during estrogen treatment were considerably milder and shorter than those during placebo. Eighteen women also completed a similar trial by Dennerstein and colleagues in which 1.5 mg estradiol gel or placebo was used daily for 7 days, beginning at least 2 days prior to the expected migraine, for four cycles.[26] The difference between estradiol gel and placebo was highly significant, favoring the estrogen gel, and less medication was used during active treatment. However, the results

were not as impressive as the study by De Lignières and colleagues. Dennerstein and colleagues commented that the reason for this might be that women in their study also experienced migraine at other times of the cycle and therefore their migraine was only partially hormone dependent.

Transdermal Estrogen Supplements

Estrogen patches have not been found to be as successful as estrogen gel in preventing migraine. Pfaffenrath studied 41 patients completing a trial of 50 μg estradiol patches versus placebo used daily from 2 days prior to the suspected onset of migraine, during a 4-month treatment phase.[27] No significant differences were seen between the two treatments although estradiol was slightly better than placebo in all parameters. Smits and colleagues also studied 50 μg patches versus placebo over three cycles in 20 women and also found no difference between estradiol and placebo.[28] Pradalier and colleagues studied two groups of 12 women using either 25 or 100 μg patches on days −4 and 0 (two patches per cycle) over two cycles and compared the results with a pretreatment cycle.[29] They found that the 100 μg dose gave a better clinical result than the 25 μg patches, raising the question of a critical level. There appears to be a dose threshold because the 100 μg estrogen patch is efficacious and the 25 and 50 μg patches have been less effective or ineffective, depending on the individual trial. The 25 and 50 μg patches result in suboptimal doses of supplemental estrogen, with estradiol serum levels of 25 pg/mL and 40 pg/mL, respectively. In contrast, the 100 μg patch effectively produces higher plasma estradiol levels that are similar to those attained using 1.5 mg percutaneous estradiol.

Long-term use of estrogens for hormone replacement therapy is associated with increased risk of thromboembolic disease, liver disease, breast cancer, and other estrogen-dependent tumors. In contrast, there is no evidence of increased risk of any of these conditions when supplemental estrogens are used in women already producing endogenous estrogen. The risks appear related to the use of estrogens in postmenopausal, not premenopausal, women. However, supplemental estrogens are not recommended for women who have estrogen-dependent tumors or other conditions, including a history of venous thromboembolism.

Perimenstrual Use of Nonsteroidal Anti-inflammatory Drugs

NSAIDs are effective prostaglandin inhibitors. They should be tried as first-line agents for migraine attacks that start on the first to third day of bleeding, particularly in the presence of dysmenorrhea and/or menorrhagia.[30]

The best evidence for NSAIDs in perimenstrual migraine prophylaxis is for naproxen sodium, but it is likely that all of the NSAIDs are effective when used in adequate doses.[31,32] The goal of this kind of therapy is to cover the window of headache vulnerability, so dosing of individual agents will depend on their half-life. Side effects include gastrointestinal disturbance. Misoprostol 800 µg or omeprazole 20 to 40 mg daily may give some gastroduodenal protection.[33] Contraindications include peptic ulcer and aspirin-induced allergy. Interactions include anticoagulants and antihypertensive agents.

There is no evidence that the new COX-2 inhibitors (rofecoxib, celecoxib, valdecoxib) are more effective than traditional NSAIDs. They are more costly but may provide a relative safety advantage for patients who need to use these agents for long periods of time and are especially prone to gastrointestinal complications. Over-the-counter versions of NSAIDs are generally less expensive than their prescription counterparts, but as their cost may not be covered by insurance, they are often more expensive for the patient.

Magnesium and Vitamin Therapy

Magnesium prolidone carboxylic acid 360 mg decreased the duration and intensity of premenstrually occurring migraine in a placebo-controlled, double-blind study of 24 women with premenstrual syndrome and migraine.[34] This study was principally aimed at identifying the effect of magnesium on a number of premenstrual problems, not just headache. The generalizability of the results to women whose menstrual headaches do not occur in association with other premenstrual symptoms is unclear. It has also been suggested that only women with a low serum ionized magnesium level will benefit from magnesium, but clear confirmation of this speculation is lacking. Magnesium compounds are well tolerated. Diarrhea is the major side effect and can sometimes be controlled by switching to other preparations. Magnesium is available over the counter, where the cost of it ranges from 30 to 40 cents per tablet.

Ergot and Derivatives

Ergotamine tartrate 1 mg qhs or bid for 5 days perimenstrually has been recommended for use.[35] Dihydroergotamine, available only in parenteral or nasal spray formulation in the United States, has been used in a specially prepared oral, time-release formulation for prevention of menstrual migraine and appeared to be helpful; unfortunately this preparation is not commercially available.[36] Ergonovine maleate, no longer available in the United States, also seemed helpful when given perimenstrually.[37] Ergots have prolonged vasoconstrictive activity and should not be used in patients with vasospastic disorders, coronary artery disease, or during pregnancy. Synergistic effects with other vasoconstrictors and pressor effects mean concomitant use with other vasoconstrictive agents should be avoided.

Because of safety concerns related to the long duration of vasoconstriction seen with ergots, and the high degree of nausea and vomiting they cause, their use has been supplanted by triptan medications. However, ergot medications are generally inexpensive and have a longer duration of action than triptans. Ergotamine tartrate costs around 80 cents per dose, and is available in a fixed combination with caffeine for oral use, and by itself for sublingual administration.

Perimenstrual Prophylaxis with Triptans

Sumatriptan 25 mg tid was used perimenstrually in an open-label trial. It appeared to be effective, with no occurrence of expected menstrual headaches in 52.4% of patients.[38] However, no placebo-controlled, double-blind trials have been performed to confirm this result. In a double-blind, placebo-controlled trial using naratriptan, 1 mg bid and 2.5 mg bid given from day -3 to $+3$, the difference between the 1 mg dose and placebo just reached statistical significance. Twenty-three percent of patients headache-free in all treated menstrual cycles, compared with 8% of placebo-treated patients, for a therapeutic gain of 15%.[39] The 2.5 mg dose was not superior to placebo. Preliminary data from a trial of over 500 patients with menstrually-associated migraine treated prophylactically with frovatriptan once or twice daily for 6 days versus placebo show modest benefit with frovatriptan (40 to 51% with menstrual migraine versus 67% with placebo; $p < .0001$).[40]

Triptan prophylaxis of menstrual migraine is costly, and trials to date suggest a modest benefit in a relatively small population. There are no trials that compare triptan prophylaxis of menstrual migraine with other lower-cost regimens. Further, use of triptans for prophylaxis limits the choice for effective acute therapy. No prophylactic strategy is 100% effective all of the time; acute therapy remains the mainstay of treatment. Thus, perimenstrual prophylaxis with triptans is not a choice for the majority of women with menstrual or menstrually-related migraine but may be considered for the subset of women with refractory menstrual migraine in whom other therapies have failed; certainly triptan prophylaxis should be tried before resorting to other regimens with even less evidence of their safety and effectiveness.

TREATMENTS FOR REFRACTORY MENSTRUAL MIGRAINE

Danazol, tamoxifen, and bromocriptine are occasionally recommended for use in menstrual migraine. However, the balance of harms and benefits of these treatments is uncertain and their use should be limited to patients who do not respond to more traditional treatment. Danazol suppresses the pituitary-ovarian axis, and doses of 200 to 600 mg per day have been studied in late luteal phase dysphoric disorder.[41] Side effects can be severe and include changes in menstrual patterns, flushing, sweating, vaginal dryness, emotional lability, and hepatic dysfunction. There have been rare cases of severe thromboembolic disorders, benign intracranial hypertension, peliosis hepatis, and benign hepatic adenomas.

No standard dose has been determined for the non-steroidal antiestrogenic agent tamoxifen; trials have used 5 to 15 mg/day for the last 7 days of the luteal phase.[42] Side effects include nausea, vomiting, vasomotor symptoms, and vaginal dryness. Continuous use of 2.5 mg of bromocriptine tid was studied, with benefit, in one small open-label trial.[43] Such approaches should be considered experimental until results of larger studies are available, along with other hormonal and nonhormonal treatments that have not been subjected to careful study.

Continuous Anovulant Regimens

Contraceptives

The use of continuous combined oral contraceptive regimens, in which an active pill is taken daily, in place of the usual method of 3 weeks of active and 1 pill-free week placebo or no therapy, has been recommended based on evidence that estrogen withdrawal provokes migraine in susceptible women. No double-blind, placebo-controlled trials, or even open-label trials, of this strategy in menstrual migraine have been performed. However, continuous oral contraceptive regimens are becoming increasingly popular and accepted by gynecologists for other indications, so there is extensive clinical acceptance of their use.[44] For women who desire contraception or have endometriosis and whose headaches are clearly linked to estrogen withdrawal, this regimen may be reasonable. If women find that continuous estrogens are associated with unacceptable breakthrough bleeding or they prefer to have a regular withdrawal 'period,' there is some evidence that supplemental estrogen used in the pill-free interval can prevent migraine at this time.[45] Contraceptive estrogens should not be used by women with migraine with aura because of the increased stroke risk.[46]

Other nonestrogen anovulant contraceptive regimens such as depot and subdermal progestogens should, in theory, be beneficial for menstrual migraine because they inhibit the normal ovarian cycle. Although there are no studies specifically on women with menstrual or menstrually-related migraine to confirm or refute this suggestion, such methods may be worth considering for women who also require contraception but for whom estrogen is contraindicated.

Gonadotropin-Releasing Hormone Analogues

There are successful case reports of "medical oophorectomy" using gonadotropin-releasing hormone (Gn-RH) analogues. Adverse effects of estrogen deficiency (eg, hot flashes) restrict the use of Gn-RH agonists as stand-alone therapy.[47] These hormones are also associated with a marked reduction in bone density and should not usually be used for longer than 6 months without regular monitoring and bone densitometry. 'Add-back' continuous combined estrogen and progestogen can be given to counter these difficulties.[48] The use of add-back estrogen is supported by results of a recent prospective study in 21 premenopausal women with menstrual migraine. In this study, minimization of hormonal fluctuations with Gn-RH agonist therapy alone did not prevent headache.[49] Addition of transdermal estradiol had a modest beneficial effect. Even the small changes in estrogen levels that occurred in this regimen, though, seemed to provoke headache. Given these limitations, in addition to increased cost, such treatment should be instigated in specialist departments and only if other treatments have failed.

Interventional Procedures

The provocative influence of hormonal cycles on migraine has led to interest in eliminating them through oophorectomy, either surgical or medical. Although reports of successful treatment with surgical oophorectomy have been published, there are also suggestions that abrupt surgical menopause may worsen migraine, and it exposes women to the risks of major surgery.[49] It has been suggested that the use of continuous estrogen replacement postoperatively may account for many reported responses to oophorectomy.[50] Certainly, one study of estradiol implants has shown efficacy.[51]

Standard Migraine Prophylaxis

Finally, women whose menstrual headaches respond poorly to acute treatment and in whom attempts at perimenstrual prophylaxis are not feasible or fail or who have menstrually-related migraine, may benefit from the use of standard prophylactic agents taken throughout the cycle.

Questions and Answers about Hormonal Headache

Question: Does the strategy for managing women who have menstrually-related migraine differ from the strategy for menstrual migraine? For example, what is the best treatment for a woman who has migraine every month with her menstrual period but who also has two or three attacks at other times of the cycle?

Answer: It is important to distinguish between menstrual migraine and menstrually-related migraine because hormonal therapies are less likely to be effective for menstrually-related migraine. If acute therapy alone does not suffice, the best approach is to try standard prophylactic strategies in the first instance—both drug and non-drug. This is because even in women with migraine regularly at the time of menstruation, nonhormonal triggers are important. Even if this approach does not improve the control of all attacks, it often reduces the frequency and severity of nonmenstrual attacks at other times of the cycle, enabling more specific management of the menstrual attacks as for menstrual migraine. For women who only have attacks of menstrual migraine, effective acute therapy is often all that is necessary. Otherwise, perimenstrual prophylaxis can be considered.

DEFINITIONS

Migraine associated with menstruation is typically migraine without aura; women who have a history of migraine with and without aura often report that menstrual attacks are without aura.

Menstrual Migraine

Migraine occurs exclusively on day 1 ± 2 of menstruation (ie, days −2 to +3) in at least two out of three menstrual cycles. The first day of menstruation is day 1 and the preceding day is day −1; there is no day 0.

Menstrually-Related Migraine

Migraine occurs on days 1 ± 2 of the menstrual cycle in at least two out of three menstrual cycles but with additional attacks of migraine at other times of the cycle.

REFERENCES

1. MacGregor EA, Chia H, Vohrah RC, Wilkinson M. Migraine and menstruation: a pilot study. Cephalalgia 1990;10:305–10.

2. Somerville BW. The role of estradiol withdrawal in the etiology of menstrual migraine. Neurology 1972;22:355–65.

3. Somerville BW. Estrogen-withdrawal migraine. Neurology 1975;25:239–50.

4. Somerville BW. The role of progesterone in menstrual migraine. Neurology 1971;21:853–9.

5. Epstein MT, Hockaday JM, Hockaday TDR. Migraine and reproductive hormones throughout the menstrual cycle. Lancet 1975;1:543–8.

6. Lichten E, Lichten J, Whitty A, Pieper D. The confirmation of a biochemical marker for women's hormonal migraine: the depo-oestradiol challenge test. Headache 1996;36:367–71.

7. MacGregor EA. "Menstrual" migraine: towards a definition. Cephalalgia 1996;16:11–21.

8. Stewart WF, Lipton RB, Chee E, et al. Menstrual cycle and headache in a population sample of migraineurs. Neurology 2000;55:1517–23.

9. Davies PTG, Eccles NK, Steiner TJ, Leathard HL, Rose FC. Plasma oestrogen, progesterone and sex-hormone binding globulin levels in the pathogenesis of migraine. Cephalalgia 1989;9 Suppl 10:143.

10. Loder E. Migraine and menstruation. J Soc Obstet Gynaecol Can 2000;22:512–7.

11. Visser WH, Jaspers NMWH, de Vriend RHM, Ferrari MD. Risk factors for headache recurrence after sumatriptan: a study in 366 migraine patients. Cephalalgia 1996;16:264–9.

12. Solbach P, Sargent J, Coyne L. Menstrual migraine headache: results of a controlled, experimental, outcome study of non-drug treatments. Headache 1984;24:75–8.

13. Gross MLP, Barrie M, Bates D, et al. The efficacy of sumatriptan in menstrual migraine. Eur J Neurol 1995;2:144–5.

14. MaasenVanDenBrink A, de Vries R, Saxena PR, et al. Coronary side-effect potential of current and prospective antimigraine. Circulation 1998;98:25–30.

15. Loder E, Tietjen GE, Marcus DA. Evaluation and management issues in migraine. J Clin Outcomes Manage 1999;6:58–74.

16. Silberstein SD, Armellino JJ, Hoffman HD, et al. Treatment of menstruation-associated migraine with the nonprescription combination of acetaminophen, aspirin and caffeine: results from three randomized, placebo-controlled studies. Clin Ther 1999;21:475–91.

17. Massiou H, Pitei D, Poole PH, Sikes C. Efficacy of eletriptan for the treatment of migraine in women with menstrually associated migraine, and in women on contraceptives or hormone replacement therapy: meta-analyses of randomized clinical trials. Poster presentation, Headache World 2000; 2000 September; London, England.

18. MacGregor EA, Keywood C. Frovatriptan is effective in menstrually associated migraine. Poster presentation, Headache World 2000; 2000 September 3–7; London, England.

19. Mathew NT, Asgharnejad M, Peykamian M, Laurenza A. Naratriptan is effective and well tolerated in the acute treatment of migraine. Results of a double-blind, placebo-controlled, crossover study. The Naratriptan S2WA3003 Study Group. Neurology 1997;49:1485–90.

20. Silberstein SD, Massiou H, LeJeunne C, et al. Rizatriptan in the treatment of menstrual migraine. Obstet Gynecol 2000;96:237–42.

21. Salonen R, Saiers J. Sumatriptan is effective in the treatment of menstrual migraine: a review of prospective studies and retrospective analyses. Cephalalgia 1999;19:16–9.

22. Loder E, Silberstein S. Clinical efficacy of 2.5 and 5 mg zolmitriptan in migraine associated with menses or in patients using non-progestogen oral contraceptives [abstract S46]. Neurology 1998;50(4 Suppl 4):A341.

23. Goadsby P. A triptan too far? J Neurol Neurosurg Psychiatry 1998;64:43–7.

24. International Headache Society Clinical Trials Subcommittee. Guidelines for controlled trials of drugs in migraine: second edition. Cephalalgia 2000;20:765–86.

25. De Lignières B, Vincens M, Mauvais-Jarvis P, et al. Prevention of menstrual migraine by percutaneous oestradiol. BMJ 1986;293:1540.

26. Dennerstein L, Morse C, Burrows G, et al. Menstrual migraine: a double-blind trial of percutaneous estradiol. Gynecol Endocrinol 1988;2:113–20.

27. Pfaffenrath V. Efficacy and safety of percutaneous estradiol vs. placebo in menstrual migraine [abstract]. Cephalalgia 1993;13 Suppl 13:244.

28. Smits MG, van der Meer YG, Pfeil JP, et al. Perimenstrual migraine: effect of Estraderm TTS and the value of contingent negative variation and exteroceptive temporalis muscle suppression test. Headache 1994;34:103–6.

29. Pradalier A, Vincent D, Beaulieu PH, et al. Correlation between oestradiol plasma level and therapeutic effect on menstrual migraine. In: Rose FC, editor. New advances in headache research. 4th ed. London: Smith-Gordon; 1994. p. 129–32.

30. Chan WY. Prostaglandins and nonsteroidal antiinflammatory drugs in dysmenorrhoea. Ann Rev Pharmacol Toxicol 1983;23:131–49.

31. Szekely B, Merryman S, Croft H, et al. Prophylactic effects of naproxen sodium on perimenstrual headache: a double blind placebo controlled study. Cephalalgia 1989;9 Suppl 10:452–3.

32. Nattero G, Allais G, De Lorenzo C, et al. Biological and clinical effects of naproxen sodium in patients with menstrual migraine. Cephalalgia 1991;11 Suppl 11:201–2.

33. Gøtzsche PC. Non-steroidal anti-inflammatory drugs. BMJ 2000;320:1058–61.

34. Facchinetti F, Montorsi S, Borella P, et al. Magnesium prevention of premenstrual migraine: a placebo controlled study. In: Rose FC, editor. New advances in headache research. 2nd ed. London: Smith-Gordon; 1991. p. 329–31.

35. Boyle CAJ. Management of menstrual migraine. Neurology 1999;53 Suppl 1:S14–8.

36. D'Alessandro R, Gamberinin G, Lozito A, Sacquegna T. Menstrual migraine: intermittent prophylaxis with a timed-release formulation of dihydroergotamine. Cephalalgia 1983;3 Suppl 1:156–8.

37. Gallagher RM. Menstrual migraine and intermittent ergonovine therapy. Headache 1989;29:366–7.

38. Newman LC, Lipton RB, Lay CL, Solomon S. A pilot study of oral sumatriptan as intermittent prophylaxis of menstruation-related migraine. Neurology 1998;51:307–9.

39. Newman L, Mannix LK, Landy S, et al. Naratriptan as short-term prophylaxis of menstrually associated migraine: a randomized, double-blind, placebo-controlled study. Headache 2001;41:248–56.

40. Tepper S, Freitag F. Prophylactic use of frovatriptan for menstrually associated migraine is effective and does not cause rebound migraine in the post dosing period. Headache 2003;43:585.

41. Lichten EM, Bennett RS, Whitty AJ, Daoud Y. Efficacy of danazol in the control of hormonal migraine. J Reprod Med 1991;36:419–24.

42. O'Dea PK, Davis EH. Tamoxifen in the treatment of menstrual migraine. Neurology 1990;40:1470–1.

43. Herzog AG. Continuous bromocriptine therapy in menstrual migraine. Neurology 1997;48:101–2.

44. Fettes I. Menstrual migraine: methods of prevention and control. Postgrad Med 1997;5:67–77.

45. MacGregor EA, Hackshaw A. Prevention of migraine in the pill-free week of combined oral contraceptives using natural oestrogen supplements. J Fam Planning Reprod Healthcare 2002;28:27–31.

46. World Health Organization. Improving access to quality care in family planning. Medical eligibility criteria for contraceptive use. 2nd ed. Geneva: WHO; 2000. p. 5–6.

47. Holdaway IM, Parr CE, France J. Treatment of a patient with severe menstrual migraine using the depot LHRH analogue Zoladex. Aust N Z J Obstet Gynaecol 1991;31:164–5.

48. Murray SC, Muse KN. Effective treatment of severe menstrual migraine headaches with gonadotrophin-releasing hormone agonist and 'add-back' therapy. Fertil Steril 1997;67:390–3.

49. Neri I, Granella F, Nappi R, et al. Characteristics of headache at menopause: a clinico-epidemiologic study. Maturitas 1993;17:31–7.

50. Martin V, Wenke S, Mandell K, et al. Medical oophorectomy with and without estrogen add-back therapy in the prevention of migraine headache. Headache 2003;43:309–21.

51. Magos AL, Zilkha KJ, Studd JWW. Treatment of menstrual migraine by oestradiol implants. J Neurol Neurosurg Psychiatry 1983;46:1044–6.

CHAPTER 11

Migraine Management During Pregnancy

Jan Lewis Brandes, MD, and Dawn A. Marcus, MD

CASE

DH is a 39-year-old woman who has experienced severe headaches since the onset of menses at age 13 years. She experienced a mixture of both migraine and tension-type headaches. As an adult, DH noted about three moderately severe headaches each week, with an incapacitating migraine about twice monthly. She was treated with verapamil and low-dose amitriptyline, with good reduction in both headache severity and frequency.

At age 32 years, DH decided to become pregnant, and her doctor tapered her preventive therapy. The return of frequent, disabling headaches with severe nausea and vomiting warranted the use of preventive therapy during conception and pregnancy. The initiation of antidepressant therapy with bupropion resulted in reduction in headaches to three mild-to-moderate headache days per week. Several months later, DH became pregnant and continued on bupropion during her first trimester. She had only one migraine during her first trimester and treated it with 800 mg of ibuprofen. Bupropion was discontinued when she entered her second trimester, and she remained headache-free for the rest of her pregnancy. One and a half weeks after delivery, she had a severe migraine and used a sumatriptan injection with success. She continued to use sumatriptan postpartum, either 6 mg injections or 100 mg orally, discarding breast milk for approximately 6 hours after dosing

and supplementing feedings with stored milk. Headaches again became frequent over the first few postpartum weeks, and preventive therapy with amitriptyline and verapamil was resumed. Magnesium therapy was also instituted. Headache severity and frequency again decreased to tolerable levels.

About 1 year later, DH decided to have her second child. She was placed on folate at 1 mg/day and continued magnesium. Preventive medications were otherwise discontinued. DH was instructed to use oxycodone as acute therapy if she became pregnant or was uncertain about pregnancy status and continued on sumatriptan, indomethacin, and prochlorperazine for acute therapy when menstruating. Within 3 months, DH became pregnant again. DH experienced only moderate headache activity during this pregnancy, with resumption of more severe headaches 1 week postpartum. Approximately 15 months later, she achieved her third pregnancy. Despite her previous pattern of headache improvement during pregnancy, headaches did not improve and actually seemed to worsen with this third pregnancy, and she was successfully managed during the first two trimesters with gabapentin. Gabapentin was discontinued before her third trimester, without the return of headaches. Postpartum, her previous headache pattern resumed after 2 weeks.

KEY CHAPTER POINTS

- Migraine improves with pregnancy for a majority of women.
- Chronic headaches often change with pregnancy because estradiol influences headache mechanisms.

- Treatment of chronic headache during pregnancy considers risks and benefits for both mother and baby.
- Breastfeeding should not be discouraged in chronic headache sufferers.

MIGRAINE IMPROVEMENT WITH PREGNANCY

Benign recurring headaches, especially migraine, typically improve during the first trimester of pregnancy, when estrogen levels are rising most dramatically. Spontaneous improvement occurs during pregnancy in 50 to 80% of women with migraine and in 30% of women with tension-type headache.[1–4] A recent prospective study of 47 pregnant women (average gestation at study initiation, 11 weeks) with migraine without aura showed a ≥ 50% headache reduction in 57% during the first trimester, 83% during the second trimester, and 87% during the third trimester.[5] Severity and duration of residual attacks, however, did not decrease significantly during pregnancy. Migraine was less likely to improve in women with menstrual migraine or complicated pregnancy.

A small (*N* = 30) prospective study of mixed headache sufferers reporting persistent headache at the end of the first trimester (mean gestation, 14 weeks) showed only an additional 30% improvement between the second and third trimesters, with a slightly greater likelihood of improvement in women with migraine.[6] This study concluded that women reporting ongoing headaches at the end of the first trimester (usually the first obstetric visit) were unlikely to experience further significant headache improvement during the remainder of their pregnancy, suggesting a need for treatment rather than observation when benign headache persists into the second trimester.

Headaches tend to recur soon after delivery. Headache occurs in 39% of all women and in 58% of migraineurs during the first postpartum week.[7,8] In the prospective study by Sances and colleagues, migraine occurred within 2 days postpartum for 4% of women, within 1 week for 34%, and within 1 month for 26%.[5] Bottle-feeding increased the risk of headache recurrence within both the first week and first month.

Determination of Serious Headache During Pregnancy

Although benign headache may begin or change in quality with pregnancy, women with a substantially changed headache pattern should receive additional evaluations, whether pregnant or not. Conditions that may mimic migraine during pregnancy and postpartum include low pressure headache related to spinal anesthesia, eclampsia/preeclampsia, cerebral venous thrombosis, subarachnoid hemorrhage, intracranial tumors, idiopathic intracranial hypertension (pseudotumor cerebri), and meningitis. A thorough history and careful medical and neurologic examination, including a funduscopic examination, usually identify women who will require additional testing.

Magnetic resonance imaging (MRI) is preferred over traditional radiographic testing during pregnancy. MRI exposure during pregnancy is generally considered to be safe, with no negative sequelae identified during evaluations of 3-year-olds exposed to MRI in utero or the offspring of female MRI technicians.[9–11] Currently, the American College of Radiology recommends MRI during pregnancy to avoid exposure to ionizing radiation when imaging studies are needed, and the results of testing may change patient care.[12] Gadolinium crosses the placenta and is generally not recommended during pregnancy. In addition, MRI angiography and venography offer noninvasive methods of visualizing cerebral vasculature.

ESTRADIOL INFLUENCES IN HEADACHE MECHANISMS

Chronic headache is hypothesized to occur as a consequence of interactions between neural and vascular tissues (Figure 11-1).[13,14] Endorphins, serotonin (5-HT), and γ-aminobutyric acid (GABA) decrease at headache onset, while norepinephrine and dopamine increase.[15–17] These changes in neurotransmitters result in dilation of meningeal blood vessels, which, when stretched, activate perivascular neurons that activate the trigeminal system. Trigeminal activation results in activation of the hypothalamus (causing cravings and stimulus sensitivities), the cervical trigeminal system (possibly increasing muscular symptoms), and pain-producing pathways in the thalamus. Calcitonin gene–related peptide (CGRP) returns signals from the activated trigeminal nucleus back to the meningeal vessels, establishing a cycle of reactivation called "neurogenic inflammation." Currently available headache therapies work by interfering with dysregulation of endorphins (eg, opioids), 5-HT (eg, triptans and antidepressants), GABA (eg, valproate and gabapentin),

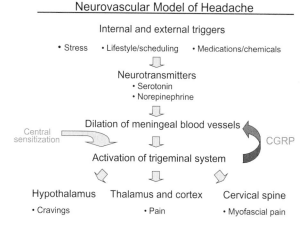

Figure 11-1 The neurovascular model of chronic headache, developed by Michael Moskowitz,[13] links changes in neurotransmitters, meningeal vessels, and trigeminal pathways to result in the headache experience. Central sensitization may result in additional excitation of the trigeminal system. CGRP = calcitonin gene–related peptide.

norepinephrine (eg, antidepressants), or dopamine (eg, antiemetics). Estradiol also influences these pain-modulating neurochemicals.

Pain symptoms are likely to change during pregnancy because of hormonal influences on neural, vascular, and psychological factors. Neural changes with pregnancy include pain threshold, neurotransmitter levels and activity, and central sensitization. CGRP, an important vascular factor in the neurovascular pathway, is also influenced by estradiol (Figure 11-2). Psychological factors can also be influenced by estrogen, although these effects appear to be modulated by cultural influences (Figure 11-3). Headache changes experienced by an individual woman during pregnancy probably result from a balance among these different factors.

Neural Factors

Pain threshold is linked to gender. Women report lower pain threshold, pain tolerance, and analgesic response after exposure to experimental pain compared with men.[18] Women with acute pain report greater pain and analgesic use than males, whereas women with chronic pain report greater pain severity, frequency, duration, and interference.[19–21] Pain threshold can be linked to sex hormones, as pain threshold increases with rising estradiol in both experimental rodent models and women during pregnancy.[22,23] Pain threshold in women also increases with estrogen elevations during the menstrual cycle.[18]

Hormonal changes occurring during pregnancy, specifically the dramatic rise in estradiol levels, contribute to significant changes in pain-provoking neuro-transmitters. Estradiol receptors exist adjacent to 50 to 80% of catecholamine receptors in the brainstem.[24] Increasing estradiol is associated with elevated levels of headache inhibitory neurotransmitters, including 5-HT and GABA.[25,26] In addition, intracellular estradiol receptors occur in the majority of enkephalin-producing neurons in superficial laminae of both the trigeminal and spinal dorsal horns.[27] Enkephalin levels increase by 68% following estrogen administration.[28] Estradiol also influences headache excitatory neurotransmitters. Whereas low-dose or pulsatile administration of estradiol increases dopamine, sustained high doses of estradiol decrease dopamine release.[29] Concentrations of both dopamine and norepinephrine measured in the rat brain decrease with pregnancy.[30] Therefore, headache inhibitory neurotransmitters are increased with increasing estradiol, whereas headache activating neurochemicals are decreased.

Central sensitization is another important factor in chronic headache. New hypotheses about the important contribution of central sensitization to migraine are currently being tested.[31] Strassman and colleagues recorded activity from primary afferents in the rat trigeminal ganglion.[32] Chemical stimulation of dural receptive fields with inflammatory agents lowered the threshold of response of mechanically sensitive neurons and provoked mechanosensitivity in neurons previously insensitive to mechanical stimulation. Burstein postulates that this enhanced mechanosensitivity results in the frequent experience of throbbing pain during migraine with minor increases in intracranial pressure (eg, cough or bending) that are too small to be noticed outside of the migraine episode.[33] In addition, migraine attacks are

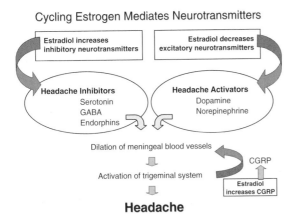

Headache

Figure 11-2 Rising estradiol during pregnancy enhances levels and activity of neurotransmitters that inhibit headache activity (eg, serotonin, GABA, and endorphins), while reducing activity of headache activators (eg, norepinephrine and dopamine). CGRP = calcitonin gene–related peptide; GABA = γ-aminobutyric acid.

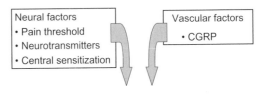

Changing headache patterns in women

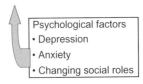

Figure 11-3 Estrogen influences a variety of factors that may affect headache patterns. Estrogen influences neurotransmitter changes to reduce probability of headache, while influencing vascular factors to increase headache probability. The role of psychological factors is moderated by cultural influences. Changes of headache for any individual woman with pregnancy depend on the balance among all of these factors. CGRP = calcitonin gene–related peptide.

associated with cutaneous allodynia (the experience of pain in response to stimulation with non-noxious heat, cold, or pressure stimuli) on the ipsilateral head in 79% of migraine patients.[34] These findings may explain the frequent reports of scalp sensitivity (difficulty brushing hair or wearing glasses or earrings) during migraine attacks. A recent report showed the reversal of signs of central sensitization in rats after trigeminal stimulation and humans with migraine-associated allodynia when treated early with triptan.[35] A sensitization model of kindling offers a well-established mechanism for the development of experimental epilepsy. Interestingly, kindling is facilitated by estrogen.[36] Other studies confirm that female rodents are more susceptible to neural sensitization than males, suggesting a testosterone inhibition of sensitization.[37] Future studies may confirm a link between estrogen and increased central sensitization in women with chronic migraine.

Estrogen influences on the neural system result in an increased likelihood of pain and headache, from lowered pain threshold and central sensitization, in women in general. Pregnancy, with its dramatic rise in estradiol, would be expected to result in improved headache activity based on acute changes in neurotransmitter levels and activity. At delivery, when estradiol levels fall precipitously, this protective effect would be lost and headache would be expected to return.

Vascular Factors

CGRP is an important vasodilator and is believed to be an important mediator of neurogenic inflammation and perpetuation of headache activity by promoting antidromic transmission from activated trigeminal neurons back to dilated meningeal vessels. Clinically, injections of CGRP into the external jugular vein in migraineurs precipitate headache.[38] This has led to the development of CGRP antagonists as possible therapies for migraine (eg, BIBN4096BS, developed by Boehringer Ingelheim).

CGRP is influenced by changes in estradiol levels. Estradiol increases CGRP concentrations and messenger ribonucleic acid (mRNA) expression in ovariectomized rodents.[39,40] In humans, CGRP levels increase during pregnancy and decrease with delivery and postpartum.[39,41,42] Pregnancy is, therefore, expected to aggravate headache activity through activation of vascular factors mediated by CGRP.

Psychological Factors

Hormonal influences may also modulate mood and other psychological factors that impact headache. Studies with menopausal women demonstrate that occurrence of somatic symptoms, including headache, with menopause are strongly influenced by cultural expectations of menopause.[43–45] The modulating impact from cultural and psychosocial variables, therefore,

must be considered when identifying headache changes with variations in estradiol.

The ability of estrogen to influence psychological factors is demonstrated indirectly by studies that negatively correlate body mass index with negative affect, as estrogen levels increase in association with increased adipose tissue.[46] In addition, mood can be improved with treatment with either monophasic oral contraceptives or estrogen replacement therapy.[47–49] A depressed mood has been strongly linked to headache activity.[50,51]

MATERNAL AND FETAL RISKS ASSOCIATED WITH CHRONIC HEADACHE TREATMENT

Medication therapy during pregnancy is limited by concerns about medication effects on the developing fetus. Updated information about medication effects during pregnancy and lactation can be obtained through pharmacists and Reprotox (accessible at http://www.reprotox.org), an Internet reproductive toxicology information source. The most serious medication effects on the fetus occur with early exposure, before many women are aware that they are pregnant. Therefore, management of young women with chronic headache needs to include an evaluation of reproductive status and contraceptive use. Fertile women not using effective contraception and at risk of pregnancy should be treated with those medications deemed safe during early pregnancy (Table 11-1).

Failure to adequately treat recurring headaches during pregnancy can result in significant disability in the mother, as well as poor hydration and nutrition if nausea occurs during headache episodes. In addition, women will usually self-medicate with available medications, even without doctor supervision. A recent survey of adolescents showed that 20% of girls would borrow or share medications with others, and 7% aged 15 to 18 years shared medications more than three times.[52] Surveys across continents have shown that during pregnancy, up to one-third of women will self-medicate for health symptoms, especially with analgesics.[53–55] Unsupervised use of analgesics can result in analgesic overuse headaches, as well as both maternal and fetal side effects.

Acute Care Medications

Acute care medication restrictions of a maximum of 3 days per week apply to both pregnant and nonpregnant headache patients. Daily or near-daily analgesic use in headache sufferers (including daily over-the-counter analgesics) results in an exacerbation of headache, with more frequent and severe headache episodes called "medication overuse headache."[56] Pregnant women are at high risk for the development of analgesic overuse headache because they often substitute daily analgesics for previously effective preventive therapy

Table 11-1 Treatment of Chronic Headache During Pregnancy or Attempted Conception

Safe During Pregnancy (FDA Risk Category A/B)	Used if Benefit > Risk (FDA Risk Category C)	Avoid During Pregnancy (FDA Risk Category D/X)
Acute therapy		
Acetaminophen, opioids, antiemetics	Triptans	Ergotamines
Preventive medication therapy		
Avoid daily or near-daily analgesics. Use beta-blockers, SSRI antidepressants, bupropion, gabapentin in early pregnancy	Tricyclic antidepressants, calcium channel blockers	Valproate
Preventive non-medication therapy		
Relaxation, biofeedback, discontinuation of nicotine, regular meals, regular sleep habits		Dietary restriction

FDA = Food and Drug Administration; SSRI = selective serotonin reuptake inhibitor.

after learning of their pregnancy. Pregnant women must be specifically advised to avoid analgesic overuse, especially if they have a pattern of frequent headache. Medication overuse headache during pregnancy is treated with discontinuation of the overused medication.

Safe acute care medications include acetaminophen, opioids, and antiemetics. Medications inhibiting prostaglandin synthesis, such as nonsteroidal anti-inflammatory drugs (NSAIDs), inhibit implantation and should be avoided during attempted conception.[57,58] In addition, NSAID use in later pregnancy is associated with premature closure of the fetal ductus arteriosus and should be avoided after gestational week 32.[59–61] Codeine has been linked with cleft palate and inguinal hernias, although these associations have not been confirmed in recent studies.[62–64] Codeine is rarely useful during pregnancy because of its constipating effects, and hydrocodone is often better tolerated. Patients must be cautioned to avoid daily opioid use to prevent the development of medication overuse headache. In addition, patients chronically using daily opioids during mid-to-late pregnancy must continue daily opioids because of the risks of fetal mortality and premature labor associated with intrauterine fetal opioid withdrawal.[65] Antiemetics (such as prochlorperazine and promethazine) are beneficial adjunctive therapy to analgesics rather than monotherapy.[66] Metoclopramide is less effective than other antiemetics.[67] Patients who fail to manage headaches at home may require intravenous rehydration and intravenous diphenhydramine, opioids, or metoclopramide.

The use of triptans during pregnancy remains controversial. Small voluntary registries collected by pharmaceutical companies have not demonstrated malformations associated with triptan use.[68,69] The largest registry by GlaxoSmithKline, containing less than 300 women, has failed to demonstrate any negative associations with triptan use during pregnancy.[70] Two large European studies reported trends toward early delivery and lower birth weight in the offspring of triptan users.[71,72] Therefore, additional data are needed before regular use of triptans during pregnancy is recommended for most women. Injectable sumatriptan can be used postpartum during lactation if women pump and discard milk obtained during the first 4 hours after sumatriptan injection and supplement feedings with stored or bottled milk.

Preventive Medications

Frequent headache (problematic episodes regularly occurring more than 2 to 3 days each week) require treatment with preventive therapy. Important considerations in women who have severe migraine and comorbid disease include issues about the metabolic changes that often occur in association with preventive medications. Antidepressants can modify weight, whereas beta-blockers increase the risk of mood disturbance. In addition, some anticonvulsants are associated with hyperinsulinemia, centripetal obesity, lipid abnormalities, and polycystic-appearing ovaries/hyperandrogenism.[73] In addition, bone health is of particular concern in women who may need to be on long-term antiepileptic drugs because of comorbid epilepsy. Antiepileptic drugs with some efficacy in migraine prophylaxis include gabapentin, valproic acid, topiramate, lamotrigine, oxcarbazepine, and levetiracetam. All manufacturers have pregnancy registries as part of their epidemiologic safety monitoring, and treating physicians can obtain this information for each drug.[74] With the exception of valproic acid, most of these drugs are classified as Food and Drug Administration pregnancy category C.

Safe preventive headache medications that can be used before and after conception and throughout pregnancy include the beta-blocker antihypertensives, selective serotonin reuptake inhibitor (SSRI) antidepressants, and bupropion.[75–81] Gabapentin may also be used while attempting to conceive and during early pregnancy, but must be discontinued in later pregnancy because of concerns about delaying fetal bony growth plate development. Tricyclic antidepressants have superior efficacy to the SSRIs, although their use in psychiatric patients has been associated with an increased risk of cardiovascular abnormalities.[82] Low-dose antidepressants may be used in patients who have disabling headaches that fail to respond to other therapy. Valproate is avoided in early pregnancy because of concerns of neural tube defects.[83] Calcium channel blockers, such as flunarizine, have not been associated with any particular teratogenic effect; however, more data are needed to establish the safe use of calcium channel blockers during pregnancy.[84,85]

Nonpharmacologic Therapy

In general, non-medication therapies can be effective in motivated patients.[86] Cordingley and colleagues compared the effectiveness of standard doses of amitriptyline to an 8-week, home-based stress management program for tension-type headache.[87] Headache activity and medication use were decreased for both groups. Headache index (calculated as an average daily headache severity score) was reduced by 58% with stress management and 33% with amitriptyline. Stress management also resulted in a superior internal locus of control, the perception that the patient can control her headache rather than the headaches being controlled by fate or healthcare providers. Greater perceived self-control of migraine and tension-type headache decreases headache-associated disability.[88] Non-medication strategies have been demonstrated to be as effective for hormonally triggered migraines as they are for nonhormonal migraines.[89,90]

Effective non-medication therapies, such as stress management, relaxation, and biofeedback, should be encouraged in motivated pregnant women to maximize both treatment efficacy and safety. Relaxation, with or without biofeedback training, is effective for 50 to 80% of motivated migraine and tension-type headache sufferers.[91,92] Treatment benefits are unrelated to the presence of comorbid psychological symptoms and are cost-effective.[93] Minimal therapist contact for relaxation with thermal biofeedback (four 1-hour training sessions) reduced headache by at least 50% in 79% of pregnant women with recurring migraine and/or tension-type headache.[94] Benefits of brief training were maintained postpartum and for 12 months after delivery.[95]

Other strategies with moderate headache efficacy and overall health benefits include discontinuation of nicotine and avoidance of fasting and sleep deprivation.[96] Dietary restriction is only beneficial for about 30% of patients and may limit adequate nutrition during pregnancy. Therefore, headache-restrictive diets (eg, tyramine-free diets) should not be prescribed during pregnancy. The benefit of herbal remedies (eg, feverfew, gingko, St. John's wort) and vitamin or mineral supplements for reducing headache has not been established. Therefore, these treatments should not be recommended during pregnancy.

Breastfeeding in Chronic Headache Sufferers

Lactation is unlikely to alter headache activity. Although there are several anecdotal reports of headache aggravation or worsening with nursing, in a large series, headache changed with lactation in only 5 of 2,500 migraineurs who were followed over 6 years.[97] Therefore, women should not be discouraged from breastfeeding because of concerns about aggravating headache.

Medication use needs to be monitored while breastfeeding in order to minimize unwanted medication exposure in the baby. Most medications that are safe during pregnancy continue to be safe while nursing. Sumatriptan can be used during lactation. Women should be advised to pump and discard milk obtained during the first 4 hours after sumatriptan injection or 6 hours after oral administration and supplement feedings with stored or bottled milk.

Summary

DH has a history of migraine without aura with significant improvement during pregnancy. She did not have spontaneous resolution of migraine, however, as is characteristic in most women with moderate to severe migraine. Postnatal headaches are reportedly common during the first postpartum week; they are generally reported to occur in 30 to 40% of women. DH did have a few fairly severe, typical migraine attacks in her early postpartum period. Like many women, DH did not experience the same pattern of headache change with each pregnancy. This may be related to changes in her own physiology or influences from confounding factors, such as added stress and sleep deprivation, during later pregnancies.

Improvement or disappearance of migraine during pregnancy has been noted in 50 to 85% of migraineurs. Migraine, however, may remain unchanged during pregnancy in 5 to 30% of migraine sufferers. Some researchers have found that improvement in migraine was limited to migraine without aura and was observed primarily in the second and third trimesters of pregnancy. Other researchers note that more severely affected migraineurs have no change during pregnancy.

In general, the beneficial effect of pregnancy on migraine is observed more frequently in women who have menstrual migraine and/or women whose migraine began at menarche.

Because migraine generally improves during pregnancy, non-pharmacologic management can be emphasized. Biofeedback, massage, avoidance of triggers, regular exercise, careful sleep, and adequate rest may all tend to minimize attack frequency and severity. Local application of ice or heat and adequate hydration may also be useful.

NSAIDs may be used as acute headache therapy after implantation and before 32 weeks. Caffeine and opioids (safety class B) alone or in combination with antiemetics, such as promethazine and ondansetron, may be useful. Rescue therapy with steroids and intravenous hydration may be necessary in extreme circumstances. The use of triptans during pregnancy has not been established, although it has recently been proposed that sumatriptan receive class B scheduling for pregnancy use. The sumatriptan pregnancy registry does not show any evidence of adverse outcomes higher than would be expected in controls. During breastfeeding, acetaminophen and NSAIDs are felt compatible with breastfeeding, although caution is required with aspirin. Sumatriptan has been used safely in this setting, with patients instructed to pump and discard breast milk for 4 to 6 hours after use before resuming feeding.

Preventive medication may be indicated in women who continue to have frequent or severe attacks, although there are no adequate well-controlled studies in pregnant women. Preventive therapy is typically tapered 4 weeks prior to delivery. Several preventive therapies, such as beta-blockers, have established safety during pregnancy.

For women during their childbearing years, clinicians have a particular opportunity to manage their migraine well around the time of conception. Management of chronic headache in women of childbearing age should consider the use of preventive therapy that is safe to continue during pregnancy: supplementation of folic acid (1 mg daily), use of magnesium 400 mg bid, or riboflavin 400 mg/day. Non-pharmacologic therapies may begin to be emphasized and the usual abortive regimen can be continued during preovulatory days. During the time when a patient is uncertain as to whether pregnancy has been achieved or is merely post-ovulation, analgesics, opioids, antiemetics, and corticosteroids can predominate as acute therapy choices.

REFERENCES

1. Callaghan N. The migraine syndrome in pregnancy. Neurology 1968;18:197–9.

2. Granella F, Sances G, Zanferrari C, et al. Migraine without aura and reproductive life events: a clinical epidemiological study in 1300 women. Headache 1993;33:385–9.

3. Chen TC, Leviton A. Headache recurrences in pregnant women with migraine. Headache 1994;34:107–10.

4. Maggioni F, Alessi C, Maggino T, et al. Primary headaches and pregnancy. Cephalalgia 1995;15:54.

5. Sances G, Granella F, Nappi RE, et al. Course of migraine during pregnancy and postpartum: a prospective study. Cephalalgia 2003;23:197–205.

6. Marcus DA, Scharff L, Turk D. Longitudinal prospective study of headache during pregnancy and postpartum. Headache 1999;39:625–32.

7. Stein GS. Headaches in the first post partum week and their relationship to migraine. Headache 1981;21:201–5.

8. Stein GS, Morton J, Marsh A, et al. Headaches after childbirth. Acta Neurol Scand 1984;69:74–9.

9. Levine D, Barnes PD, Edleman RR. Obstetric MR imaging. Radiology 1999;211:609–17.

10. Baker P, Johnson I, Harvey P, Mansfield P. A three-year follow-up of children imaged in utero using echo-planar magnetic resonance. Am J Obstet Gynecol 1994;170:32–3.

11. Kanal E, Gillen J, Evans J, et al. Survey of reproductive health among female MR workers. Radiology 1993;187:395–9.

12. ACR standards: MRI safety and sedation. Available at: http://www.acr.org (accessed July 28, 2003).

13. Moskowitz MA. The neurobiology of vascular head pain. Ann Neurol 1984;16:157–68.

14. Marcus DA. Serotonin and its role in headache pathogenesis and treatment. Clin J Pain 1993;9:159–67.

15. Marcus DA. Interrelationships of neurochemicals, oestrogen, and recurring headache. Pain 1995;62:129–39.

16. Kruger H, Luhmann HJ, Heinemann U. Repetitive spreading depression causes selective suppression of GABAergic function. Neuroreport 1996;7:2733–6.

17. Fanciullaci M, Alessandri M, Del Rosso A. Dopamine involvement in the migraine attack. Funct Neurol 2000;15:171–81.

18. Hellstrom B, Lundberg U. Pain perception to the cold pressor test during the menstrual cycle in relation to estrogen levels and a comparison with men. Integr Physiol Behav Sci 2000;35:1377–9.

19. Zeichner A, Loftin M, Panopoulos G, et al. Sex differences in pain indices, exercise, and use of analgesics. Psychol Rep 2000;86:129–33.

20. Unruh AM. Gender variations in clinical pain experience. Pain 1996;65:123–67.

21. Unruh AM, Ritchie J, Merskey H. Does gender affect appraisal of pain and pain coping strategies? Clin J Pain 1999;15:31–40.

22. Dawson-Basoa MB, Gintzler AR. 17-Beta-estradiol and progesterone modulate an intrinsic opioid analgesic system. Brain Res 1993;601:241–5.

23. Cogan R, Spinnato JA. Pain and discomfort thresholds in late pregnancy. Pain 1986;27:63–8.

24. Heritage AS, Stumpf WE, Sar M, Grant L. Brainstem catecholamine neurons are target sites for sex hormones. Science 1980;207:1377–9.

25. Joy KP, Tharakan B, Goos HJ. Distribution of gamma-aminobutyric acid in catfish (*Heteropneustes fossilis*) forebrain in relation to season, ovariectomy and E2 replacement, and effects of GABA administration on plasma gonadotropin-II level. Comp Biochem Physiol A Mol Integr Physiol 1999;123:369–76.

26. Lagrange AH, Ronnekleiv OK, Kelly MJ. The potency of mu-opioid hyperpolarization of hypothalamic arcuate neurons is rapidly attenuated by 17-beta-estradiol. J Neurosci 1994;14:6196–204.

27. Amandusson A, Hermanson O, Blomqvist A. Colocalization of oestrogen receptor immunoreactivity and preproenkephalin mRNA expression to neurons in the superficial laminae of the spinal and medullary dorsal horn of rats. Eur J Neurosci 1996;8:2440–5.

28. Amandusson A, Hallbeck M, Hallbeck AL, et al. Oestrogen-induced alterations of spinal cord enkephalin gene expression. Pain 1999;83:243–8.

29. Fabre-Nys C. Steroid control of monoamines in relation to sexual behavior. Rev Reprod 1998;3:31–41.

30. Glaser J, Russell VA, Taljaard JJ. Rat brain hypothalamic and hippocampal beta-adrenergic receptor changes during pregnancy. Brain Res 1992;557:293–9.

31. Bendtsen L. Sensitization: its role in primary headache. Curr Opin Invest Drugs 2002;3:449–53.

32. Strassman AM, Raymond SA, Burstein R. Sensitization of meningeal sensory neurons and the origin of headaches. Nature 1996;384:560–4.

33. Burstein R. Deconstructing migraine into peripheral and central sensitization. Pain 2001;89:107–10.

34. Burstein R, Yarnitsky D, Goor-Aryeh I, et al. An association between migraine and cutaneous allodynia. Ann Neurol 2000;47:614–24.

35. Burstein R, Collins B, Bajwa Z, Jakubowski M. Triptan therapy can abort migraine attacks if given before the establishment or in the absence of cutaneous allodynia and central sensitization: clinical and preclinical evidence. Headache 2002;42:390–1.

36. Edwards HE, Burnham WM, Mendonca A, et al. Steroid hormones affect limbic afterdischarge threshold and kindling rates in adult female rats. Brain Res 1999;838:136–50.

37. Hennessy JW, Levin R, Levine S. Influence of experiential factors and gonadal hormones on pituitary-adrenal response of the mouse to novelty and electric shock. J Comp Physiol Psychol 1977;91:770–7.

38. Lassen LH, Haderslev PA, Jacobsen VB, et al. CGRP may play a causative role in migraine. Cephalalgia 2002;22: 54–61.

39. Gangula PR, Wimalawansa SJ, Yallampalli C. Pregnancy and sex steroid hormones enhance circulating calcitonin gene-related peptide concentrations in rats. Hum Reprod 2000;15:949–53.

40. Gangula PR, Lanlua P, Wimalawansa S, et al. Regulation of calcitonin gene-related peptide expression in dorsal root ganglia of rats by female sex steroid hormones. Biol Reprod 2000;62:1033–9.

41. Stevenson JC, Macdonald DW, Warren RC, et al. Increased concentration of circulating calcitonin gene related peptide during normal human pregnancy. BMJ 1986;293:1329–30.

42. Saggese G, Bertelloni S, Baroncelli GI, et al. Evaluation of a peptide family encoded by the calcitonin gene in selected healthy pregnant women. A longitudinal study. Horm Res 1990;34:240–4.

43. Flint M. The menopause: reward or punishment? Psychosomatics 1975;16:161–3.

44. Matthews KA, Wing RR, Kuller LH, et al. Influences of natural menopause on psychological characteristics and symptoms of middle-aged women. J Consult Clin Psychol 1990;58:345–51.

45. Avis NE, Kaufert PA, Lock M, et al. The evolution of menopausal symptoms. Baillieres Clin Endocrinol Metab 1993;7:17–32.

46. Oinonen KA, Mazmanian D. Does body fat protect against negative moods in women? Med Hypotheses 2001;57:387–8.

47. Oinonen KA, Mazmanian D. To what extent do oral contraceptives influence mood and affect? J Affect Disord 2002;70:229–40.

48. Rasgon NL, Altshuler LL, Fairbanks LA, et al. Estrogen replacement therapy in the treatment of major depressive disorder in perimenopausal women. J Clin Psychiatry 2002;63 Suppl 7:45–8.

49. Soares CN, Almeida OP, Joffe H, Cohen LS. Efficacy of estradiol for the treatment of depressive disorders in perimenopausal women: a double-blind, randomized, placebo-controlled trial. Arch Gen Psychiatry 2001;58: 529–34.

50. Sheftell FD, Atlas SJ. Migraine and psychiatric comorbidity: from theory and hypotheses to clinical application. Headache 2002;42:934–44.

51. Miranda H, Ortiz G, Figueroa S, et al. Depression scores following migraine treatment in patients attending a specialized center for headache and neurology. Headache 2001;41:680–4.

52. Daniel KL, Honein MA, Moore CA. Sharing prescription medication among teenage girls: potential danger to unplanned/undiagnosed pregnancies. Pediatrics 2003;111:1167–70.

53. Gomes KR, Moron AF, Silva R, Siqueira AA. Prevalence of use of medicines during pregnancy and its relationship to maternal factors. Rev Saude Publica 1999;33:246–54.

54. Fonseca MR, Fonseca E, Bergsten-Mendes G. Prevalence of drug use during pregnancy: a pharmacoepidemiological approach. Rev Saude Publica 2002;36:205–12.

55. Damase-Michel C, Lapeyre-Mestre M, Moly C, et al. Drug use during pregnancy: survey in 250 women consulting at a university hospital center. J Gynecol Obstet Biol Reprod (Paris) 2000;29:77–85.

56. Baumgartner C, Wessely P, Bingol C, et al. Long-term prognosis of analgesic withdrawal in patients with drug-induced headache. Headache 1989;29:510–4.

57. Carp HJ, Fein A, Nebel L. Effect of diclofenac on implantation and embryonic development in the rat. Eur J Obstet Gynaecol Reprod Biol 1988;28:273–7.

58. Kanayama K, Osada H, Nariai K, Endo T. Inhibitory effects of indomethacin on implantation and its related phenomena. J Int Med Res 1996;24:258–62.

59. Momma K, Hagiwara H, Konishi T. Constriction of fetal ductus arteriosus by non-steroidal anti-inflammatory drugs: study of additional 34 drugs. Prostaglandins 1984;28:527–36.

60. Rein AJ, Nadjari M, Elchalal U, Nir A. Contraction of the fetal ductus arteriosus induced by diclofenac. Case report. Fetal Diagn Ther 1999;14:24–5.

61. Zenker M, Klinge J, Kruger C, et al. Severe pulmonary hypertension in a neonate caused by premature closure of the ductus arteriosus following maternal treatment with diclofenac: a case report. J Perinat Med 1998;26:231–4.

62. Bracken MB, Holford TR. Exposure to prescribed drugs in pregnancy and association with congenital malformations. Obstet Gynecol 1981;58:336–44.

63. Saxen I. Association between oral cleft and drugs taken during pregnancy. Int J Epidemiol 1975;4:37–44.

64. Saxen I. Epidemiology of cleft lip and palate: an attempt to rule out chance correlations. Br J Prev Soc Med 1975;29:103–10.

65. Drug use and dependence. In: The Merck manual of diagnostics and therapeutics. 17th ed. Section 15. Chapter 195. Available at: http://www.merck.com/pubs (accessed July 28, 2003).

66. Jones J, Pack S, Chun E. Intramuscular prochlorperazine versus metoclopramide as single-agent therapy for the treatment of acute migraine headache. Ann Emerg Med 1996;14:262–4.

67. Coppola M, Yealy DM, Leibold RA. Randomized, placebo-controlled evaluation of prochlorperazine versus metoclopramide for emergency department treatment of migraine headache. Ann Emerg Med 1995;26:541–6.

68. Schuhaiber S, Patusak A, Schick B, et al. Pregnancy outcome following first trimester exposure to sumatriptan. Neurology 1998;51:581–3.

69. O'Quinn S, Ephross SA, Williams V, et al. Pregnancy and perinatal outcomes in migraineurs using sumatriptan: a prospective study. Arch Gynecol Obstet 1999;263: 7–12.

70. Sumatriptan and naratriptan pregnancy registry data on file at GlaxoSmithKline. Available at: http://pregnancyregistry.gsk.com/naratriptan.html. (accessed October 5, 2003).

71. Olesen L, Steffensen FH, Sorensen HT, et al. Pregnancy outcome following prescription for sumatriptan. Headache 2000;40:20–4.

72. Kallen B, Lygner PE. Delivery outcome in women who used drugs for migraine during pregnancy with special reference to sumatriptan. Headache 2001;41:351–6.

73. Morrell MJ. The new anti-epileptic drugs in women: efficacy, reproductive health, pregnancy, and fetal outcome. Epilepsia 1996;37:S34–44.

74. Reiff-Eldrigde R, Heffner CR, Ephross SA, et al. Monitoring pregnancy outcomes after prenatal drug exposure through prospective pregnancy registries: a pharmaceutical company commitment. Am J Obstet Gynecol 2000;182:159–63.

75. Bank J. A comparative study of amitriptyline and fluvoxamine in migraine prophylaxis. Headache 1994;34:476–8.

76. Black KJ, Sheline YI. Paroxetine as migraine prophylaxis. J Clin Psychiatry 1995;56:330–1.

77. Kulin NA, Pastuszak A, Sage SR, et al. Pregnancy outcome following maternal use of the new selective serotonin reuptake inhibitors: a prospective controlled multicenter study. JAMA 1998;279:609–10.

78. D'Amato CC, Pizza V, Marmolo T, et al. Fluoxetine for migraine prophylaxis: a double-blind study. Headache 1999;39:716–9.

79. Amelin AV, Skoromets AA, Korenko KA, et al. A comparative efficiency of amitriptyline, fluoxetine, and maprotiline in prevention of migraine in attack-free period. Zh Nevropatol Psikhiatr Im S S Korsakova 2000; 100:20–3.

80. Goodman JF. Treatment of headache with bupropion. Headache 1997;37:256.

81. Pinsker W. Potentially safe and effective new treatment for migraine? Headache 1998;38:58.

82. Simpkins JW, Field FP, Torosian G, Soltis EE. Effects of prenatal exposure to tricyclic antidepressants on adrenergic responses in progeny. Dev Pharmacol Ther 1985; 8:17–33.

83. Thomas SV, Indrani L, Devi GC, et al. Pregnancy in women with epilepsy: preliminary results of Kerala registry of epilepsy and pregnancy. Neurol India 2001; 49:60–6.

84. Gulmezoglu AM, Hofmeyr GJ. Calcium channel blockers for potential impaired fetal growth. Cochrane Database Syst Rev 2000;2:CD00049.

85. Sorensen HT, Czeizel AE, Rockenbauer M, et al. The risk of limb deficiencies and other congenital abnormalities in children exposed in utero to calcium channel blockers. Acta Obstet Gynecol Scand 2001;80:397–401.

86. Marcus DA. Nonpharmacologic treatment of migraine. TEN 2001;3:50–5.

87. Cordingley G, Holrody K, Pingel J, et al. Amitriptyline versus stress management therapy in the prophylaxis of chronic tension headache. Headache 1990;30:300.

88. French DJ, Holroyd KA, Pinell C, et al. Perceived self-efficacy and headache-related disability. Headache 2000;40:647–56.

89. Solbach P, Sargent J, Coyne L. Menstrual migraine headache: results of a controlled, experimental, outcome study of non-drug treatments. Headache 1984;24:75–8.

90. Gauthier JG, Fournier AL, Roberge C. The differential effects of biofeedback in the treatment of menstrual and nonmenstrual migraine. Headache 1991;31:82–90.

91. Warner G, Lance JW. Relaxation therapy in migraine and chronic tension headache. Med J Aust 1975;1:298–301.

92. Daly EJ, Donn PA, Galliher MJ, Zimmerman JS. Biofeedback applications to migraine and tension headache: a double-blinded outcome study. Biofeedback Self Regul 1983;8:135–52.

93. Blanchard EB, Andrasik F, Appelbaum KA, et al. The efficacy and cost-effectiveness of minimal-therapist-contact, non-drug treatments of chronic migraine and tension headache. Headache 1985;25:214–20.

94. Marcus DA, Scharff L, Turk DC. Nonpharmacologic management of headaches during pregnancy. Psychosom Med 1995;57:527–33.

95. Scharff L, Marcus DA, Turk DC. Maintenance of effects in the nonmedical treatment of headaches during pregnancy. Headache 1996;36:285–90.

96. Payne TJ, Stetson B, Stevens VM, et al. Impact of cigarette smoking on headache activity in headache patients. Headache 1991;31:329–32.

97. Wall VR. Breastfeeding and migraine headaches. J Hum Lact 1992;8:209–12.

CHAPTER 12

Menopause and Migraine

Stephen D. Silberstein, MD, FACP

CASE

MS, a 47-year-old woman, had a lifelong history of migraine. Her headaches began with her first period at age 16 years. The headaches were typically bilateral, throbbing in quality, and associated with nausea. They ranged in severity from mild with no disability to severe when she was bedridden. Throughout her life, MS averaged one to two attacks per month, often associated with her menstrual period. She was headache-free during each of her pregnancies. Her periods became irregular when she was 43 years of age. Associated with this was an increase in her headache frequency. Her periods ceased at age 46 years and her headaches became less frequent. Her gynecologist gave her conjugated estrogens for hot

flashes, which, again, were associated with increased migraine attacks. After conversion to a transdermal formulation, her headaches and hot flashes both came under control.

MS's story is very typical of many women who experience significant headache changes throughout their reproductive life cycle as hormonal levels are changing. Women often experience an unexpected increase in migraine during the early perimenopausal period and again after treatment with estrogen replacement therapy. Treating both somatic and migraine symptoms after menopause requires consideration of both headache activity and the somatic risks and benefits from hormonal supplementation.

KEY CHAPTER POINTS

- **Strategies for prescribing hormonal replacement depend on a variety of risks factors.**
- **Progestins protect the endometrium of the intact uterus.**
- **Headache management in women using hormone replacement therapy (HRT) may require adjustment of estrogen.**
- **Risks of ovarian and breast cancer may be increased with HRT.**
- **Risks of cardiovascular disease may be increased with HRT.**
- **Estrogen replacement therapy (ERT) increases thromboembolic risk twofold.**
- **HRT reduces overall risk of vertebral and nonvertebral fracture by about 25%.**
- **Cognitive benefits from ERT are uncertain.**

At menopause, the permanent cessation of menstruation, sex steroid hormone levels are low and

gonadotropin levels are elevated. The average age of menopause is between 51 and 52 years, with a range of 40 to 60 years. The timing of menopause is both genetically and environmentally influenced. It occurs about 2 years earlier in women who smoke cigarettes than in those who do not smoke.[1] The prevailing view has been that normal menopause results from depletion of ovarian follicles that can be stimulated to ovulate. An alternative view is that age-related changes in the central nervous system initiate menopause, and the exhaustion of ovarian follicles is a consequence of the altered temporal organization of neural signals.[2]

Ovarian function decreases gradually; the time between the onset of menstrual irregularity and menopause is called "the perimenopause." In the perimenopausal period, plasma concentrations of follicle-stimulating hormone are elevated and are associated with increased levels of serum estradiol and urine estrogen conjugates. As the follicles become depleted and inhibin levels remain low, they no longer respond to elevated follicle-stimulating hormone levels and estradiol levels fall. This leads to the failure of endometrial development and the absence of uterine bleeding.

Menopause is associated with both early and late symptoms (Table 12-1).[3,4] Hot flushes, a vasomotor change, correlate with bursts of activity in hypothalamic pacemaker neurons, leading to pulses of gonadotropin-releasing hormone and, thus, luteinizing hormone.[5,6] A community study in the United Kingdom found the peak prevalence of flushing in the 45- to 50-year and 50- to 55-year age groups to be at 40% and 50%, respectively. For every 5-year age-band from 40 to 65 years, the prevalence was above 20%.[7]

Although migraine prevalence decreases with advancing age, migraine can either regress or worsen at menopause.[8,9] Neri and colleagues investigated 556 consecutive postmenopausal women attending an outpatient clinic and found that headache was present in 13.7%.[10] Most (82%) had had headaches prior to the onset of menopause. Many (62%) had migraine without aura; the remainder had tension-type headaches. None of the women had migraine with aura or cluster headache. Two-thirds of women with prior migraine improved with physiologic menopause. In contrast, two-thirds of women who had surgical menopause had a worsening of migraine. Other studies have shown that hysterectomy or oophorectomy is not an effective treatment for migraine at any age, despite recent suggestions to the contrary.[11–14] ERT and HRT (ERT in combination with progestins) can exacerbate migraine or, alone or with testosterone, relieve it.[15–19] This has been confirmed in one, but not another, double-blind study.[20,21] Menopausal women who do not need ERT should be prescribed migraine drugs based on their cardiac and renal status.[22]

RISKS FACTORS IN HORMONAL REPLACEMENT THERAPY

HRT aims to restore physiologic levels of estrogen in order to prevent estrogen deficiency symptoms and diseases resulting from menopause. The benefits of ERT may be modified by the addition of progestogens, which are necessary to protect the endometrium in a woman with an intact uterus. There is no evidence that migraine is a risk factor for ischemic stroke in women over age 45 years. There are insufficient data to support an increased risk of ischemic stroke in women who have any type of migraine and are using HRT. Migraine alone is not a contraindication for HRT.[23]

ERT, alone or in combination with progestins (HRT), is often used to treat menopausal symptoms and prevent osteoporosis.[24,25] ERT decreases the risk of osteoporotic fracture (including hip and vertebral), but long-term, unopposed ERT increases the risk of endometrial carcinoma.[26,27] The increased endometrial cancer risk can be avoided by adding a progestin to the

Table 12-1 Menopausal Symptoms

Early

Hot flushes
- Associated with pulses of hypothalamic activity that lead to pulses of luteinizing hormone
- Atrophic vaginitis

Psychological and somatic complaints
- Depression
- Anxiety
- Fatigue
- Dizziness
- Insomnia
- Altered libido
- Loss of concentration
- Headache

Late

Dyspareunia

Hirsutism

Reduced breast size

Dry skin

Osteoporosis

Arteriosclerotic cardiovascular disease

estrogen regimen for women who have a uterus.[26,28–30] Menopause presents a particular set of problems for women for whom ERT is indicated, but its use leads to a worsening of migraine symptoms. Women should use the lowest dose of estrogen that will relieve vasomotor symptoms, prevent vaginal and urethral epithelial atrophy, maintain the collagen content of the skin, and reduce the rate of bone resorption. ERT use is no longer believed to delay the onset and decrease the risk of Alzheimer's disease and improve cognition.[31,32] The effect of ERT on the risk of breast cancer is no longer uncertain; recent results suggest an increased risk with long-term use.[26–29]

The most commonly used estrogen, Premarin, is a mixture of conjugated estrogens of equine (CEE) origin (Table 12-2).[33] Pure estrones, estradiols, and synthetic ethinyl estradiol are also available.[34] ERT should be physiologic not pharmacologic.[1] The optimal long-term estrogen dose given to asymptomatic women to reduce the risk of osteoporosis (physiologic replacement dose) is 0.625 mg of CEE or estrone sulfate or 1 mg of micronized estradiol and probably 0.05 mg transdermally. Higher estrogen doses may be needed for 1 or 2 years to relieve hot flushes.

Estrogens can be taken sequentially for 25 days a month with the addition of a progestational agent on

Table 12-2   Hormonal Preparations

Estrogens

Conjugated steroidal estrogens

Estrones

- Conjugated equine estrogens (Premarin; estrone sulfate, equilin sulfate, and 17-dihydroequilenin)
  - Oral 0.3 mg, 0.625 mg, 0.9 mg, 1.25 mg, 2.5 mg
  - Vaginal cream 0.00625%
- Esterified estrogens (Estratab, Menest, Cenestin)
  - Oral 0.3 mg, 0.625 mg, 1.25 mg, 2.5 mg
- Estrone
  - Intramuscular 2 mg or 5 mg
- Estropipate (Ogen, Ortho-est)
  - Oral 0.625 mg, 1.25 mg, 2.5 mg
  - Vaginal cream 0.15%

Estradiol

- Oral (Estrace) 0.5 mg, 1 mg, 2 mg
- Estrogen ring (Estring) 2 mg
- Vaginal cream (Estrace) 0.01%
- Transdermal (Estraderm, Climara, FemPatch, Vivelle)
  - 0.025 μg, 0.375 μg, 0.05 μg, 0.075 μg, 0.1 μg once or twice a week
- Estradiol pellet (Estrapel) 25 mg; investigational
- Estradiol cypionate (Depo-Estradiol, Depogen, Estro-Cyp, depGynogen, Gynogen, Dioval)
  - Injection 1 mg/mL or 5 mg/mL
- Estradiol valerate (Delestrogen, Estraval)
  - Injection 10 mg/mL, 20 mg/mL, 40 mg/mL

Nonconjugated steroidal estrogens

17-Ethinyl estradiol (Estinyl)

- Oral 0.02 mg, 0.05 mg

17-Ethinyl estradiol-3-cyclopentoether (Quinestrol; Estrovis)

- Oral 0.1 mg

Synthetic estrogen analogues (nonsteroidal)

Dienestrol (Ortho, Estragard)

- Vaginal cream 0.01%

Progestins

Medroxyprogesterone acetate (Amen, Cycrin, Provera)

- Oral 2.5 mg, 5 mg, 10 mg

Norethindrone acetate (Aygestin)

- Oral 5 mg

Progesterone

- Micronized (Prometrium) 100 mg or 200 mg
- Vaginal gel (Crinone) 4% (45 mg) and 8% (90 mg)

Hydroxyprogesterone (Hylutin, Hyprogest)

- Intramuscular 125 mg or 250 mg/mL

Continued

Table 12-2 *Continued*

Combination Products

Conjugated estrogen/medroxyprogerestrone (Premphase, Prempro)
- Oral 0.625 mg/2.5 mg, 0.625 mg/5 mg

Esterified estrogens/methyltestosterone (Estratest)
- Oral 0.625 mg/1.25 mg, 1.25 mg/2.5 mg

Estradiol/norethindrone (CombiPatch)
- Transdermal patch 50 mg/0.14 mg, 50 mg/0.25 mg

days 16 to 25 to induce bleeding; alternatively, estrogens and progesterone can be taken continuously.[35] Estrogens can also be given for 5 days each week (skipping the weekend) to control breast tenderness. Estrogens are available orally or parenterally in the form of injection, vaginal cream, estrogen ring, or transdermal patches.[33] Experimental implants and transdermal patches provide stable blood estrogen levels.[6,24,36] In addition, parenteral administration of estrogens produces fewer hepatic effects and a higher, more physiologic serum estradiol to estrone ratio than oral administration.[34,37]

CEE was initially used short-term (generally less than 3 years), often in relatively young, hysterectomized or oophorectomized women. The first surveys published in the 1970s showed an increase in the frequency of vascular accidents, particularly myocardial infarction and stroke, in CEE users.[38,39] Since then, studies have suggested that the dosing was an essential problem: doses of CEE twofold lower than those used in the 1960s appeared to produce strong vascular protection.[40] However, as with the oral contraceptives, healthy users were carefully selected, but this selection process did not avoid the increase in thromboembolic deep venous, pulmonary, and cerebral accidents that continues.[41–47] The first prospective, randomized, placebo-controlled study using a combination of CEE and a progestin has shown no protective effect in women who are at high vascular risk. Users not only had more venous thromboembolic accidents but also tended to have more myocardial infarcts and death during the first year of the study.[47]

Despite low bioavailability, oral estradiol, in micronized or valerate form, produces therapeutic effects, specifically the reestablishment of physiologic vasomotoricity. Because of the strong first-pass hepatic effect, a dose of 1 to 2 mg (7 to 14 times more than the intramuscular dose) is required to reproduce the effects of endogenous production of around 100 µg of estradiol. Low bioavailability is due to the rapid metabolism of estradiol in the digestive tract into barely active or inactive metabolites: 20 to 25% of estradiol is metabolized by the intestinal wall and around 70% by the liver.

The hepatic cells receive the impact of 75 to 80% of the active form of the steroid, whereas the peripheral target tissues share only 5 to 10% of bioavailable estradiol.[48] This produces changes in estrogen-dependent hepatic metabolism (as occurs with CEE) similar to those that occur during pregnancy: an increase in the estrone to estradiol ratio, sex hormone–binding globulin, angiotensinogen, and triglycerides; a decrease in antithrombin; and an increase in fragments 1 and 2 of prothrombin.[49,50]

Cutaneous estradiols in gel form (daily application) or in patch form (once or twice weekly application) closely simulate the physiologic ovarian model. They deliver 17β-estradiol into the vessels of the dermis, then into the general circulation. There is no first-pass hepatic effect in estradiol metabolism; the estrone to estradiol ratio and regulation of hepatic metabolism are more physiologic. In particular, a slow increase in high-density lipoprotein cholesterol occurs without a parallel increase in triglycerides; a decrease in low-density lipoprotein cholesterol occurs without a decrease in low-density lipoprotein particle size; and a decrease in fibrinogen and plasminogen activator inhibitor occurs without an increase in factor VII and a decrease in antithrombin III.[49–51] Subcutaneous estradiol implants reproduce, in primates, all the antiatherogenic and vasodilator effects of endogenous estradiol.[52] The favorable effects on lipids, hemostasis, and vasodilation are clearly dose-dependent and require an estradiol plasma concentration greater than 60 pg/mL.[53–55] Individual adaptation of the dose is essential because the patch systems only deliver small quantities of estradiol and there is great interindividual variability in estrogen bioavailability by any route of administration.[51,56] Gel formulations are invisible, can be applied on large skin surfaces, and are better adapted to delivering doses that maintain serum estradiol levels ≥ 60 pg/mL. No studies have been performed in a sufficient number of users of cutaneous estradiol to assess the incidence of vascular accidents.[57]

Adjunct hormones include progesterone for prevention of endometrial cancer (not needed after hysterectomy) and androgens to combat decreased libido and sexual responsiveness and, perhaps, fatigue, depression, and headache.[11,58] Progesterone itself is associated with side effects, including increased headache and other central nervous system side effects and, in women using progesterone for contraception, is one of the major reasons for discontinuation. Contraindications to ERT include breast or endometrial cancer, active thrombophlebitis, and undiagnosed abnormal uterine bleeding. A prior history of thromboembolic events associated with exogenous estrogen is also a contraindication.[1]

Women without a uterus are not at risk of endometrial cancer and can use estrogens unopposed, either cyclically or continuously. Progestins are administered either sequentially or continuously to postmenopausal women with a uterus. In the sequential regimen, the progestin is given daily for the first 10 to 14 days of the month. In the combined regimen, both the estrogen and the progestin are given daily. The cyclic regimens produce monthly withdrawal bleeding in about 80% of women. The continuous regimen, where estrogens and progestins are given daily, usually results in irregular bleeding and spotting during the first 3 months, but with longer use, nearly all women become amenorrheic.[59] Estrogen and progestogens are available in combination oral tablets and in a transdermal patch containing estradiol and norethindrone acetate.

EFFECT OF PROGESTINS ON THE ENDOMETRIUM

The progestogen most commonly used in North America to protect the endometrium of nonhysterectomized postmenopausal women is medroxyprogesterone acetate (MPA), which is different than natural progesterone. It negates the antiatheroma and vasodilator benefits of estrogens. In contrast, natural progesterone maintains all of estrogen's benefits; they are only negated at supraphysiologic concentrations.[52,60–64] The longest prospective controlled study, Postmenopausal Estrogen Progestin Interventions, shows a significant decrease in high-density lipoprotein cholesterol without the reduction in triglycerides and perturbation of the 2-hour glucose test that is provoked in MPA users. Whereas oral micronized progesterone users had no metabolic side effects at doses ensuring identical results on the endometrium.[61] The choice of the progestogen may, therefore, be as important as the choice of the estrogen in the modulation of cardiovascular effects of HRT.[52,57]

Progestins, used to prevent endometrial hyperplasia, can cause headache in addition to other symptoms of premenstrual syndrome, particularly if used cyclically. Giving a lower dose of a progestin (medroxyprogesterone, 2.5 mg versus 7.5 mg) continuously can often control this effect. Another strategy is to change the type of progestin. Women who received norethindrone had less depression than those who received MPA.[65]

Women with a uterus who have intolerable mental symptoms with progestins may use an estrogen-only regimen in conjunction with an annual endometrial biopsy or vaginal ultrasonography to measure the endometrial thickness. If the endometrial echo complex is less than 4 mm, it may not be necessary to perform a biopsy because the risk of endometrial cancer is very low.[1]

Another strategy is to use targeted drug delivery. The new adhesive vaginal gel that contains micronized progesterone in an emulsion system was designed to maximize progesterone's therapeutic effect on the uterus while minimizing the potential for systemic side effects. The vaginal route is traditionally used for local therapy or as an alternative route for systemic drug administration. However, the uterine effects of vaginal progesterone gels exceed the response due to circulating levels of progesterone because of a direct first-pass effect. It has been shown experimentally that radiolabeled progesterone applied to the cuff of vaginal tissue remaining attached to the cervix after hysterectomy diffused to the entire uterus in the absence of systemic circulation.[66] Endometrial progesterone extraction was higher in the luteal phase than in the proliferative phase. Progesterone vaginal gel absorption has a long absorption half-life of 25 to 50 hours, an elimination half-life of 5 to 20 minutes, and a dose-dependent bioavailability of 20 to 28%. The direct uterine progesterone delivery allows lower systemic progestin levels and provides endometrial protection with fewer progesterone side effects. It is available as a 4% (45 mg) and 8% (90 mg) formulation (Crinone) that can be given every other day.[67]

HEADACHE MANAGEMENT IN WOMEN USING HORMONE REPLACEMENT THERAPY

Headache management of women who require HRT for menopausal symptoms but develop headaches as a result of the therapy can be difficult. Several empiric strategies may be used to control headache in women with menopausal symptoms (Table 12-3). Reducing the dose of estrogen or changing the type of estrogen from a conjugated estrogen to pure estradiol, to synthetic ethinyl estradiol, or to a pure estrone may significantly reduce headache. Almost all HRT preparations will relieve hot flushes if a sufficient dose is given; however, many women get relief from low doses of estrogen (1 mg oral estradiol or equivalent). Changing from interrupted to continuous administration may be very effective if the headaches are associated with estrogen withdrawal. Techniques may be combined. Kudrow reported a 58% improvement in headache control with a reduced, continuous dose of estrogen.[15] Parenteral estrogens, with or without adjunct hormones, can be effective. Greenblatt and Bruneteau studied postmenopausal women with oral estrogen-induced headaches and found that their headaches could be

Table 12-3 Treatment of Hormonal Replacement Headache

Estrogens

1. Reduce estrogen dose
2. Change estrogen type from conjugated estrogen to pure estradiol to synthetic estrogen to pure estrone
3. Convert from interrupted to continuous dosing
4. Convert from oral to parenteral dosing
5. Add androgens
6. Switch to selective estrogen receptor modulator

Progestin

1. Switch from interrupted (cyclic) to continuous lower dose
2. Change progestin type
3. Change delivery system (oral to vaginal)
4. Discontinue progestin (periodic endometrial biopsy or vaginal ultrasound)

improved by switching from oral to parenteral estrogens (estradiol) and adding androgens (testosterone).[19] The estradiol cutaneous patch, which provides a physiologic ratio of estradiol to estrone and a steady-state concentration of estrogen, has been associated anecdotally with fewer headache side effects.[33,68,69] Postmenopausal women were randomly given two different HRT formulations: transdermal estradiol 50 μg or oral CEE 0.625 mg/day plus MPA for 14 days. Women with migraine had a significant increase in attack frequency and headache days with oral, but not transdermal, estrogen.[70] The new selective estrogen receptor modulator, raloxifene, can also be used if a woman requires, but cannot tolerate, nonselective estrogen.

RISKS OF CANCER WITH HORMONE REPLACEMENT THERAPY

The Women's Health Initiative (WHI) Hormone Replacement Trial was a prospective, randomized, controlled primary prevention trial of nearly 16,608 postmenopausal women treated with CEE 0.625 mg plus MPA 2.5 mg, or placebo (1:1 randomization).[27] The trial was terminated because of a 26% increased risk of breast cancer in the estrogen plus progestin group (38 versus 30 per 10,000 person-years) almost reached nominal statistical significance. The weighted test statistic used for monitoring was highly significant. Colorectal cancer rates were reduced by 37% in the HRT group (10 versus 16 per 10,000 person-years), also reaching nominal statistical significance. Endometrial cancer incidence was not affected, nor was lung cancer incidence (54 versus 50, respectively, in the HRT group; hazard ratio [HR], 1.04; 95% confidence interval [CI], 0.71 to 1.53) or total cancer incidence.

The American Cancer Society's Cancer Prevention Study II was a prospective US cohort study with mortality follow-up from 1982 to 1996.[71] Women who used ERT at baseline had higher death rates from ovarian cancer than women who had never used ERT (relative risk [RR], 1.51; 95% CI, 1.16 to 1.96). Risk was slightly, but not significantly, increased among former estrogen users (RR, 1.16; 95% CI, 0.99 to 1.37). The risk of fatal ovarian cancer was related to both duration and recency of hormone use. The risk of death from ovarian cancer was approximately doubled in women who had used estrogens for 10 or more years within the 15 years prior to enrollment in the study. Lifetime risk of ovarian cancer, however, is low (1.7%).

The association between ERT and HRT and ovarian cancer was also analyzed using data from the Breast Cancer Detection Demonstration Project follow-up study.[72] Women who used ERT, particularly for 10 or more years, were at significantly increased risk of ovarian cancer. Women who used short-term HRT were not at increased risk, but risk associated with longer-term HRT warrants further investigation.[72]

RISKS OF CARDIOVASCULAR DISEASE WITH HORMONE REPLACEMENT THERAPY

The American Heart Association reviewed cardiovascular disease in women.[73] Old prospective studies showed a consistent reduced risk (35 to 50%) of coronary heart disease (CHD) and a less consistent reduced risk of stroke in women using ERT.[26,74,75] This reduction is probably due to selection artifact.

Two US trials were designed to quantitate the cardioprotective effect of ERT, unconfounded by healthy women selection bias. The Heart and Estrogen/Progestin Replacement Study (HERS) is a 5-year, randomized, placebo-controlled secondary prevention trial of CEE plus MPA in 2,763 postmenopausal women who already have CHD.[47] Unopposed estrogen is not being evaluated. The primary outcome was the occurrence of nonfatal myocardial infarction or CHD death. Secondary cardiovascular outcomes included coronary revascularization, unstable angina, congestive heart failure, resuscitated cardiac arrest, stroke or transient ischemic attack, and peripheral arterial disease. All-cause mortality was also considered. During an average follow-up of 4.1 years, treatment with oral CEE plus MPA did not reduce the overall rate of CHD events in postmenopausal women with established coronary disease. The treatment did increase the rate of thromboembolic events and gall bladder disease. Based on the finding of no overall cardiovascular benefit and a pattern of early increase in risk of CHD events, the authors did not recommend starting this treatment for the purpose of secondary prevention of CHD. However, in the hormone group, findings did suggest a higher risk of CHD events during the first year and a decreased risk during years 3 to 5.

HERS II is an unblinded 2.7-year follow-up of HERS. Ninety-three percent of those surviving consented to follow-up in HERS II. Participants were randomly assigned to receive CEE 0.625 mg/day of conjugated estrogens and 2.5 mg of MPA ($n = 1,380$) or placebo ($n = 1,383$) during HERS; personal physicians used their discretion to prescribe open-label HRT during HERS II. There were no significant decreases in rates of primary CHD events or secondary cardiovascular events among women assigned to the hormone group compared with the placebo group in HERS, HERS II, or overall. The unadjusted relative hazard (RH) for CHD events in HERS was 0.99 (95% CI, 0.81 to 1.22); HERS II, 1.00 (95% CI, 0.77 to 1.29); and overall, 0.99 (95% CI, 0.84 to 1.17). The overall RHs were similar after adjustment for potential confounders and differential use of statins between treatment groups (RH, 0.97; 95% CI, 0.82 to 1.14) and in analyses restricted to women who were adherent to randomized treatment assignment (RH, 0.96; 95% CI, 0.77 to 1.19). Lower rates of CHD events among women in the hormone group in the final years of HERS did not persist during additional years of follow-up. After 6.8 years, HRT did not reduce the risk of cardiovascular events in women with CHD. Postmenopausal HRT should not be used to reduce the risk of CHD events in women with CHD.[76]

The WHI Hormone Replacement Trial was terminated because of increased risk of breast cancer.[27,77] In the WHI trial, 16,608 postmenopausal women aged 50 to 79 years with an intact uterus at baseline were recruited between the years 1993 to 1998. Participants received CEE, 0.625 mg/day plus MPA 2.5 mg/day in one tablet ($n = 8,506$) or placebo ($n = 8,102$). The primary outcome was CHD (nonfatal myocardial infarction and CHD death), with invasive breast cancer as the primary adverse outcome. Estimated HRs (nominal 95% CIs) were as follows: CHD, 1.29 (1.02 to 1.63) with 286 cases; breast cancer, 1.26 (1.00 to 1.59) with 290 cases; stroke, 1.41 (1.07 to 1.85) with 212 cases; pulmonary embolus (PE), 2.13 (1.39 to 3.25) with 101 cases; colorectal cancer, 0.63 (0.43 to 0.92) with 112 cases; endometrial cancer, 0.83 (0.47 to 1.47) with 47 cases; hip fracture, 0.66 (0.45 to 0.98) with 106 cases; and death due to other causes, 0.92 (0.74 to 1.14) with 331 cases. Corresponding HRs (nominal 95% CIs) for composite outcomes were 1.22 (1.09 to 1.36) for total cardiovascular disease (arterial and venous disease), 1.03 (0.90 to 1.17) for total cancer, 0.76 (0.69 to 0.85) for combined fractures, 0.98 (0.82 to 1.18) for total mortality, and 1.15 (1.03 to 1.28) for the global index. Absolute excess risks per 10,000 person-years attributable to estrogen plus progestin were seven more CHD events, eight more strokes, eight more PEs, and eight more invasive breast cancers, whereas absolute risk reductions per 10,000 person-years were six fewer colorectal cancers and five fewer hip fractures. The absolute

excess risk of events included in the global index was 19 per 10,000 person-years.

Overall CHD rates were low. The rate of women experiencing CHD events was increased by 29% for women taking estrogen plus progestin relative to placebo (37 versus 30 per 10,000 person-years), reaching nominal statistical significance (at the $p = .05$ level). Most of the excess was in nonfatal myocardial infarction. No significant differences were observed in CHD deaths or revascularization procedures (coronary artery bypass grafting or percutaneous transluminal coronary angioplasty). Stroke rates were also higher in women receiving estrogen plus progestin (41% increase; 29 versus 21 per 10,000 person-years), with most of the elevation occurring in nonfatal events. Women in the estrogen plus progestin group had twofold greater rates of venous thromboembolism as well as deep vein thrombosis and PE individually, with almost all associated CIs excluding one.

The WHI finding that estrogen plus progestin does not confer a benefit for preventing CHD among women with a uterus concurs with the HERS findings among women with clinically apparent CHD. The excess risk of stroke in the HRT group was not present in the first year but appeared during the second year and persisted through the fifth year. Venous thromboembolism is an expected complication of postmenopausal hormones, and the pattern over time in WHI is consistent with the findings from HERS and several observational studies.

On the basis of HERS and other secondary prevention trials, the American Heart Association recommended against initiating postmenopausal hormones for the secondary prevention of cardiovascular disease. Results from WHI indicate that the combined postmenopausal hormones, CEE 0.625 mg per day plus MPA 2.5 mg per day, should not be initiated or continued for the primary prevention of CHD. In addition, the substantial risks of cardiovascular disease and breast cancer must be weighed against the benefit for fracture in selecting from the available agents to prevent osteoporosis.[27]

RISKS OF VENOUS THROMBOSIS WITH ESTROGEN REPLACEMENT THERAPY

The risk of venous thromboembolism with postmenopausal ERT was recently assessed by using a literature review and meta-analysis.[78] The absolute rate increase was 1.5 venous thromboembolic events per 10,000 women in 1 year. Six case-control studies that reported risk according to duration of use found that risk was highest in the first year of use (RR, 3.49; 95% CI, 2.33 to 5.59). Current use of postmenopausal estrogen is associated with a twofold increased risk of venous thromboembolism (RR 2.14; 95% CI, 1.64 to 2.81). With a baseline risk of venous thromboembolism of 1.3 per 10,000 woman-years, based on a study with 10,000 controls, an additional 1.5 events per 10,000 women each year would be expected. The absolute incremental risk was 3.2 additional events for the first 12 months and 1.2 additional events after 12 months.

The absolute excess risk (or risk reduction) attributable to estrogen plus progestin is low. Over 1 year, 10,000 women taking estrogen plus progestin compared with placebo might experience seven more CHD events, eight more strokes, eight more pulmonary emboli, eight more invasive breast cancers, six fewer colorectal cancers, and five fewer hip fractures. Combining all the monitored outcomes, women taking estrogen plus progestin might expect 19 more events per year per 10,000 women than women taking placebo. Over a longer period, more typical of the duration of treatment that would be needed to prevent chronic disease, the absolute numbers of excess outcomes would increase proportionately.

The results do not necessarily apply to lower dosages of these drugs, to other formulations of oral estrogens and progestins, or to estrogens and progestins administered through the transdermal route. It remains possible that transdermal estradiol with progesterone, which more closely mimics the normal physiology and metabolism of endogenous sex hormones, may provide a different risk-benefit profile.

Risks of Fractures with Hormone Replacement Therapy

A systematic review of all randomized trials of HRT that have reported or collected nonvertebral fracture data showed an overall 27% reduction in nonvertebral fractures in a pooled analysis (reduction favoring HRT in RR, 0.73; 95% CI, 0.56 to 0.94; $p = .02$). This effect was greater among women randomly assigned to HRT who had a mean age younger than 60 years (RR, 0.67; 95% CI, 0.46 to 0.98; $p = .03$). Among women with a mean age of 60 years or older, there was no significantly reduced effect (RR, 0.88; 95% CI, 0.71 to 1.08; $p = .22$). For hip and wrist fractures alone, the effectiveness of HRT appeared more marked (RR, 0.60; 95% CI, 0.40 to 0.91; $p = .02$), particularly for women younger than 60 years (RR, 0.45; 95% CI, 0.26 to 0.79; $p = .005$). The meta-analysis of randomized controlled trials of HRT noted a statistically significant reduction in nonvertebral fractures. However, this effect may be attenuated in older women.[79]

In the WHI trial, women treated with HRT experienced low hip fracture rates (10 per 10,000 person-years in the estrogen plus progestin group versus 15 per 10,000 person-years in the placebo group).[27] Estrogen plus progestin reduced the observed hip and clinical vertebral fracture rates by one-third compared with placebo, both nominally significant. The reductions in other osteoporotic fractures (23%) and total fractures

(24%) were statistically significant (all associated CIs excluding one).[27,77]

Cognitive Benefits from Estrogen Replacement Therapy

Yaffe and colleagues reviewed the literature on the effects of ERT on cognitive function and dementia in postmenopausal women.[32] Five observational studies and eight trials addressed the ERT effect on cognitive function in nondemented postmenopausal women. Cognition improved in perimenopausal women, possibly because menopausal symptoms improved, but there was no clear benefit in asymptomatic women. Ten observational studies measured the effects of ERT use on the risk of developing dementia. Meta-analysis of these studies suggests a 29% decreased risk of developing dementia among estrogen users, but the findings of the studies are heterogeneous. Four positive trials of ERT in women with Alzheimer's disease were small, of short duration, nonrandomized, or uncontrolled. All of the studies have methodologic problems and have produced conflicting results, reflecting, in part, the healthy women bias.

Exposure to ERT was not associated with a reduced risk of Alzheimer's disease in a population-based, nested, case-control study.[80] Among the 59 newly diagnosed cases of Alzheimer's disease, 15 (25%) were current estrogen users, whereas among the controls, 53 (24%) were current users. The adjusted odds ratio comparing all current estrogen recipients with nonrecipients was 1.18 (95% CI, 0.59 to 2.37). In estrogen users who took the drug for 5 years or longer compared with nonusers, the odds ratio was 1.05 (95% CI, 0.32 to 3.44). Odds ratios were similar for estrogen recipients who received estrogens alone and recipients who received combined estrogen plus progestin treatment. The use of ERT in women after the onset of menopause was not associated with a reduced risk of developing Alzheimer's disease.

Summary

Meta-analyses of observational studies indicated summary RRs for CHD incidence and mortality that were significantly reduced among current HRT users only, although risk of incidence was not reduced when only studies that controlled for socioeconomic status were included. The WHI reported increased CHD events (HR, 1.29; 95% CI, 1.02 to 1.63). Stroke incidence, but not mortality, was significantly increased among HRT users in both the meta-analysis and the WHI trial. The meta-analysis indicted that risk was significantly elevated for thromboembolic stroke (RR, 1.20; 95% CI, 1.01 to 1.40) but not for subarachnoid or intracerebral stroke. Risk of venous thromboembolism among current HRT users was increased overall (RR, 2.14; 95% CI, 1.64 to 2.81) and was highest during the first year of use (RR, 3.49; 95% CI, 2.33 to 5.59) according to a meta-analysis of 12 studies. Protection against osteo-porotic fractures is supported by a meta-analysis of 22 estrogen trials, cohort studies, results of the WHI trial, and trials with bone density outcomes. Current estrogen users have an increased risk of breast cancer that increases with duration of use. Endometrial cancer incidence, but not mortality, is increased with unopposed estrogen use but not with estrogen plus progestin. A meta-analysis of 18 observational studies showed a 20% reduction in colon cancer incidence among women who had ever used HRT (RR, 0.80; 95% CI, 0.74 to 0.86), a finding supported by the WHI trial. Women symptomatic from menopause had improvement in certain aspects of cognition. Current studies of estrogen and dementia are not definitive. In a cohort study, current HRT users had an age-adjusted RR for cholecystitis of 1.8 (95% CI, 1.6 to 2.0), increasing to 2.5 (95% CI, 2.0 to 2.9) after 5 years of HRT use. Benefits of HRT include prevention of osteoporotic fractures and colorectal cancer, while prevention of dementia is uncertain. Harms include CHD, stroke, thromboembolic events, breast cancer with 5 or more years of HRT use, and cholecystitis.[81]

Conclusion

There is a link between estrogen and progesterone, the female sex hormones, and migraine.[8,82–85] Migraine prevalence decreases with advancing age but may either regress or worsen at menopause. Women with natural menopause usually improve, whereas those with surgical menopause usually worsen.[8–10] ERT can change the character and frequency of migraine.[15,86]

The case summary of MS illustrates common changes in headache activity experienced during a woman's life cycle and with menopause. Determining how to treat her ongoing postmenopausal headache will need to consider the risks versus the continuing benefits of HRT, both on her headaches and on her other organ systems. Women should be monitored in conjunction with their gynecologists.

References

1. Mishell DR, Stenchever MA, Droegemueller W, et al. Menopause: endocrinology, consequences of estrogen deficiency, effects of hormonal replacement therapy, treatment regimens. In: Mishell DR, Stenchever MA, Droegemueller W, Herbst AL, editors. Comprehensive gynecology. 3rd ed. St. Louis (MO): Mosby; 1997. p. 1159–98.

2. Wise PM, Krajnak KM, Kashon ML. Menopause: the aging of multiple pacemakers. Science 1996;273:66–70.

3. Utian WH. Overview on menopause. Am J Obstet Gynecol 1987;156:1280–3.

4. Utian WH. The fate of the untreated menopause. Obstet Gynecol Clin North Am 1987;14:1–11.

5. Rebar RW, Spitzer IB. The physiology and measurement of hot flushes. Am J Obstet Gynecol 1987;156:1284–8.

6. Ravnikar V. Physiology and treatment of hot flushes. Obstet Gynecol 1990;75:S3–8.

7. Bungay GT, Vessey MP, McPherson CK. Study of symptoms in middle life with special reference to the menopause. BMJ 1980;281:181–3.

8. Goldstein M, Chen TC. The epidemiology of disabling headache. In: Critchley M, editor. Advances in neurology. 33rd ed. New York (NY): Raven Press; 1982. p. 377–90.

9. Whitty CWM, Hockaday JM. Migraine: a follow-up study of 92 patients. BMJ 1968;1:735–6.

10. Neri I, Granella F, Nappi RMGC, et al. Characteristics of headache at menopause: a clinico-epidemiologic study. Maturitas 1993;17:31–7.

11. Utian WH. Estrogen, headache and oral contraceptives. S Afr Med J 1974;48:2105–8.

12. Alvarez WC. Can one cure migraine in women by inducing menopause? Report on forty-two cases. Mayo Clin Proc 1940;15:380–2.

13. Casson P, Hahn PM, Van Vugt DA, et al. Lasting response to ovariectomy in severe intractable premenstrual syndrome. Obstet Gynecol 1990;162:99–105.

14. Casper RF, Hearn MT. The effect of hysterectomy and bilateral oophorectomy in women with severe premenstrual syndrome. Am J Obstet Gynecol 1990;162:105–9.

15. Kudrow L. The relationship of headache frequency to hormone use in migraine. Headache 1975;15:36–49.

16. Aylward M, Holly F, Parker RJ. An evaluation of clinical response to piperazine estrone sulphate ("Harmogen") in menopausal patients. Curr Med Res Opin 1974;2:417–23.

17. Kaiser HJ, Meienberg O. Deterioration or onset of migraine under estrogen replacement therapy in the menopause. J Neurol 1993;240:195–7.

18. Martin PL, Burnier AM, Segre EJ, et al. Graded sequential therapy in the menopause: a double-blind study. Am J Obstet Gynecol 1971;111:178–86.

19. Greenblatt RB, Bruneteau DW. Menopausal headache – psychogenic or metabolic? J Am Geriatr Soc 1974;283:186–90.

20. Campbell S. Double-blind psychometric studies on the effects of natural estrogens on postmenopausal women. In: Campbell S, editor. The management of the menopause and postmenopausal years. Baltimore (MD): University Park Press; 1976. p. 149–58.

21. Coope J. Double-blind cross-over study of estrogen replacement therapy. In: Campbell S, editor. The management of the menopause and postmenopausal years. Baltimore (MD): University Park Press; 1976. p. 159–60.

22. Dennerstein L, Laby B, Burrows GD, et al. Headache and sex hormone therapy. Headache 1978;18:146–53.

23. Bousser MG, Conard J, Kittner S, et al. Recommendations on the risk of ischemic stroke associated with use of combined oral contraceptives and hormone replacement therapy in women with migraine (The International Headache Society Task Force on Combined Oral Contraceptives and Hormone Replacement therapy). Cephalalgia 2000;20:155–6.

24. Shoemaker ES, Forney JP, MacDonald PC. Estrogen treatment of postmenopausal women. JAMA 1977;238:1524–30.

25. LaRosa JC. Has HRT come of age? Lancet 1995;345:76–7.

26. Grady D, Rueben SM, Pettiti DB, et al. Hormone therapy to prevent disease and prolong life in postmenopausal women. Ann Intern Med 1992;117:1016–37.

27. Writing Group for the Women's Health Initiative Investigators. Risks and benefits of estrogen plus progestin in healthy postmenopausal women: principal results from the Women's Health Initiative randomized controlled trial. JAMA 2002;288:321–33.

28. Grady D, Gebretsadik T, Kerlikrowske K, et al. Hormone replacement therapy and endometrial cancer risk: a metaanalysis. Obstet Gynecol 1995;85:304–13.

29. Martin KA, Freeman MW. Postmenopausal hormone replacement therapy. N Engl J Med 1993;328:1115–7.

30. Nablusi AA, Folsom AR, White A, et al. Association of hormone replacement therapy with various cardiovascular risk factors in postmenopausal women. N Engl J Med 1993;328:1069–75.

31. Tang MX, Jacobs D, Stern Y, et al. Effect of oestrogen during menopause on risk and age at onset of Alzheimer's disease. Lancet 1996;348:429–32.

32. Yaffe K, Sawaya G, Lieberburg I, et al. Estrogen therapy in postmenopausal women: effects on cognitive function and dementia. JAMA 1998;279:688–95.

33. Stumpf PG. Pharmacokinetics of estrogen. Obstet Gynecol 1990;75:9–17.

34. Cedars MI, Judd HL. Nonoral routes of estrogen administration. Obstet Gynecol Clin North Am 1987;14:269–98.

35. Wentz AC. Management of the menopause. In: Jones HW, Wentz AC, Burnett LS, editors. Novak's textbook of gynecology. 11th ed. Baltimore: Williams and Wilkins; 1985. p. 397–442.

36. Whitehead MI, Hillard TC, Crook D. The role and use of progestogens. Obstet Gynecol 1990;75:S59–76.

37. Studd J, Magos A. Hormone pellet implantation for the menopause and premenstrual syndrome. Obstet Gynecol Clin North Am 1987;14:229–49.

38. McDowell F, Louis S, McDevitt E. A clinical trial of premarin in cerebrovascular disease. J Chronic Dis 1967;20:679–84.

39. Stern MP, Brown BW, Haskell WL, et al. Cardiovascular risk and use of estrogens or estrogen-progestagen combinations. JAMA 1976;235:811–5.

40. Grodstein F, Stampfer MJ, Manson JE, et al. Postmenopausal estrogen and progestin use and the risk of cardiovascular disease. N Engl J Med 1996;453–61.

41. Petitti DB. Hormone replacement therapy and heart disease prevention: experimentation trumps observation. JAMA 1998;280:650–2.

42. Daly E, Vessey MP, Hawkins MM, et al. Risk of venous thromboembolism in users of hormone replacement therapy. Lancet 1996;348:977–80.

43. Jick H, Derby LE, Myers MW, et al. Risk of hospital admission for idiopathic venous thromboembolism among users of postmenopausal estrogens. Lancet 1996;348:981–3.

44. Vandenbroucke JP, Helmerhorst FM. Risk of venous thrombosis with hormone replacement therapy. Lancet 1996;348:972.

45. Grodstein F, Stampfer MJ, Goldhaber SZ, et al. Prospective study of exogenous hormones and risk of pulmonary embolism in women. Lancet 1996;348:983–7.

46. Pedersen AT, Lidegaard O, Kreiner S, et al. Hormone replacement therapy and risk of nonfatal stroke. Lancet 1997;350:1277–83.

47. Hulley S, Grady D, Bush T, et al. Randomized trial of estrogen plus progestin for secondary prevention of coronary heart disease in postmenopausal women. JAMA 1998;280:605–13.

48. Kuhnz W, Gansau C, Mahler M. Pharmacokinetics of estradiol, free and total estrone, in young women following single intravenous and oral administration of 17β-estradiol. Arzneimittelforschung 1993;43:966–73.

49. DeLignières B. The case for nonplasma lipoprotein etiology of reduced vascular risk in estrogen replacement therapy. Curr Opin Obstet Gynecol 1993;5:389–95.

50. Scarabin PY, Alhenc-Gelas M, Plu-Bureau G, et al. Effects of oral and transdermal estrogen/progesterone regimens on blood coagulation and fibrinolysis in postmenopausal women. Arterioscler Thromb Vasc Biol 1997;17:3071–8.

51. Lindoff C, Peterson F, Lecander I, et al. Transdermal estrogen replacement therapy: beneficial effects on hemostatic risk factors for cardiovascular disease. Maturitas 1996;24:43–50.

52. Clarkson T. Progestogens and cardiovascular disease. A critical review. J Reprod Med 1999;44:180–4.

53. Hashimoto M, Akishita M, Eto M, et al. Modulation of endothelium-dependent flow-mediated dilatation of the brachial artery by sex and menstrual cycle. Circulation 1995;92:3431–5.

54. LaRosa JC. Triglycerides and coronary risk in women and the elderly. Arch Intern Med 1997;157:961–8.

55. Clarkson TB, Anthony MS, Jerome CP. Lack of effect of raloxifene on coronary atherosclerosis of postmenopausal monkeys [author's response]. J Clin Endocrinol Metab 1998;83:3002–4.

56. Scott RT, Ross B, Anderson C, et al. Pharmacokinetics of percutaneous estradiol: a crossover study using a gel and a transdermal system in comparison with oral micronized estradiol. Obstet Gynecol 1991;77:758–64.

57. DeLignieres B, Silberstein SD. Pharmacodynamics of oestrogens and progestogens. Cephalalgia 2000;20:200–7.

58. Greenblatt RB. The use of androgens in the menopause and other gynecic disorders. Obstet Gynecol Clin North Am 1987;14:251–68.

59. Droegemueller W. Postoperative counseling and management: patient evaluation, informed consent, infection prophylaxis, avoidance of complications. In: Mishell DR, Stenchever MA, Droegemueller W, Herbst AL, editors. Comprehensive gynecology. 3rd ed. St. Louis (MO): Mosby; 1997. p. 719–66.

60. Miyagawa K, Rosch J, Stanczyk F, et al. Medroxyprogesterone interferes with ovarian steroid protection against coronary vasospasm. Nat Med 1997;3:324–7.

61. The Writing Group for the PEPI Trial. Effects of estrogen or estrogen/progestin regimens on heart disease risk factors in postmenopausal women. JAMA 1995;273:199–208.

62. Sullivan JM, Shala BA, Miller LA, et al. Progestin enhances vasoconstrictor responses in postmenopausal women receiving estrogen replacement therapy. J Am Menopause Soc 1995;2:193–9.

63. Giraud GD, Morton MJ, Wilson RA, et al. Effects of estrogen and progestin on aortic size and compliance in postmenopausal women. Am J Obstet Gynecol 1996; 174:1708–18.

64. Gerhard M, Walsh BW, Tawaqkol A, et al. Estradiol therapy combined with progesterone and endothelium-dependent vasodilation in postmenopausal women. Circulation 1998;98:1158–63.

65. Smith RNJ, Holland EFN, Studd JWW. The symptomatology of progestogen intolerance. Maturitas 1994;18:87.

66. Bulletti C, DeZiegler D, Flamigni C, et al. Target drug delivery in gynecology: the first uterine pass effect. Hum Reprod 1997;12:1073–9.

67. Medical Economics Company. Physicians' desk reference. 53rd ed. Montvale (NJ): Medical Economics Company; 1999.

68. Anonymous. Transdermal estrogen. Med Lett Drugs Ther 1986;28:119–20.

69. Judd H. Efficacy of transdermal estradiol. Obstet Gynecol 1987;156:1326–31.

70. Nappi RE, Cagnacci A, Granella F, et al. Course of primary headaches during hormone replacement therapy. Maturitas 2001;38:157–63.

71. Rodriguez C, Patel AV, Calle EE, et al. Estrogen replacement therapy and ovarian cancer mortality in a large prospective study of US women. JAMA 2001;285: 1460–5.

72. Lacey JV, Mink PJ, Lubin JH, et al. Menopausal hormone replacement therapy and risk of ovarian cancer. JAMA 2002;288:334–41.

73. Mosca L, Manson JE, Sutherland SE, et al. Cardiovascular disease in women: a statement for healthcare professionals from the American Heart Association (American Heart Association scientific statement). Circulation 1997;96:2468–82.

74. Barrett-Connor E, Bush TL. Estrogen and coronary heart disease in women. JAMA 1991;265:1861–7.

75. Stampfer MJ, Colditz GA. Estrogen replacement therapy and coronary heart disease: a quantitative assessment of the epidemiologic evidence. Prev Med 1991;20:47–63.

76. Grady D, Herrington D, Bittner V, et al. Cardiovascular disease outcomes during 6.8 years of hormone therapy: Heart and Estrogen/Progestin Replacement Study Follow-up (HERS II). JAMA 2002;288:49–57.

77. Rossouw JE, Finnegan LP, Harlan WR, et al. The evolution of the Women's Health Initiative: perspectives from the NIH. J Am Med Wom Assoc 1995;50:50–5.

78. Miller J, Chan BK, Nelson HD. Postmenopausal estrogen replacement and risk for venous thromboembolism: a systematic review and metaanalysis for the US Preventive Services Task Force. Ann Intern Med 2002;136: 680–90.

79. Torgerson DJ, Bell-Syer SE. Hormone replacement therapy and prevention of nonvertebral fractures: a meta-analysis of randomized trials. JAMA 2001;285:2891–7.

80. Seshadri S, Zornberg GL, Derby LE, et al. Post-menopausal estrogen replacement therapy and the risk of Alzheimer disease. Arch Neurol 2001;58:435–40.

81. Nelson HD, Humphrey LL, Nygren P, et al. Post-menopausal hormone replacement therapy: scientific review. JAMA 2002;288:872–81.

82. Epstein MT, Hockaday JM, Hockaday TDR. Migraine and reproductive hormones throughout the menstrual cycle. Lancet 1975;1:543–8.

83. Raskin NH. Headache. 2nd ed. New York (NY): Churchill-Livingstone; 1988.

84. Selby G, Lance JW. Observation on 500 cases of migraine and allied vascular headaches. J Neurol Neurosurg Psychiatry 1960;23:23–32.

85. Silberstein SD, Merriam GR. Estrogens, progestins, and headache. Neurology 1991;41:775–93.

86. Bickerstaff ER. Neurological complications of oral contraceptives. Oxford: Clarendon Press; 1975.

CHAPTER 13

Oral Contraception, Estrogen Replacement Therapy, Migraine, and Stroke

Gretchen E. Tietjen, MD, and Robin L. Brey, MD

CASE

TX is a 40-year-old migraineur who presented with acute onset aphasia and right hemiplegia associated with severe headache beginning immediately after orgasm. She was diagnosed with an ischemic stroke and her subsequent evaluation was remarkable for the presence of a patent foramen ovale. Antiphospholipid antibody screen was negative. Although she had previously undergone tubal ligation, at the time of the stroke she had been taking an oral contraceptive containing 30 µg estradiol for the past several months as treatment for menstrual migraines. She has a longstanding history of migraine with typical 30-minute-long visual auras preceding about one-half of her bimonthly attacks, usually those associated with her menstrual period. She had not noted a difference in the migraine frequency or characteristics since starting the pill. She does not smoke and considers herself healthy although her poststroke evaluation showed an elevated cholesterol and blood pressure.

KEY CHAPTER POINTS

- **Hormone supplementation may be related to migraine.**
- **Migraine is an independent risk factor for stroke.**
- **Oral contraceptives increase stroke risk.**
- **The risk of stroke in migraineurs using oral contraceptives is increased.**
- **Is estrogen replacement safe for TX?**

HORMONE SUPPLEMENTATION

Migraine affects 18% of females, with the prevalence peaking at 30% in the 40-year-old woman.[1,2] Although declining after menopause, the prevalence in women after age 65 years is still a sizable 15%.[3] Oral contraceptives (OCs) and estrogen replacement therapy (ERT) are used by hundreds of millions of women worldwide, and given the high prevalence of migraine, many women using hormone supplementation will also have migraine. Developed to prevent pregnancy, OCs are used by 25 million women in the United States. In addition to contraception, OCs are widely used to treat menorrhagia, irregular menses, peri-menopausal symptoms, and, as in the case of TX, menstrual migraine. ERT, used by an estimated 6 million postmenopausal women in the United States, is commonly prescribed to prevent osteoporosis and alleviate symptoms of menopause, including hot flashes, night sweats, insomnia, and mood swings.[4]

Although the majority of women with preexisting migraine who take OCs experience no difference in their migraine pattern, new onset of migraine is significantly more common in women taking OCs than in those who are not.[5–7] For women who do experience an increase in frequency or severity of migraine attacks while taking OCs, there is a tendency for attacks to occur in the drug-free interval of the cycle, when there is a decrease in estrogen.[8] Those with migraine with aura (MA) are more likely to experience a worsening with OCs than those with migraine without aura (MO) (MA, 56.4%; MO, 25.3%; odds ratio [OR], 3.8; confidence interval [CI], 1.6 to 9.3).[9] It has been hypothesized that OC use alters vasomotor function in the cases in which OC use induces or worsens migraine.[10] Estrogen and progesterone also induce increased secretion of prostaglandins, which inhibit central norepinephrine release, antagonize morphine analgesia, sensitize pain receptors, and increase neurogenic inflammation.[11] The influence of the composition of OCs on migraine remains uncertain.

It has been estimated that about 3% of women starting ERT therapy complain of new onset migraine or worsening of migraine.[12] One study of patients with MO beginning ERT demonstrated a worsening in both frequency and days of headache within 3 months of treatment and more so with the oral as compared to the transdermal route.[13] Recommendations for dealing with migraine that worsened with ERT include lowering the estrogen dose, using continuous dosing if possible, and even adding androgens.

Although migraine onset or worsening may be associated with hormone supplementation, OCs and ERT have been used to treat migraine. Percutaneous estradiol gel started 48 hours before the anticipated onset of the migraine attack and continued daily for 7 days was well tolerated and efficacious in double-blind, placebo-controlled studies in women with menstrual migraine.[14] Second- or third-generation OCs with 20 µg of ethinyl estradiol combined with a low-dose ERT during the OC placebo week is effective for some migraineurs with worsening of migraine around menstruation.[15] Alternative hormone strategies include using either a 0.1 mg 17 β-estradiol patch for the week of the menses or receiving an injection of depot progestogen.[16]

MIGRAINE AND STROKE

The first suggestion that migraine was an independent risk factor for stroke came in 1975 from the Collaborative Group for the Study of Stroke in Young Women (Table 13-1).[17] In that study, migraine was associated with a significant relative risk (RR, 2.0) of thrombotic stroke using neighbor controls but not hospital controls (RR, 1.2). An ongoing, large-scale epidemiologic study in the United States found the risk of stroke doubled (OR, 2.1) in migraineurs, but that migraine-associated risk declined with increasing age.[2] A Danish case-control study of 497 women with a diagnosis of cerebral thromboembolism found an increased risk of stroke in women with migraine (OR, 2.8).[18] A French case-control study also found that migraine was a stroke risk factor but only in women less than 45 years of age.[19] An Italian case-control study suggested migraine to be a risk factor for stroke in women less than 35 years of age.[20] MA had a stronger association with stroke than MO in three case-control studies,

Table 13-1 Migraine as a Risk Factor for Stroke

Study	Population	Case:Control	Risk Ratio (RR)/ Odds Ratio (OR)
Collaborative Group for the Study of Stroke in Young Women[17]	Women, 15–44 years	430:429	RR = 2.0 (neighbor), RR = 1.2 (hospital), RR = 5.9 (+ OCP)
Henrich and Horowitz[21]	Men and women, 15–65 years	89:179	OR = 1.3 without aura, OR = 2.6 with aura
Tzourio et al[19]	Men and women, 18–80 years	212:212	OR = 1.3, OR = 4.3 (women < 45)
Tzourio et al[22]	Women, < 45 years	72:173	OR = 3.0 without aura, OR = 6.2 with aura, OR = 10.9 (+ smoking), OR = 13.9 (+ OCP)
Lidegaard[18]	Women, 15–44 years	497:1370	OR = 2.8
Carolei et al[20]	Men and women, < 45 years	308:591	OR = 1.0 without aura, OR = 8.6 with aura, OR = 3.7 (women < 35)
Chang et al[76]	Women, 20–44 years	291:736	OR = 3.0 without aura, OR = 3.8 with aura, OR = 17 (+ OCP), OR = 34 (OCP, smoking)
National Health and Nutrition Examination Survey[2]	Men and women, 25–74 years	12,220 (cohort)	OR = 2.1

OCP = oral contraceptive pill.

including one limited to women less than 45 years of age.[20–22] In that study, the stroke risk was sixfold for MA and threefold for MO.[21] Based on this risk calculation, and recent data of stroke incidence in a large population of young women, the expected incidence of ischemic stroke (strokes per 100,000 women per year) for a 40-year-old woman with MA is 70, which is nearly sixfold higher than women without migraine of similar ages and ninefold higher than the risk of the migraineur at age 20 years.[22–24] Although varying widely by age, the absolute risk of stroke in migraineurs is estimated at 17 to 19 per 100,000 women-years.[25] Given the 21 million female migraineurs in the United States, the number of strokes per year attributed to migraine could approach 4,000.

Most strokes in migraineurs occur remote in time from the typical migraine attack, but there are also cases in which stroke occurs during the course of the migraine attack. This has been referred to as migrainous or migraine-related infarction and implies a causal relationship. The incidence of migraine-related infarction (per 100,000 persons per year) was estimated at 1.44 (95% CI, 0 to 3.07) from the Oxfordshire, England, prospective community registry and at 1.7 from a retrospective review of Mayo Clinic records from nearly 5,000 migraineurs under age 50 years.[26,27] In 1988, the International Headache Society (IHS) migraine classification defined migrainous infarction as stroke occurring during a typical attack of MA.[28] In series published since the introduction of the IHS criteria, the percentage of stroke under age 45 years attributed to migrainous infarction ranges from 1.2 to 14%.[29–32] The stroke of our patient, TX, who has migraine with visual aura, occurred in association with a migraine-like headache, but given the absence of aura at the time, it would not meet the IHS criteria for migrainous infarction.[28] A recent study examined the migraine-stroke relationship without the artifice of the current classification schema, comparing all stroke patients with active migraine (at least two attacks in the previous 2 months) to those without active migraine.[33] The prevalence of active migraine in ischemic stroke was 3.7%, which is substantially lower than the prevalence of migraine in the general population. In the study subset of stroke in those less than 45 years of age, however, the prevalence of active migraine was 15% and three times higher in women than in men. Other predictors of migraine in that study included patent foramen ovale (PFO) and the use of OCs. This closely matches the profile of TX.

Mechanisms of Stroke in Migraine

Stroke in women under age 45 years appears related primarily to cardiac embolism,[34] hypercoagulability, and arterial dissection, all mechanisms that have been implicated in migraine-related stroke. PFO, a well-established risk factor for ischemic stroke in the young,[35] has been found to be more common in those young ischemic stroke patients with migraine.[33,36] PFO has also been associated with MA in individuals without stroke.[37–39] The basis for the association of PFO and MA is uncertain, but there is evidence that both migraine and PFO have a genetic predisposition.[37,40] A recent intriguing finding that PFO closure reduced or abolished migraine suggests a causal relationship. It has been hypothesized that shunted microbubbles trigger migraine, possibly by creating a surface for coagulation and platelet activation or by liberation of vasoactive substances.[41] Of note is the fact that TX had many fewer migraines after transcatheter PFO closure and initiation of daily aspirin therapy.

The issue of hypercoagulability in migraine has remained unresolved despite over 30 years of study. Platelets, in the context of the pathoetiology of migraine, have been the focus of much of the attention, but platelet aggregation studies have yielded conflicting results.[42] Findings of an elevation of an endothelial glycoprotein, von Willebrand's factor, in migraineurs, both during[43] and between attacks,[44] suggest that migraine-induced endothelial changes may activate platelets and predispose to thrombosis. Antiphospholipid antibodies (aPL), a risk marker for stroke in young women,[45] have also been implicated as the link between migraine and stroke, as many people with primary and secondary aPL syndrome have headache and transient focal neurologic events. Two small studies of aPL in migraine-related infarction were conflicting in their findings.[46,47] A large, prospective case-control study of migraine, both with and without aura, in people under age 60 years and without a clinical history of stroke, failed to substantiate an independent connection between migraine and aPL. aPL antibody-positive migraineurs with aura were, however, more likely to have silent ischemic lesions demonstrated on neuroimaging scans than the aPL antibody-negative cohort.[48] The precise mechanism by which aPL leads to thrombosis is uncertain, but, aPL, like other prothrombotic risk factors studied in migraine,[49–52] has greater importance for clotting in the venous system than in the arterial system. Positive findings may be of interest in the evaluation of migraine-associated stroke, in light of the migraine-PFO link. Vasospasm and prolonged cortical spreading depression with oligemia have also been implicated as mechanisms for stroke in migraineurs but usually in reference to migrainous infarction.[53]

ORAL CONTRACEPTIVES AND STROKE RISK

Assessment of the risk of stroke associated with combined OCs is difficult because their composition has changed substantially over the 40 years since they were introduced. The estrogen content has decreased at least fivefold (from 150 μg to 20 to 35 μg), in attempts to decrease the risk of thrombosis. The type of progestogen has changed as well. Second-generation OCs contain levonorgestrel, and third-generation OCs contain gestagen or desogestrel, which are less androgenic and have a tendency to increase high-density lipoprotein (HDL) cholesterol levels.[54] Several studies, however, have suggested at least a twofold increased risk of venous thrombosis with the newer generation OCs,[55–58] and a meta-analysis has supported the link between third-generation OCs and an increased risk of venous thrombosis.[59]

Cerebral Venous Thrombosis

Cerebral venous thrombosis (CVT) is more rare than arterial stroke, but studies suggest that CVT is strongly and independently associated with the use of OCs (OR, 13[60]; OR, 22[61]). OC users with congenital thrombophilia, including factor V Leiden and the prothrombin gene mutation, are at even higher risk. The risk of CVT for women with the prothrombin gene mutation increases dramatically in OC users (OR, 149).[61] However, because the thrombophilic mutations are present in less than 5% of the population and the incidence of CVT is likely less than 1 per 1,000 persons per year, screening for these mutations prior to prescribing OCs is arguably not cost-effective.[61]

Cerebral Ischemic Infarction (Arterial)

The improved safety of lower-dose estrogen with respect to stroke risk is illustrated by a number of studies. The World Health Organization (WHO) study of OCs was a multicenter hospital-based, case-control study with centers throughout Europe and in developing countries in Asia, Africa, and Latin America. Although in the developing countries the risk of stroke was increased regardless of the pill dosage, in the European countries, risk of stroke was elevated fivefold for women using OC preparations with estrogen greater than 50 μg but was negligible (OR, 1.53; CI, 0.71 to 3.31) with formulations containing less than 50 μg.[62] Similarly, a Danish case-control study reported an increased risk of thrombotic stroke with formulations containing 50 μg estrogen (OR, 2.9) and 30 to 40 μg estrogen (OR, 1.8) but not with those containing 20 μg.[63] The Royal College of General Practitioners' (RCGP) study showed that for normotensive, nonsmoking women, the less than 50 μg estrogen OC was not associated with an increased risk of stroke (OR, 0.6; CI, 0.1 to 2.9). In this study, the risk was significantly higher with 50 μg (OR, 2.9; CI, 1.7 to 5.0) and greater than 50 μg (OR, 5.8; CI, 1.5 to 22.8) preparations.[64] In the Oxford Family Planning Association Study, no thrombotic strokes occurred in women using OCs with less than 50 μg estrogen.[65] A California health maintenance organization-based case-control study of less than 50 μg estro-

gen OCs and stroke showed a nonsignificant adjusted OR of 1.18 (CI, 0.54 to 2.59).[23] When these data were pooled with a similar US population-based case-control study,[66] analysis suggested that the risk of ischemic stroke (adjusted pooled odds ratio (pOR), 0.66; CI, 0.20 to 1.47) in low-dose OC users was not greater than for the cohort that had never used OCs, even in those who smoked cigarettes (pOR, 0.72; CI, 0.17 to 3.02), were obese (pOR, 0.59; CI, 0.16 to 2.12), or were older than 35 years (pOR, 0.61; CI, 0.13 to 2.08). Although the OC estrogen content was not specified, in the US Health and Nutrition Survey of 12,000 people, there was no increased risk of ischemic stroke in OC users.[2]

The recently published Risk of Arterial Thrombosis in Relation to Oral Contraceptives (RATIO) study, a multicenter, population-based, case-control study in the Netherlands, found that OC users, including those taking third-generation low-estrogen formulations, have a twofold risk of first ischemic stroke, increasing the incidence from 3 to 6 in 10,000.[67] To compare the effects of the ethinyl estradiol dose, controlling for the type of progestogen, they analyzed the subset of women using second-generation OCs. Users of 50 μg ethinyl estradiol had a risk of 2.7 (CI, 1.0 to 7.6), users of 30 μg 2.4 (CI, 1.4 to 4.1). Direct comparison of the 30 and 50 μg doses yielded the OR of 0.7, supporting the contention that lower doses of estrogen are associated with a lower stroke risk.

Subarachnoid and Intracerebral Hemorrhage

The effects of OCs on the vasculature and coagulation system do not appear to predispose to an increased risk of primary hemorrhage, but studies examining the risk of subarachnoid hemorrhage (SAH) in users of combined OCs have yielded conflicting results. A recent meta-analysis of 11 observational studies suggests that even when controlling for smoking and hypertension, there is an increase in the risk of SAH in current OC users (RR, 1.57; CI, 1.25 to 1.99), with no significant difference based on estrogen content.[68] In the WHO study, an increased risk of hemorrhagic stroke in women over 35 years using OCs was significant in developing countries but not in Europe.[69]

Additional Stroke Risk in Oral Contraceptive Users

The risk of stroke with OC use is affected by advancing age and established vascular risk factors such as hypertension, cigarette smoking, and hypercholesterolemia.

Advancing Age

The expected incidence (strokes per 100,000 women per year), assuming a twofold increase in risk with OC use, based on unadjusted data from the large Kaiser Permanente study of low-dose OC use in women of reproductive age, is 3 at age 20 years, 5 at age 30 years, and increases dramatically to 23 at age 40 years.[24]

Hypertension

The risk of ischemic stroke in hypertensive OC users doubled in the RCGP study,[64] and rose sevenfold in the European arm of the WHO study[62] and the RATIO study.[67] The effect of hypertension on intracerebral hemorrhage risk was similar.[69] The impact of hypertension in developing countries, where the overall risk with the OCs is higher, was also substantial (OR, 14).[69] The mechanism by which the interaction of OC use and hypertension increases stroke risk is unclear and confounded by the fact that OC use may lead to an elevation in blood pressure.

Cigarette Smoking

Overall, in women of childbearing age, smoking increases the risk of both cerebral ischemia (OR, 2.5) and cerebral hemorrhage (OR, 5). In women smokers over 35 years of age, studies have also consistently shown a substantial increase in stroke risk with OC use.[62,67,69]

Hypercholesterolemia

The RATIO study showed a ten-fold risk of ischemic stroke in OC users with hypercholesterolemia, a risk that for many may go undetected.[67]

Mechanisms of Stroke with Oral Contraceptive Use

Beneficial effects of hormone supplementation include improved endothelial vascular function, reduction of Lp(a) lipoprotein, reduction of plasma levels of low-density lipoprotein (LDL), and an increase in plasma levels of HDL.[70] The adverse effect of OCs that increases stroke risk, both in the arterial and venous circulations, is most likely related to the effects on hemostasis: the equilibrium of coagulation and fibrinolysis.[71] In persons on synthetic ethinyl estradiol–containing OCs, hypercoagulability is related to elevated levels of fibrinogen and coagulation factors (VII, VIII, and X), as well as to decreased levels of physiologic anticoagulants (antithrombin III, protein S, protein C) and acquired activated protein C resistance. These effects are balanced by increased fibrinolysis related to increased plasminogen and a decrease in its physiologic inhibitor, plasminogen activating inhibitor 1 (PAI-1).[72–74] In total, these changes are more likely to affect the venous than the arterial system. Progesterone, the other component in the combined OC, adversely affects lipids and lipid metabolism, possibly increasing atherogenic potential. Progestogen-only contraception does not affect coagulation or fibrinolysis, and there are no data suggesting that they predispose to thromboembolism.[75]

RISK OF STROKE IN MIGRAINEURS WITH ORAL CONTRACEPTIVE USE

A retrospective case-control study in Denmark involving 497 women with stroke and 1,370 controls found that migraine is associated with a threefold increase in the risk of stroke that is independent of OC usage.[18] No synergism existed between OCs, smoking, and migraine in relation to stroke. The Collaborative Stroke Study suggested the relative stroke risk for women with migraine using OCs was 5.9 compared with women without migraine who did not use OCs (see Table 13-1).[17] In the Italian case-control study, the combination of migraine and OC (high-estrogen preparation) use occurred in seven female patients (4.8%) and none of the controls.[20] In examining the risk of stroke associated with migraine in women younger than 45 years, all cases of stroke occurred in OC users, although the risk of stroke associated with migraine did not reach statistical significance.[2] The case-control study of Tzourio and colleagues showed an OR of 13.9 for women with migraine using OCs.[22] Based on these data it has been estimated that OC use will increase the number of strokes per 100,000 women-years by 10 for those with MO and by 20 for those with MA.[24] For the 40-year-old woman with MA taking OC (like our patient, TX), the incidence of stroke is 139 per 100,000 women-years, 12-fold greater than for the 40-year-old woman without these risk factors.[24] The data from the WHO substudy also suggest a similarly elevated stroke risk for migraineurs using OC (OR, 16.9), although the risk was lower (OR, 6.6) with less than 50 µg estrogen formulations.[76] With the additional risk from cigarette smoking, the OR for ischemic stroke was 34.4. In the WHO study, OC use did not change the frequency or type of migraine.

IS ESTROGEN REPLACEMENT THERAPY SAFE FOR TX?

TX suffered an ischemic stroke in an arterial distribution just after orgasm. The mechanism is presumed to be cardioembolism via a right to left shunt through the PFO during Valsalva's maneuver. Hypercoagulability related to migraine and OC use may have played a role. Subsequent to the stroke, she underwent transcatheter closure of the PFO, discontinued OCs, and remained on low-dose aspirin. Her neurologic deficit has nearly resolved and her migraines have been much less frequent in the intervening months. She has, however, noted vaginal dryness and hot flashes. Because she is approaching menopause, and given her recent symptoms and family history of osteoporosis, she inquires about whether ERT is an option for her.

Risk of Stroke with Estrogen Replacement Therapy

Postmenopausal ERT is used by approximately 6 million women in the United States to treat the symptoms associated with menopause and to prevent osteoporosis after menopause. Postmenopausal ERT is not without risk. Similar to synthetic estrogen-containing OCs, oral conjugated equine estrogens and oral 17β-estradiol

ERT predispose to thrombosis by decreasing anti-thrombin III, protein S, and causing abnormal activated protein C (APC) resistance. Profibrinolytic effects of ERT include a decrease in PAI-1 and a decrease in fibrinogen.[71] A shift toward hypercoagulability appears to increase with an increasing dose of conjugated estrogen.[77] Favorable alterations of LDL and HDL levels with oral estrogens at doses of both 0.625 and 1.25 mg/day have been reported.[78] The decrease in LDL levels resulted from accelerated LDL catabolism, and an increase in triglycerides resulted from an increased production of large, triglyceride-rich very-low-density lipoprotein (VLDL). This large VLDL fraction is cleared directly from the circulation and not converted into small VLDL or LDL. Postmenopausal estrogens also have beneficial effects on serum glucose and insulin levels and blood pressure.[79,80] Transdermal 17β-estradiol preparations may lack deleterious effects on hemostasis,[81] but their benefits are also less certain.

Observational studies have yielded conflicting information with regards to ERT-associated stroke risk, with some showing an increase,[82] decrease,[83–87] or no effect.[88–95] Observational studies are confounded by the fact that patients receiving ERT are, in general, better educated and healthier.

The Heart and Estrogen Replacement Study (HERS) trial was a randomized trial of estrogen plus progestin for secondary prevention of coronary artery disease in 2,763 postmenopausal women with an average follow-up of 4.1 years. It did not show a significant difference in the main outcome of nonfatal myocardial infarction (MI) or coronary heart disease and death although there was a beneficial effect on lipid levels.[95] The highest risk of nonfatal MI was within the first year of treatment, suggesting that an early adverse effect on coagulation may increase the risk of MI before longer-term beneficial effects of ERT on lipid levels or atherogenesis could be realized. This is supported by observational data from the Nurse's Health Study,[96] in which the risk of short-term use, comparable to the first year of follow-up in HERS, was increased compared with patients who had never had ERT. However, after longer-term use the rate was lower than in patients who had never had ERT. No differences were seen between users of estrogen alone compared with estrogen plus progestin. The HERS investigators also looked at prespecified secondary end points, transient ischemic attacks, and ischemic and hemorrhagic strokes.[97] The main finding was the absence of any significant beneficial or detrimental effect of ERT on the risk of cerebrovascular disease events with coronary disease over 4 years of follow-up. Unlike the pattern observed for nonfatal MI and death in the initial report, there was neither an early

increased risk of stroke in the ERT group nor a later decrease.

Looking specifically at secondary stroke risk, the Women's Estrogen Stroke Trial (WEST) was a prospective, randomized, controlled trial of 17β-estradiol (without progestin) compared with placebo in women who had experienced a transient ischemic attack or nondisabling stroke.[98] This trial found no effect of estrogen on recurrent strokes overall but some increase in the first 6 months. Women randomly assigned to estrogen therapy had a higher risk of fatal stroke (RR, 2.9; CI, 0.9 to 9.0), and nonfatal strokes were associated with slightly worse neurologic and functional deficits.

The data from randomized studies suggest that patients such as TX who have had a stroke should not use ERT. What about ERT for women without prior stroke? The Women's Health Initiative Study, designed to be the largest and most definitive long-term study of ERT (Prempro, a tablet containing 0.625 mg of conjugated equine estrogen and 2.5 mg medroxyprogesterone acetate) was halted in July 2002 due to an increased incidence of breast cancer and vascular events (heart attacks, blood clots in legs and lungs, and strokes).[99] This study enrolled 16,608 women, aged 50 to 79 years who were randomly assigned to ERT or placebo, and followed them for 5 years. The incidence of stroke was 41% higher in the group using ERT and occurred just as commonly in apparently healthy women as those with stroke risk factors. There are insufficient data to comment on whether migraine confers an even greater risk of stroke in ERT users.[25]

RECOMMENDATIONS

Migraine treatment and stroke prevention must be individualized, but the following recommendations are made with the intention of minimizing stroke risk:

- Avoid estrogen-containing OCs if you have MA.
- If you have MO, stop OCs if aura appears.
- If you have had a transient ischemic attack, stroke, or MI, do not use OCs or ERT.
- If there is a family history of clotting disorders, undergo screening prior to OC use.
- If you use OCs, have your cholesterol checked, monitor your blood pressure, and do not smoke.
- Stop OC use at or before age 40 years, when the incidence of stroke in migraineurs rises dramatically.

Although there is no evidence that aspirin is effective in the primary treatment of stroke, given the safety and low cost of aspirin, as well as the evidence of platelet activation and increased prevalence of PFO in migraine, this is an area deserving of further research.

REFERENCES

1. Lipton RB, Stewart WF, Diamond S, et al. Prevalence and burden of migraine in the United States: data from the American Migraine Study II. Headache 2001;41:646–57.

2. Merikangas KR, Fenton BT, Cheng SH, et al. Association between migraine and stroke in a large-scale epidemiological study of the United States. Arch Neurol 1997;54:362–8.

3. Henry P, Michel P, Brochet B, et al. A nationwide survey of migraine in France: prevalence and clinical features in adults. Cephalalgia 1992;12:229–37.

4. Keating NL, Cleary PD, Rossi AS, et al. Use of hormone replacement therapy by postmenopausal women in the United States. Ann Intern Med 1999;130:545–53.

5. Larsson-Cohn U, Lundberg PO. Headache and treatment with oral contraceptives. Acta Neurol Scand 1970; 46:267–78.

6. Nilsson L, Solvell L. Clinical studies on oral contraceptives: a randomized, double-blind, cross-over study of 4 different preparations (Anovlar mite, Lyndiol mite, Ovulen, and Volidan). Acta Obstet Gynaecol Scand 1967;46 Suppl 8:3–31.

7. Cullberg J. Mood changes and menstrual symptoms with different gestagen/estrogen combinations: a double blind comparison with a placebo. Acta Psychiatr Scand 1972;236 Suppl:259–76.

8. Whitty CWM, Hockaday JM, Whitty MM. The effect of oral contraceptives on migraine. Lancet 1986;1:856–9.

9. Granella F, Sances G, Pucci E, et al. Migraine with aura and reproductive life events: a case control study. Cephalalgia 2000;20:701–7.

10. Hockaday JM, Macmillan AL, Whitty CM. Vasomotor-reflex response in idiopathic and hormone-dependent migraine. Lancet 1967;1:1023–6.

11. Moskowitz MA. The neurobiology of vascular head pain. Ann Neurol 1984;16:157–68.

12. Kaiser HJ, Meienberg O. Deterioration or onset of migraine under oestrogen replacement therapy in the menopause. J Neurol 1993;240:195–7.

13. Nappi RE, Cagnacci A, Granella F, et al. Course of primary headache during hormone replacement therapy. Maturitas 2001;38:157–63.

14. Dennerstein L, Morse C, Burrows G, et al. Menstrual migraine: a double blind trial of percutaneous estradiol. Gynecol Endocrinol 1988;2:113–20.

15. Mannix LK, Calhoun AH. Menstrual migraine. Designing a treatment strategy. Female Patient 2001;26:46–51.

16. MacGregor A. Migraine associated with menstruation. Funct Neurol 2000;15 Suppl 3:143–53.

17. Collaborative Group for the Study of Stroke in Young Women. Oral contraceptives and stroke in young women. JAMA 1975;231:718–22.

18. Lidegaard O. Oral contraceptives, pregnancy and the risk of cerebral thromboembolism: the influence of diabetes, hypertension, migraine and previous thrombotic disease. Br J Obstet Gynaecol 1995;102:153–9.

19. Tzourio C, Iglesias S, Hubert JB, et al. Migraine and risk of ischemic stroke: a case-control study. BMJ 1993;308: 289–92.

20. Carolei A, Marini C, De Matteis G. History of migraine and risk of cerebral ischaemia in young adults. Lancet 1996;347:1503–6.

21. Henrich JB, Horowitz RI. A controlled study of ischemic stroke risk in migraine patients. J Clin Epidemiol 1989;42:773–80.

22. Tzourio C, Tehindrazanarivelo A, Iglesias S, et al. Case-control study of migraine and risk of ischemic stroke in young women. BMJ 1995;310:830–3.

23. Pettiti DB, Sidney S, Bernstein A, et al. Stroke in users of low-dose oral contraceptives. N Engl J Med 1996;335:8–15.

24. Becker WJ. Use of oral contraceptives in patients with migraine. Neurology 1999;53(4 Suppl 1):S19–25.

25. The International Headache Society Task Force on Combined Oral Contraceptives and Hormone Replacement Therapy. Recommendations on the risk of ischaemic stroke associated with the use of combined oral contraceptives and hormone replacement therapy in women with migraine. Cephalalgia 2000;20:155–6.

26. Henrich JB, Sandercock PAG, Warlow CP, et al. Stroke and migraine in the Oxfordshire Community Stroke project. J Neurol 1986;23:257–62.

27. Broderick JP, Swanson JW. Migraine-related strokes: clinical profile and prognosis in 20 patients. Arch Neurol 1987;44:868–71.

28. Headache Classification Committee of the International Headache Society. Diagnostic criteria for headache disorders, cranial neuralgias and facial pain. Cephalalgia 1988;8 Suppl 7:20.

29. Sacquegna AT, Andreoli A, Baldrati A, et al. Ischemic stroke in young adults: the relevance of migrainous infarction. Cephalalgia 1989;9:255–8.

30. Carolei A, Marini C, Ferranti E, et al, and the National Research Council Study Group. A prospective study of cerebral ischemia in the young. Analysis of pathogenic determinants. Stroke 1993;24:362–7.

31. Kittner SJ, Stern BJ, Wozniak M, et al. Cerebral infarction in young adults. The Baltimore-Washington Cooperative Young Stroke study. Neurology 1998;50:890–4.

32. Bogousslavsky J, Pierre P. Ischemic stroke in patients under age 45. Neurol Clin 1992;10:113–24.

33. Milhaud D, Bogousslavsky J, van Mell G, Liot P. Ischemic stroke and active migraine. Neurology 2001;57:1805–11.

34. Thorvaldsen P, Asplund K, Kuuasmaa K, et al. Stroke incidence, case fatality, and mortality in the WHO MONICA project: the WHO MONICA project. Stroke 1995;26:361–7.

35. Overell JR, Bone I, Lees KR. Interatrial septal abnormalities and stroke: a meta-analysis of case-control studies. Neurology 2000;55:1172–9.

36. Lamy C, Giannesini C, Zuber M, et al. Clinical and imaging findings in cryptogenic stroke patients with and without patent foramen ovale. The PFO-ASA Study. Stroke 2002;33:706–11.

37. Del Sette M, Angeli S, Leandri M, et al. Migraine with aura and right to left shunt on transcranial Doppler: a case-control study. Cerebrovasc Dis 1998;8:327–30.

38. Anzola GP, Magoni M, Guindani M, et al. Potential source of cerebral embolism in migraine with aura: a transcranial Doppler study. Neurology 1999;52:1622–5.

39. Wilmhurst P, Nightingale S. Relationship between migraine and cardiac and pulmonary right-to left shunts. Clin Sci 2001;100:215–20.

40. Arquizan C, Coste J, Touboul PJ, Mas JL. Is patent foramen ovale a family trait? A transcranial Doppler sonographic study. Stroke 2001;32:1563–6.

41. Wilmhurst P, Nightingale S, Walsh KP, Morrison WL. Effect on migraine of closure of cardiac right-to-left shunts to prevent recurrence of decompression illness or stroke or for hemodynamic reasons. Lancet 2000;356:1648–51.

42. Crassard I, Conrad J, Bousser M-G. Migraine and haemostasis. Cephalalgia 2001;21:630–6.

43. Cesar JM, Garcia-Avello A, Vecino AM, et al. Increased levels of plasma von Willebrand factor in migraine crisis. Acta Neurol Scand 1995;91:412–3.

44. Tietjen GE, Al-Qasmi MM, Athanas K, et al. Increased von Willebrand factor in migraine. Neurology 2001;57:334–6.

45. Brey RL, Stallworth CL, McGlasson DL, et al. Antiphospholipid antibodies and stroke in young women. Stroke 2002;33:2396–401.

46. Montalban J, Titus F, Ordi J, et al. Anticardiolipin antibodies and migraine-related strokes [letter]. Arch Neurol 1988;45:603.

47. Silvestrini M, Matteis M, Troisi E, et al. Migrainous stroke and antiphospholipid antibodies. Eur Neurol 1994;34:316–9.

48. Tietjen GE, Day M, Norris L, et al. Role of anticardiolipin antibodies in young persons with migraine and transient focal neurological events. Neurology 1998;50:1433–40.

49. Haan J, Kapelle LJ, de Ronde H, et al. The factor V Leiden is not a major risk factor for migrainous cerebral infarction. Cephalalgia 1997;17:605–7.

50. Soriani S, Borgna-Pignatti C, Trabetti E, et al. Frequency of Factor V Leiden in juvenile migraine with aura. Headache 1998;38:779–81.

51. Corral J, Iniesta JA, Gonzales-Conejero R, et al. Migraine and prothrombotic risk factors. Cephalalgia 1998;18: 27–60.

52. D'Amico F, Moschiano F, Leone M, et al. Genetic abnormalities of the protein C system: shared risk factors in young adults with migraine with aura and with ischemic stroke? Cephalalgia 1998;18:618–21.

53. Tietjen GE. Mechanisms of migraine-related brain ischemia. Semin Headache Manage 1997;2:1–14.

54. Speroff L, DeCherney A. Evaluation of a new generation of oral contraceptives: the Advisory Board for the New Progestins. Obstet Gynecol 1993;81:1034–47.

55. World Health Collaborative Study of Cardiovascular Disease and Steroid Hormone Contraception. Venous thromboembolic disease and combined oral contraceptives: results of international multi-center case-control study. Lancet 1995;346:1575–82.

56. Jick H, Jick SS, Gurewich V, et al. Risk of idiopathic cardiovascular death and nonfatal venous thromboembolism in women using oral contraceptives with differing progestagen components. Lancet 1995;346: 1589–93.

57. Bloemenkamp KWM, Rosendaal FR, Helmenhorst FM, et al. Enhancement by factor V Leiden mutation of risk of deep-vein thrombosis associated with oral contraceptives containing a third generation progestagen. Lancet 1995;346:1593–6.

58. Spitzer WO, Lewis MA, Heinemann LAJ, et al. Third generation oral contraceptives and risk of venous thromboembolic disorders: an international case-control study: the Transnational Research Group on Oral Contraceptives and the Health of Young Women. BMJ 1996;312:83–8.

59. Kemmeren JM, Algra A, Grobbee DE. Third generation oral contraceptives and risk of venous thrombosis: meta-analysis. BMJ 2001;323:131–4.

60. De Bruijn SFTM, Stam J, Koopman MM, et al. Case-control study of risk of cerebral sinus thrombosis in oral contraceptive users and in carriers of hereditary pro-thrombotic condition. The Cerebral Venous Sinus Thrombosis Study Group. BMJ 1998;316:589–92.

61. Martinelli I, Sacchi E, Landi G, et al. High risk of cere-bral-vein thrombosis in carriers of a prothrombin-gene mutation and in users of oral contraceptives. N Engl J Med 1998;338:1793–7.

62. WHO Collaborative Study. Cardiovascular disease and steroid hormone contraception. Ischemic stroke and combined oral contraceptives: results of an interna-tional, multicentre, case-control study. Lancet 1996;348:498–505.

63. Lidegaard O. Oral contraception and risk of a cerebral thromboembolic attack: results of a case control study. BMJ 1993;306:956–63.

64. Hannaford PC, Croft PR, Kay CR. Oral contraception and stroke: evidence from the Royal College of General Prac-tioners' oral contraception study. Stroke 1994;25:935–42.

65. Vessey MP, Lawless M, Yeates D. Oral contraceptives and stroke: findings in a large prospective study. BMJ 1984;289:530–1.

66. Schwartz SM, Petitti DB, Siscovick DS, et al. Stroke and use of low-dose oral contraceptives in young women. A pooled analysis of two US studies. Stroke 1998;29:2277–84.

67. Kemmeren JM, Tanis BC, Maurice AAJ, et al. Risk of arterial thrombosis in relation to oral contraceptives (RATIO) Study. Oral contraceptives and the risk of ischemic stroke. Stroke 2002;33:1202–8.

68. Johnston SC, Colford JM, Gress DR. Oral contraceptives and the risk of subarachnoid hemorrhage. A meta-analysis. Neurology 1998;51:411–8.

69. WHO Collaborative Study of Cardiovascular disease and steroid hormone contraception. Haemorrhagic stroke, overall stroke risk, and combined oral contraceptives: results of an international, multicentre, case-control study. Lancet 1996;348:505–10.

70. Herrington DM, Reboussin DM, Brosnihan KB, et al. Effects of estrogen replacement on the progression of coronary artery atherosclerosis. N Engl J Med 2000;343:522–9.

71. Conrad J, Samama MM. Oral contraceptives, hormone replacement therapy and haemostasis. Cephalalgia 2000;20:175–82.

72. Cohen H, Mackie IJ, Walshe K, et al. A comparison of the effects of two triphasic oral contraceptives on haemosta-sis. Br J Haematol 1988;69:259–63.

73. Rosing J, Tans G, Nicolaes GAD, et al. Oral contracep-tives and venous thrombosis: different sensitivities to activated protein C in women using second and third generation oral contraceptives. Br J Haematol 1997;97:233–8.

74. Rakoczi I, Gero G, Demeter J, et al. Comparative meta-bolic effects of oral contraceptive preparations contain-ing different progestogens. Effects of desogestrel and ethinylestradiol on the haemostatic balance. Drug Res 1985;35:630–3.

75. Kuhl H. Effects of progestogens on haemostasis. Matu-ritas 1996;24:1–19.

76. Chang CL, Donaghy M, Poulter N. World Health Organi-zation Collaborative Study of cardiovascular disease and steroid hormone contraception. Migraine and stroke in young women: case-control study. BMJ 1999;318:13–8.

77. Caine YG, Bauer KA, Barzegar S, et al. Coagulation acti-vation following estrogen administration to post-menopausal women. Thromb Haemost 1992;4:392–5.

78. Walsh BW, Schiff I, Rosner B, et al. Effects of post-menopausal estrogen replacement on the concentrations and metabolism of plasma lipoproteins. N Engl J Med 1991;325:1196–204.

79. Barrett-Connor E. Putative complications of estrogen replacement therapy: hypertension, diabetes, throm-bophlebitis, and gallstones. In: Korenman SG, editor. The menopause; biological and clinical consequence of ovarian failure; evolution and management. Norwel (MA): Serono Symposi; 1990. p.199–209.

80. Lobo RA. Estrogen replacement therapy and hyperten-sion. Postgrad Med 1987;14:48–54.

81. Conrad J, Samama M, Basdevant A, et al. Differential AT III response to oral and parenteral administration of 17beta estradiol. Thromb Haemost 1983;49:245.

82. Wilson PWF, Garrison RJ, Castelli WP. Postmenopausal estrogen use, cigarette smoking and cardiovascular mor-bidity in women over 50: the Framingham Study. N Engl J Med 1985;313:1038–43.

83. Falkeborn M, Persson I, Terent A, et al. Hormone replacement therapy and the risk of stroke: follow-up of a population-based cohort in Sweden. Arch Intern Med 1993;153:1201–9.

84. Finucane FF, Madans JH, Bush TL, et al. Decreased risk of stroke among postmenopausal hormone users: results from a national cohort. Arch Intern Med 1993;153:73–9.

85. Henderson BE, Paganini-Hill A, Ross RK. Decreased mortality in users of estrogen replacement therapy. Arch Intern Med 1991;151:75–8.

86. Hunt K, Vessey M, McPherson K. Mortality in a cohort of long-term users of hormone replacement therapy: an updated analysis. Br J Obstet Gynaecol 1990;97:1080–6.

87. Schairer C, Adami H-O, Hoover R, et al. Cause-specific mortality in women receiving hormone replacement therapy. Epidemiology 1997;8:59–65.

88. Stampfer MJ, Coldwitz GA, Willett WC, et al. Postmenopausal estrogen therapy and cardiovascular disease. Ten-year follow-up from the nurses' health study. N Engl J Med 1991;325:756–62.

89. Lindenstrom E, Boysen G, Nyboe J. Lifestyle factors and risk of cerebrovascular disease in women: the Copenhagen City Heart Study. Stroke 1993;24:1468–72.

90. Folsom AR, Mink PJ, Sellers TA, et al. Hormonal replacement therapy and morbidity and mortality in a prospective study of postmenopausal women. Am J Public Health 1995;85:1128–32.

91. Grodstein F, Stampfer MJ, Manson JE, et al. Postmenopausal estrogen and progestin use and the risk of cardiovascular disease. N Engl J Med 1996;335:453–61.

92. Pedersen AT, Lidegaard O, Kreiner S, et al. Hormone replacement therapy and risk of non-fatal stroke. Lancet 1997;350:1277–83.

93. Petitti DB, Sidney S, Quesenberry CP, et al. Ischemic stroke and use of estrogen and estrogen/progestogen as hormone replacement therapy. Stroke 1998;29:23–8.

94. Grodstein F, Stampfer MJ, Falkeborn M, et al. Postmenopausal hormone therapy and risk of cardiovascular disease and hip fracture in a cohort of Swedish women. Epidemiology 1999;5:476–80.

95. Hulley S, Grady D, Bush T, et al. Randomized trial of estrogen plus progestin for secondary prevention of coronary heart disease in postmenopausal women. JAMA 1998;280:605–13.

96. Grodstein F, Manson JE, Stampfer MJ. Postmenopausal hormone use and secondary prevention of coronary events in the Nurses' Health Study: a prospective, observational study. Ann Intern Med 2001;135:1–9.

97. Simon JA, Hsia J, Cauley JA, et al, for the HERS Research Group. Postmenopausal hormone therapy and risk of stroke: the Heart and Estrogen-progestin Replacement Study (HERS). Circulation 2001;103:638–42.

98. Viscoli CM, Brass LM, Kernan WN, et al. A clinical trial of estrogen-replacement therapy after ischemic stroke. N Engl J Med 2001;345:1243–9.

99. Writing Group for the Women's Health Initiative Investigators. Risks and benefits of estrogen plus progestin in healthy postmenopausal women: principal results from the Women's Health Initiative randomized controlled trial. JAMA 2002;288:321–33.

CHAPTER 14

Psychiatric and Psychological Factors in Headache

Gay L. Lipchik, PhD, and Jeanetta C. Rains, PhD

CASE

PR, a 27-year-old woman, was referred to a multidisciplinary headache clinic for evaluation and treatment of chronic daily headaches. With a 13-year chronicity, headaches began in her early teens, with escalation in frequency in recent years, following significant psychosocial stressors (eg, marital separation and unemployment following a work-related repetitive motion injury). At the time of presentation, her headache frequency was 7 days per week. Two distinct headache types were presented. The daily tension-type headache emerged from a dull ache at onset, to a pressing, tightening pain. This headache would originate in the occipital region and radiate forward to the temporal area bilaterally. PR denied photophobia, phonophobia, nausea, or vomiting with these daily headaches, instead reporting that stress and anxiety were the triggers. Daily headaches were associated with increased irritability and poor sleep. She believed her daily headaches were limiting her ability to find employment. She reported minimal medication use for daily headaches (ie, approximately four doses of nonsteroidal anti-inflammatory drugs [NSAIDs] per week) because she found medication to be of little benefit. In addition to the daily headache, PR was also diagnosed with migraine. Migraine headache occurred one to two times per month, characterized by unilateral, throbbing pain, with accompanying photophobia, phonophobia, nausea, and rarely vomiting. Migraine often occurred around the time of menses and responded to triptans. Her family history was positive for migraine. PR denied the use of alcohol, illicit drugs, nicotine, and caffeine.

On the Primary Care Evaluation of Mental Disorders (PRIME-MD) Patient Questionnaire (available at <http://www.neclinicians.org/pdf/depression/PrimeMDPATIENTQUESTIONNAIRE.pdf>), PR endorsed a sad mood, anhedonia, worry, nervousness, and anxiety attacks.[1] During the PRIME-MD interview using the Clinician Guide, she reported symptoms of depression including sad mood, discouragement about the future, sleep disturbance (early morning wakening), worthlessness, and fleeting suicidal ideation. PR also reported experiencing unexpected panic attacks at least once per week, accompanied by shortness of breath, increased heart rate, sweating, trembling, fear she may be dying, and worry about panic attack reoccurrence. No medical cause for these episodes had been identified. Additionally, PR described herself as always feeling nervous, anxious, irritable, and aware of muscle tension in her neck and shoulders. She reported that she was unable to control her worry about many different things. Her responses were consistent with the diagnoses of major depression, panic disorder, and generalized anxiety disorder.

Responses to the Beck Depression Inventory (BDI; available at <http://www.psychcorp.com/>) were suggestive of a moderate level of depression.[2] Symptoms on the BDI included sad mood, discouragement about the future, sense of failure, guilt, disappointment in self, anhedonia (loss of interest or pleasure), anergia, fleeting suicidal ideation without suicidal intent or plan, indecision, early morning wakening, increased irritability, fatigue, and decreased libido. Total score on the Trait Anxiety Inventory (TAI; available at <http://www.mindgarden.com/Assessments/Info/staiinfo.htm>) was at the 98th percentile for same-age women.[3] Responses to the TAI indicated significant symptoms of psychological distress and anxiety including nervousness, restlessness, dysphoria, irritability, fatigue, near-constant worry, tension, feeling overwhelmed by current situation, indecision, and negative self-evaluation.

PR stated that she was most concerned about her daily headaches and was apprehensive about taking medications to address all of her symptoms. She requested non-pharmacologic treatment. She did agree to undergo a trial of medication for headache prophylaxis. She was advised that additional medication might be recommended in the future to assist in managing depression and anxiety, if optimal results were not achieved with non-pharmacologic treatment.

Amitriptyline 10 mg PO qhs was initiated and titrated to 75 mg. PR also participated in cognitive-behavioral headache management, which incorporated cognitive-behavioral interventions for anxiety, panic disorder, and depressive symptoms. She attended six 1-hour individual therapy sessions at 1-month intervals, which included additional telephone contacts with the therapist between sessions. A stress-management workbook and audiotapes were provided to facilitate skills acquisition and practice. Treatment included progressive muscle relaxation training, neck stretching exercises, and brief relaxation techniques. PR was also instructed in the use of abdominal breathing, relaxation techniques, and cognitive coping to abort panic attacks. She identified interpersonal conflicts with her mother and ex-husband and the stress of raising her son as current stressors and likely headache triggers. Coping skills were taught, including assertiveness training and cognitive restructuring to challenge cognitive distortions associated with stress appraisal and self-image.

PR was compliant with pharmacologic treatment as well as cognitive-behavioral therapy. With relaxation and cognitive coping skills, the panic attacks resolved, and sleep improved. Her daily tension-type headaches and episodic migraine headaches were reduced by approximately 75%. Her self-esteem improved and she sought employment. At the 6-month follow-up evaluation, PR no longer met diagnostic criteria for depression or panic disorder, and her generalized anxiety was much more manageable. Following 9 months of pharmacologic treatment, she was successfully weaned from the amitriptyline. At a 3-year follow-up visit, PR had continued to improve: her headache diaries indicated an 85% reduction in headache activity, and she no longer met diagnostic criteria for any psychiatric disorder nor had she experienced any recurrences of depression or panic attacks. She reported continuation of the relaxation and cognitive coping skills learned in treatment, and she was employed full-time.

Psychological factors are highly relevant to the evaluation and treatment of headache. Although population-based studies indicate that most headache sufferers do not exhibit severe psychopathology, associations between migraine and mood disorders have been identified in a sizable minority of patients. In addition, nonpathologic psychological factors (eg, stress and inadequate coping responses) are relevant to many patients with headache. This chapter reviews the current literature on comorbidity of psychiatric illness and primary headache disorders and provides pharmacologic and behavior treatment recommendations. Particular attention is placed on major depression and panic disorder because of the high rates of comorbidity with headache disorders. Although the prevalence rates are much lower for somatoform disorders and borderline personality disorder, they are briefly addressed because they are difficult to treat and are associated with a poorer prognosis. Tools for assessing comorbid psychiatric disorders are reviewed. Headache precipitants are discussed, with a focus on behavioral and stress-related factors. The most commonly used cognitive-behavioral interventions for the treatment of recurrent headache disorders are described, and a review is included of their use for the treatment of hormonally-related headaches.

KEY CHAPTER POINTS

- Depression and anxiety are comorbid with migraine and chronic tension-type headache, and co-occurrence increases headache-associated disability.
- Psychological treatments are important adjuncts to medication withdrawal when treating analgesic-overuse headache.
- Headache sufferers, especially migraineurs, are physiologically hyperresponsive to a variety of internal and external stimuli, including psychological stress that triggers individual headache episodes.
- Cognitive-behavioral treatments may be highly effective in the management of headache and should be individualized to the patient's particular symptoms, incorporating skills for headache management as well as general psychological functioning (eg, mood, assertiveness, interpersonal relationships, self-esteem).
- The addition of cognitive-behavioral treatments to standard headache pharmacologic therapy maximizes treatment efficacy.

DEPRESSION AND ANXIETY DISORDERS

Migraine

More than 30% of migraineurs, compared with 10% of individuals without migraine, have a lifetime prevalence of major depression; 11% of migraineurs, compared with 2% of individuals without migraine, have a lifetime prevalence of panic disorder.[4] The lifetime prevalence of specific psychiatric disorders with an elevated risk for migraineurs appears in Table 14-1.

Migraine with comorbid depression is often complicated by an anxiety disorder. In individuals with migraine, major depression, and an anxiety disorder, the onset of anxiety generally precedes the onset of migraine and may be present as early as childhood.[5,6] In contrast, the onset of major depression typically follows the onset of migraine.[7]

Anxiety and depression are more prevalent among *both* women and men with migraine than among those without recurrent headaches, although women with migraine are more likely to experience anxiety or depression than men with migraine.[8–15] For example, Breslau and colleagues followed a random sample of young adults 21 to 30 years of age for 3.5 years.[15] Women were significantly more likely than men to receive lifetime diagnoses of both migraine (24% versus 9%) and major depression (24% versus 13%) by age 30 years, with the relative female risk increasing for migraine in the late teens and for major depression after about age 20 years. Longitudinal data indicated that women were fourfold more likely to develop migraine and twofold more likely to develop major depression than men. It is noteworthy that migraine dramatically increased the risk of depression, tripling the probability of developing major depression. As a result, by age 33 years, the majority (53%) of migraineurs, but fewer than one in six individuals without migraine, received a lifetime diagnosis of major depression. In older women, active migraine is strongly associated with a history of depression at any time during life, high levels of stress susceptibility, and high levels of anxiety.[16] Comorbid depression substantially increases the disability associated with migraine, suggesting the importance of identification and management of comorbid psychiatric disorders in patients with migraine.[12]

The exact nature of the relationship between migraine and mood disorders remains unclear. It is unlikely that depression results simply as a result of the burden of living with a recurrent painful condition. Several epidemiologic studies suggest that the relationship is bidirectional, with the presence of major depression or anxiety also increasing the likelihood of subsequently developing migraine.[11,15,17] It is generally believed that comorbidity most likely arises from the shared pathophysiology of migraine and mood disorders. Glover and colleagues have reviewed features common to the biology of major depression and migraine, and it has been hypothesized that a dysfunction in the serotonergic system increases the risk of both disorders.[18]

Tension-Type Headache

The prevalence of mood and anxiety disorders does not appear to be elevated in episodic tension-type headache.[13] This finding, however, cannot be generalized to

Table 14-1 Lifetime Prevalence of Migraine and Affective and Anxiety Disorders

Diagnosis	Migraine Group (%)	Control Group (%)	Odds Ratio*
Major depression	34	10	4.5
Dysthymia	9	2	4.4
Bipolar II†	4	1	5.1
Manic episode	5	1	5.4
Panic disorder	11	2	6.6
Generalized anxiety disorder	10	2	5.7
Obsessive-compulsive disorder	9	2	5.1
Phobia	40	21	2.6
Illicit drug use	20	10	2.2
Nicotine dependence	33	18	2.2

Adapted from Breslau N and Davis GC[4] and Breslau N et al.[8]
*Odds ratios adjusted for gender.
†The hypomanic episode does not result in marked impairment.

chronic tension-type headache (CTTH). More than 40% of patients with CTTH in primary care settings and as many as 65% of patients with CTTH seen in specialty settings are diagnosed with mood or anxiety disorders.[19-21] Comorbid mood or anxiety disorder increases the disability associated with CTTH, suggesting the importance of identification and management of comorbid psychiatric disorders in patients with headache. As with migraine, women with CTTH are more likely than men with CTTH to experience comorbid depressive or anxiety disorders.[14,20,21]

Chronic Daily Headache

Chronic daily headache (CDH) refers to a heterogeneous group of headaches characterized as near-daily headaches with primarily migrainous features (chronic migraine) or primarily tension-type features (CTTH). CDH is a descriptive clinical diagnosis widely employed in research and practice, rather than a diagnosis within the official nomenclature of the International Headache Society. Psychiatric comorbidity has been reported in up to 90% of patients with primary CDH in clinical samples, with anxiety and mood disorders being the most common diagnoses.[22,23] Clinical experience suggests that for some patients, comorbid depression improves as headaches improve.[14] In specialty centers, patients with intractable CDH report a high prevalence of physical, emotional, and sexual abuse and a history of parental alcohol abuse/dependence.[24] CDH tends to be refractory to standard monotherapy with either pharmacologic or behavioral therapies, and multimodal treatment has been found to yield the best results.[25,26]

Depression: Overview and Treatment Recommendations

Major depression is a common disorder that affects at least 20% of women and 10% of men over their lifetime.[27] In primary care settings, the rate of dysthymia (chronic, low-grade depression) is similar to the rate of major depression. Depression has been described as the "the neglected major illness" with costs estimated to be $44 billion (US) per year in the United States alone.[28] Most of the cost of depression is derived from inadequate treatment of the illness that leads to lowered job productivity and lost income from missed workdays and suicide. Obviously, successful headache management is unlikely if comorbid depression is not recognized and effectively treated.

Major depression is defined by the American Psychiatric Association in the *Diagnostic and Statistical Manual of Mental Disorders* (DSM-IV) by a collection of symptoms resulting in significant functional impairment.[29] At least five of the symptoms, outlined in Table 14-2, must be present during the same 2-week period, and at least one of the symptoms must be either

Table 14-2 Symptoms of Major Depression

A. Five or more symptoms present for the same 2-week period, including listed points 1 and 2 below:

1. Depressed mood most of the day, nearly every day (feeling sad or empty, appears tearful; for children or adolescents, can be irritable mood)
2. Loss of interest or pleasure in most activities
3. Significant weight loss without dieting, or decrease in appetite; with atypical depression: weight gain, increased appetite
4. Insomnia or hypersomnia
5. Psychomotor agitation or retardation
6. Fatigue or loss of energy
7. Feelings of worthlessness or excessive, inappropriate guilt
8. Impaired concentration, slowed thinking, or indecision
9. Suicidal thoughts (with or without a plan) or a suicide attempt

B. Symptoms cause clinically significant distress or impairment in functioning

C. No prior manic or hypomanic episode

D. Symptoms are not due to the following:

1. The direct physiologic effects of a substance (medication or drug of abuse)
2. A general medical condition (eg, hypothyroidism)
3. Bereavement

Adapted from American Psychiatric Association.[29]

depressed mood or loss of interest or pleasure (anhedonia). Dysthymia (sad mood lasting a minimum of 2 years) is more chronic, but less intense, than major depression. In addition to sad mood, the patient also experiences at least two of the symptoms listed in Table 14-2. Mood disorders have a high comorbidity with anxiety disorders and substance abuse.

Although major depression with symptoms of depressed affect, tearfulness, and psychomotor retardation is easily recognizable in isolation, the diagnosis may be obscured by additional somatic and emotional symptoms in the medically ill. Inquiry into all of the symptoms that constitute major depression is critical for the diagnosis of depression. The PRIME-MD Patient Questionnaire and BDI can be used to facilitate the recognition of depression.[1,2] (See "Assessment of Comorbid Psychiatric Disorders" section below.)

Pharmacologic treatment of major depression focuses on the use of adequate doses of antidepressants. Tricyclic and related cyclic antidepressants are effective in the treatment of headache disorders but are currently less commonly used in the treatment of depression because of side effects (eg, sedation, weight gain, cardiac arrhythmias) that occur at the higher doses required to treat depression. Newer selective serotonin reuptake inhibitors (SSRIs) have more benign side effect profiles, are better tolerated than the tricyclic antidepressants (TCAs), and are less likely to prove lethal in cases of overdose. Thus, consideration of an SSRI is recommended when headache and major depression are comorbid, although few controlled studies have investigated the efficacy of SSRIs in headache prophylaxis. Anecdotal evidence suggests that fluoxetine and some newer antidepressants such as bupropion, nefazodone, and venlafaxine are effective for migraine prophylaxis, as well as in the treatment of depression.[30] The doses of newer antidepressants used to treat migraine are the same as those usually prescribed for depression. Because the efficacy of antidepressants is essentially equivalent, the choice of medication should be based on side effect profile and symptom configuration. SSRIs and TCAs are contraindicated when mania is present or suspected. The anticonvulsant valproate is effective in treating migraine and comorbid manic-depression (bipolar disorder). The beta-blockers, typically used in migraine prophylaxis, are contraindicated when depression is also present.

Dysthymia is typically treated with psychological interventions. Antidepressants may be used in patients with dysthymia if the patient fails to respond to psychotherapy or has depressive symptoms typically responsive to antidepressants (eg, sleep onset or sleep maintenance problems).

The Agency for Health Care Policy and Research developed guidelines in 1993 for treating major depression.[31] Once a diagnosis has been made, treatment should be monitored every few weeks. Response to treatment should be assessed at week 6, and when the patient shows clear improvement, the treatment should be continued for at least an additional 6 weeks. When there is complete remission of symptoms, medication is continued for 4 to 9 months to prevent relapse, and maintenance treatment is considered because a single episode of depression carries at least a 50% risk of recurrence. Evidence supports ongoing treatment for a period of several years, if not indefinitely, to reduce the likelihood of relapse and recurrence. When a patient is only partially improved at 6 weeks, a dose adjustment can be made. Treatment should be continued and monitored at 2-week intervals. If remission has not occurred by week 12, a psychiatric referral, treatment change, or augmentation of the current medication should be considered.

Combined psychological and pharmacologic treatments should be considered for patients with comorbid headache and depressive and/or anxiety disorders.[32]

Behavioral interventions, such as maintaining a regular schedule and increasing pleasant activities, getting adequate sleep and exercise, and discontinuing the use of tobacco, are often beneficial. It is noteworthy, however, that patients with chronic depression *may* notice a *transient* increase in depressive symptoms following nicotine discontinuation.[33,34] Relaxation training and biofeedback may provide a nonthreatening means of introducing the patient to psychological treatments, and may encourage the patient to acknowledge psychological difficulties and accept treatment for psychological disorders. Empirically validated cognitive-behavioral interventions for depression can be incorporated easily into cognitive-behavioral interventions for headache management.[35–37] The addition of cognitive-behavioral therapy to pharmacotherapy for the treatment of depression has been found to be more effective than medication alone at preventing relapse.[38]

In settings where access to psychologists is limited, self-help manuals for the cognitive treatment of depression (eg, that of Greenberger and Padesky[39]) may be somewhat helpful. Burns' popular book, *Feeling Good*, instructs patients in some of the cognitive therapy techniques and has been shown to be an effective form of bibliotherapy, demonstrating that cognitive therapy for depression can be delivered efficiently in some cases.[40,41]

Basic descriptions of cognitive-behavioral therapy can be found in the books by Beck and colleagues (1979), Beck and Emery (1985), Beck (1995), and Greenberger and Padesky (1995).[35,39,42,43] Briefly, cognitive-behavioral treatment combines two psychological treatment approaches—cognitive therapy and behavior therapy. When used in combination, cognitive-behavioral treatments attempt to change overt behavior by altering thoughts, interpretations of events, assumptions, and usual behavior strategies of responding to events. Cognitive therapy asserts that an individual's cognitions and fundamental belief system play a substantial role in their emotional reactions and a powerful role in maintaining dysfunctional moods and behaviors regardless of their origins. Characteristic dysfunctional cognitions and beliefs accompany various mood states. Depressive cognitions and beliefs are typically self-critical ("It's all my fault. I'm no good. I'm a failure. I'm worthless"), negative about the world ("Nobody cares about me"), and hopeless about the future ("Things will never get any better"). Anxiety is typically accompanied by thoughts of danger, vulnerability, and anger, with thoughts of violation and unfairness. For example, an individual prone to depression may interpret an essentially benign event (eg, not getting offered a position following a job interview) as confirmation of negative self-beliefs. The individual's automatic thoughts and underlying beliefs may include self-statements such as, "They didn't select me for the

fic, instead of clenching one's teeth and tensing one's neck and shoulder muscles, patients are instructed to relax these muscles, use gentle muscle-stretching exercises, and breathe deeply while subvocalizing the word "relax."

Biofeedback Training

The two most widely used biofeedback training modalities for headaches are 1) thermal biofeedback or *hand-warming* feedback quantifying skin temperature from a finger, and 2) EMG biofeedback or *muscle-tension* feedback of electrical activity from the scalp, neck, or trapezius muscles.[77] Biofeedback training for headache is commonly administered in conjunction with relaxation training, either concurrently or sequentially, and a dozen or more biofeedback training sessions may be needed. The number of training appointments may be reduced by providing home instructions, a simple hand-held thermometer, and practice sheets. As with relaxation training, patients typically are instructed to practice the self-regulation skills at home daily.

Cognitive-Behavioral Therapy or Stress-Management Training

The rationale for cognitive-behavioral therapy or stress-management training in headache management derives from the observation that the way in which individuals cope with everyday stresses can precipitate, exacerbate, or maintain headaches and increase headache-related disability and distress.[89–91] Cognitive-behavioral therapy focuses on the cognitive, emotional, and behavioral components of headache, and it is typically administered in conjunction with relaxation or biofeedback training, which focus on the physiologic components of headache.

Cognitive-behavioral interventions educate patients about the relationships between stress, coping, and headaches and alert them to the role that their cognitions play in their response to stress. Patients are taught to identify the specific psychological or behavioral factors that trigger or aggravate their own headaches and to employ more effective strategies for coping with headache-related stress. For example, patients may be instructed to replace stress-generating thoughts and beliefs (eg, "I'll never meet my sales goal this month. I'm letting the company down. I'm a failure") with adaptive coping statements and more realistic stress appraisals ("At this point, there is no way to tell how far I'll get this month, and there is no evidence to indicate I can't meet the goal. I'll focus on the task at hand and see how far I get. Missing the goal one month does not detract from all the times I have met the sales goals for the company. Ann missed her goal last month, and I don't think of her as a failure; so most likely, no-one will think of me as a failure if I don't meet the goal this

month"). By assisting patients to more effectively manage stress, cognitive-behavioral therapy can help to limit the disability, anxiety, and depression that often afflict patients with more frequent and severe headaches.

Integration of Behavioral and Pharmacologic Treatments

An integrated "multimodal" treatment approach combining behavioral and pharmacologic treatments is often the treatment of choice in specialty headache centers. Here, in addition to the best of the pharmacologic treatment strategies described elsewhere in this volume, behavioral interventions are tailored to provide patients with the strategies for headache prevention and management described above, as well as skills for the effective use of medications. Strategies for selecting the appropriate prescribed medication (eg, acute care or preventive medications) and dosing schedule for headaches of various patterns and severity and using this information to individualize medication treatment plans, have already been incorporated into some behavioral headache management programs, with documented benefits in terms of improved compliance and enhanced outcomes.[92,93] The often high cost of headache medications, particularly over many years of headache chronicity, and concerns regarding complications from medication overuse, suggest that methods for helping patients to use these medications in an optimal fashion are necessary.[94]

Efficacy of Behavioral Treatments for Headache
Migraine

In 1999, the US Agency for Healthcare Research and Quality (AHRQ), formally the Agency for Health Care Policy and Research, released a series of technical reports that systematically reviewed all controlled trials of pharmacologic, behavioral, and physical treatments for migraine published between 1966 and 1996. The meta-analysis of behavioral treatments for migraine identified 355 published articles describing behavioral and physical treatments for migraine, including 70 controlled clinical trials of behavioral treatments for migraine in adults.[95] The 39 prospective and randomized trials that met all of the stringent research design and data extraction requirements yielded 60 treatment groups, evaluating relaxation training (10 trials), temperature biofeedback training (5 trials), temperature biofeedback plus relaxation training (10 trials), EMG biofeedback training (5 trials), cognitive-behavioral therapy (stress-management training) (7 trials), cognitive-behavioral therapy plus temperature biofeedback (5 trials), hypnotherapy (2 trials), wait-list control (12 trials), and various other control conditions (4 trials).

Based on a composite headache index or headache frequency measures, treatment outcome data were calculated: 1) "effect size score"—the standardized difference between group means, and 2) average percentage headache improvement from pre- to post-treatment (weighted by sample size). The behavioral interventions yielded a 32 to 49% reduction in migraine versus a 5% reduction for no-treatment controls. The conservative effect size estimates indicated that relaxation training, thermal biofeedback combined with relaxation training, EMG biofeedback, and cognitive-behavioral therapy were all statistically more effective than wait list control.

An evidence-based guideline based on the AHRQ technical reviews was developed by a multidisciplinary consortium (US Headache Consortium) from the American Academy of Family Physicians, American Academy of Neurology, American Headache Society, American College of Emergency Physicians, American College of Physicians, American Osteopathic Association, and the National Headache Foundation.[96] The Consortium's recommendations pertaining to behavioral interventions for migraine were as follows: 1) relaxation training, thermal biofeedback combined with relaxation training, EMG biofeedback, and cognitive-behavioral therapy may be considered as treatment options for prevention of migraine, and 2) behavioral therapy may be combined with preventive drug therapy to achieve added clinical improvement for migraine.

Findings of the AHRQ review were consistent with prior meta-analyses using broader inclusion of the available research, where behavioral treatments for migraine yielded a 30 to 55% headache reduction (Figure 14-1).[95,97,98]

The best of the preventive pharmacologic and behavioral therapies appear equally as effective for uncomplicated migraine patients. Meta-analyses have shown that virtually identical improvement in migraine has been reported with propranolol (arguably the preventive pharmacologic therapy most widely employed in the United States and among the most effective for migraine; 32 trials), flunarizine (a calcium channel blocker widely used for migraine prophylaxis in Canada and Europe; 31 trials), and combined relaxation and biofeedback training (35 trials), whereas the average patient receiving a placebo pill for migraine showed only a 12% improvement.[97,99–101]

Meta-analyses indicate that approximately three-quarters of participants in the research of behavioral treatments were women.[97,102,103] This is expected because the majority of migraine headache sufferers are women. Most studies have not reported gender differences in treatment outcome. When gender differences have been examined in individual studies, significant gender differences in response to behavioral treatments have generally not been observed.[81,92,104] At this time, it is

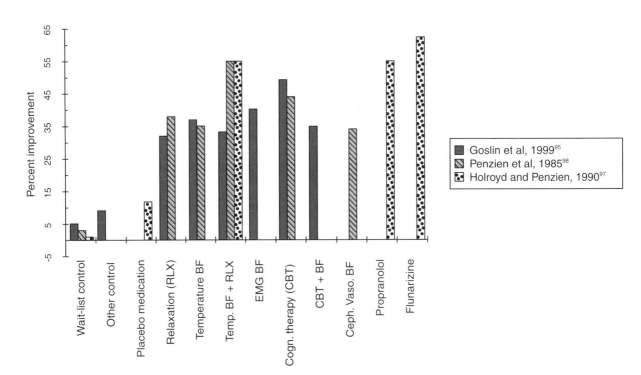

Figure 14-1 Meta-analyses of behavioral and pharmacologic treatments for migraine: percent improvement scores by treatment condition. BF = biofeedback; CBT = cognitive-behavioral treatment; Ceph. Vaso. BF = cephalic vasomotor biofeedback; EMG = electromyographic; RLX = relaxation training.

generally believed that women and men respond similarly to behavioral interventions for headache.

Although behavioral and pharmacologic treatments are often administered in combination in the specialty headache settings, this combined treatment approach has not been extensively researched. Only two studies have been published that evaluated combined treatment for migraine. Both found the combination of propranolol and behavioral (ie, relaxation, biofeedback) treatments to be highly effective, yielding an average reduction in headache of at least 70% and more effective than behavioral treatment alone.[105,106] Although data are limited, the AHRQ deemed the data sufficient to recommend behavioral therapy to be combined with preventive drug therapy to achieve added clinical improvement for migraine.[107]

Tension-Type Headache

A meta-analysis of the randomized controlled trials of behavioral treatments for tension-type headache was recently completed using parallel methodology to the AHRQ review.[95,108] The 35 prospective and randomized trials published between 1966 and 1999 yielded 77 treatment groups, including relaxation training (19 trials), EMG biofeedback training (14 trials), EMG biofeedback plus relaxation training (7 trials), cognitive-behavioral therapy (13 trials), wait-list control (13 tri-

als), and other controls (11 trials). Treatment outcome data were calculated, including summary effect size estimates and average percentage improvement at post-treatment.

Behavioral interventions for tension-type headache yielded 37 to 50% reduction in headache versus 2% reduction for no-treatment and 9% for other controls. The effect size estimates indicated that all of the behavioral interventions were statistically more effective than wait-list control. Results are consistent with prior meta-analyses of the behavioral tension-type literature, with behavioral treatments for tension-type headache showing typical reductions of 35 to 55% in headache post-treatment and all treatment conditions statistically more effective than control conditions (Figure 14-2).[102,103,109]

For comparison purposes, McCrory and colleagues searched for all controlled trials of amitriptyline, arguably the most commonly prescribed medication for prophylaxis of tension-type headache.[108] Three controlled trials of amitriptyline for tension-type headache were identified and they yielded, on average, a 33% reduction in headache activity, which is on the low end of the range achieved by behavioral therapies.

As with migraine, research concerning the combined use of pharmacologic and behavioral treatment of tension-type headache has been minimal. Only one

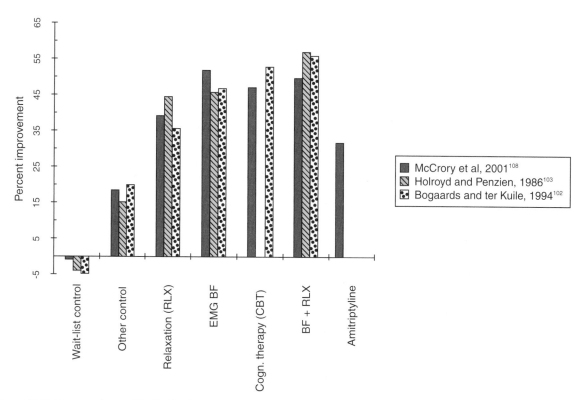

Figure 14-2 Meta-analyses of behavioral and pharmacologic treatments for tension-type headache: percent improvement scores by treatment condition. BF = biofeedback; CBT = cognitive-behavioral treatment; EMG = electromyographic; RLX = relaxation training.

large-scale direct clinical comparison has been published. Holroyd and colleagues randomly assigned over 200 chronic tension-type headache patients to one of four conditions: 1) TCA medication (amitriptyline to 100 mg/day), 2) stress-management training, 3) combined antidepressant and stress-management, or 4) medication placebo.[25] Medication and behavioral therapy each produced larger reductions in headache activity, analgesic medication use, and headache-related disability than placebo, but the medication condition yielded more rapid improvements in headache activity. The combined therapy was more likely to produce clinically meaningful reductions in headache (64% of patients) than either isolated medication (38%) or stress-management training (35%), indicating that, whereas both isolated treatment strategies are modestly effective, the combined therapy may improve outcomes. In a recently completed retrospective analysis of these data, Holroyd and colleagues found that both antidepressant medication and stress-management demonstrated the greatest response in patients with a comorbid mood or anxiety disorder, high intensity headaches, and high levels of disability.[110]

Alternate Formats for Behavioral Treatments
Minimal Therapist-Contact Treatment
Most of the published clinical trials of behavioral treatments for headache have been administered in a clinic, requiring 10 to 12 clinic sessions with a healthcare professional. As an alternative to these more intensive clinic-based treatments, the minimal therapist-contact or "home-based" behavioral treatment format provides an economical and efficient mode of service delivery. In a minimal-contact treatment format, self-regulation skills are introduced in face-to-face clinic sessions, but the training primarily occurs at home with the patient guided by written materials and audiotapes. Minimal therapist-contact treatments typically have only three or four monthly clinic sessions.

Meta-analyses of minimal-contact behavioral interventions for headache have demonstrated the use of the minimal-contact treatment approach, indicating that for many patients, such treatments can be as effective as those delivered in a clinic setting for uncomplicated headache patients.[79,111,112] Notably, the minimal therapist-contact approach may be poorly suited for more complicated patients, including those who are overusing analgesic medications, are clinically depressed, or have particularly refractory headache problems. Complicated patients would continue to require more therapist-intensive treatments to achieve optimal results.

Group Treatment Format
Behavioral interventions for headache may be administered in small groups rather than individually. A meta-analysis has identified 10 studies where behavioral treatments were administered in a group format.[112] The 53% improvement associated with the group format was similar to that reported when the same interventions were individually administered. Where patient flow is adequate, group rather than individual administration of treatment allows the cost of treatment to be reduced and professional time to be efficiently allocated.

Behavioral Treatment of Hormonally Influenced Headaches
It has generally been assumed that headaches associated with hormonal changes, or aggravated by hormonal preparations, are less responsive to behavior therapy than are other primary headaches. However, there is some evidence to suggest that behavior therapy may be effective in the treatment of hormonally influenced headaches and may be especially useful for headaches during pregnancy.[113]

Menstrual Migraine
Few studies have evaluated the efficacy of behavioral treatment for menstrual migraine, and these studies have yielded conflicting results (Table 14-5). Of the three studies that have examined the effects of relaxation or biofeedback therapy specifically on menstrual migraine, two studies have reported reasonable reductions in menstrual migraines.[114,115] However, one study (study 2, Kim and Blanchard) reported only minimal reductions in menstrual migraines.[116] Two additional studies have investigated the efficacy of relaxation or biofeedback therapies on overall headache activity in women who experienced both menstrual and nonmenstrual migraines. One study (study 1, Kim and Blanchard) reported reasonable improvement, and one study reported almost no improvement in overall headache activity.[116,117] These studies differed in their definition of menstrual migraine. Thus, all headaches that were considered menstrually-related in one study were not considered menstrually-related in another study. The inability to unambiguously identify menstrually-related migraine and the use of slightly different definitions of menstrual migraine in different studies make it difficult to compare results across studies.

There is some evidence that menstrually-related migraines need not be refractory to behavior therapy. Gauthier and colleagues compared improvements in headaches associated with menstruation (occurring within 3 days of the beginning of menstruation period) and in headaches occurring at other times in women who received either thermal or cephalic vasomotor biofeedback training.[114] Similar improvements were observed in menstrual and nonmenstrual headaches, with about one-half of women showing clinically significant improvement (greater than 50% reduction in

Table 14-5 Response of Menstrual Migraines to Behavioral Treatment

Authors	Definition of MM	Results	Comments
Gauthier et al[114] (1991) (N = 39)	−3 to +3 days from onset of menstruation	MM = NMM; 49% patients > 50% reduction in MM	Unclear if subjects on oral contraceptives were excluded
Szekely et al[115] (1986) (N = 8)	−7 to +7 days from start of menstruation	MM = NMM; 50% patients > 50% reduction in MM	Cluster and tension headaches included; improvements not significant
Kim and Blanchard[116] (1992) Study 1 (N = 98)	Self-identification	MM = NMM; 42% MM patients > 50% reduction in headaches	MM and NMM not distinguished in diary recordings
Kim and Blanchard[116] (1992) Study 2 (N = 15)	Self-identification + verification by diary	MM = NMM; 27% patients > 50% reduction in MM	Reductions in neither MM nor NMM significant
Solbach et al[117] (1984) (N = 136)	−3 to +3 days from start of menstruation	Direct comparison not reported.* Approximately 13% reduction in headaches in MM sufferers†	MM and NMM not distinguished in diary recordings

MM = menstrual migraine headache; NMM = nonmenstrual migraine headache.
*Indirect comparison suggested MM < NMM.
†Reduction in frequency from pretreatment to final 12-week block.

headache activity) in each type of headache. Improvements in menstrual and nonmenstrual headaches were equally likely to be maintained at a 6-month follow-up.

Pregnancy

Behavioral interventions are attractive for managing headaches during pregnancy because, unlike medications, behavioral interventions pose no risks to the developing fetus. Moreover, behavioral interventions may reduce the nausea and vomiting associated with pregnancy. For some women, migraines remit during the second or third trimester without treatment making it difficult to evaluate the effectiveness of headache therapies during pregnancy. Uncontrolled studies provide limited information about the efficacy of behavior therapy for headaches during pregnancy.

In a randomized controlled study, Marcus and colleagues found behavior therapy to be a promising treatment during pregnancy.[118] In this study, 31 pregnant women were randomly assigned to either a 2-month (8 session) treatment that included relaxation or thermal biofeedback training and physical therapy exercises, or to a pseudotherapy control treatment that included much of the same educational material and thermal biofeedback training to *decrease* (rather than increase) finger temperature. For most women, the treatment program was initiated during the second trimester (eighteenth week of pregnancy on average) and was completed before delivery. Women who received

the active treatment showed substantially larger mean reductions in headache activity (81% versus 33% reduction) and were more likely to show clinically significant improvement (73% versus 29% of women) following treatment than women in the control condition. Additionally, improvements were maintained throughout the perinatal period and at 3- and 6-month follow-up evaluations.[119] These findings encourage greater experimentation with the use of behavioral intervention to manage headaches during pregnancy.

Menopause

Little attention has been paid to the evaluation of behavior therapies in postmenopausal women. Clinical trials that have been large enough to include a reasonable sample of postmenopausal women have failed to report results specifically for this subgroup of women.

Candidates for Behavioral Treatments or Combined Behavioral and Pharmacologic Treatment

The US Headache Consortium concluded that behavioral treatments may be particularly well-suited for patients having one or more of the following characteristics: patient preference of a non-pharmacologic approach; pharmacologic treatment cannot be tolerated or is medically contraindicated; the response to pharmacologic treatment is absent or minimal; the patient is pregnant, has plans to become pregnant, or is nursing; the patient has a long-standing history of frequent or excessive use of analgesic or acute medications that can aggravate headache; or the patient is faced with significant stressors or has deficient stress-coping skills.[107] Patients with these characteristics should be at least considered for referral to behavioral treatment. In certain cases, the combination of pharmacologic and behavioral approaches may be employed to achieve maximal efficacy and minimize untoward effects.

Ideally, pharmacologic and behavioral treatments would be justly allocated to patients based on their individual headache characteristics, medical condition, psychosocial factors, and preferences. Unfortunately, there are no empirically-based algorithms available to date to determine which specific patients are likely to be most responsive to behavioral versus pharmacologic versus combination behavioral and pharmacologic treatments. Future research should target this area of medical decision-making.

Addition of Cognitive-Behavioral Treatments to Standard Headache Pharmacologic Therapy

Psychological factors are highly relevant to headache patients. All headache patients should receive at least a preliminary psychosocial screening as a facet of their medical evaluation at the point of primary care service (where most headache patients enter the healthcare system). The average headache patient would benefit from at least basic education (in house) about headache triggers, self-regulation, and medication management. This has been termed by some as "headache school," and it can be carried out in a variety of cost-effective delivery formats (eg, nonmedical office staff, videotaped instruction, computer interactive programs, small patient groups). Those patients with higher frequency or more disabling headache should be directed toward preventive behavioral treatments (perhaps a minimal therapist-contact behavioral intervention) and/or prophylactic medication with limits on the use of symptomatic medications (to flag and reduce the risk of analgesic overuse and rebound headache). Similarly, patients with largely stress-related headaches should be enrolled in the more intensive stress-management treatment to decrease stress-related headache and reduce the risk of medication complications. Major mood disorders and severe psychopathology are relatively uncommon among headache patients. However, when present, psychiatric comorbidities impact prognosis, and individualized treatment regimens are needed to maximize efficacy. Patients with significant depression, anxiety, or other psychopathology should be referred for more intensive psychological interventions.

Behavioral treatments are effective and on par with the better pharmacologic treatments for headache prophylaxis. Behavioral treatments are most often provided by mental health professionals (usually clinical psychologists) within specialty headache programs, medical school or university-based healthcare facilities, or private practice settings. In some communities, especially rural areas, it may be challenging to identify providers of behavioral services. Sometimes, assistance in identifying appropriate providers can be gathered from professional organizations for headache, pain management, and behavioral medicine (eg, American Council for Headache Education Web site, available at <http://www.achenet.org>).

To date, behavioral interventions have been designed for patients with complicated and difficult headache problems. Patients with less difficult headache problems, however, may well benefit from simplified behavioral interventions, requiring much less therapist time and assistance. Recently, some attempts have been made to integrate behavioral interventions into the primary care setting. Administration of behavioral treatment within primary care can help to counter stigmas that sometimes are associated with services provided within psychiatric and psychological facilities and may increase the probability of patients following through with referral recommendations.[120]

Development of appropriate written and audio or video materials (for review by patients in the office setting and at home) designed specifically for use in primary care settings would go a long distance toward reducing the commitment of staff time, as well as the cost of the intervention. These same interventions also could readily be tailored to facilitate compliance with and effective use of the pharmacologic therapies prescribed by the primary care physician and thus the patient would receive an integrated pharmacologic–non-pharmacologic treatment package. Creative integration of behavioral therapies into primary care settings could be of substantial benefit to headache sufferers who likely otherwise would not have access to this form of care.

References

1. Spitzer RL, Williams JB, Kroenke K, et al. Utility of a new procedure for diagnosing mental disorders in primary care: the PRIME MD 1000 study. JAMA 1994;272:1749–56.

2. Beck AT, Ward CH, Mendelson M, et al. An inventory for measuring depression. Arch Gen Psychiatry 1961;4:561–71.

3. Spielberger CD. State-trait anxiety inventory for adults (Form Y). Palo Alto (CA): Mind Garden/Consulting Psychologists; 1983.

4. Breslau N, Davis GC. Migraine, physical health and psychiatric disorder: a prospective epidemiologic study in young adults. J Psychiatr Res 1993;27:211–21.

5. Merikangas KR, Angst JR, Isler H. Migraine and psychopathology: results of the Zurich cohort study of young adults. Arch Gen Psychiatry 1990;47:849–53.

6. Waldie KE, Poulton R. Physical and psychological correlates of primary headache in young adulthood: a 26 year longitudinal study. J Neurol Neurosurg Psychiatry 2002;72:86–92.

7. Silberstein SD, Lipton RB, Breslau N. Migraine: association with personality characteristics and psychopathology. Cephalalgia 1995;15:358–69.

8. Breslau N, Merikangas K, Bowden CL. Comorbidity of migraine and major affective disorders. Neurology 1994;44 Suppl 7:S17–22.

9. Brandt J, Celentano D, Stewart WF. Personality and emotional disorder in a community sample of migraine headache sufferers. Am J Psychiatry 1990;147:303–8.

10. Breslau N, Davis GC. Migraine, major depression and panic disorder: a prospective epidemiologic study of young adults. Cephalalgia 1992;12:85–90.

11. Breslau N, Schultz LR, Stewart WF, et al. Headache and major depression: is the association specific to migraine? Neurology 2000;54:308–13.

12. Lipton RB, Hamelsky SW, Kolodner KB, et al. Migraine, quality of life, and depression: a population-based case-controlled study. Neurology 2000;55:629–35.

13. Merikangus KR, Merikangus JR, Angst J. Headache syndromes and psychiatric disorders: association and familial transmission. J Psychiatr Res 1993;27:197–210.

14. Mitsikostas DD, Thomas AM. Comorbidity of headache and depressive disorders. Cephalalgia 1999;19:211–7.

15. Breslau N, Davis GC, Schultz LR, Peterson EL. Migraine and major depression: a longitudinal study. Headache 1994;34:387–93.

16. Mattson P, Ekselius L. Migraine, major depression, panic disorder, and personality traits in women aged 40–74: a population-based study. Cephalalgia 2002;22:543–51.

17. Breslau N, Schultz LR, Stewart WF, et al. Headache types and panic disorder: directionality and specificity. Neurology 2001;56:350–4.

18. Glover V, Jarman J, Sandler M. Migraine and depression: biologic aspects. J Psychiatr Res 1993;27:918–24.

19. Holroyd K, Stensland M, Lipchik GL, et al. Psychosocial correlates and impact of chronic tension-type headaches. Headache 2000;40:3–16.

20. Guidetti V, Galli F, Fabrizi P, et al. Headache and psychiatric comorbidity: clinical aspects and outcome in an 8-year follow-up study. Cephalalgia 1998;18:455–62.

21. Puca F, Genco S, Prudenzano MP, et al. Psychiatric comorbidity and psychosocial stress in patients with tension-type headache from headache centers in Italy. Cephalalgia 1999;19:159–64.

22. Sandrini G, Verri AP, Barieri E, et al. Psychiatric comorbidity in chronic daily headache. Cephalalgia 1995;15 Suppl 14:163.

23. Verri AP, Cecchini AP, Galli C, et al. Psychiatric comorbidity in chronic daily headache. Cephalalgia 1998;18 Suppl 21:45–9.

24. Mathew NT, Kurman R, Perez F. Intractable chronic daily headache: a persistent neurobehavioral disorder. Cephalalgia 1989;Suppl 10:180–1.

25. Holroyd KA, O'Donnell FJ, Stensland M, et al. Management of chronic tension-type headache with tricyclic antidepressant medication, stress management therapy, and their combination: a randomized controlled trial. JAMA 2001;285:2208–15.

26. Saper JR, Lake AE III, Madden SF, et al. Comprehensive/tertiary care for headache: a 6-month outcome study. Headache 1999;39:249–63.

27. Kessler RC, McGonagle KA, Zhao S, et al. Lifetime and 12-month prevalence of DSM-III-R disorders in the United States: results from the National Comorbidity Survey. Arch Gen Psychiatry 1994;51:8–19.

28. Greenberg PE, Stiglin LE, Finkelstein SN, Berndt ER. The economic burden of depression in 1990. J Clin Psychiatry 1993;4:405–18.

29. American Psychiatric Association. Diagnostic and statistical manual of mental disorders. 4th ed. Washington (DC): American Psychiatric Association; 1994.

30. Silberstein SD, Saper JR, Freitag FG. Migraine: diagnosis and treatment. In: Silberstein SD, Lipton RB, Dalessio DJ, editors. Wolff's headache and other head pain. 7th ed. New York (NY): Oxford University Press; 2001. p. 121–237.

31. Agency for Health Care Policy and Research. Depression in primary care. Vol 2. Treatment of major depression. Rockville (MD): AHCPR; 1993.

32. Holroyd KA, Lipchik GL, Penzien DB. Psychological management of recurrent headache disorders: empirical basis for clinical practice. In: Dobson KS, Craig KD, editors. Empirically supported therapies: best practice in professional psychology. Thousand Oaks (CA): Sage Publications; 1998. p. 187–236.

33. Ward MM, Swan GE, Jack LM. Self-reported abstinence in the first month after smoking cessation. Addict Behav 2001;26:311–27.

34. Thorsteinsson HS, Gillin JC, Patten CA, et al. The effects of transdermal nicotine therapy for smoking cessation on depressive symptoms in patients with major depression. Neuropsychopharmacology 2001;24:350–8.

35. Beck AT, Rush AJ, Shaw BF, et al. Cognitive therapy for depression. New York (NY): Guilford Press; 1979.

36. Dobson KS. A meta-analysis of the efficacy of cognitive therapy for depression. J Consult Clin Psychol 1989;57: 414–9.

37. Robinson LA, Berman, JS, Neimeyer RA. Psychotherapy for the treatment of depression: a comprehensive review of controlled outcome research. Psychol Bull 1990;108: 30–49.

38. Williams JMG. Depression. In: Clark DM, Fairburn CG, editors. Science and practice of cognitive behaviour therapy. New York (NY): Oxford University Press; 1997. p. 259–83.

39. Greenberger D, Padesky CA. Mind over mood: a cognitive therapy treatment manual for clients. New York (NY): Guilford Press; 1995.

40. Burns DD. Feeling good: the new mood therapy. New York (NY): Signet; 1980.

41. Jamison C, Scogin F. The outcome of cognitive bibliotherapy with depressed adults. J Consult Clin Psychol 1995;63:644–50.

42. Beck AT, Emery G. Anxiety disorders and phobias: a cognitive perspective. New York (NY): Basic Books; 1985.

43. Beck JS. Cognitive therapy: basics and beyond. New York (NY): Guilford Press; 1995.

44. Markowitz JS, Weissman MM, Oullette R, et al. Quality of life in panic disorder. Arch Gen Psychiatry 1989;46: 984–92.

45. Lum M, Fontaine R, Elie R. et al. Divalproex sodium's antipanic effect in panic disorder: a placebo-controlled study. Biol Psychiatry 1990;27:164A–5A.

46. Woodman CL, Noyes R. Panic disorder: treatment with valproate. J Clin Psychiatry 1994;55:134–6.

47. Gould RA, Otto MW, Pollack MH. A meta-analysis of treatment outcome for panic disorder. Clin Psychol Rev 1995;15:819–44.

48. Barsky AJ. A 37 year-old man with multiple somatic complaints. JAMA 1997;278:673–9.

49. Looper KJ, Kirmayer LJ. Behavioral medicine approaches to somatoform disorders. J Consult Clin Psychol 2002;70:810–27.

50. Weissman MM. The epidemiology of personality disorders: a 1990 update. J Pers Disord 1993;7:44–62.

51. Silk K, Lee S, Hill E, Lohr N. Borderline personality disorder symptoms and severity of sexual abuse. Am J Psychiatry 1995;152:1059–64.

52. Hegarty AM. The prevalence of migraine in borderline personality disorder. Headache 1993;33:271.

53. Saper JR, Lake AE. Borderline personality disorder and the chronic headache patient: review and management recommendations. Headache 2002;42:663–74.

54. Mongini F. Personality traits, depression, and migraine in women: a longitudinal study. Cephalalgia 2003;23: 186–92.

55. Beck AT, Steer RA. Beck anxiety inventory. San Antonio (TX): Psychological Corporation; 1993.

56. Mathew NT, Reuveni V, Perez F. Transformed or evolutive migraine. Headache 1987;27:102–6.

57. Mathew NT, Kurman R, Perez F. Drug-induced refractory headache: clinical features and management. Headache 1990;30:634–8.

58. Mathew NT. Medication misuse in headache. Cephalalgia 1998;18 Suppl 21:34–6.

59. Wang SJ, Fuh JL, Lu SR, et al. Chronic daily headache in Chinese elderly: prevalence, risk factors, and biannual follow-up. Neurology 2000;54:314–9.

60. Rapoport AM. Analgesic rebound headache. Headache 1988;28:662–5.

61. Saper J, Sheftell F. Headache in the abuse-prone individual. In: Olesen J, Tfelt-Hansen P, Welch KMA, editors. The headaches. 2nd ed. Philadelphia (PA): Lippincott Williams & Wilkins; 2000. p. 953–8.

62. Kudrow L. Paradoxical effects of frequent analgesic use. Adv Neurol 1982;33:335–41.

63. Michultka DM, Blanchard EB, Appelbaum KA, et al. The refractory headache patient II: high medication consumption (analgesic rebound) headache. Behav Res Ther 1989;27:411–20.

64. Baumgartner C, Wesseley P, Bingol C, et al. Long-term prognosis of analgesic withdrawal in patients with drug-induced headaches. Headache 1989;29:510–4.

65. Blanchard EB, Taylor AE, Dentinger MP. Preliminary results from the self-regulatory treatment of high-medication consumption headache. Biofeedback Self Regul 1992;71:179–202.

66. Diener HC, Dichgans J, Scholz E, et al. Analgesic-induced chronic headache: long-term results of withdrawal therapy. J Neurol 1989;236:9–14.

67. Grazzi L, Andrasik F, D'Amico D, et al. Behavioral and pharmacologic treatment of transformed migraine with analgesic overuse: outcome at 3 years. Headache 2002;42:483–90.

68. Rasmussen BK. Migraine and tension-type headache in a general population: precipitating factors, female hormones, sleep pattern and relation to lifestyle. Pain 1993; 53:65–72.

69. DeBenedittis G, Lorenzetti A. Minor stressful life events (daily hassles) in chronic primary headache: relationship with MMPI personality patterns. Headache 1992;32:330–4.

70. Srikiathachorn A, Phanthumchinda KP. Prevalence and clinical features of chronic daily headache in a headache clinic. Headache 1997;37:277–90.

71. Edhe DM, Holm JE. Stress and headache: comparisons of migraine, tension, and headache-free subjects. Headache Q 1992;3:54–60.

72. Holm JE, Holroyd KA, Hursey KG, Penzien DB. The role of stress in recurrent tension headache. Headache 1986;26:160–7.

73. DeBenedittis G, Lorenzetti A, Pieri A. The role of stressful life events in the onset of chronic primary headache. Pain 1990;40:65–76.

74. Edinger JD, Wohlgmuth WK, Radtke RA, et al. Cognitive behavior therapy for treatment of chronic primary insomnia. JAMA 2001;285:1856–64.

75. Robbins L. Precipitating factors in migraine: a retrospective review of 494 patients. Headache 1994;34:214–6.

76. Medina JL, Diamond S. The role of diet in migraine. Headache 1978;18:31–4.

77. Holroyd KA, Penzien DB, Lipchik GL. Behavioral management of headache. In: Silberstein SD, Lipton RB, Dalessio DJ, editors. Wolff's headache and other head pain. 7th ed. New York (NY): Oxford University Press; 2001. p. 562–98.

78. Holroyd KA, Penzien DB. Psychosocial interventions in the management of recurrent headache disorders—I: overview and effectiveness. Behav Med 1994;20:53–63.

79. Rowan AB, Andrasik F. Efficacy and cost-effectiveness of minimal therapist contact treatments for chronic headache: a review. Behav Ther 1996;27:207–34.

80. Penzien DB, Rains JC, Holroyd KA. Psychological assessment of the recurrent headache sufferer. In: Tollison CD, Kunkel RS, editors. Headache: diagnosis and treatment. Baltimore (MD): Williams and Wilkins; 1993. p. 39–49.

81. Blanchard EB, Andrasik F. Management of chronic headaches: a psychological approach. Elmsford (NY): Pergamon Press; 1985.

82. Martin PR. Psychological management of chronic headaches: a functional perspective. New York (NY): Guilford Press; 1993.

83. Lipchik GL, Holroyd KA, Nash JM. Cognitive-behavioral management of recurrent headache disorders: a minimal-therapist-contact approach. In: Turk DC, Gatchel RJ, editors. Psychological approaches to pain management: a practitioner's handbook. 2nd ed. New York (NY): Guilford Press; 2002. p. 365–89.

84. Bernstein DA, Borkovec TD. Progressive relaxation training: a manual for the helping professions. Champaign (IL): Research Press; 1973.

85. Jacobson E. Progressive relaxation: a physiological and clinical investigation of muscular states and their significance in psychology and medical practice. Chicago (IL): University of Chicago Press; 1929.

86. Jacobson E. Progressive relaxation. Chicago (IL): University of Chicago Press; 1934.

87. Schultz JH, Luthe V. Autogenic training. Vol 1. New York (NY): Grune and Stratton; 1969.

88. Benson H. The relaxation response. New York (NY): William Morrow and Company; 1975.

89. Holroyd KA, Andrasik F. A cognitive-behavioral approach to recurrent tension and migraine headache. In: Kendall PE, editor. Advances in cognitive-behavioral research and therapy. New York (NY): Academic Press; 1982.

90. Holroyd KA, Appel M, Andrasik F. A cognitive-behavioral approach to the treatment of psychophysiological disorders. In: Meichenbaum D, Jaremko M, editors. Stress prevention and management: a cognitive-behavioral approach. New York (NY): Plenum Press; 1982. p. 219–57.

91. Holroyd KA, Holm JE, Penzien DB. Clinical issues in the behavioral treatment of recurrent headache. In: Keller PA, Heyman SR, editors. Innovations in clinical practice: a source book. Sarasota (FL): Professional Resource Exchange; 1988. p. 433–57.

92. Holroyd KA, Holm JE, Hursey KG, et al. Recurrent vascular headache: home-based behavioral treatment vs. abortive pharmacological treatment. J Consult Clin Psychol 1988;56:218–23.

93. Holroyd KA, Cordingley GE, Pingel JD, et al. Enhancing the effectiveness of abortive therapy: a controlled evaluation of self-management training. Headache 1989;29:148–53.

94. Silberstein SD, Lipton RB. Chronic daily headache, including transformed migraine, chronic tension-type headache, and medication overuse. In: Silberstein SD, Lipton RB, Dalessio DJ, editors. Wolff's headache and other head pain. 7th ed. New York (NY): Oxford University Press; 2001. p. 247–84.

95. Goslin RE, Gray RN, McCrory DC, et al. Behavioral and physical treatments for migraine headache. Technical review 2.2. National Technical Information Service; 1999. NTIS Accession No.: 127946. Contract No: 290-94-2025. Prepared for the Agency for Health Care Policy and Research

96. Silberstein SD. Practice parameter: evidence-based guideline for migraine headache (an evidence-based review). Neurology 2000;55:754–63.

97. Holroyd KA, Penzien DB. Pharmacological vs. non-pharmacological prophylaxis of recurrent migraine headache: a meta-analytic review of clinical trials. Pain 1990;42:1–13.

98. Penzien DB, Holroyd KA, Holm JE, Hursey KG. Behavioral management of migraine: results from five-dozen group outcome studies. Headache 1985;25:162.

99. Davis MK, Holroyd KA, Penzien DB. Flunarizine and propranolol: comparative effectiveness in the treatment of migraine headaches. Headache 1999;39:349.

100. Holroyd KA, Penzien DB, Rokicki LA, Cordingley GE. Flunarizine vs. propranolol: a meta-analysis of clinical trials. Headache 1992;32:256.

101. Holroyd KA, Penzien DB, Cordingley GE. Propranolol in the prevention of recurrent migraine: a meta-analytic review. Headache 1991;31:333–40.

102. Bogaards MC, ter Kuile MM. Treatment of recurrent tension headache: a meta-analytic review. Clin J Pain 1994;10:174–90.

103. Holroyd KA, Penzien DB. Client variables and the behavioral treatment of recurrent tension headache: a meta-analytic review. J Behav Med 1986;9:515–36.

104. Blanchard EB, Andrasik F, Evans DD, et al. Behavioral treatment of 250 chronic headache patients: a clinical replication series. Behav Ther 1985;16:308–27.

105. Holroyd KA, Cordingley GE, France JL, et al. Enhancing the effectiveness of relaxation-thermal biofeedback training with propranolol hydrochloride. J Consult Clin Psychol 1995;63:327–30.

106. Mathew NT. Prophylaxis of migraine and mixed headache: a randomized controlled study. Headache 1981;21:105–9.

107. Campbell JK, Penzien DB, Wall EM. Evidence-based guidelines for migraine headaches: behavioral and physical treatments. 2000. Available at: http://www.aan.com/professionals/practice/pdfs/g10089.pdf (accessed July 12, 2003).

108. McCrory DC, Penzien DB, Hasselblad V, Gray RN. Evidence report: behavioral and physical treatments for tension-type and cervicogenic headache. Des Moines (IA): Foundation for Chiropractic Education and Research (Product No. 2085); 2001.

109. Blanchard EB, Andrasik F, Ahles TA, et al. Migraine and tension-type headache: a meta-analytic review. Behav Ther 1980;11:613–31.

110. Holroyd KA, Malinoski PE, O'Donnell FJ, et al. Antidepressant medication and cognitive-behavioral therapy for CTTH: predictors of treatment response and dose-response relationships. Headache 2002;42:456–7.

111. Haddock CK, Rowan AB, Andrasik F, et al. Home-based behavioral treatments for chronic benign headache: a meta-analysis of controlled trials. Cephalalgia 1996;17:113–8.

112. Penzien DB, Rains JC, Holroyd KA. A review of alternative behavioral treatments for headache. Mississippi Psychol 1992;17:8–9.

113. Holroyd KA, Lipchik GL. Sex differences in headache. In: Fillingim RB, editor. Sex, gender, and pain. Progress in pain research and management. Vol 17. Seattle (WA): IASP Press; 2000. p. 251–79.

114. Gauthier JG, Fournier A, Roberge C. The differential effects of biofeedback in the treatment of menstrual and non-menstrual migraine. Headache 1991;31:82–90.

115. Szekely B, Botwin D, Eidelman BH, et al. Nonpharmacological treatment of menstrual headache: relaxation-biofeedback, behavior therapy and person-centered insight therapy. Headache 1986;26:86–92.

116. Kim M, Blanchard EB. Two studies of the non-pharmacological treatment of menstrually-related migraine headaches. Headache 1992;32:197–202.

117. Solbach P, Sargent J, Coyne L. Menstrual migraine headache: results of a controlled, experimental outcome study of non-drug treatments. Headache 1984;24:75–8.

118. Marcus DA, Scharff L, Turk DC. Nonpharmacological management of headache during pregnancy. Psychosom Med 1995;57:527–35.

119. Scharff L, Marcus DA, Turk DC. Maintenance of effects in the nonmedical treatment of headaches during pregnancy. Headache 1996;36:285–90.

120. McGrady AV, Andrasik F, Davies T, et al. Psychophysiologic therapy for chronic headache in primary care. Prim Care Comp J Clin Psychiatry 1999;1:96–102.

121. Blau JN, Thavapalan M. Preventing migraine: a study of precipitating factors. Headache 1988;28:481–3.

CHAPTER 15

A Sociologic Perspective on Migraine in Women

Joanna Kempner, MA

CASE

JM, a 35-year-old advertising executive, presents with periodic headaches of moderate severity. She is divorced and lives with her 5-year-old son. Vital signs and a physical examination were normal. She reports that her headaches occur up to three times per month and that they are not related to her menstrual cycle. JM's headaches begin at the base of her head and spread up the left side of her head to her eye. The pain is steady, not throbbing, and is accompanied by photo- and phonophobia. She occasionally is nauseated during her headaches. She reports that her headaches are triggered by certain odors, lack of sleep, and changes in the weather. A year ago, she consulted a physician for her headaches and was given a diagnosis of tension-type headaches and directed to begin stress-reduction activities. No medication was prescribed. She reports that she was dissatisfied with this treatment regimen and felt that the physician did not believe her triggers. She said that she was hesitant to consult a physician this time, but her headaches were disrupting her work life. She often leaves work early to pick up her son and is reluctant to tell her employer when she has a headache. The last time that she called off from work, her employer remarked that he wished he could take off every time his head hurt and once made a comment about her inability to deal with stress.

JM's prior experiences with physicians and her employer made her reluctant to report her pain and was anxious about the perceived legitimacy of her symptoms. Like all patients, she brings her experiences and concerns into the clinical encounter, where they influence her expectations about how she might be perceived and how she ought to be treated. Likewise, her physicians also come to the medical encounter with their own set of expectations about how to treat headache disorders and their own predispositions about their patients who report these symptoms. Although we may tend to view doctor–patient interactions in terms of the clinical encounter, this is just a brief moment in the lives of both the physician and the patient. The stage for this interaction is set during a lifetime of experiences that shape both participants' expectations for what may occur.

KEY CHAPTER POINTS

- **Contextual clues influence the doctor–patient relationship.**
- **Migraine is perceived as a female-gendered illness.**
- **Medicine historically has understood migraine as a psychosomatic condition of women.**
- **Framing migraine as a woman's disease may unduly perpetuate gendered social and cultural stereotypes.**
- **Potential gender bias influences the medical treatment of migraine.**
- **Stress influences on headache vary by gender.**

INFLUENCE OF CONTEXTUAL CLUES ON THE DOCTOR–PATIENT RELATIONSHIP

This chapter discusses cultural influences on the medical view of migraine. Migraine is often represented as a "woman's disease" in the medical literature and by advertisements and the mass media. In a culture that has not always valued the contributions of women or seriously considered women's illnesses, the identification of migraine as a women's disease can influence how both physicians and patients understand the disorder. Understanding migraine to be a woman's disease may take on a significance that extends beyond diagnosis and treatment and into the process of decision-making, patient experience, patient perceptions, and the doctor–patient relationship.

Migraine is not a gender-neutral disorder; on the contrary, assumptions about migraine and women underlie how headaches are represented in the media and understood by physicians and the public. Without sufficient reflection on how gender may bias perceptions about headaches, physicians may not provide headache patients with the most effective care. This chapter explores the ways that subtle gender stereotypes may affect the medical encounter. It examines the culturally-embedded ideas associated with headache and migraine, then looks briefly at the historic association between migraines and women. Finally, it examines the role of gender in contemporary research on migraine and suggests how gender may influence the medical treatment of headache. Because little research has addressed the social and cultural aspects of migraine, the information in this chapter is culled from a more general literature on gender and pain, as well as sociologic and anthropologic theory.

GENDER-ASSOCIATED PERCEPTIONS OF MIGRAINE

The medical literature represents headache as a biologic disease process. When framed from a biomedical perspective, headache is an objective category that describes a deviation from the normal, healthy body and is largely thought to be absent of social meanings. The physician's job is to reconfigure patient reports of symptoms into recognized diagnoses and to prescribe an appropriate treatment protocol. The most important aspects of headache are its symptoms, diagnosis, etiology, pathophysiology, and treatment.

Most physicians recognize that framing headache as a purely biologic phenomenon is simplistic. Like all disorders, headache exists in a social and cultural context that affects every aspect of treatment. Headache is a biopsychosocial condition; to focus solely on the biology of headache excludes the important influence of social and cultural factors on the course of the condition, patient experience, and the doctor–patient relationship. As in JM's case, both patient and physicians have formed opinions about headache before they ever meet in a clinical encounter. Patients' ideas come from the world in which they live, including media representations of headache, conversations with people in their social networks, explorations on the Internet, and previous interactions with physicians. Likewise, physicians come to the medical encounter with their own set of notions about what a headache is and what the typical headache sufferer looks like. Physician knowledge is derived from medical training, medical literature, and contacts with pharmaceutical companies but is also informed by the same cultural representations about headache and ideas about the world that inform

patient perspectives. How patients and physicians make sense of symptoms and choose to treat them is culturally patterned; there is a shared sense about appropriate ways of being ill that arises out of the cultural milieu.[1–7]

In some part, responses to illness are dependent on the shared understanding of what certain conditions mean. Cancer, for example, strikes fear into the patient, as it elicits notions of extreme pain, a lack of control, invasive treatments, and death. Cancer is so frightening that it is used to describe anything unwanted and difficult to control, for example, complex and insidious political situations.[8] The fight against cancer elicits militaristic images that are carried over into invasive treatment modalities. The human immunodeficiency virus (HIV) also elicits vivid imagery that imbues the disease with attendant meanings, such as divine punishment or sinful behavior. The powerful meanings associated with cancer and HIV provide two examples that disease is more than an objective category requiring medical attention; furthermore, these examples highlight how meanings serve as the subtext of patient experience and the medical encounter.

Headache may be less severe than cancer or HIV but carries no fewer metaphoric meanings. The head is a sensitive area in which to experience pain. In a Cartesian era ruled by the dictum, "I think, therefore I am," the head is often considered the center of personality and individual distinction in Western societies. Expressing pain when it occurs elsewhere is difficult but can be unbearable when affecting the head. Because headaches strike so central a feature of personhood, they may be a deep source of concern for the patient and physician who sort out whether the symptom is indicative of a more serious underlying pathology or a result of worries and strong emotions. More often, headache is used as a metaphor for something irritating, perhaps interfering, but not of grave concern, for example, bad traffic, overwhelming workload, and stressful situations. Reference to headache is often made in deferring normal social obligations, for example, calling out of work or leaving early from a function.

The metaphor of headache as an excuse has the most salience as an avoidance strategy from sex, as evidenced by the classic punchline, "Not tonight honey, I have a headache." This is a clear example of how the attendant meanings of headache are "gendered." To say that an illness is gendered means that a condition has associated connotations that are patterned through, and in terms of a distinction between male and female, masculine and feminine.[9] An illness is gendered female when it is primarily portrayed as affecting women or conveys some sense of femininity, for example, weakness or an inability to cope with certain life stressors. Other conditions elicit images of masculinity, such as alcoholism. Media saturated with images of women with headache or a common joke about women with headache contributes to the gendering of migraine. The old joke "not tonight honey" might seem inconsequential, but given its pervasiveness, it strongly genders migraine female.

Gendering headache adds to the already tenuous legitimacy of the patient's complaint. In general, women are often not taken seriously when they complain of pain, in part because they are viewed as overly emotional and even hysterical at times.[10] Because headaches are invisible and lack an objective diagnostic test, treatment demands that the healthcare practitioner trusts the person reporting that pain. Hoffman and Tarzian suggest that "the subjective nature of pain requires health-care providers to view the patient as a credible reporter, and stereotypes or assumptions about behavior in such circumstances (over-sensitivity, complaining, stoicism) add to the likelihood of undertreatment of some groups and over-treatment of others" (p. 20).[10] It is difficult for any patient to convey the quality of their pain; this task may be more difficult when reported by a woman. If the available research on pain is any indication, a woman with migraine is less likely to be believed by her physician. If she anticipates a lack of credibility, she may also be less likely to report her pain.

Much social science research has found that as an illness becomes linked with other social identities, it can absorb the stigma associated with that group.[11–13] *Who* we think of as the stereotypic headache sufferer plays a large role in the cultural meanings of migraine. Representations of headache sufferers as women who are sometimes neurotic or possible malingerers may have a significant role in how people with migraine report their symptoms and how physicians diagnose and treat those symptoms. Headache advocacy groups understand how destructive this stereotype can be and have tried to mitigate its effects by publicizing migraine as a real and biologic condition.[14] Nevertheless, popular and medical understandings of who gets head pain create a cultural mood that forms the backdrop in which we think about migraine. This is not to say that there is a linear connection between these metaphors and the ways that physicians and patients approach migraine treatment, but preconceived impressions can color our subconscious profile of who gets migraine and what this might say about the migraine sufferer as a person.

HISTORIC MEDICAL PERCEPTIONS OF MIGRAINEURS

The frameworks that researchers use to understand illness may absorb and reflect other issues of importance during that time.[15] In the case of migraine, one can see that researchers drew on gender stereotypes of their era to describe their patients.

This tendency to describe the migraine patient as a particular type of person becomes evident after 1873.[16] The writing of this era often described the migraineur as a male, perhaps because many of the male authors had migraine. This migraine sufferer was portrayed as a well-bred intellectual, one who used his mind. Physicians considered migraines to primarily affect the "cultured classes."[17] In 1873, Edward Liveing published his monograph, which was the first to envision migraine as a type of "nerve storm," or sudden electric discharge primarily originating in the nervous system. In doing so, Liveing directly compared migraine to epilepsy and considered the two conditions to be close correlates. Liveing described certain behaviors that may trigger an attack.[18] He blamed

> ... [mental] exertion, if too close or continuous, and especially if attended with anxiety ... the malady is often first developed by close application to books, coupled with a deficiency of out-door life. The same thing happens in later years to literary and professional men when overworked and over-anxious in business.

P.W. Latham, a contemporary of Liveing, took issue with Liveing's comparison of migraine with epileptics but offered a similar account of their social status. Latham described migraineurs as prominent and well-born, whereas epileptics were more generally considered to be low-class and shunned. Latham indicated in his lectures that he had discussed this association with Liveing and mentioned that if Liveing's theory was correct, then migraine has "a relationship, though happily a very distant one, to epilepsy."[19] Latham offered the following description of the migraineur:

> The sufferers possess what is called the nervous temperament; their brains are very excitable, their senses acute, and their imaginations free. The attacks are induced by prolonged mental work, protracted mental excitement, or any intense strain on the feelings.[19]

Frequently through his lectures, Latham described migraineurs as suffering from mental exhaustion and "a general want of tone."[19] Latham evinced a subtle, but important rhetorical shift from Liveing. Where Liveing described overworking as a trigger of migraine, Latham located the etiology of migraine in the particular person's attributes; that is, people with nervous temperaments.

The notion that migraineurs were certain types of people flourished in the early twentieth century. In the 1930s and 1940s, the research of Harold G. Wolff helped turn the migraine personality into scientific and popular gospel in the United States. Wolff, considered the father of modern headache research, engaged in two long-lasting avenues of research from 1930 to his death in 1962. First, with elaborate experiments, he physically demonstrated that cranial blood vessels were dilated during migraine headaches and provided much evidence supporting constriction theories of aura. These experiments, measuring the vascular changes in migraine headache, ensured Wolff's prominent place in medical history. Wolff continued his research, however, because he viewed the vascular action of migraine as the mechanism of pain but not the true cause. Instead, he thought of the body as responsive to the emotions and personality and located the cause of the pain in the migraine patients' psyche and personality. He dedicated much of his research to uncovering the migraine personality.

Wolff examined the personality profiles of his research subjects who suffered from vascular headaches, including patients, friends, colleagues, and medical students.[20] Wolff, himself a migraine sufferer, characterized their personalities as ambitious, successful, perfectionist, and efficient.[21] He believed that these tendencies toward perfectionism and hard work began in childhood:

> The individual with migraine aims to gain approval by doing *more than* and *better than* his fellows through 'application' and 'hard work' and to gain security by holding to a stable environment and a given system of excellent performance, even at high cost of energy. This brings increasing responsibility and admiration, but gains little love, and greater resentment at the pace he feels obliged to maintain. Then the tension associated with repeated frustration, sustained resentment, and growing anxiety is often followed by prostrating fatigue, the setting in which the migraine attack occurs [sic].[20]

In an era that valued men as good providers and stable earners, the migraine personality had something of a positive bent to it. As a prolific researcher and highly regarded clinician, Wolff personally related to the ambitious migraineur and suggested that his patients follow his lead and break every day for a game of squash.

However, the tenor of the migraine personality shifted less favorably when Wolff applied it to women.[16] Wolff described the migrainous woman as unwilling to accept the female role.[22] He described 80% of his female sample as sexually dissatisfied, particularly because of dissatisfaction with sexual experiences. "Orgasm was seldom attained and the sex act was accepted, as at least a reasonable marital duty."[22] Furthermore, the migrainous woman was sometimes "reluctant to accept . . . the consequences of maternity."[22] In contrast, Wolff's male patients were reported to be sexually well adjusted, except "three migrainous men with vigorous sex drive who were married to sexually indifferent or frigid wives."[22]

Walter C. Alvarez, a great admirer of Wolff and a gastroenterologist at the Mayo Clinic, captured the female migraine personality in his articles. Alvarez expressed distress that so many migrainous women sought diagnostic tests and spent so much money on doctors, when doctors had few effective migraine treatments.[23] He argued that a more appropriate role for the physician would be to spend time with the patient "in talking over her life problems and in showing her how to live more calmly and happily, than in making useless examinations."[23] He explained, "It is an axiom with me that whenever a woman is having three attacks of migraine a week, it means that she is either psychopathic or else she is overworking or worrying or fretting, or otherwise using her brain wrongly."[23] Alvarez's description of the female migraine patient focused on a specific personality. "[T]he women have a peculiar migrainous temperament. They are more alike than are most sisters, and their troubles are due to their unusual sensitiveness, their nervous tension, and their easy fatigability."[23]

The idea of migraine personality began to fade in the 1960s when Lance and Anthony argued that while many migraineurs do share Wolff's migraine personality, a similar proportion of the unaffected population also have this personality.[24] In addition, the popularity of psychological and psychosomatic theories of migraine declined because the psychosomatic medicine movement declined more generally.[15] Psychoanalysis proved ineffective for treating migraines, especially compared with increasingly effective pharmaceuticals. In contrast to earlier conceptions about who had migraine, new studies have found that migraines are actually more prevalent among less educated and lower income groups. Nevertheless, references to the migraine personality regularly appeared in the medical and popular literature well into the 1970s.[25,26] The migraine personality may now seem like a quaint relic from the past, but, in retrospect, we can see how the migraine personality was borne out of biased clinical samples and how it reflected gender roles of the time.

Today, a gendered view of migraine is still apparent, even though our understanding of headaches has changed dramatically. Advances in brain imaging technology, pharmacology, and genetics are transforming migraine from a condition of the mind to one of the brain. The biopsychosocial model, which dominated for most of the twentieth century, is moving closer to a neurobiologic model that emphasizes a more objective, value-neutral, disease-oriented description of migraine. Contemporary researchers believe that new medical and technologic advances in migraine treatment have freed women from the oppressive gender stereotyping that occurred in the past. Although this might be true, gender is still a central organizing construct in the medical literature on migraine.

GENDER BIAS IN MEDICAL TREATMENT

Contemporary medical literature portrays migraine as a woman's disease. As common as it is to view migraine as a woman's disease, we rarely scrutinize this assumption. If men, women, and children suffer from migraines, how can we tell if it belongs to the purview of one gender over the other? This question is important because framing migraine as a woman's disease may unduly perpetuate gendered social and cultural meanings, which in turn may indirectly delegitimize migraine as a medical condition.

The most prevalent logic for thinking of migraine as a woman's disease comes from the epidemiologic reality that migraine is far more common among women than men. Nearly all epidemiologic studies conducted around the world have found that women are three times more likely to get migraine than men. In the United States, 18% of women have migraine, as compared to 6% of men.[27–29] The gender difference in migraine prevalence is remarkably consistent, even as prevalence estimates fluctuate. Furthermore, the effects of migraine in women tend to be more severe and frequent than in men.[30]

In addition to this basic statistical association, the strong relationship between migraine incidence and hormonal milestones provides the most compelling evidence that migraine is a woman's disease. Most researchers identify sex hormones as explaining the gender difference in the prevalence of migraine.[31,32] A substantial body of literature has documented a relationship between hormonal fluctuations and migraine incidence. For example, in children younger than 12 years of age, little gender difference exists in the prevalence of migraine. After pubescence, the rate of migraine among females increases steadily, until it peaks between the ages of 40 and 50 years. The prevalence of migraine in men also increases after puberty but at a much lower rate. In addition, migraine in women often improves during the second and third trimesters of pregnancy when estrogen levels are highest.[33]

If the barometer for testing whether migraine is a woman's condition is either hormonal or statistical, then the answer is a resounding "yes, migraine is a woman's condition." But, are these two measures enough evidence to assign migraine to the providence of women? An estimated 6% of American men have migraine and many experience great associated disability.[29,34] In fact, men experience migraine more than diabetes, diseases of the prostate, and ulcers.[35] Men tend to have other forms of headache at a similar rate to women; for example, in the United States, 42% of men and 36% of women have episodic tension-type headache, bringing the gender prevalence ratio down to 1.16.[36] Enough men suffer from migraine to question whether migraine ought to be considered a woman's disease. Nevertheless, media representations of headache overwhelmingly portray the migraine sufferer as a woman. While women constitute the largest segment of their marketing base, these media images may perpetuate the idea that only women can get migraine.

Coronary heart disease (CHD) provides a useful cautionary tale for the dangers of viewing a condition as affecting just men or women. In the past decade, there has been an increasing awareness of how the gendering of CHD significantly altered how researchers, physicians, and patients understood, and continue to understand, the condition. Even though it is the leading cause of death of American women, CHD was traditionally viewed as a "man's disease."[37,38] By the mid-1990s, medical researchers had realized that CHD posed a large burden of illness for women. Women develop cardiac problems later in life than men but die of CHD at a much greater rate.[37] Yet, women's risk of CHD lacked sufficient attention in the medical and epidemiologic literature. Medical practices reflected and reinforced the notion that CHD was a male condition. Evidence began to emerge that men and women were receiving unequal treatment in hospitals; women's symptoms were not recognized as myocardial infarction or were treated less aggressively.[39,40] Bernadine Healy, past director of the National Institutes of Health, referred to this sex bias as the "Yentl" phenomenon.[41] Just as Yentl had to impersonate a boy to gain entrance to a yeshiva, a woman had to have a massive heart attack like a man to receive comparable medical treatment.

Problems of gender bias in CHD research and treatment were well publicized in major newspapers and medical journals.[42–45] Nevertheless, for some patients, the residual effects of gender bias remain significant barriers to obtaining effective care, leaving researchers to conclude that subconscious biases may contribute to treatment disparities.[46,47] In addition, the laity continues to understand CHD as something that primarily happens to men.[48] A 1995 Gallup poll indicated that 4 of 5 women and 1 of 3 general practitioners did not realize that CHD was the primary killer of women.

Thinking of CHD as a man's condition has serious implications for the care of those with the disorder. This phenomenon is captured in the sociologic adage that when people define situations as real, they are real in their consequences.[49] We can see this principle in action with research and treatment of CHD. Because researchers and physicians thought of CHD as a male condition, it was more difficult to identify, diagnose, and treat women with CHD. Similarly, an uncritical reliance on the paradigm of migraine as a woman's disease may reify the relationship between migraine and women, even when it is not justified. Because the cultural ideas surrounding male and female, masculinity and femininity, resound so strongly in our culture, thinking of a condition as primarily affecting women can have serious implications for setting research agendas, treatment, diagnosis, and for how patients experience and report illness. The following section examines the evidence to see if a gender bias in the treatment of migraine exists.

POTENTIAL GENDER BIAS IN THE MEDICAL TREATMENT OF MIGRAINE

As the case of CHD illustrates, social and cultural biases sometimes creep into medical care practices. This is not an isolated case; subjectivity and uncertainty are inherent in the practice of medicine.[50] As physicians have increasingly less time to spend with their patients, they may rely on subjective impressions of who gets what disorder and how they respond to treatment.[51,52] Not enough research has systematically explored how physicians diagnose migraine. Nevertheless, there is some evidence that the gender of the patient does influence how both physicians and headache specialists approach the migraine patient.

Gendering migraine female may lead to the underdiagnosis of migraine in men. Lipton and colleagues have found that women receive diagnoses from physicians more often than men, even after controlling for gender difference in prevalence.[53] By using symptom-based reporting in a random sample of the population, Lipton and his colleagues were able to compare the sociodemographic characteristics of people who reported a physician-diagnosed migraine versus those who had migraine according to the International Headache Society's (IHS) diagnostic standards. While 41% of women with IHS-defined cases of migraine reported that they received a diagnosis of migraine, only 29% of men with IHS-defined cases of migraine reported a physician-diagnosed case of migraine. This study suggests both a low concordance of diagnostic criteria with medical practice and a gender gap in the application of migraine as a diagnosis. The clinical utility of the IHS criteria is discussed elsewhere, but very little research has explicitly examined the role of gender in assigning headache diagnoses. Some research suggests that the gender difference in diagnosis can be explained in part by gendered patterns in help-seeking and symptom reporting,[54] for which Lipton and colleagues did not control in their study. The retained belief among physicians that migraine is a woman's disease, however, may make it less likely for men and more likely for women to receive a migraine diagnosis.

Women are also put at a disadvantage when physicians have entrenched perceptions about migraine and women. For example, the association of migraine as a woman's disease may elevate the role of gender and hormones in the diagnostic criteria used by physicians, even though neither characteristic is included in official IHS diagnostic criteria. In a study by Marcus and colleagues, headache specialists were asked to rank 16 patient and headache characteristics in order of importance for making a headache diagnosis.[55] Respondents reported that headaches with a relationship to hormonal fluctuations were ranked to be more important for the diagnosis of migraine than two IHS-approved diagnostic criteria. In addition, gender was ranked as more important than one IHS feature.

There is also some evidence that men and women receive different treatments once diagnosed with migraine. In a clinical sample, Loder and Beluk found that women with migraine were more likely than men to be prescribed antidepressants and tranquilizers for their condition.[56] Their findings mirror an emerging consensus among pain researchers; physicians prescribe less pain medication for women, even though women experience more pain than men.[10,57] There is evidence that women receive less pain medication because physicians often blame emotional factors for women's pain but not for men's.[58]

A large body of research has demonstrated that gender can influence how physicians diagnose and treat patients. Part of this is good Bayesian deduction; women get more migraines, report symptoms more often, and are therefore more likely to present migrainous symptoms to their physicians. Research has indicated that gender plays a pervasive role in the clinical encounter. The robust findings of this research do suggest that the gendering of migraine is a crucial factor in the medical encounter. More systematic research needs to explore how gendered assumptions about migraine affect patient experience and treatment outcomes.

STRESS INFLUENCES ON HEADACHE

Migraine is a complex, multifactorial condition. Even though leading biomedical theory suggests that the gender difference in migraine prevalence is largely due to the influence of sex hormones, other triggers of migraine, such as stress, alcohol consumption, and sleep disturbances, may also have a differential effect on men and women. Indeed, most research indicates that stress is the most common trigger of migraine.[59,60] Socially and culturally embedded gender differences in exposure to stress may help explain some of the gender gap in migraine prevalence.

Stress is a vague concept and difficult to operationalize but is implicated as an aggravating factor in many conditions. Stressful situations can arise from difficult personal changes, for example, moving, changing jobs, divorce, or sudden loss. Stress also arises from routine daily hassles, such as making ends meet, negotiating multiple roles, or working in high-demand, low-power jobs. Women consistently report more extreme levels of distress than men. Laboratory studies suggest that some of the reason why women experience more distress is biologic; women have a lower threshold and tolerance for experimental pain and report more discomfort than men.[10,61] These experiments indicate that women's lower threshold for distress and their attendant pain response is in some ways biologic and related to gender differences in central processing of sensory information or to hormonal fluctuations.[62,63] Similarly, experimental studies are beginning to discover that migraineurs are physiologically more responsive to stress than controls, a finding that might be properly attributed to differences in nervous response.[64,65]

However, distress is as social as it is biologic and social conditions expose men and women to different levels of stress. In the aggregate, men and women differ in their exposure and responses to various life stressors. For example, women may report more distress because women's roles expose them to more life stressors.[66] As women enter into the workforce in greater numbers, they tend to adopt multiple roles and responsibilities. At the same time, men's roles have in some ways become less stressful, as the "good provider" role has begun to diminish as a mark of masculinity. In Hochschild's classic study of dual-income households, she found that women perform almost all of the domestic work and child-rearing, in addition to their full-time jobs.[67] She estimated that women work as much as an extra month per year more than their husbands, leading to chronic exhaustion, increased stress, and higher divorce rates. Other studies indicate that women may experience higher symptom levels than men when they are overloaded with work and family demands or when they experience low power as a consequence of being out of the labor market.[68] Whereas these psychological stressors are often thought of as experiences of an individual, some populations are exposed to more life stressors than others. Individual stress may be thought of as a mediating mechanism linking social context with personal experience.

Men and women differ so much in social context (from disparate incomes to exposures to violence and abuse to occupational hazards) that there may be non-biologic reasons for why men and women have a differential experience of migraine. Rather than assume that all gender differences in incidence are caused by underlying physiologic dysfunction (ie, hormonal or genetic), it is worthwhile to examine some of the external social forces that men and women experience.

SUMMARY

Migraine is a highly prevalent and disabling condition that disproportionately affects women. In some respects, it may be appropriate to consider migraine a woman's disease, however, researchers and physicians should be aware of the social and cultural consequences of linking migraine with women. Because we live in a culture that frequently discounts and delegitimizes the experiences of women, women's conditions may be ignored or not taken seriously by physicians. This problem is exacerbated by a historic legacy of psychosomatic medicine that portrayed headache sufferers as hysterical women who lacked the psychological strength to cope with everyday life. These social and cultural meanings of headache may contribute to some patients' reluctance to report their pain to healthcare practitioners. They may be concerned that their pain is not severe enough to warrant medical attention, or they might worry that they will be labeled as hysterical or hypochondriacal. Healthcare practitioners should be sensitive to these concerns in the medical encounter and seek to understand how social and cultural influences affect the individual patient's experience.

ACKNOWLEDGMENTS

The author would like to thank Charles L. Bosk, Michelle Kempner, Helen Lee, and Jason Schnittker for their comments on an earlier draft.

REFERENCES

1. Kleinman A. Writing at the margin: discourse between anthropology and medicine. Berkeley (CA): University of California Press; 1995.

2. Lorber J. Gender and the social construction of illness. Thousand Oaks (CA): Sage Publications; 1997.

3. Lupton D. Medicine as culture: illness, disease and the body in western societies. London: Sage Publications; 1994.

4. Angel RJ, Thoits P. The impact of culture on the cognitive structure of illness. Cult Med Psychiatry 1987;11:465–94.

5. Blaxter M. Health and lifestyles. London: Travistock/Routledge; 1990.

6. Hunt LM, Jordan B, Irwin S. Compliance and the patient's perspective: controlling symptoms in everyday life. Cult Med Psychiatry 1989;13:315–34.

7. Morris DB. Illness and culture in the postmodern age. Berkeley (CA): University of California Press; 1998.

8. Sontag S. Illness as metaphor. New York (NY): Farrar, Straus and Giroux; 1978.

9. Acker J. Hierarchies, jobs, bodies: a theory of gendered organizations. Gender Soc 1990;4:139–58.

10. Hoffman DE, Tarzian AJ. The girl who cried pain: a bias against women in the treatment of pain. J Law Med Ethics 2001;29:13–27.

11. Crandall CS, Moriarty D. Physical illness stigma and social rejection. Br J Soc Psychol 1995;34:67–83.

12. Rush LL. Affective reactions to multiple social stigmas. J Soc Psychol 1998;138:421–30.

13. Ware NC. Suffering and the social construction of illness: the delegitimation of illness experience in chronic fatigue syndrome. Med Anthropol Q 1992;6:347–61.

14. Phillips P. Migraine as a woman's issue—will research and new treatments help? JAMA 1998;280:1975–6.

15. Aronowitz RA. Making sense of illness. Cambridge: University of Cambridge Press; 1998.

16. Segal J. Patient lives and rhetorical encounters. Halifax (NS): Society for the Social Studies of Science; 1998.

17. Reilly TF. Headache: its causes and treatment. Philadelphia (PA): P. Blakiston's Sons and Company; 1926.

18. Liveing E. On megrim, sick-headache and some allied disorders: a contribution to the pathology of nerve-storms. London: J. and A. Churchill; 1873.

19. Latham PW. On nervous or sick-headache: its varieties and treatment. Cambridge: Deighton, Bell, and Company; 1873.

20. Goodell H. Thirty years of headache research in the laboratory of the late Dr. Harold G. Wolff. Headache 1967;6:158–71.

21. Goodell H, Wolff IB. The influence on medicine and neurology of Harold G. Wolff. Cornell Univ Med Coll Q 1970;Spring.

22. Wolff HG. Headache and other head pain. 2nd ed. New York (NY): Oxford University Press; 1963.

23. Alvarez WC. The migrainous woman and all her troubles. Alex Blain Hosp B 1945;4:3–8.

24. Lance JW, Anthony M. Some clinical aspects of migraine. A prospective survey of 500 patients. Arch Neurol 1966;15:356–61.

25. Crisp A, Kalucy R, McGuinness B, et al. Some clinical, social and psychological characteristics of migraine subjects in the general population. Postgrad Med J 1977;53:691–7.

26. Freese AS. Pain. New York (NY): Penguin Books; 1975.

27. Stewart W, Lipton R, Celentano D, Reed M. Prevalence of migraine headache in the United States: relation to age, income, race and other sociodemographic characteristics. JAMA 1992;267:64–9.

28. Rasmussen BK. Epidemiology of migraine. Biomed Pharmacother 1995;49:452–5.

29. Lipton RB, Stewart WF, Diamond S, et al. Prevalence and burden of migraine in the United States: data from the American Migraine Study II. Headache 2001;41:646–57.

30. Stewart WF, Schechter A, Lipton RB. Migraine heterogeneity: disability, pain intensity, and attack frequency and duration. Neurology 1994;4:S24–39.

31. Rasmussen BK, Stewart WF. Epidemiology of migraine. In: Olesen J, Tfelt-Hansen P, Welch KMA, editors. The headaches. 2nd ed. Philadelphia (PA): Lippincott Williams & Wilkins; 2000. p. 227–33.

32. Stewart W, Schecter A, Rasmussen B. Migraine prevalence: a review of population-based studies. Neurology 1994;44:S17–23.

33. Abu-Arefeh I, Russell G. Prevalence of headache and migraine in schoolchildren. BMJ 1994;309:765–9.

34. Stewart W, Lipton R, Simon D. Work-related disability: results from the American migraine study. Cephalalgia 1996;16:231–8.

35. Current estimates from the National Health Interview Survey, 1996. Hyattsville (MD): National Center for Health Statistics; 1996.

36. Schwartz BSM, Stewart W, Simon D, Lipton R. Epidemiology of tension-type headache. JAMA 1998;279:381–3.

37. Minino AM, Smith BL. National vital statistics reports. Washington: US Department of Health and Human Services; 2001. p. 49.

38. Wenger NK, Speroff L, Packard B. Cardiovascular health and disease in women. N Engl J Med 1993;329:247–56.

39. Ayanian J, Epstein A. Differences in the use of procedures between women and men hospitalized for coronary heart disease. N Engl J Med 1991;325:221–5.

40. Steingart R, Packer M, Hamm P, et al. Sex differences in the management of coronary artery disease. Survival and Ventricular Enlargement Investigators. N Engl J Med 1991;325:226–30.

41. Healy B. The Yentl syndrome. N Engl J Med 1991;325:274–6.

42. Altman LK. Study finds heart treatment differs for men and women. The New York Times 1991 Nov 13; Late final edition: p. 18.

43. Toward healthy women. The New York Times 1991 Sept 9; Late final edition: p. 14.

44. Krucoff C. Equal opportunity killer; heart disease a greater risk to women than commonly recognized. The Washington Post 1994 July 15; Final edition: Sect. Z:16.

45. Roan S. Medicine turning its attention to women and heart disease. The Los Angeles Times 1993 Apr 6: p. 1.

46. Johnson PA, Goldman L, Orav JE, et al. Gender differences in the management of acute chest pain: support for the "Yentl Syndrome." J Gen Intern Med 1996;11:209–17.

47. Sheifer SE, Escarce JJ, Schulman KA. Race and sex differences in the management of coronary artery disease. Am Heart J 2000;139:848–57.

48. Emslie C, Hunt K, Watt G. Invisible women? The importance of gender in lay beliefs about heart problems. Soc Health Illness 2001;23:203–33.

49. Thomas WI, Thomas DS. The child in America: behavior problems and programs. New York (NY): Knopf; 1928.

50. Fox RC. Medical uncertainty revisited. In: Albrecht GL, Fitzpatrick R, Scrimshaw SC, editors. Handbook of social studies in health and medicine. London: Sage Publications; 2000. p. 409–25.

51. McKinlay JB, Potter DA, Feldman HA. Non-medical influences on medical decision-making. Soc Sci Med 1996;42:769–76.

52. Balsa AI, McGuire TG. Statistical discrimination in health care. J Health Econ 2001;20:881–907.

53. Lipton RB, Stewart WF, Celentano D, Reed M. Undiagnosed migraine headaches: a comparison of symptom-based and reported physician diagnosis. Arch Intern Med 1992;152:1273–8.

54. Celentano DD, Linet MS, Stewart WF. Gender differences in the experience of headache. Soc Sci Med 1990;30:1289–95.

55. Marcus DA, Nash JM, Turk DC. Diagnosing recurring headaches: IHS criteria and beyond. Headache 1994;34:329–36.

56. Loder EW, Beluk S. The influence of gender on evaluation and treatment of migraine. Headache 1999;39:366.

57. Crook J, Tunks E. Women with pain. In: Tunks E, Bellissimo A, Roy R, editors. Chronic pain: psychosocial factors in rehabilitation. Malabar (FL): R.E. Krieger Publishing Company; 1990.

58. Elderkin-Thompson V, Waitzkin H. Differences in clinical communication by gender. J Gen Intern Med 1999;14:112–21.

59. Spierings E, Ranke A, Honkoop P. Precipitating and aggravating factors of migraine versus tension-type headache. Headache 2001;41:554–8.

60. Robbins L. Precipitating factors in migraine: a retrospective review of 494 patients. Headache 1994;34:214–6.

61. Barsky AJ, Peekna HM, Borus JF. Somatic symptom reporting in women and men. J Gen Intern Med 2001;16:266–75.

62. Derbyshire S. Sources of variation in assessing male and female responses to pain. New Ideas Psychol 1997;15:83–95.

63. Fillingim R, Maixner W, Girdler S, et al. Ischemic but not thermal pain sensitivity varies across the menstrual cycle. Psychosom Med 1997;59:512–20.

64. Hassinger HJ, Semenchuk EM, O'Brien WH. Cardiovascular responses to pain and stress in migraine. Headache 1999;39:605–15.

65. Rainero I, Amanzio M, Vighetti S, et al. Quantitative EEG responses to ischaemic arm stress in migraine. Cephalalgia 2001;21:224–9.

66. Almeida DM, Kessler RC. Everyday stressors and gender differences in daily distress. J Pers Soc Psychol 1998;75:670–80.

67. Hochschild AR. The second shift. New York (NY): Avon Books; 1990.

68. Rosenfield S. The effects of women's employment: personal control and sex differences in mental health. J Health Soc Behav 1989;30:77–91.

CHAPTER 16

Ethnic and Cultural Factors in Women's Headaches

Elizabeth Loder, MD, FACP

CASE

CC is a 28-year-old Mexican-American woman who experiences severe headache on average twice a month. She is otherwise healthy, a fact that she describes as "lucky because I don't have health insurance." She is the single mother of two children and works part-time as a hotel maid, a job that does not provide health benefits. She uses over-the-counter analgesics to treat her headaches, but roughly four times a year experiences severe vomiting in association with the headache that precludes the use of oral treatment. For these headaches, she seeks care in a local emergency department (ED), where she generally receives an injectable opioid for treatment. CC's headaches meet the criteria for migraine without aura, but a review of ED records shows a diagnosis of only "severe benign headache."

Ethnic and cultural factors play an important, though largely unexplored, role in the experience of female headache sufferers. This chapter reviews the complex interactions of these variables.

KEY CHAPTER POINTS

- **Migraine prevalence varies by ethnicity, although headache features, triggers, and treatment response are similar across groups.**
- **Cultural and socioeconomic factors influence treatment-seeking behavior, pain expression and reporting, and treatment acceptance and adherence.**
- **Ethnic, socioeconomic, and cultural factors interact in a complex way with gender to influence the clinical presentation of migraine.**

MIGRAINE PREVALENCE AND ETHNICITY

Headache Prevalence by Ethnicity

In the United States, migraine prevalence is lowest in Asian-Americans (9.2% in women, 4.8% in men), intermediate in African-Americans (16.2% in women, 7.2% in men), and highest in Caucasians (20.4% in women, 8.6% in men).[1] These differences presumably reflect genetic influences on migraine susceptibility that vary by ethnic group. Other investigations confirm ethnic differences in migraine rates. For example, migraine prevalence in Nigerian blacks was found to be lower than that in Caucasians living in that country; in that study, socioeconomic factors did not appear to influence headache risk.[2]

A recent study of the prevalence of headache in Puerto Rico, with a predominantly Caribbean population, showed a 1-year headache prevalence of 35.9% and a 1-year migraine prevalence of 13%. In all age groups, migraine prevalence was highest in women. In women, migraine prevalence peaked in the 40 to 49 year age group, whereas in men, it peaked in the 30 to 39 year age group.[3]

A review of epidemiologic studies of headache in Asia showed that the prevalence of migraine and tension-type headache, as defined by International Headache Society criteria, was remarkably consistent among the various Asian countries despite what the authors referred to as "diverse cultural backgrounds and development." The finding of a lower prevalence of migraine in Asians compared with other ethnic groups persists in other studies as well.[4]

Cultural, gender, and socioeconomic factors undoubtedly play an important, though difficult to determine, role in migraine susceptibility within ethnic groups as well. That genetic factors alone do not account for all ethnic variability is demonstrated by a study of migraine prevalence among Mexican-Americans. This study showed that migraine prevalence in Mexican-born Mexican-Americans was higher than the prevalence in those born in the United States — a statistically significant doubling of risk.[5] The prevalence rate for migraine appears to be somewhat lower among Asians living in Asia than in Asians living in Western countries, another demonstration that ethnic influences on migraine prevalence can be modified by cultural and environmental factors.[6]

Gender, socioeconomic status, and age also modulate the expression of migraine within ethnic groups. Among Mexican-Americans over 45 years of age, self-reported migraine was twice as common in women as it was in men; in African-Americans, migraine is four times more prevalent in women than in men. Migraine prevalence in all studied groups (Mexican-Americans, Caucasians, and African-Americans) declines with age and is inversely related to socioeconomic status. This study indicated that the age range at which peak prevalence of migraine occurs differs among ethnic groups. White Americans in the 65- to 74-year age group had the highest prevalence of migraine, compared with the 45- to 54-year age group for African-Americans and Mexican-Americans.[5]

Genetic factors that influence vulnerability to migraine are heterogeneous and may not be the same in all ethnic groups. The mitochondrial deoxyribonucleic acid (DNA) 11084 A to G transition that is a risk factor for migraine in Caucasians, for example, is more common in Japanese subjects but is not a risk factor for migraine in the Japanese population.[7]

Headache Features and Triggers by Ethnic Group

The self-reported frequency of migraine trigger factors in a Mexican-American population is similar to that reported by non-Hispanic migraineurs. Among women, these included missing meals (identified as a trigger by 58.9% of Hispanic women with migraine), weather changes (54.4%), menstruation (53.6%), post-crisis letdown (52.7%), and fatigue (51.8%). Seventy-three percent of the Hispanic female migraineurs reported that the period just prior to the onset of menses was a trigger for migraine, compared to a figure from a separate study of 67% of Caucasian women in a Danish sample.[5,8] Hispanic women with menstrual migraine and Raynaud's phenomenon appeared to be most sensitive to environmental triggers for migraine.[5]

Treatment Response and Adverse Events by Ethnic Group

There is little evidence that the efficacy or tolerability of pharmacologic treatments for migraine is significantly influenced by ethnicity. A study of sumatriptan injection in 150 non-Caucasians (46 Blacks, 68 Hispanics, and 36 others) showed headache response and adverse events to the treatment similar to those seen in Caucasians. In addition, headache recurrence was similar among groups, with one important exception: non-Caucasians reported more severe pain and clinical disability and waited longer before initiating treatment than did Caucasians. Non-Caucasians reported less nausea than Caucasians, but when nausea was present in the non-Caucasian group, it was more resistant to treatment. Placebo response was also increased among non-Caucasians in this study, although the authors speculated that this may have been due to spontaneous headache resolution in this group of patients who waited so long to be treated.[9] This study suggests that clinicians should consider emphasizing the importance of timely treatment of migraine to non-Caucasian migraineurs.

A study of chest pain occurring with subcutaneous sumatriptan administration was performed in 62 Japanese subjects. As has been suggested in other ethnic groups, symptoms of chest pain did not correlate with objective measures of coronary ischemia.[10] Ethnicity has little effect on the pharmacologic effects of drugs. For example, the pharmacokinetics of zolmitriptan were similar in Japanese and Caucasian subjects. Japanese females had higher plasma concentrations of the drug than did Japanese males; this gender discrepancy was observed in Caucasians as well.[11] No differences in response or adverse event rates between Japanese and non-Japanese populations emerged in studies of the drug, and a special analysis showed no adverse events that were unique to Japanese subjects. Two-hour response rates for 5 mg of zolmitriptan in Japanese subjects were 66.2% compared with 71.7% in non-Japanese subjects, not a statistically significant difference.[12] A study of 402 Japanese subjects who received eletriptan showed no clinically important differences in drug response, adverse events, or pharmacokinetics compared with non-Japanese subjects.[13]

CULTURAL AND SOCIOECONOMIC INFLUENCES

Influences on Treatment-Seeking Behavior, Pain Expression, and Reporting

In the United States, migraine prevalence has been shown to increase as income or highest level of education decreases.[14,15] In other studies, however, a positive relationship between migraine prevalence and income was found.[16,17] Patients of lower socioeconomic status generally have less access to health care for migraine and other health problems and may be less likely to seek or be aware of treatment for migraine even if they have access to it.

Willingness to seek treatment for migraine or other pain problems is strongly influenced by ethnic and cultural factors. A Singapore study showed that Malays were more likely than non-Malays to seek medical attention for headache, although no significant gender predisposition for treatment-seeking was noted. The authors of this study remarked that because many patients consulting for headache reported a good treatment response to nonprescription medications, the likely purpose of the consultation was to relieve "anxieties regarding the diagnosis rather than to obtain symptomatic relief."[18] The prevalence of complaints of some pain syndromes, notably whiplash, varies markedly depending on the social acceptability of the diagnosis. Whiplash is a common source of disability in Western nations, where it is legitimized, but acknowledged cases of whiplash are rare in countries where social sanctions against this diagnosis exist.[19] A nationwide survey of migraine in Japan found that 69.4% of patients with migraine had never consulted a physician, despite the fact that 74.2% reported impairment of daily activities due to migraine, and 56.9% of patients were using only over-the-counter medications.[20] Stoicism and the cultural and gender acceptability of admitting pain or seeing a physician because of pain undoubtedly influence presentation for treatment.

The type of treatment used for headache is also strongly influenced by cultural factors. Nontraditional treatments or folk treatments for headache remain in common use in many cultures. In the United States, this largely takes the form of herbs and nutritional supplements, but more dramatic and invasive treatments persist in isolated cultures. For example, headache is a prominent reason for the use of a crude form of craniotomy in the Kisii tribe of Kenya, although the authors of the report speculate that the practice is "probably destined to disappear within this generation."[21] Tactful inquiry about the use of nonstandard, folk, or alternative treatment for headache is important in all patients but may be even more so in patients from cultures or ethnic groups where such practices are widespread. Eighty-three percent of Cambodian headache sufferers, for example, used traditional Cambodian treatments for their headache.[22]

Understanding the cultural, ethnic, and sociodemographic influences on patients' "explanatory models" for headache can improve diagnosis, as well as patient compliance and satisfaction. There are relatively few studies that examine these models in various cultures. One such study, of 76 older Cambodian refugees, found that headache was the most common symptom and complaint in both psychiatric and nonpsychiatric subjects. Headache was significantly more frequent among those with depression and was explained by most sufferers as a result of sadness, grief, and anxiety. The authors of this study concluded that headache is very prevalent among older Cambodian refugees, and that in this group, it was often a somatic manifestation of depression.[22]

In some cultures, certain diagnoses are stigmatized or unacceptable, and the labels used for some symptoms have a cultural rather than a medical or scientific basis. German patients with symptoms such as headache and dizziness, for example, are often diagnosed with "hypotension" rather than migraine or depression. Thus, one explanation for varying rates of clinical diagnoses of migraine and other illnesses might be that frequent and vague symptoms such as headache result in different diagnostic labels, depending on culturally sanctioned ways of presenting and labeling distress.[23]

Patients' pain reports and the words used to describe pain may vary considerably depending on cultural and social factors. A study of 150 Chinese subjects with headache given the McGill Pain Questionnaire showed that Chinese patients used fewer and different words to report their pain than patients reported in the western literature.[24] Because the diagnosis of benign headache syndromes such as migraine is heavily dependent on elicitation of historic features and pain descriptors, providers must be especially alert to the problems that such differences in word use can pose. The use of medically knowledgeable translators should be considered in non–English-speaking patients, unless a medical provider fluent in that language is available.

Influences on Treatment Access, Acceptance, and Adherence

A study examining predictors of medical consultation for headache was conducted in Taiwan. Physician consultation was more likely in migraineurs than nonmigraineurs, where 12% of the migraineurs and 6% of the non-migraineurs accounted for half of all consultations for headache. In addition to diagnosis, low copayments, low educational levels, and unrestricted access to medical care also increased the incidence of seeking medical care for headache.[25]

Socioeconomic status significantly affects access to care. Low-income migraineurs are less likely than those of higher income to have insurance coverage for medical care or to make regular medical visits to a consistent medical provider. One study demonstrated that middle-aged women of upper socioeconomic status were more likely to respond to an offer of free treatment and examination for headache related to temporomandibular joint dysfunction.[26]

Migraineurs who do not speak English may be especially likely to remain undiagnosed because headache diagnosis is heavily dependent on historic features. They may be especially likely to seek episodic care in EDs during headache crises. If such patients with chronic headache do seek or obtain regular care for headache, socioeconomic factors have not been demonstrated to affect treatment dropout but may affect the ability to afford the treatment prescribed.[27]

INTERACTION OF ETHNICITY, SOCIOECONOMICS, CULTURE, AND GENDER ON THE CLINICAL PRESENTATION OF MIGRAINE

The influences of ethnic and cultural factors on headache are difficult to disentangle from other factors such as gender and socioeconomic status. These variables interact in complicated ways to influence migraine presentation and treatment. For example, the inverse relationship between income, education, and migraine prevalence noted in many studies does not hold true for African-Americans, where the highest migraine prevalence occurs in the group with the highest, not lowest, educational level and is higher in mid- than low-income groups. The authors speculated that the higher rate of migraine in this group "may be due to the social stresses incumbent in an upwardly mobile or upwardly aspirant population."[4]

Socioeconomic circumstances often determine exposure to other headache triggers. For example, female children from economically disadvantaged backgrounds are more likely than other children to be the victims of sexual assault. A review of five different population samples showed that sexual assault occurring in childhood (but not adulthood) raises the risk of subsequent headache problems, as well as a wide range of other physical symptoms.[28] Whereas gender and ethnicity did not change the likelihood of developing headache as a result of assault, these factors certainly influence the chance of being assaulted as a child. Disadvantaged ethnic groups may be more likely to encounter environmental pollutants, severe psychosocial stress, or occupational factors that provoke or aggravate headache. Such indirect effects on migraine will change over time as the status and economic circumstances of the group change. Increased exposure to a variety of adverse environmental circumstances that act to increase the expression of migraine genes may explain the increased risk of disabling primary headache in lower socioeconomic groups. In fact, the higher prevalence of migraine in low-income groups has been attributed to their poorer diets, increased stress related to poor living conditions and financial difficulties, and higher rates of smoking, as well as their poorer access to health care.[29]

Gender also interacts with social class, ethnicity, and culture. A study of children in Iceland showed that headache prevalence was significantly higher among younger children, girls, and those of lower socioeconomic status, with interactions between social class and gender; young girls of low socioeconomic status were especially likely to experience headache.[30] In a study conducted in the Netherlands, however, social status did not appear to correlate with headache in a sample of 2,300 children between the ages of 10 and 17 years.[31]

Headache triggers may be differentially present depending on cultural and environmental factors unique to certain groups of patients. A study of Japanese nurses and administrators who worked in high-stress jobs showed that 40.6% of nurses and only 19.1% of administrators reported recurrent headaches, a prevalence the investigators believed was larger than in the general female population. The prevalence of headache in female administrators was higher than that in their male counterparts. There are so few male nurses in Japan that the gender prevalences within that group could not be studied. The group of nurses who reported headache scored higher than the non-headache group on a variety of measures, including stressful life events, decreased work motivation, and "nervous behavior." The authors speculated that psychological or work stress, especially characteristic of Japanese life, appeared to be related to the high prevalence of headaches in the studied groups. They noted that the work of nurses is believed in Japan to be both mentally and physically challenging, as is the work of middle managers and administrators.[32]

Much has been made of gender effects on pain tolerance and expression; a variety of studies have demonstrated lower pain thresholds and tolerance in females than males. It is often speculated that these gender differences reflect biologic factors such as hormonal effects or differences in gene expression between males and females. A recent study suggested, however, that these measured gender differences in pain threshold may reflect gender role expectations; that is, a cultural, rather than biologic, cause. In this study, the pain threshold and tolerance of male and female subjects to a standard cold pressor test were examined. Subjects who were given only general instructions about the test showed the expected gender differences in pain tolerance. A separate group of subjects received instructions about the test that included statements about the pain tolerance "of the average male/female." Females who were given specific time estimates of expected pain tolerance for women before the test showed a pain tolerance and threshold that was much higher than that of females not given such instructions; in fact, their results were statistically indistinguishable from those of male subjects receiving similar instructions. These male subjects showed no difference in pain threshold compared with male subjects not given such instruction. In other words, the pain threshold of female subjects (but not of male subjects) was greatly increased by manipulating their expectations and beliefs about the ability of females to tolerate pain. This suggests that cultural expectations of behavior have significant influence on pain perception and reporting in women. It underscores the need for thoughtful and cautious interpretation of gender, ethnic, and cultural differences in the general pain and headache literature.[33]

SUMMARY

Genetic susceptibility to migraine varies depending on ethnicity, but migraine prevalence is high in all groups. Exposure to many of the environmental factors that trigger or aggravate migraine is heavily dependent on culture, socioeconomic status, and gender. In addition, all of these factors influence the tendencies to report headache; to seek, access, and accept treatment for it; and to adhere to that treatment. Females from economically disadvantaged ethnic groups may be particularly likely to experience migraine and least likely to receive appropriate treatment for it.

REFERENCES

1. Stewart WF, Lipton RB, Liberman J. Variation in migraine prevalence by race. Neurology 1996;47:52–9.

2. Osuntokun BO, Adeuja AO, Nottidge VA, et al. Prevalence of headache and migrainous headache in Nigerian Africans: a community-based study. East Afr Med J 1992;69:196–9.

3. Miranda H, Ortiz G, Figueroa S, et al. Prevalence of headache in Puerto Rico. Headache 2003;43:774–8.

4. Wang SJ, Liu HC, Fuh JL, et al. Prevalence of headaches in a Chinese elderly population in Kinmen: age and gender effect and cross-cultural comparisons. Neurology 1997;49:195–200.

5. Molgaard CA, Rothrock J, Stand PE, Golbeck AL. Prevalence of migraine among Mexican Americans in San Diego, California: survey 1. Headache 2002;42:878–82.

6. Wang SJ. Epidemiology of migraine and other types of headache in Asia. Curr Neurol Neurosci Rep 2003;3:104–8.

7. Takeshima T, Fukuhara Y, Adachi Y, et al. Leukocyte mitochondrial DNA A to G polymorphism at 11084 is not a risk factor for Japanese migraineurs. Cephalalgia 2001;21:987–9.

8. Rasmussen BK. Migraine and tension-type headache in a general population: precipitating factors, female hormones, sleep pattern and relation to lifestyle. Pain 1993;53:65–72.

9. Burke-Ramirez P, Asgharnejad M, Webster C, et al. Efficacy and tolerability of subcutaneous sumatriptan for acute migraine: a comparison between ethnic groups. Headache 2001;41:873–82.

10. Tomita M, Suzuki N, Igarashi H, et al. Evidence against strong correlation between chest symptoms and ischemic coronary changes after subcutaneous sumatriptan injection. Intern Med 2002;41:622–5.

11. Yates RA, Tateno M, Nairn K, et al. The pharmacokinetics of the antimigraine compound zolmitriptan in Japanese and Caucasian subjects. Eur J Clin Pharmacol 2002;58:247–52.

12. Sakai F, Iwata M, Tashiro K, et al. Zolmitriptan is effective and well tolerated in Japanese patients with migraine: a dose-response study. Cephalalgia 2002;22:376–83.

13. Eletriptan steering committee in Japan. Efficacy and safety of eletriptan 20 mg, 40 mg, and 80 mg in Japanese migraineurs. Cephalalgia 2002;22:416–23.

14. Lipton RB, Stewart WF, Diamond S, et al. Prevalence and burden of migraine in the United States: data from the American Migraine Study II. Headache 2001;41:646–57.

15. Lipton RB, Stewart WF. Migraine in the United States: a review of the epidemiology and health care use. Neurology 1993;Suppl 30:S6–10.

16. Gobel H, Petersen-Braun M, Soyka D. The epidemiology of headache in Germany: a nationwide survey of a representative sample on the basis of headache classification of the International Headache Society. Cephalalgia 1994;14:97–106.

17. O'Brien B, Goeree R, Streiner D. Prevalence of migraine headache in Canada: a population-based survey. Int J Epidemiol 1994;23:1020–6.

18. Anttila P, Metsahhonkala L, Helenius H, Sillanpaa M. Predisposing and provoking factors in childhood headache. Headache 2000;40:351–6.

19. Balla JI. The late whiplash syndrome: a study of an illness in Australia and Singapore. Cult Med Psychiatry 1982;6:191–210.

20. Sakai F, Igarashi H. Prevalence of migraine in Japan: a nationwide survey. Cephalalgia 1997;17:15–22.

21. Furnas DW, Sheikh MA, van den Hombergh P, et al. Traditional craniotomies of the Kisii tribe of Kenya. Ann Plast Surg 1985;15:538–56.

22. Handelman L, Yeo G. Using explanatory models to understand chronic symptoms of Cambodian refugees. Fam Med 1996;28:271–6.

23. Donner-Banzhoff N, Kreienbrock L, Baum E. Hypotension—does it make sense in family practice? Fam Pract 1994;11:368–74.

24. Hui YL, Chen AC. Analysis of headache in a Chinese patient population. Anaesthesiol Sinica 1989;27:13–8.

25. Wang SJ, Fuh JL, Young YH, et al. Frequency and predictors of physician consultations for headache. Cephalalgia 2001;21:25–30.

26. Heloe B. Response to an offer of consultation concerning TMJ disorder. Scand J Dent Res 1976;84:413–7.

27. Tsushima WT, Stoddard VM, Tsushima VG, Dalyb J. Characteristics of treatment drop-outs among two samples of chronic headache patients. J Clin Psychol 1991; 47:199–205.

28. Golding JM. Sexual assault history and headache: five general population studies. J Nerv Ment Dis 1999;187: 624–9.

29. Stewart WF, Linet MS, Celentano DD, et al. Age and sex-specific incidence rates of migraine with and without visual aura. Am J Epidemiol 1991;134:1111–20.

30. Kristjansdottir G, Wahlberg V. Sociodemographic differences in the prevalence of self-reported headache in Icelandic school-children. Headache 1993;33:376–80.

31. Passchier J, Orlebeke JF. Headaches and stress in school-children: an epidemiological study. Cephalalgia 1985; 5:167–76.

32. Nadaoka T, Kanda H, Oiji A, et al. Headache and stress in a group of nurses and government administrators in Japan. Headache 1997;37:386–91.

33. Robinson ME, Gagnon CM, Riley JL, Price DD. Altering gender role expectations: effects on pain tolerance, pain threshold, and pain ratings. J Pain 2003;4:284–8.

CHAPTER 17

Patient Educational Resources

Lynne O. Geweke, MD, and Dawn A. Marcus, MD

CASE

JM reports the following:

> When I was pregnant, I couldn't walk down the aisle in the grocery store without hearing pregnancy advice from other women. Now that my doctor has diagnosed me with migraines, it's almost as bad! Everywhere I go, people give me all sorts of hints for curing my headaches. I've been told to take a painkiller every day before my headache starts and to avoid daily pain medicines. I've been told that exercise and certain foods can and can't trigger headaches. Now I'm so confused! I just wish there was someplace where I could find reliable information.

Surveys of headache sufferers show that what patients want most from their doctors is information about their headaches; consumers rank education higher than doctor expertise and compassion.[1] Doctors incorrectly believe that patients are most interested in having a doctor who is compassionate and an expert in the condition being treated. Doctors incorrectly rank education as having a low desirability. Fortunately, there are a wide variety of accurate resources available to provide educational materials to headache patients.

Studies show that patient education is an effective tool for reducing headaches. Interdisciplinary self-management education significantly reduced headaches in 70% of recalcitrant headache patients, with a 71% overall reduction in medication use as well.[2]

Less intense headache education efforts are also effective. Holroyd and colleagues randomized migraineurs, all of whom received standard acute care migraine medication, into groups either with or without additional brief headache education.[3] Headache education consisted of a 30-minute session with an allied healthcare worker and three follow-up telephone calls. The 30-minute session included describing migraine education and strategies for appropriate medication use. The three telephone calls identified and corrected problems discovered at home. After 2 months, headache activity was reduced by 47% in the education group and by only 18% in the standard treatment group.

Self-education may also be effective. A multimedia educational program, including educational information, relaxation, and autogenic training techniques with written materials and television and radio programs, was provided to 164 headache sufferers over 10 weeks.[4] The number of headache days decreased by 50% as a result of education, by 30% as a result of analgesic use, and by 54% after preventive medication. In addition, there was a 45% decrease in work absence and a 61% decrease in doctor visits. A recent pilot project reported the effectiveness of headache education administered via the Internet.[5]

KEY CHAPTER POINTS

- **Caution should be exercised in making dietary recommendations to women with migraine.**
- **Diaries provide useful tools for assessing headache activity and treatment response.**
- **Patient educational materials are available online.**
- **Patient educational materials may be individualized for each medical practice.**

DIETARY MIGRAINE TRIGGERS AND WOMEN

Caution should be exercised in making dietary recommendations to female migraineurs. Nearly every lay and medical book about headaches, as well as televi-

Table 17-1 Sample 2-Week Diary

Date	Headache Severity*	Headache Duration	Trigger	Pain Medications	Menstrual Days†

*Use the following severity scale: 0 = no headache; 1 = mild headache—able to continue with routine activities; 2 = moderate headache—activities restricted; and 3 = severe headache—unable to perform usual daily activities.
†Women should record any days with menstrual flow, whether or not they have a headache on that day.

sion, magazine, and newspaper reviews of migraine, include a list of foods commonly believed to trigger migraine. In general, these recommendations are well intentioned and probably seem harmless. For many of the foods included on these lists, however, there is little or no scientific validation that they are in fact common migraine triggers. Exceptions to this include aspartame (very high intake has been convincingly linked to migraine exacerbation), caffeine (in small amounts, caffeine is helpful for headache, but caffeine *withdrawal* in migraineurs using it regularly is a well-known headache precipitant), and alcohol. Recommendations to avoid or moderately use these substances are reasonable and evidence-based.

However, few other dietary recommendations can be made with confidence of their scientific validity. Many "migraine diet" recommendations include broad, sweeping generalizations about entire food or nutrient groups. These groups include some that are important for a healthy and varied diet. Dairy products, for example, are commonly included in these lists, as are citrus fruits and many kinds of vegetables. There are obvious and important long-term health implications to the recommendation that female migraineurs avoid these food groups. Therefore, restrictive diets should be maintained for several weeks. During this time, women can test which foods might be triggers for them.

The evidence that chocolate is a trigger of migraine is weak, and one study of migraineurs who identified chocolate as a trigger for headache failed to show any association.[6] Current thinking is that craving for chocolate or other foods may be caused by brain changes that occur early in migraine; thus, the chocolate craving occurs because of the headache, and the chocolate itself does not trigger the headache at all.

However, every migraine patient is different. For some, food triggers may be of more importance than they are for the average migraineur. For others, traditional treatment methods may be contraindicated or ineffective; in these situations, more detailed attention to potentially modifiable environmental triggers may

be warranted. In these cases, careful elimination diets may be helpful in identifying suspect foods. A typical "migraine-free diet" is included in Appendix 17-C.

Food is one of the great pleasures of life, and it is important to avoid reinforcing unnecessary dietary scrutiny in patients who are unlikely to benefit from it. Attention to food as a possible trigger of migraine is understandable because diet is one of the few things under a patient's immediate control. Most migraineurs have a strong desire to be able to do something—anything—to assist in controlling attacks that may make them feel helpless. Perhaps this is why at least one study of a special migraine diet showed that migraine improved on several different diets; it was not the diet itself but *simply being on a diet* that seemed to be therapeutic.[7]

In addition, the association between dietary factors and headache can sometimes be coincidental. Because most people eat many times each day, every time a woman has a headache, she is likely to have recently eaten something. It is thus natural that dietary factors should frequently come under suspicion. Association does not prove causation, however, and, for this reason, suspected food triggers should be analyzed more carefully with the use of an elimination diet and headache diary. The woman can eliminate individual food items or groups from her diet for several weeks and then reintroduce those items, all the while keeping careful track of headache frequency, intensity, and timing in relation to food intake. If a food item is an important trigger of headache, the relationship between its intake and headache attacks should become obvious with this method.

HEADACHE DIARY

The headache diary is an effective tool for identifying headache patterns, headache triggers, and response to treatment. Diaries can be instructive for both patients and their healthcare providers. Without the help of diaries, patients may miss important headache patterns, such as headache frequency and medication overuse. In addition, they may endorse false associations between headache activity and trigger factors. For example, women often falsely identify the menstrual

Table 17-2 Completed Sample Diaries with Headache Diagnoses

Date	Headache Severity	Headache Duration	Trigger	Pain Medications	Menstrual Days
Sunday	0				X
Monday	0				X
Tuesday	0				
Wednesday	2	2 pm – 9 pm	Skipped meals; red wine	Excedrin: Two at 2 pm and two at 7 pm	
Thursday	0				
Friday	0				

Diagnosis: episodic migraine, nonmenstrual.

Date	Headache Severity	Headache Duration	Trigger	Pain Medications	Menstrual Days
Sunday	2	10 am – 8 pm	Placebo pills in birth control		
Monday	1	4 pm – 9 pm	Placebo pills		
Tuesday	2	3 pm – 9 pm	Placebo pills		X
Wednesday	0				X
Thursday	0				X
Friday	0				X

Diagnosis: headache aggravated by estrogen withdrawal from oral contraceptive.

Date	Headache Severity	Headache Duration	Trigger	Pain Medications	Menstrual Days
Sunday	1	4 am – 9 pm	Stress	Six aspirin	
Monday	1	6 am – 10 pm		Six aspirin	
Tuesday	2	All day	Lack of sleep	Three Tylenol; four Aleve	
Wednesday	1	All day		Eight Tylenol	
Thursday	2	4 am – 2 pm		Four aspirin	

Diagnosis: analgesic overuse headache.

Date	Headache Severity	Headache Duration	Trigger	Pain Medications	Menstrual Days
Sunday	3	12 am – 1 am	Sleep		
Monday	3	12:05 am – 1 am	Sleep		
Tuesday	3	11:30 pm – 12 am	Sleep		
Wednesday	3	11 pm – 11:30 pm	Sleep		

Diagnosis: cluster headache.

cycle as a headache trigger, only to find that their headaches fail to respond to hormonal therapy. In these cases, diaries may fail to identify a consistent link between menses and headache activity.[8]

Diaries should record data about headache frequency, duration, severity, possible triggers, and medication use (Table 17-1). Evaluating data from several weeks of diary recording may help determine a headache diagnosis, for example, intermittent versus constant headache, incapacitating episodic migraine versus mild but frequent tension-type headache, or chronic daily headache versus analgesic-overuse headache (Table 17-2). Trigger factors may also be identified. Pre- and post-treatment diaries are the most effective tools for determining treatment response, as memory for painful experiences is notoriously poor and inaccurate.[9]

Alternative diaries may be accessed at the healthcare provider section of the National Headache Foundation Web site (http://www.headaches.org) and through the American Council for Headache Education (ACHE) Web site (http://www.achenet.org/resources/diary.php). In addition, patients can develop a computerized diary through the ACHE Web page at <http://www.achenet.org/your/diary2.php>.

ONLINE PATIENT EDUCATIONAL MATERIALS

A variety of reliable Web sites are available that provide accurate and up-to-date headache information to both patients and healthcare providers. Below are listed several excellent sites developed by major headache organizations:

- The American Council for Headache Education—http://www.achenet.org
- The patient educational materials section of the American Headache Society Web site—http://www.ahsnet.org/resources/patient.php
- The National Headache Foundation Web site that includes a section for patients (including educational materials) and healthcare providers—http://www.headaches.org

Internet sites are also available to provide preliminary assessments of headache impact and diagnosis:

- Headache impact
  - The Headache Impact Test (HIT-6) questionnaire may be completed online by patients at <http://www.amihealthy.com>
  - The Migraine Disability Assessment Survey (MIDAS) may be downloaded from <http://www.midas-migraine.net/About_Midas/questionnaire5.pdf>

- Diagnosis
  - An individualized headache diagnostic screen can be accessed online through Dr. Jerry Goldstein's, San Francisco Headache Clinic Web site at <http://www.sfcrc.com/html/headache.htm>

INDIVIDUALIZED PATIENT EDUCATIONAL MATERIALS

Patients appreciate receiving written materials that reinforce messages from their doctors. Standardized forms may be used or forms may be individualized for different medical practices. A sampling of educational forms is included in the appendixes.

APPENDIXES

A. Medication educational sheets: migraine and tension-type headaches (Tables 17-3 and 17-4)
B. Medication educational sheets: cluster headache (Tables 17-5 and 17-6)
C. Headache-free diet
D. Drug rebound or analgesic-overuse headache educational sheets
E. Mechanism of chronic headache educational sheet

REFERENCES

1. Lipton RB, Stewart WF. Acute migraine therapy: do doctors understand what patients with migraine want from therapy? Headache 1999;39 Suppl 2:S20–6.

2. Scharff L, Marcus DA. Interdisciplinary outpatient group treatment of intractable headache. Headache 1994;34:73–7.

3. Holroyd KA, Cordingley GE, Pingel JD, et al. Enhancing the effectiveness of abortive therapy: a controlled evaluation of self-management. Headache 1989;29:148–53.

4. de Bruijn-Kofman AT, van de Wiel H, Groenman NH, et al. Effects of a mass media behavioral treatment for chronic headache: a pilot study. Headache 1997;3:415–20.

5. Strom L, Pettersson R, Andersson G. A controlled trial of self-help treatment of recurrent headache conducted via the Internet. J Consult Clin Psychol 2000;68:722–7.

6. Marcus DA, Scharff L, Turk DE, Gourley LM. A double-blind provocative study of chocolate as a trigger of headache. Cephalalgia 1997;17:855–62.

7. Medina JL, Diamond S. The role of diet in migraine. Headache 1978;18:31–4.

8. Loder E. Menstrual migraine. Curr Treat Options Neurol 2001;3:189–200.

9. Linton SJ. Memory for chronic pain intensity: correlates of accuracy. Percept Mot Skills 1991;72:1091–5.

APPENDIX 17-A: HEADACHE MEDICATION GUIDE FOR MIGRAINE AND TENSION-TYPE HEADACHES

Table 17-3 Acute Care Medications for Migraine and Tension-Type Headaches
(To be used for infrequent, severe headaches [less than 3 days per week])

Medication	Uses	Dose	Side Effects
Anti-inflammatory: aspirin, ibuprofen, naproxen, Excedrin	Arthritis, swelling, pain, blood thinner	Aspirin: 650 mg (2 tabs) every 3–4 hours; daily maximum 4 g Ibuprofen: 400 mg (2 Advil tabs) every 4–6 hours Naproxen: 440 mg (2 Aleve tabs) every 8 hours Excedrin: 2 tabs every 6 hours	Stomach upset, dizziness, fluid retention, bleeding, ringing in the ears, hearing loss, kidney or liver damage
Analgesics: Tylenol	Pain	Tylenol: 650 mg every 4 hours; daily maximum 3.5 g	Kidney or liver damage, bleeding
Antinausea: Reglan, Compazine, Thorazine, Tigan	Nausea, migraine	Reglan: 10 mg by mouth or IM injection Compazine: 25 mg rectally	Drowsiness, dystonia, parkinsonism; rarely tardive dyskinesia or neuroleptic malignant syndrome
Isometheptene: Midrin *Avoid if taking MAOI or uncontrolled high blood pressure or glaucoma*	Headache	2 tabs initially, then 1 in 1 hour if needed. No more than 5 pills per day and 10 pills per week	Drowsiness, dizziness, rash
Ergotamine: Cafergot *Avoid with Inderal*	Migraine	½–1 (2 mg) rectal suppository. May repeat in 1 hour. No more than 2 pills per attack and 5 pills per week	Numbness in fingers/toes, leg cramps, stomach cramps/diarrhea, vertigo, fainting, tremor, blue fingers/toes, chest pain
Dihydroergotamine: DHE-45, Migranal *Avoid with erythromycin*	Migraine	Nasal spray: 1 spray (0.5 mg) in each nostril. May repeat in 15 minutes. Maximum 4 sprays per day, 8 sprays per week	Nausea, chest tightness, leg cramps, vomiting, increased blood pressure
Triptans: Imitrex, Maxalt, Zomig, Relpax, Axert, Amerge, Frova	Severe headache	Imitrex pills: 50–100 mg. May repeat once in 2 hours	Tingling, anxiety, nausea, sedation, weakness, chest/neck tightness. *Avoid if heart disease or uncontrolled high blood pressure*

Remember:
1. Many pain medications contain aspirin or Tylenol. Include these when calculating daily dose.
2. Don't use several anti-inflammatory medications together. They counteract each other and have similar side effects.
3. Take acute care medicines at the *beginning* of a bad headache attack.
4. If you have warning signs before a headache starts, use these pills when the warning signs occur.
5. Limit acute care medications to no more than *3 days per week* to avoid drug rebound headache.
6. Take smaller doses of medications at the suggested frequency, rather than big doses infrequently. Excessive doses less frequently will not work as well.

IM = intramuscularly; MAOI = monoamine oxidase inhibitor.

Table 17-4 Preventive Medications for Migraine and Tension-Type Headaches
(For prevention of frequent headache [more than 3 days per week])

Medication	Uses	Dose	Side Effects

Antidepressant
  Tricyclic: Elavil, Tofranil
  SSRI: Paxil
  Avoid tricyclic if glaucoma
	Depression, anxiety, chronic pain	Elavil or Tofranil: 25–100 mg 2 hours before bed; Paxil: 5–20 mg twice daily	Sedation, dry mouth, dizziness, weight change, sexual dysfunction, blurred vision, urine retention

Beta-blocker: Inderal, Tenormin	High blood pressure, heart disease, headache	Inderal: 80–160 mg daily. Long-acting form may be used once daily	Depression, sedation, constipation, dizziness
Calcium channel blocker: Calan	High blood pressure, heart disease, headache	Calan: 240–480 mg daily. Long-acting form may be used once daily	Constipation, diarrhea, dizziness, fluid retention
Anti-inflammatory: Naproxen, Relafen, Celebrex, Vioxx	Drug rebound, menstrual headache	Naproxen: 250–500 mg twice daily. Daily for rebound. Preovulation/ menstrually for menstrual headache	Stomach upset, dizziness, fluid retention, bleeding, ringing in the ears, hearing loss, kidney or liver damage
Antiseizure: Depakote, Neurontin, Topamax	Epilepsy, migraine, chronic pain	Depakote: 250–500 mg twice daily; Neurontin: 100–800 mg 2–3 times daily	Weight gain, hair thinning, tremor, bleeding, nausea, dizziness, rash
Antihistamine: Periactin *Avoid if glaucoma or using MAOI*	Allergies, headache	Periactin: 4 mg 2–3 times daily	Drowsiness, weight gain, dry mouth, constipation

Remember:
1. Don't expect headache reduction for at least 2 to 3 weeks after starting preventive medications.
2. Take preventive medications *every day*. Acute care medications can also be used for infrequent, severe headaches.
3. Once headaches are controlled, take preventive medications for 4 to 6 months before trying to taper dose. If headaches return with taper, return to previously effective dose. Retry taper in 6 months.

MAOI = monoamine oxidase inhibitor; SSRI = selective serotonin reuptake inhibitor.

APPENDIX 17-B: HEADACHE MEDICATION GUIDE FOR CLUSTER HEADACHES

Table 17-5 Acute Care Medications for Cluster Headaches

Medication	Uses	Dose	Side Effects
Oxygen		100% oxygen at 7–8 L/min for 10 minutes by face mask. May repeat up to 4 times daily	Generally well tolerated
Dihydroergotamine: DHE-45, Migranal *Avoid with erythromycin*	Headache	Nasal spray: 1 spray (0.5 mg) in each nostril. May repeat in 15 minutes. Maximum 4 sprays per day, 8 sprays per week	Nausea, chest tightness, leg cramps, vomiting, increased blood pressure
Triptans: Imitrex	Headache	Imitrex injection: 6 mg subcutaneously	Tingling, anxiety, nausea, sedation, weakness, chest/neck tightness. *Avoid if heart disease or uncontrolled high blood pressure*
Lidocaine	Anesthetic, headache	4% intranasal lidocaine: 1 mL in nostril on painful side. Lie with head extended for 1 minute. May repeat once	Generally well tolerated
Steroid: Dexamethasone		Dexamethasone: 8 mg single dose	High blood pressure, increased blood sugar, confusion, tremor, stomach ulcers. More serious side effects include cataracts, bone thinning and necrosis